S0-AUJ-351

Consumers against Capitalism?

Consumers against Capitalism?

Consumer Cooperation in Europe, North America, and Japan, 1840-1990

edited by
Ellen Furlough
and
Carl Strikwerda

ROWMAN & LITTLEFIELD PUBLISHERS, INC.
Lanham • Boulder • New York • Oxford

ROWMAN & LITTLEFIELD PUBLISHERS, INC.

Published in the United States of America
by Rowman & Littlefield Publishers, Inc.
4720 Boston Way, Lanham, Maryland 20706

12 Hid's Copse Road
Cumnor Hill, Oxford OX2 9JJ, England

Copyright © 1999 by Rowman & Littlefield Publishers, Inc.

All rights reserved. No part of this publication may be reproduced,
stored in a retrieval system, or transmitted in any form or by any
means, electronic, mechanical, photocopying, recording, or otherwise,
without the prior permission of the publisher.

British Library Cataloguing in Publication Information Available

Library of Congress Cataloging-in-Publication Data

Consumers against capitalism? : consumer cooperation in Europe, North
  America, and Japan, 1840–1990 / edited by Ellen Furlough and Carl
  Strikwerda.
    p. cm.
  Includes bibliographical references and index.
  ISBN 0-8476-8648-5 (cloth : alk. paper). — ISBN 0-8476-8649-3
(pbk. : alk. paper)
    1. Consumer cooperatives—History. I. Furlough, Ellen, 1953–
II. Strikwerda, Carl.
HD3271.C67 1999   98-31615
334' .5'09034—dc21   CIP

Printed in the United States of America

⊖™ The paper used in this publication meets the minimum requirements of American
National Standard for Information Sciences—Permanence of Paper for Printed Library
Materials, ANSI Z39.48–1984.

To Two Advisors and Friends

Joan Wallach Scott

and

Louise Audino Tilly

Contents

Acknowledgments

The editors wish to thank the Council for European Studies and its Director, Iannis Sinanaglou, for generously providing support in the form of a Workshop Grant, which supported a small conference held at the University of Kansas in March 1990. The conference brought together a number of the contributors and other activists and scholars interested in consumer cooperation and provided the impetus for this volume. We are grateful for the stimulating insights at that conference of Dana Frank, presently at the University of California, Santa Cruz, and Ann Hoyt of the University of Wisconsin, Madison. The Office of International Programs, the Hall Center for the Humanities, the Department of History, the College of Liberal Arts and Sciences, and Professors Victor Bailey, Gail Bossenga, Angel Kwolek-Folland, and John Sweets, all of the University of Kansas, also deserve our thanks for their financial or intellectual support. A number of other scholars elsewhere have been very helpful with advice and support, among them Jonathan Birchall of Brunel University, Marcel van der Linden of the International Institute for Social History in Amsterdam, Wolfgang Maderthaner of Vienna, John Walton of the University of Central Lancashire, Timothy Guinnane of Yale University, and Michael Hanagan of Vassar College and the New School for Social Research.

The Wescoe Word Processing Center of the University of Kansas, and its staff, Paula Courtney, Pam LeRow, and Lynn Porter, produced numerous versions of the manuscript, including camera-ready copy, with unfailing professionalism and energy. Steve Wrinn, a former student of one of the editors and now a friend of both of them, has been more than an excellent editor to work with at Rowman and Littlefield; he's been an inspiration. All scholars should be so lucky as to have editors such as Steve.

The editors owe a particular debt to their very patient contributors, who bore up under a very long process of editing, rewriting, and book production. Michael Grant did the index with excellent care and thoughtfulness.

Finally, the editors must each acknowledge a debt to each other. Ten years, with only two very brief face-to-face meetings, have seen a surprisingly active collaboration carried out via the post, fax, and email, despite numerous interruptions caused by the demands of family and other professional and scholarly commitments. Despite all the challenges of bringing together different styles and points of view, and in spite of all the disruptions, we have always enjoyed an intellectually fruitful and personally satisfying relationship. It is worth it to cooperate.

Chapter 1

Economics, Consumer Culture, and Gender: An Introduction to the Politics of Consumer Cooperation

Ellen Furlough and Carl Strikwerda

Why the History of Consumer Cooperation?

As capitalist free enterprise and individualistic consumerism appear to sweep the globe at the end of the twentieth century, it may seem odd to devote scholarly attention to consumer cooperation, a movement that for much of its history saw itself as an alternative to capitalist consumer practices and ideologies. Because capitalist consumerism, with its emphases on individual decision making, sophisticated advertising, and a seemingly infinite range of choices, is sometimes taken to be a quintessential mark of modernity, alternatives to capitalism are usually seen as vestiges of the past, as noble but flawed eccentricities, or simply as failures appropriately swept aside by efficiency and progress. Thus consumer cooperation—the provision of consumer goods through private, collectively owned institutions—more often than not appears as a footnote in modern history. Yet cooperation was important in its own right, and for a time, was much more significant than most observers today realize.

Consumer cooperation emerged in almost every European country and in the Americas from the early to mid-nineteenth century. As Japan industrialized at the turn of the century, consumer cooperation spread there as well. Consumer cooperation particularly flourished in industrializing Europe and North America within tightly defined working-class cultures in which labor movements were growing and consumer capitalism had not yet achieved its final form. Large and well-funded cooperative stores were commercial centers of urban working class communities across Europe. Their "social capital" financed labor militancy and worker education projects, and their cultural activities ranged from children's choruses, marching bands, and all-night balls to theatrical productions. Rural cooperatives marketed a vast array of products, and in some cases powerfully influenced the nature and volume of agricultural production and distribution. Cooperative pharmacies, credit institutions, and housing programs proliferated. By the early twentieth century, the consumer cooperative movement boasted impressive wholesaling and retailing networks and was organized internationally within the International Cooperative Alliance. As industrialization began within Asia, Latin America, and Africa in the early twentieth century, European cooperators helped spread the "gospel of cooperation" there as well.

By the middle of the twentieth century, however, the consumer cooperative movement was stagnating in North America and in many countries in Europe, buffeted by various challenges—an increasingly pervasive consumer capitalism, hostile political regimes, and an aging membership. It is no coincidence that there has been relatively little recent work on consumer cooperation, and virtually no comparative studies on its transnational dimensions and impact.[1]

This volume argues, however, that consumer cooperation deserves a long second look by historians, social scientists, and those interested in economic institutions and consumer cultures. We are particularly interested in situating the consumer cooperative movement within the historical development of consumer institutions, identities, and what has been called a "consumer society." Recent studies on the history of retailing and marketing, specific consumer goods, and consumption patterns of different genders and social groups demonstrate a profound similarity in consumer activity. Across the industrialized world, the dominant structures, meanings, and ideology of consumerism have become capitalist, individualist, acquisitive, and oriented toward notions of pleasure and desire.[2] This particular consumerist ethos was, as the study of consumer cooperation will demonstrate, neither inevitable nor universally embraced, and there have been (and continue to be) competing visions and practices. The form of capitalist consumerism that has immense power and influence today is a peculiar historical development, not a linear and inevitable "end of history." In order to understand it, we need to see its history against its rivals, among which consumer cooperation was one of the most important. For, as Mary Douglas has argued, "consumption is the very arena in which culture is fought over and licked into shape."[3]

The history of consumer cooperation is important not only because it was a significant economic and cultural counterpoint to emergent forms of capitalist commerce and at the center of working-class cultures and politics from the 1880s through the 1930s, but because cooperation exerted a powerful appeal within the era's political and intellectual imagination. As we shall see in this volume's subsequent chapters, cooperation was integral to the utopian socialists' project of the 1820s and 1830s. Radicals of the 1840s saw in producers cooperatives a key element of economic independence and the preservation of their skills. Liberal reformers, following the revolutionary upheavals of 1848 and rising discontent associated with industrialization and urbanization, envisioned consumer and credit cooperatives as a way to encourage "self-help" and savings and thus (they hoped) avoid class conflict as well. For the late-nineteenth- and early-twentieth-century labor movement, consumer cooperation was a democratic model of the future society, one of the "three pillars of socialism," along with trade unionism and political socialism. It was meant to emancipate workers from exploitation as consumers, producers, and citizens. Consumer cooperation was often a major arena of political experimentation—or political conflict. During the early years of the Russian Revolution, the new government experimented with turning over distribution of consumer goods to consumer cooperatives, and the Stalinist regime used consumer cooperatives as an arm of the State. During the 1920s and 1930s, fascist governments in Germany, Italy, and Japan, seeking to assuage their lower-middle-class supporters and fearing the power of consumer cooperation as a site of working class mobilization, took control of the cooperative movement in order to harness it to their regimes.

Consumer cooperation was also the focus of lively and extensive discussion in the early twentieth century by European and North American intellectuals, many of whom were active in the cooperative movement—activists whom we would today call "engaged intellectuals." Intellectuals of the later nineteenth century, for example Peter Kropotkin and Karl Marx, had been preoccupied with issues such as the role of cooperation within mutual aid, the efficacy of producers cooperation as opposed to consumers cooperation, or the revolutionary potential of cooperation. By the turn of the century, however, discussions increasingly focused on the "Cooperative Commonwealth" (sometimes referred to as the "Cooperative Republic"). While the origins of this notion remain unclear and deserve further investigation, there is no doubt that intellectuals on an international scale were preoccupied with the cooperative movement's potential as the vehicle for a profound reorganization of the economy and society, a "middle way" between capitalism and socialism that was to be realized gradually rather than through revolutionary means. Intellectuals including Louis de Brouckère in Belgium, Richard Ely in the United States, Charles Gide in France, and Leonard Woolf in England thought that a "Cooperative Commonwealth" was a genuine possibility.[4] The French pacifist Jean Prudhommeaux even hoped that cooperation might be able to bring together all organized economic interests "in the universal cooperative republic, the uniform and supreme expression of *human* consumption, just as the great nations concentrated in the part of the globe which we inhabit will end up creating the United States of Europe."[5]

One reason for cooperation's breadth of influence was its ideological flexibility. Within different national contexts, the ideological focus of consumer cooperation varied widely. As Peder Aléc explains in his chapter in this volume, the argument that cooperation represented a "third way" between liberalism and state socialism played a prominent role within the elaboration of Swedish social democracy. Kathleen Donohue, on the other hand, demonstrates the ways in which intellectuals in the United States interpreted consumer cooperation in a particularly "American" manner that was consistent with ideologies of liberal individualism. Most agreed, however, as French coopera- tor Ernest Poisson put it in the mid-1920s, that the "production of wealth will be directed by the association of the consumers" and that the means for the gradual realization of the Cooperative Republic were to be the "co-ordination of effort so as to effect an organic unity, and knowledge on the part of co- operative leaders of the goal at which they should aim."[6]

The history of consumer cooperation also bears further study for what it can tell us about the underlying assumptions of most labor and socialist move- ments. The traditional focus by labor historians on socialist parties and trade unions has muted the extent and richness of working-class mobilization that emerged in the late nineteenth century. The cooperative movement was vitally important for fostering and enriching a vibrant working-class culture with political implications. In many countries, cooperatives were the wealthiest working-class institutions—"the milk cows of the movement," as one Socialist put it—and they generously funded political parties, trade unions, and exten- sive worker education efforts. Control of the local cooperative was often a stepping-stone for control of municipalities as well as a political training ground for national politics. Widening the lens of analysis to include coopera- tion in studies of labor history and working-class cultures and politics not only reveals a great deal about the underlying assumptions of most labor and socialist movements, but also renders their concerns and preoccupations more complex. For example, it has long been argued that most working-class move- ments were fundamentally productivist in their orientation. And indeed, wages, working conditions, and the control over the profits of production were vitally important concerns in a time when workers were losing control over their work. These concerns, however, were generally defined in terms of male workers, whereas most women workers were simultaneously wage earners and consumers in ways in which many men were not. What has been missed by historians is the degree to which working-class people were also struggling within a wage economy to maintain control over issues of consumption. The history of consumer cooperation reveals extensive mobilization of working- class men and women around issues of consumption, as well as the elaboration of a vast range of institutions that expressed their visions for a more just and nonexploitive social order and mode of consumption.[7]

Finally, the history of consumer cooperation is important because it both articulated notions of a consumer identity that were not fundamentally rooted in appeals to diversion and self-indulgent pleasure, and because it gave voice to moral and ethical commitments, ones that have been, in part, reinvented within modern consumer affairs movements. Analysis of consumer cooperation demonstrates not only the extent to which working people have organized around issues of consumption, but also highlights their attempts to control patterns of consumption during what has been called the "consumer revolution" from the mid-nineteenth to the mid-twentieth century. While there are studies of the historical growth of department stores, advertising, and other capitalist consumer institutions, as well as analyses of the positions of bourgeois intellectuals on consumption, working-class practices and attitudes toward consumption are only beginning to be studied. We argue that it was within the consumer cooperative movement that urban working-class people and rural farmers first organized themselves as consumers into a large-scale movement. As consumers they demanded fair prices, unadulterated foodstuffs, and goods made under just conditions by unionized workers. As consumers, they built institutions that returned profits on the basis of consumer purchases rather than on the basis of shares owned. As consumers they constructed vast wholesaling enterprises, founded political parties, and debated the nature of the good society of the future. The cooperative movement still inspires a variety of other forms of collective economic activity, for example credit unions, employee and union-owned enterprises, and housing cooperatives, and remains a particularly active force in the so-called "developing" countries.

Why then did the movement stagnate and decline in most of Europe and North America? The usual explanations are largely incorrect, and these misperceptions, in turn, obscure the sources of capitalist consumerism's success. Consumer cooperation did not suffer necessarily from failures to exploit economies of scale, from a lack of capital, or from an overdependence on socialism. Consumer cooperatives were often pioneers in their size, financing, and use of the branch store format. While there were indeed business failures of individual cooperatives due to poor management, difficulties associated with rapid growth, and so forth, these problems were not unlike those that plagued other forms of retailing during this period. As for their political associations, cooperatives were linked to a wide range of political and even religious perspectives—liberal, paternalist, Catholic, etc. Furthermore, for most of its history, the consumer cooperative movement insisted upon its political "neutrality." As several chapters in this collection demonstrate, those cooperatives who were overtly socialist generally found this to be an asset in an era where socialism was strong and active in working-class communities; cooperatives were typically aided rather than constrained by socialist ideology.

The great challenge for cooperation, and in retrospect capitalist consumerism's real comparative advantage, was in the selling of "dream worlds," and more particularly, in the emergence and consolidation of a profit and pleasure-oriented mass consumer culture. The chapters in this volume bring to light a vast and complicated series of responses to an emergent culture of consumption. They help to undermine assumptions that rising incomes and mass-produced goods were all that was needed for working people simply to imitate bourgeois consumption models. Rather, we believe that capitalist and cooperative commerce represent different models of consumer culture, models that for a time exercised different appeals. Several of the chapters in this volume discuss how leaders of the consumer cooperative movement struggled with how to preserve the culture and character of cooperation and yet respond effectively to the powerful commercial and cultural challenges of capitalist consumer culture. Their responses may, in the end, reveal less about the so-called "weakness" of consumer cooperation than about the strength and appeal of capitalist consumerism.

Consumer Cooperation: An Historical Sketch

The history of Euro-American consumer cooperation is inextricably enmeshed within the vast transformations associated with the growth and maturation of industrial economies and societies from the mid-eighteenth century. The spread of commercialized market economies, transformations in production that expanded the variety and availability of consumer goods, the rise of family wage economies, and the proliferation of new models of distribution and of consumption (the latter based within, and constitutive of, class) all provide the context for the the development of consumer cooperatives.[8] The "consumer revolution" in the early modern period that a number of historians have described—as important as it was—still usually affected primarily the urban middle class. Nonetheless, this increased buying and marketing indicated that larger numbers of people were giving up home production, responding to new kinds of products, and becoming more aware of taste, fashion, and new modes of consumer information such as advertisements.[9]

For working people, the growth of proto-industrialization and then full industrialization created a larger population of wage earners who depended on buying a wider range of food items and domestic goods from retail shops. The "proletarians in the countryside" who made cloth, nails, or straw hats for urban merchants were often really wage earners in and near small towns who had to buy an increasingly large part of their food and other items in markets.[10] As long as these workers lived in or near the countryside, they could keep a small garden or hire themselves out for harvest work and at least obtain their food outside of markets. The enormous increase in factories and mines in the early nineteenth century in Britain, Belgium, and eventually other areas of continental Europe and North America, created much larger numbers of workers in densely populated towns who had no choice but to buy most of their food and household items within a market economy. It was also not uncommon for owners of factories or mines to provide "company stores" for their workers. In part, this was because their factories or mines sprung up in areas where there was not sufficient retail trade to supply the workers. These stores more often became a means to control workers by creating systems of dependence upon the companies.[11]

Other forces compelled workers in early industrial towns to create cooperatives. The growth of industrialized economies and increasing urbanization created intense social and economic dislocations. The large and growing population of wage earners depended upon sporadic and low pay for inadequate housing in unhealthy cities. Strained family economies meant that people tended to rely on credit to purchase often adulterated foodstuffs. Until the end of the nineteenth century, there was little social welfare available. Because workers lacked insurance and pensions, it was difficult to provide for major moments in the life cycle—birth and deaths—as well as unexpected illness or disability. Furthermore, even if one had a job, factory and mine work was unpredictable. Workers' families knew that even when there was full employment, hard times might come again within a few months.

The first cooperatives grew out of traditions of solidarity between workers and artisans. Mutual insurance and friendly societies in England, France, and the Low Countries provided associations to enable working people to save for times of extra expense and penury and were seed beds for cooperative buying ventures.[12] Early cooperatives were associations for mutual self-help, often organized around bread and other essential foodstuffs. Studies of English cooperatives, for example, have documented the efforts of the urban poor to establish cooperative flour mills, flour clubs, and corn-milling societies from the late eighteenth century on. These efforts to assert control over aspects of distribution and consumption paralleled efforts to retain control over production. Workers being squeezed by the processes of industrialization founded early producer cooperatives in the late eighteenth and early nineteenth centuries. Many of these early cooperatives, such as the one at Hull, England, founded in 1795, were meant to provide unadulterated and inexpensive bread. Others, in the early to mid-nineteenth century, were producer cooperatives formed by members of specific trade to assert control over their labor and liberate themselves from economic exploitation.[13] These institutions were founded in an era of new openness to association and new forms of sociability as older, more formal types of sociability such as villages, guilds, clientage, and the established churches weakened. The very term "society," meaning a voluntary organization of equal individuals, was an invention of the period as was the related concept of the modern public sphere.[14] And, it was within the proliferation of institutions for "self-help" beginning in the late eighteenth century and "cooperative association" in the early nineteenth century from which inventive new visions of "society" would emerge.[15]

By the 1820s in England, the Owenite movement linked the practice of founding cooperatives with new visions of community and a reordering of society.[16] These efforts provided an ideological critique of emergent industrial capitalism, a radical vocabulary, and institutional experiments that envisioned a "new moral world," a society and an economy to be built upon, to use Peter Gurney's felicitous phrase, "the art of association." The Owenites also generated a body of committed activists who provided both expertise and institutional memory for the full-fledged cooperative movement later in the century. What workers tried to do was to create economic organizations to advance their interests as middle-class people had, but to make these new institutions be democratic and profit-sharing, rather than hierarchical and exclusive. At the same time, utopian thinkers in France such as Henri Saint Simon and Charles Fourier preached a variety of socialist programs, which included communal and cooperative ventures as ways to end economic inequality.[17]

The legacy of utopian socialism was strongly evident in the subsequent cooperative movement in which cooperators attempted to "build a bridge, materially and ideologically, between the competitive present and the cooperative future." A number of Chartists in the 1830s and early 1840s created consumer cooperative stores while working to reform the British political system.[18] Elsewhere, in France and several German states, associationist impulses, along with the economic distress of the 1840s, fueled the founding of consumer and producer cooperatives. These cooperatives were formally constituted, democratically managed, and jointly owned economic organizations dedicated to education and mutual self-help among working people.[19] With the failure of Chartism in the early 1840s in Britain and the revolutions of 1848 on the continent, associational activities were channeled into cooperative activities. Many activists saw cooperation as "economic" and "social" while the confrontational tactics of Chartism and 1848 were explicitly "political." These notions were consistent with earlier beliefs that the key to economic and social transformation lay with education and mutual self-help. Utopian socialist ideas of thinkers such as Charles Fourier and Etienne Cabet, which emphasized communal solidarity as the salvation of humanity, encouraged workers and artisans in Continental Europe to embrace cooperation.[20]

We can see the confluence of these early developments within the history of what was the most influential consumer cooperative in European and American history—the Equitable Pioneers of Rochdale, England, founded in 1844. A textile town, Rochdale had long been the center of labor protest as the power loom displaced handloom weavers. Artisans and workers in the town supported radical politics as discontent with the passivity of local oligarchy mounted. Rochdale had also been the site of early cooperative activities, including the "Rochdale Friendly Co-operative Society" founded in 1830 by handloom weavers to offset the high prices and adulterated food being sold by local merchants. The Owenites were also active in Rochdale. As historian Brett Fairbairn emphasizes, the creators of the Equitable Pioneers of Rochdale in 1844—Owenites, weavers, some ex-Chartists, and a few temperance campaigners—were "thinkers, activists, and leaders who functioned within a network of ideas and institutions."[21] Motivated by ideals of a more just social order, as well as by pragmatic economic concerns, the first statutes of the society testify to the Pioneers' desires to link vision and practice, economic goals with social purposes. The Rochdale Pioneers saw their economic activities as sequential; first they intended to open a cooperative store, and the profits from the store would mobilize capital for cooperative housing and cooperative production. Producer cooperatives were then to provide employment for the members, and the goods they produced were to be sold in the store. The final goal was the creation of a community based in cooperation rather than competition, a "new moral world" to replace the "old immoral world"—a vision clearly inspired by Owenism. The Rochdale Pioneers, in sum, reformulated "self-help" in collective rather than individualist terms, and envisioned cooperation as a practical strategy for the achievement of new order of society and economy.

The Rochdale Pioneers were especially important because of the cooperative's influential principles and organization. Its statutes, gleaned from earlier Owenite models and duly registered with government authorities under the Friendly Societies Act, set forth principles that have been retained by subsequent cooperatives and that have served as an important foundation for the later cooperative movement. The cooperative was to be democratically controlled and to avoid the evils of capitalist enterprise. It was to be a member-owned business, with capital based on members' purchase of shares. Officers were to be elected. Sales were for cash only, not credit. This meant that the familiar tragedy of working people falling into debt and being trapped financially for years was to be avoided. Share capital was to receive only a limited return, and profits (after meeting expenses and interest charges) were to be distributed to members on the basis of their purchases (rather than on shares). Over the years, additional statutes stipulated that each member was to have only one vote—an important expression of democracy, that a portion of the profits of the cooperative was to be used for education, and that both sexes were to have equality of rights regarding membership.

The Rochdale cooperative, which began selling basic foodstuffs and simple household items (sugar, flour, oatmeal, candles, and the like), rapidly expanded its operations and its membership (from seventy-four members in 1845 to six hundred members only five years later). And, while a cooperative community along Owenite lines was never realized, the Rochdale cooperative diversified its operation into production, wholesaling (The Co-operative Wholesale Society, or CWS, was founded in 1863), and an extensive network of educational endeavors and social works. The development of large wholesaling institutions was especially important. Not only did the CWS, and its Scottish counterpart the Scottish Cooperative Wholesale Society (SCWS, founded in 1868) allow for economies of scale and scope, but it also meant that the cooperative societies themselves joined together in a federation-type arrangement by which they entrusted not only wholesale purchasing, but eventually production and import trade, to the wholesale society on behalf of the affiliated societies. As a result, by the early twentieth century, the British cooperative movement was not only the largest and financially strongest in the world, it was also a model for an interconnected movement with strong central agencies. [22] Whether or not the turn from visions of a new moral world to the purportedly more pragmatic matters of building a strong consumer-oriented institution was a reformist retreat or, as Peter Gurney and other revisionist historians have recently argued, remained a profoundly radical cultural enterprise, remains an open question.

The spectacular success of the Rochdale Pioneers inspired efforts to create cooperatives elsewhere and provided a powerful example of how to blend practical economic initiative with social and educational goals. As we shall see in many of the chapters in this collection, cooperatives inspired by Rochdale served as the origin for cooperative movements in numerous countries in the second half of the nineteenth century. Knowledge about the "Rochdale system" of cooperation spread in a variety of ways. Particularly important was the publication in the 1850s of a series of articles by cooperator George Jacob Holyoake in the London *Daily News*, which was soon published in book form and translated into many languages. Word spread as well among political exiles in England in the 1850s who returned home to continental European countries and founded cooperatives, and also among interested social reformers who journeyed to England to see the British cooperatives first hand. Brett Fairbarn's chapter in this volume recounts the influence of Rochdale on various founders of German cooperatives. For example, Victor-Aimée Huber, a conservative German writer, traveled to England and then promoted consumer cooperation in Germany as a solution to the "social question." Eduard Pfeiffer, who also visited Rochdale in the early 1860s, subsequently published a book on consumer cooperation and promoted consumer cooperatives in Württemberg as working-class institutions dedicated to "participation, democracy, and transformation of society." [23] In Peder Alex's chapter on Sweden in this volume, we learn how various writers introduced the British and French cooperative movement in Sweden during the 1850s. In the Americas, workers of British background who had experience with consumer cooperation founded a Rochdalian cooperative in the mining town of Stellarton, Nova Scotia, in 1861, the first of dozens founded in mining and industrial communities in Canada. [24] In the United States, the impetus for consumer cooperatives on the Rochdale model came primarily from European immigrants, especially those from the Scandinavian countries, as well as within immigrants from the British Isles in the agricultural and working-class movements such as the Grange and the Knights of Labor. [25]

The intentions of the founders of new cooperatives, however, as well as the uses to which they were put, were not always consistent with Rochdalian goals and principles. In general, the chapters in this volume highlight the uneven application of the "Rochdale System" and explore the variegated forms of cooperation that evolved in light of national and regional particularities, notably the timing and intensities of industrial development, urbanization, and the growth of an urban working class, and the shape of politics and political cultures. Consumer cooperatives in the mid-nineteenth century were often founded by middle-class reformers eager to promote cooperation as a means of self-help among groups being squeezed by an emergent capitalist market economy.

The aim of these reformers, however, was not to oppose the market. They saw cooperatives as a way ultimately to ease the disadvantaged groups' transition into a liberal capitalist order. Hermann Schulze-Delitzsch in Germany, for example, saw cooperation as a way for the *Mittelstand* (lower-middle classes) as well as waged laborers to band together within cooperatives, pool their individual and collective capital, pull themselves by their own efforts, and become "honest citizens." In Sweden, Abraham Rundbeck founded a cooperative in 1867 based on Rochdale principles and intended to educate workers in self-sufficiency and "moral" development. Austrian cooperatives in the 1860s and 1870s were meant to increase the purchasing power of economically disadvantaged individuals; as one cooperator put it "to provide the little man with as many of the advantages of large capital as possible."[26] The Danish clergyman H. C. Sonne was instrumental in founding cooperatives meant to raise the educational and "moral" level of workers by improving their material well-being and fostering "respectability." In France, liberals, including prominent liberal economists such as Léon Walras, saw consumer cooperatives as an avenue for individual self-help; workers were to save their dividends from cooperatives, become "small capitalists," and thus find state aid, revolutions (a particular concern in France), and trade unions unnecessary.[27] Many of the early exponents of cooperation in this era, then, envisioned cooperation as a liberal means of economic association intended to promote social peace and to ameliorate material distress and social tensions; consumer cooperatives were thus to provide an antidote to worker radicalism. Class conciliation, individual saving, moralization, and self-improvement were the watchwords of this generation of liberal cooperation. Cooperation in this view was an alternative to socialism, a perspective that helps explain the hostility toward cooperation shown by some of the leaders of the emergent socialist movements, particularly Karl Kautsky, in the latter part of the century.[28]

This era saw the multiplication of different kinds of cooperative societies as well as different understandings of the uses and purposes of cooperation. Accelerating in the 1850s, savings and credit societies, along the models provided by Germans Hermann Schulze-Delitzsch and Friedrich Wilhelm Raiffeisen, and later Wilhelm Haas, were especially strong in Central Europe. Designed to bring credit and capital within the reach of people of modest means—particularly self-employed artisans and peasant-farmers—their efforts became People's Banks, multipurpose village cooperative stores, and special-purpose cooperatives such as those for dairy products.[29] In Italy, Luigi Luzzatti, a Venetian economist and politician, founded a People's Bank (*Banca*

Popolare) in Milan in 1864.[30] In Liège, Belgium, a *Banque populaire*, founded in the 1860s, by 1889 claimed 2,706 members, more than half of whom were workers and artisans.[31] Adapted from Schulze-Delitzsch's model, shareholders could obtain loans and enjoyed limited liability. In Italy, rural savings banks (*casse rurali*) inspired by the Raiffeisen cooperatives were established by Leone Wollemborg, a middle-class reformer who became a government minister beginning in 1883.[32]

Mutual insurance societies, known in the British Isles as "Friendly Societies" or "Benefit Societies," were also often closely related to consumer cooperatives. The economic principle behind these societies was similar to those in modern insurance companies, indeed many private companies today in the United States and elsewhere began as "mutuals." Individuals paid small amounts each year or each quarter to insure that if they incurred an accident or death, their family would receive some larger benefit. Unlike private companies but like cooperatives, the societies were to be run by representatives of the beneficiaries, not an owner or small group of shareholders.[33] Building societies were a variant of the same principle; individuals paid into the building society in order to have the right to borrow money to build or buy housing. As Patrick Joyce argues for the textile industrial areas of England, "In their provision of benefit and fellowship, the friendly societies were perhaps the central institution of working class life."[34] Outside Britain where wages were higher for workers and building societies and mutual insurance societies were particularly strong, however, these groups did not always reach a working-class constituency as much as consumer cooperation did. In many industrial areas on the Continent, only the better-off workers had enough money to invest in a building society or mutual insurance fund. In turn of the century Bochum, Germany, for example, a city heavily dependent on manual work in coal mining or iron-smelting, the cooperative housing movement was largely a lower- middle-class movement.[35] Even in Britain, E. J. Hobsbawm argues, until the last twenty-five years before World War I, cooperatives and friendly societies, like trade unions, were predominantly the work of the best-paid workers, the so-called "labour aristocrats."[36]

Agricultural cooperation among farmers emerged at the same time and, around the world, in the twentieth century has usually been the strongest example of cooperative economic enterprises. Farmers, both renters and those who owned their own land, formed cooperatives designed to market agricultural products, purchase seed and implements, and provide credit. In Denmark, as Niels Finn Christiansen points out in his chapter in this volume, such cooperatives helped transform the country's agriculture in the face of the collapse of European grain prices because of the influx of cheap New World and Russian grain.[37] Similar cooperatives spread in Germany, Belgium, and France.[38] These purchasing and marketing cooperatives frequently began selling household goods and later food in order to further assist their members.

This retailing, however, was and has usually continued generally to be a secondary activity to the goal of strengthening the agricultural activities of the farmer members.

Cooperatives, both consumer cooperatives and those for credit or agriculture buying or marketing, were also used for political and religious purposes. For example, consumer and credit cooperatives within Austria-Hungary were often quite political and organized among ethnic and religious groups to further their interests within the Empire. In Slovenia, for example, cooperative organizations were seen as a way to strengthen the economic position of Slovenes and to gain more economic independence from German-Austrians. One description of the Slovenian credit cooperatives characterized their nationalist motives as "economic self-reliance and independence of the Slovenian nation from German capital. . . . Let us get rid of the foreign capital which exploits us. Let us start saving institutions out of which banks will develop. As long as we don't have our own financial institutions, we are still far away from national freedom."[39] The Catholic cooperative movement, as well as other cooperatives based on religious goals and principles, also gained in influence although it was slower to develop and usually did not become as large as neutral or Socialist movements.[40] Belgium, for example, which had the strongest Catholic labor movement in Europe, also developed a Catholic consumer cooperative federation as did France and Germany. Italy has remained the most divided country in terms of cooperation, but it is also one where Catholic cooperatives' membership is today the largest.[41]

In the last third of the nineteenth century, there was still a strong belief in the potential for producer cooperatives to return knowledge and economic power to artisans and workers. The Knights of Labor in the United States, described by Steve Leikin in this volume, was one of many movements in the industrialized world that saw a "cooperative system" of worker-controlled enterprises as reform for society.[42] Nonetheless, the increasing costs of capital investment and the complexities of obtaining capital and marketing goods made creating successful producers' cooperatives more difficult. The tensions within cooperation between putting scarce resources into producer cooperatives or founding consumer cooperatives as a way to provide capital for the eventual founding of producer cooperatives remained a major issue of debate for decades.

Most cooperative movements in the mid- to late nineteenth century began with some productive operation as a vital part of the enterprise or at least as a goal. Yet, by and large, early producers' cooperation generally failed, or at least certainly grew much less than did the consumer side of the movement.[43] Kathleen Donohue illustrates this shift in her chapter in this volume where she analyzes discussions among intellectuals and movement activists. She explores, for example, how the late-nineteenth century economist and Christian socialist Richard Ely in the United States advocated cooperation, and especially producers' cooperatives, as a way to unite labor and capital and eliminate class conflict. By the early twentieth century, however, cooperative theorists were attracted to the work of the British writer Beatrice Potter (Webb) and influenced by Potter's argument that consumer rather than producer cooperatives could more easily transform the economy as a whole. The French cooperator, economist, and professor Charles Gide was also influential in this regard. He insisted upon the potential economic power of associated consumers, power that would enable them to organize distribution and production to meet the needs of consumers and to provide auxiliary services such as banking, insurance, and housing.

In important ways, the new perspectives of Potter, Gide, and others who were constructing a theory of "consumer sovereignty" formed part of a larger shift in economic theory. "Classical" political economy had arisen in a world of apparent scarcity; the major concern of most economic thinkers until late in the nineteenth century was to explain how more goods could be produced and the few goods available could be better distributed. According to the classical view, production set prices. Beginning in the late nineteenth century, economic theory was moving away from scarcity, production, and supply toward the "neo-classical" concern with explaining why producers produced what they did and how production and consumption meshed within whole societies. In this neo-classical view, demand as determined by customs, set prices. Older emphases on production and supply were giving way to arguments that every act of exchange influenced the values of all goods within an economic system. Although the individual remained a central focus in the new theories, there was an increased importance placed on consumers, households, and firms. In other words, it was not primarily the labor put into a product that regulated its value, but the quantity and quality available in relation to the demand for it by consumers.[44]

Theorists of consumer cooperation agreed with the increasing importance placed on demand and on the power of consumption to influence production. Still, they also differed in important ways from most neo-classical economists. They stressed the role of *associations* of consumers rather than *individual* consumers in the creation of that demand. Cooperators also reinterpreted profit, arguing that cooperatives "redistributed" profits among members according to their purchases rather than the amount of individual shares. Not capital, then, but the needs of consumers ruled cooperatives. Workers employed by cooperatives, furthermore, were to be paid trade union wages and to share in the distribution of profits within the cooperative as *consumers*.

Yet, nagging questions remained. If the ascendancy of consumer cooperation by the late nineteenth century was based on the power of workers as consumers, did this leave cooperation open to the charge that it was not really fully a challenge to capitalism? If production, distribution, and finance remain capitalist, was consumer cooperation simply a cooperative branch grafted awkwardly on the capitalist trunk of the economy? For many critics, consumer cooperation was seen as always vulnerable to capitalism's control of politics and the rest of the society, and as an insufficient lever for any radical economic and social transformation of vital modes of production.

One place in which these debates were heatedly and passionately discussed was within the International Cooperative Alliance (ICA), founded in 1895. By the late nineteenth century, information regarding cooperation had long flowed across national boundaries, and the exchange of delegations of cooperators routinely attended national cooperative congresses. At the London meeting of 1895, which constituted the ICA, the founding institutions and individuals represented the diversity of understandings of cooperation, with delegates from consumer cooperatives, credit cooperatives, agricultural cooperatives, profit-sharing societies, and producers cooperatives. A wide variety of political perspectives—liberal reformist, socialist, and Catholic—also were present. The diversity of perspectives at the initial meeting was indicative of the cooperative movement at the time, although the more conservative interests rather than the socialists dominated the ICA in its first several years. The subsequent constitution adopted by the ICA did not resolve all the fundamental differences of purpose and interpretation among cooperators (notably concerning profit-sharing, the relative balance among the different forms of cooperation, and the "true principles" of cooperation), but it did promulgate an article that has remained a constant within the movement, i.e., that of political and religious neutrality.[45]

Over the years, consumer cooperation became the dominant form within the ICA, especially after the withdrawal from the ICA in 1904 of German and Austrian agricultural cooperatives and credit banks of the Schulze-Delitzsch and Raiffeisen models. Strengthening the emphasis on consumer cooperation was the gradual abandonment by cooperative theorists of the notion that consumer cooperation was a step toward the culminating goal of producers' cooperatives. Consumer cooperation instead came to be seen as a means by which the planned and systematic organization of consumers would work toward a new economic and cultural system. This new system would complement in the economic sphere the advancing democracy of the political sphere. By late nineteenth century, then, the emergence of national cooperative organizations as well as the growth of the ICA worked to streamline the varieties and definitions of consumer cooperation. They also contributed to the ascendancy of notions of collective "consumer sovereignty" as a way to envision a more just society and economy.

The relations between socialism and cooperation had several major variations across the industrialized world and went through some important changes in the nineteenth and twentieth centuries. Cooperation in Britain, as in the rest of the English-speaking world, has been careful to insist upon its political neutrality, although many of its leaders have identified with the labor union movement and with Labour politics.[46] By the end of the nineteenth century, however, during a general acceleration of working class militancy and political mobilization, there was an important reevaluation of the relationship between socialism and cooperation elsewhere in the industrialized world, especially continental Europe. As many of the chapters in this volume note, many Socialists had been opposed or were indifferent to cooperation both for theoretical reasons and because of the long-standing interest in consumer cooperation by bourgeois, liberal reformers, and industrialists. In the 1860s German socialist Ferdinand Lassalle had argued that consumer and credit cooperatives would do little to change workers' conditions because wages tended toward the level of subsistence set by capitalists. Lassalle was more hopeful about producers' cooperatives, but recognized that they needed to obtain large amounts of capital (which he felt would ideally be obtained from a democratic state) in order to compete effectively with large-scale capitalist enterprises. Karl Marx had warned against cooperation becoming a reformist alternative to the only true solution to workers' problems, nationalization of industry by a proletarian government. German socialist Karl Kautsky declared in an 1897 pamphlet that consumer cooperatives did not offer any answer to the social question. National leaders of socialist parties were deeply suspicious of consumer cooperation for other reasons as well, including its historic links to liberal self-help, the fear that support of consumer cooperation would encourage "reformism" within socialism, and continued ambivalence concerning the petit-bourgeoisie as potential socialist supporters (especially of the position of shopkeepers who saw consumer cooperatives as economic rivals).[47] Meanwhile, the national cooperative organizations generally were not reaching out to the socialists; until after 1895 in France and 1903 in Germany, the largest consumer cooperative movements were neutral and reformist. Economist Charles Gide inspired and led the Cooperative Union (*Union coopérative*) in France while the General Union (*Allgemeine Verband*) in Germany had been founded by Schulze-Delitzsch and was led by his liberal followers for decades.

Workers who were often both politically sympathetic to socialism as well as supporters of trade unionism, however, were responsible for a grassroots transformation of this equivocal relationship. As we see in more detail in the chapters in this volume, local people moved ahead of their national leaders by founding cooperatives that were closely aligned with other socialist organizations. The large and important cooperative *Produktion* was founded in Hamburg, Germany, in 1899, for example, after a strike of port workers. The cooperative then grew through the efforts of trade unionists and expanded into worker housing and production. In the coal and steel towns of the Ruhr in Germany, cooperation came eventually to be as central a part of working class life as labor unions.[48] By 1910, the international organizations of both cooperation and socialism recognized their mutual interests. The 1910 Congress of the Second International, at which socialist cooperators such as Adolf von Elm of Berlin, Germany, and Edouard Anseele of Ghent, Belgium, had taken part, recognized that consumers cooperatives were economic institutions working toward the democratization and socialization of the economy. The Congress affirmed that consumer cooperation was a weapon of the working class in its struggle to achieve political and economic power. A resolution of the Congress demanded that all socialists and trade unionists should become active members of consumer cooperatives, and that the cooperatives in turn should ensure fair working conditions for their employees and sell products produced under just conditions. A few days later, the ICA, meeting at the Congress of Hamburg, adopted by a large majority a resolution declaring its approval of and agreement with this assertion of the Second International.[49] By the twentieth century, the Socialist Cooperative Exchange (*Bourse des Coopératives Socialistes*) in France and the socialist-aligned Central League of German Consumer Associations (*Zentralverband Deutscher Konsumvereine*) in Germany became the largest in their respective countries. The Scandinavian movements went through a similar shift, but without splitting cooperative ranks. The closer relationship of consumer cooperation with the labor and socialist movements both heightened the radical possibilities of consumer cooperation and galvanized and financially sustained the labor unions and socialist parties.

What the chapters in this volume demonstrate is that a radical, politicized, and politically engaged notion of consumer cooperation that emerged within working class communities was subsequently officially recognized as one of the "three pillars of socialism" by socialist and trade union leaders. In Belgium, where socialists went the furthest toward integrating cooperation as a full part of their movement, cooperatives kept the socialist party and labor union movement alive before 1914. It was the leading socialist of Flemish Belgium, Edouard Anseele, who said cooperatives were to be the "milk cows of the party." A certain percentage, generally 2 percent, of the profits of the socialist cooperatives in Belgium and in parts of France, went directly into socialist party coffers. Belgian cooperation pioneered the practice of inscribing workers automatically on socialist party rolls when they became members of the cooperative. Belgian cooperatives provided a model of integrating all working class organizations in a locality together and bringing together economic action, politics, art and music, and leisure as in clubs, tourism, and sports. The largest Belgian consumer cooperatives, the *Maison du Peuple* of Brussels and *Vooruit* of Ghent, for example, sponsored art exhibits, popular lectures, theatrical performances, tours to galleries, and musical evenings, and housed within their large and magnificent buildings the consumer cooperative and socialist party headquarters as well as presses, cafés, pharmacies, and later movie theaters.[50] Not surprisingly, Emile Vandervelde, leader of the Belgian socialist party, was the leading advocate in the late nineteenth and twentieth centuries among continental socialists for rejecting political neutrality and allying cooperation with Socialism—either formally as in Belgium or de facto as the French, German, and Scandinavian socialist cooperators did.[51] The example of Belgian cooperation was an inspiration for other continental cooperative movements, as in France where cooperators traveled to Belgium for advice much as a generation earlier cooperative enthusiasts had traveled to Rochdale.[52]

The links between consumer cooperation and an emergent working class movement were especially potent as cooperatives expressed and made manifest many of labor's goals and assumptions. Socialist consumer cooperatives not only financially sustained other aspects of the labor movement, but they participated in the elaboration of an alternative culture. As Peter Gurney explains, cooperation was competing with capitalist forms of business, learning, and pleasure.[53] Large, urban consumer cooperatives—many with the red flag of socialism proudly flying over the building—were places bustling with activity and energy in the early twentieth century. Not only were cooperatives centers for a range of worker education initiatives, but they provided opportunities for working class mobility. The cooperative provided skills in store management and jobs in the wide range of institutions connected with consumer cooperatives (often for workers fired after strikes). As historian Stephen Yeo has observed, consumer cooperation entailed an "identification of class with activity and confidence rather than submission . . . with capacity rather than with apathy."[54] We argue here that consumer cooperatives can be seen as the site of an alternative culture, one which linked working-class consumers' economic, social, and political concerns. By 1914, consumer cooperation was the largest and strongest working class movement in Europe—larger in membership than either the labor unions or political parties.[55]

During World War I, consumer cooperatives in continental Europe were often seen by wartime governments as ways both to ensure food distribution and to help provision postwar society. In part, this reflected the entry of labor and socialist leaders into the wartime governments. The patronage of government, however, also points out cooperation's strengths. Cooperatives often had lower costs and could operate more efficiently than private retailers, but they did so by offering a narrower range of goods and by doing less in terms of advertising or other services. During wartime, under conditions of scarcity, cooperation's strengths were real advantages. Private shopkeepers in Germany often complained bitterly about the government encouragement of cooperation by, for example, rationing out large wholesale purchases that favored cooperatives.[56] In Russia and the Ukraine, during and immediately after the war, cooperatives, especially in rural areas, became essential to supply basic food necessities. By 1919, there were an estimated 4 million members of consumer cooperatives in the Ukraine.[57]

The War also radicalized many cooperators and encouraged them to become more political. Ironically, in Britain, where cooperation was the strongest, the government often ignored the cooperatives until the height of the food crisis due to the German submarine blockade in late 1917.[58] As a result, in Britain, where political neutrality had always been upheld, the cooperative movement shifted sharply to the left. A "Co-operative Party" even formed as part of a coalition with the Labour Party.[59] In Russia, the Bolsheviks who came to power in 1917 distrusted the voluntary, decentralized cooperative movement and preferred a state-controlled distribution system. Lenin and Trotsky initially hoped to centralize the cooperative movement and create one nationwide "cooperative." Between March 1919 and April 1921, the cooperatives were officially nationalized, although the chaos of the Civil War meant that many local cooperatives escaped the effect of this decree. Once creating a single, government, controlled system proved impractical, however, and the cooperatives proved valuable in simply keeping food accessible to consumers, the government reversed itself. As part of Lenin's "New Economic Policy" beginning in 1921, consumer cooperatives became a mainstay of a new communist system of distribution.[60] Until Stalin drastically—and this time, thoroughly—renationalized the cooperatives in the process of the industrialization and collectivization drive in the 1930s, the Russian cooperatives were among the most successful in the world.

In many ways, in terms of numbers of members and proportion of retail trade under their control, the cooperatives in Europe had their greatest time of success in the interwar era. In 1920, cooperatives accounted for approximately 18 to 20 percent of total national sales of groceries and household items in Britain, while approximately 35 percent of the population belonged to cooperatives. In Germany, members of the cooperatives leaped from 1.8 million members in 1914 to 3.5 million in 1924. In 1921, over 20 percent of the German population belonged to cooperatives.[61] The new Weimar government in Germany after World War I, which in its early years had substantial Social Democratic support, encouraged the expansion of consumer cooperatives in order to bring down retail prices. During the most catastrophic inflation in world history in 1923, the German government guaranteed the credits of the Prussian Central Cooperative Bank in order to save the cooperative movement's finances.[62] The association of cooperation with socialist and Labour governments boosted the prestige of the movement worldwide. Even Canadian cooperators used the photo of consumer cooperative goods being delivered to 10 Downing Street when Ramsay MacDonald was briefly in office as Labour Prime Minister in 1924.[63]

The First World War and its aftermath, however, began several major shifts that slowly brought about immense changes in the world of cooperatives. As discussed in more detail in a later section, capitalist companies found new ways to stimulate demand through advertising, entertainment, and credit buying. All these had been less important for cooperatives, which were primarily interested in satisfying consumers' essential needs at the lowest price. The shift in the position of cooperation within working class movements was also important. Before 1914, cooperatives usually had their greatest success when they were parts of tightly knit working class subcultures, as for example, in Austria, Belgium, Britain, France, Germany, and Sweden. Cooperatives, along with labor unions and Socialist and Labour parties, were outside the centers of power in society, but were poised, many observers believed, to move together with other working class movements into a position of real power. In fact, the First World War brought about the selective integration of Labour and socialist parties into government and of labor unions into the economy. This selective integration left cooperation somewhat isolated. Unemployment and health insurance and collective bargaining appeared to many activists to guarantee a minimum level of income better than inexpensive goods from cooperatives. Thus, the gains brought about by social welfare systems sometimes lessened working-class activists' view of cooperation as essential to workers' emancipation.

At the same time, consumer cooperation's identification as a manifestation of working-class communities and an arm of the working class movement was challenged by a new ideal of consumer activism and advocacy. The cooperative ideal was that consumers could be best protected in a capitalist society by having recourse to their own retail system run by cooperative, not capitalist principles. Even if cooperation did not absorb a great majority of retail trade, its very existence served as an alternative to private capitalist enterprise and prevented capitalist firms from having a monopoly. In the new visions of consumer advocacy, consumers could protect their interests by lobbying governments, publicizing information about retail goods and services, and pressuring capitalist firms through public opinion and boycotts. Initially, many consumer cooperatives also supported consumer advocacy, but eventually the logic of the two approaches often led to tensions within the movement in many countries. It may be no coincidence that the United States, as both Steve Leikin and Kathleen Donohue point out in their chapters in this volume, had the weakest consumer cooperative movement in the industrialized world already before World War I, but soon had one of the strongest consumer advocacy movements. The Consumer Union, organized in 1936 but whose oldest ancestor organization was founded in 1920, helped lead to a broader consumer movement in the United States that later, under the leadership of Ralph Nader in the 1970s and 1980s, was a model for the rest of the industrialized world.[64]

Consumer cooperative movements tried to respond to the new situation after the First World War with a variety of strategies. National cooperative movements struggled to merge many small, local cooperatives into increasingly larger units. At the same time, the movements tried to strengthen wholesale operations. The giant British operation, the Cooperative Wholesale Society (CWS), already before 1914 had begun setting up production facilities and shipping depots in continental Europe, the United States, and Canada. It expanded its activities in the 1920s and 1930s so that by 1939 the CWS had 60,000 workers in 182 factories and depots in Britain and abroad.[65] Swedish cooperators expanded production facilities in order to break capitalist monopolies and bring down prices for items as diverse as margarine, gasoline, and galoshes.[66] The consolidation of small cooperatives into a larger one, however, was the major goal. For activists who had created cooperatives in the pre-World War I period as grassroots organizations based in local neighborhoods, consolidation was often a painful process. It could also be painfully slow. In England, the 24 largest societies had 25 percent of the membership in 1900; by 1939, after many mergers, they had 37 percent.[67] Tensions over local versus central control have continued to the present. Centralization meant less democratic governance, but, for the most part, increased efficiency and economies of scale and scope.[68] Cooperative movements also tried to meet the challenges of the post-World War I world by increasing offerings to members in the areas of insurance, banking, entertainment, and leisure.

The very success of cooperation in many areas in the interwar period elicited responses from competitors, responses that became more insistent in the Depression of the 1930s. Ironically, consumer cooperatives were often lumped with department stores, chain stores, and banks as enemies of the lower-middle-class shopkeepers. These enemies, the shopkeepers charged, destroyed the independent retailer and left society all the more vulnerable to big business.[69] This charge was often brought by fascists and Nazi movements in the 1920s and 1930s, but it built on long-standing complaints about cooperatives' non-profit or tax-exempt status in many countries. In France and Belgium already in the late nineteenth century, private retailers demanded that cooperatives pay the *patente*, the tax that allowed one to operate a business.[70] Even in the interwar era, anticooperative sentiment went well beyond fascist or reactionary movements. In 1919, the British National Chamber of Trade declared:

> The enormous growth of the co-operative movement during recent years [means that] an ever-increasing volume of trade is yearly passing out of the taxable area and becoming a menace to the state by making it more and more difficult for the Chancellor of the Exchequer to balance the nation's account.[71]

The economic difficulties of the 1920s and especially the Great Depression stimulated anticooperative feeling to a new height.[72] Mussolini's Fascists attacked consumer cooperatives before their rise to power in the 1920s, ransacking their buildings as a way to win support from lower-middle-class shopkeepers.[73] In both democratic Belgium and Nazi-controlled Germany during the 1930s, governments imposed so-called "padlock laws," which gave them the power to control or limit the opening of retail outlets. This shackled the department and chain stores, but also prevented cooperatives from exploiting their natural advantage of economies of scale.[74]

The Depression also weakened cooperatives by weakening or even bankrupting the credit institutions that working-class movements had formed and that had helped finance the consolidation of consumer cooperatives. In both Austria and Belgium, the "Labor Banks" went bankrupt. Hundreds of cooperatives as well as labor union locals and individual workers lost their savings.[75] The decline of consumer cooperation is a larger part of the story of working class mobilization than many historians or social scientists have realized. Subsidies from cooperatives to Socialist parties declined and then disappeared after the early 1930s. Up to the 1930s, cooperatives had often had surplus funds that they used to grant subsidies or loan money to Socialist parties or labor unions. Outside Scandinavia and Britain, cooperatives now instead tended to be weaker financially than parties or unions that could now rely on political patronage or mandatory dues.

The greatest challenge to cooperation came from hostile political regimes, usually in countries where the movements had first been weakened by high unemployment among workers. As Gabriella Hauch and Brett Fairbairn explain in their chapters in this volume, for example, fascism and Nazism destroyed or took over cooperatives in Austria and Germany, as they did in Italy, Czechoslovakia, Spain, and Japan.[76] Already before the Depression, the German Socialist cooperative movement's membership had fallen from its peak after the War, but the Depression accelerated this trend. Membership fell from 3.5 million to 2.8 million between 1924 and 1933. Soon after their takeover, the Nazis forced both Socialist and Christian cooperative movements into a new Nazi-party dominated organization, while also closing seventy-three cooperatives that had a membership of over a million members. By the time the Second World War broke out, membership and sales had fallen still more. Finally, in 1941, the War provided an excuse to close the cooperatives down completely.[77] In the case of Austria, during the 1930s and 1940s, dictatorships—first Christian authoritarian and then, after 1938, Nazi—took over the cooperatives for their own purposes. Cooperatives remained useful as economic enterprises because of their relatively efficient operation. Their leisure organizations survived, but under state control. The leaders of the cooperatives were purged, however, and cooperatives were taxed and not allowed to expand.[78]

Consumer cooperation in the post-World War II period went through another series of transformations, largely conditioned by larger social, political, and economic forces. The erosion of working class communities undermined consumer cooperation's historical membership base. The political divisions of the Cold War meant that consumer cooperatives in Eastern Europe underwent extensive redefinition and transformations as they were effectively taken over by the state just as those in the Soviet Union had been by Stalin in the interwar era. The onset of social welfare states in much of Western Europe resulted in cooperation becoming more of a consumer advocacy group in some countries, while in others—notably in Sweden—the historical weight of cooperation as a "Third Way" had helped make it a vital part of the emergent social democratic state since the 1930s.[79]

By 1958, which could be taken as the apogee of the immediate post-World War II success of the cooperatives, one can distinguish roughly three groups of countries where cooperatives were strongly implanted, had a modest presence, or were only weakly represented (see table 1). In countries such as Finland, Israel, Sweden, and Great Britain, cooperatives were a significant part of the entire economy, while in Belgium and Italy they had a presence but not real power, whereas in the United States and the Netherlands, they had only marginal importance.

Table 1. *Cooperatives' Turnover as Percentage of GNP* (1958)

Finland	19.7	Norway	5.4
Israel	6.7	Denmark	4.7
Sweden	6.0	Switzerland	3.9
Britain	5.5		
Austria	2.2	Italy	1.5
Germany	1.6	France	1.4
Belgium	1.6		
Netherlands	.8	Japan	.2
Canada	.6	India	.2
USA	.3		

Source: Jean Meynaud, *Les consommateurs et le pouvoir* (Paris, 1964), 40.[80]

Finally, the acceleration and increased velocity of capitalist consumer economy and culture, discussed below, made it increasingly difficult to sustain cooperative institutions that offered economic and cultural alternatives to capitalist consumerism. Despite a flurry of interest in consumer cooperation during the 1960s in both the United States and Europe, the movement's influence in Europe receded from the 1980s, its membership often committed but

aging, its mission as a harbinger of a new social and economic order diminished, its self-definition framed primarily in terms of consumer advocacy, and
its economic activities limited to a small cooperative sector. The Austrian,
Belgian, French, and German consumer cooperative federations all, in effect,
collapsed in the 1980s and 1990s, although a number of local and regional
cooperatives still continue. The growth of small, countercultural consumer
cooperatives in the United States since the 1960s and the extension of federal
credit guarantees to consumer cooperatives has left some experiments still
thriving, but they are a tiny part of the retail market.[81] Ironically, some of the
recent interest in cooperatives in North America and Western Europe has been
among one of the traditional enemies of consumer cooperation: lower-middle-
class operators of small businesses. By forming cooperatives to purchase
wholesale goods or obtain equipment, groups of small, private businesses in
the United States, Germany, and other countries have hoped to fend off the
challenge of monstrous multistore chains such as Wal-Mart and C&A. These
discussions of cooperatives, however, involve little of the idealism or social
vision of the traditional cooperative movement, but rather questions of economic survival for small businesses.[82]

One could argue that as Europe and North America moved, in the postwar
period, away from an economy of scarcity and austerity and toward managed
economic growth and social welfare provisions, the locus of cooperation
shifted to the non-European world. The most important area of growth for
consumer cooperation is the newly industrializing nations of Africa, Asia, and
Latin America. The spread of consumer cooperation from Europe to other
continents was part of a long-lasting international dimension to cooperation.
Since the age of pioneers who first spread the news of Rochdale to other
countries, more successful cooperative movements have often fostered cooperation elsewhere. In 1913, the British CWS loaned the capital to the French
cooperators to start the FNCC wholesale company.[83] After World War I,
Belgian cooperatives loaned money to French socialists to start their own
newspaper after the pre-World War I French socialist daily, L'Humanité, was
taken over by Communists.[84] During the interwar period, the cooperative
movements that were in the strongest position in their own countries could also
experiment with international production. Swedish cooperators challenged the
international light bulb cartel formed by capitalist producers by creating their
own firm, Luma. They then brought in the Danish, Norwegian, and Finnish
cooperative movements and expanded their market.[85]

The spread of cooperation beyond Europe has been a part of this tradition.
British cooperative activists first introduced consumer cooperation to India
around 1900.[86] The American businessman Edward Filene who became a
leading propgandist for cooperation in the United States "became interested in
the idea when he was in India in 1908, on a trip around the world, where he
met W. R. Gourlay, an Englishman, who was assisting in establishing credit

societies."[87] By 1912, the British Government of India introduced a Cooperative Societies Act, modeled after the original Provident and Friendly Societies
Act in Britain, which allowed cooperatives to obtain legal recognition and set
standards for their financial accounting.[88] Information about the successful
cooperatives in Europe led to the founding of cooperatives by both middle-
class reformers and working-class activists in countries such as Japan before
World War I, but most of these had limited success.[89]

The inclusion of the formerly private International Labour Office in the
new League of Nations after World War I was a major impetus to the spread
of cooperation. The French Socialist Albert Thomas, as Director of the ILO,
established an Office of Cooperation in the ILO, which published information
on cooperation and organized visits of cooperators to countries worldwide.[90]
The International Cooperative Alliance became the world's largest non-govern-
mental international organization and actively encouraged cooperative efforts
especially in Africa and Asia. As parts of these efforts, the ICA in 1923
created an International Cooperative Flag, also known as the Rainbow Flag,
and designated the second Saturday in July as "International Cooperative Day."
Before World War II, most of the efforts to create cooperatives outside Europe
and North America, however, bore modest fruits, although agricultural and
credit cooperatives did better than consumer cooperation. Because of British
influence, for example, India had the longest history of consumer cooperation
outside the industrialized world. Yet in 1939, there were only 385 cooperative
stores with some 60,000 members.[91]

The real growth of consumer cooperation outside Europe has been since
the Second World War. Communist control in Russia and Eastern Europe and
the takeover of cooperative movements by right-wing dictatorships in Argentina and Greece were setbacks, but otherwise cooperatives grew quickly in India
and Japan as well as in countries such as Mexico, Nigeria, Sri Lanka, and
Indonesia.[92] By 1960, the number of non-European countries represented in
the ICA outnumbered European ones for the first time. As recently as 1992,
two-thirds of the consumer cooperators in the ICA still came from Europe, although there are important groups of consumer cooperators outside Europe
who belong to non-ICA organizations. Given the heavily agricultural and
capital-starved economies of much of the non-European world, the greatest
impetus for cooperative efforts was to create purchasing and distribution
cooperatives for farmers and credit unions for the general public. But consumer
cooperation also grew as activists for farmer cooperatives and credit unions
began organizing consumers alongside these organizations and as the cooperative idea spread. In many cases, the same government subsidies, tax advantages, and favorable laws that helped farmers and credit unions also facilitated
consumer organizing into cooperatives.[93]

Besides the growth in Asia and Africa, there are still strong signs of the
appeal and adaptability of the cooperative ideal. In the Scandinavian coun-

tries—Denmark, Finland, Norway, and Sweden—consumer cooperatives have successfully weathered the challenges of chain stores and continued to be the preferred places to shop for about a fifth of the population. Although its market share has shrunk to only about 10 percent, British cooperation as a whole is the biggest purveyor of food in the country. Some of Europe's strongest cooperatives are in countries where the cooperative movement had never existed or been wiped out before 1945. Spain under Franco's dictatorship was completely cut off from the International Cooperative Alliance. Yet beginning in the 1950s, a Basque priest, José Mariá Arizmendiarreta, who had heard of Rochdale, helped workers around the town of Mondragon create a huge complex of production, agricultural, housing, and consumer cooperatives. By 1985, there were 111 consumer and production cooperatives with a workforce of 19,200. The enterprises typically depended on workers acting as self-employed investors, not on total cooperative ownership, but nonetheless democratic control was maintained via elected boards.[94] Although less dramatic, Italy's network of small cooperative ventures also demonstrates that cooperative practices can be adapted to a variety of ends.[95] Other efforts also demonstrate cooperation's appeal. Farmers' cooperatives flourish all across the globe from Canada, France, and Israel to India and Japan.[96] The financial sector is the largest in the International Cooperative Alliance. Some 60 million Americans belong to credit unions, while credit cooperatives represent 12 percent of the German banking sector. Funeral cooperatives have sprung up in Canada and the United States. Co-op America sponsors a credit card service and long-distance service—Working Assets Long Distance (WALD)—in the United States, while recently car sharing cooperatives have sprung up in Switzerland and Germany.[97]

Yet these efforts' success raise the question of why consumer cooperation, once the most common form of cooperation and one founded on the most ubiquitous of economic activities, that is, shopping for daily food, should not have had more success. The chapters in this volume explore, in ten different national contexts, the successes and failures of consumer cooperation in order to see what the history of cooperation can reveal about the evolution of economic practices and attitudes, social movements, and the distribution of power. American consumer activist Ralph Nader has written that there is much to learn from the history of consumer cooperation for modern consumers seeking economic power and justice:

> the theory behind consumer cooperatives possesses powerful attractions. . . . Under this theory, consumers band together to start their own business which they are supposed to own and control. Thus combined, consumers can not only vastly expand their bargaining power vis-a-vis manufacturers and wholesalers, but they can also determine what they want to sell to themselves and under which

standards. They can condition the terms of purchase from suppliers well beyond price to include quality, safety, nutrition, warranty, durability . . . They can federate into larger cooperative networks to move into the wholesaling and even the manufacturing sectors. They can use their cash flow to add ancillary services and leverage their membership into their own insurance, media, travel, and adult education enterprises. Where economic issues are shaped by political decisions, cooperatives can inform and organize their membership to participate in a highly informed and persistent manner.[98]

Since meanings of cooperation have historically derived both from the local and international context, surely any newer manifestations will be both similar and different from those that have gone before. The future of consumer cooperation will doubtless be influenced by the legacy of earlier consumer cooperative movement, with its historical commitment to community self-reliance, democratic governance, profits returned to consumers rather than corporations, and economic justice.

Cooperative Commerce

If markets have been almost as ubiquitous in modern history as civilization itself, why should cooperatives exist? Does the dramatic decline in recent years of consumer cooperation in countries such as Germany, Belgium, and Austria—countries where the movement had once known great success—mean that consumer cooperation is inherently unworkable in economic terms? The best way to attempt to answer these questions is to compare cooperatives to capitalist enterprises in order to see their similarities and differences and to examine whether consumer cooperatives are in any way inherently ineffective economically. In the process, it is crucial also to examine the impact of capitalist consumer culture in the twentieth century and the role of gender in the evolution and the decline of the consumer cooperative movement in the industrialized world. First, however, it is useful to define what consumer cooperation is more precisely and to review what the indictment of consumer cooperation has been.

In economic terms, we can define consumer cooperatives as democratically run, collectively owned, private enterprises, which return a share of their profits to the customers and members who collectively own the organizations or whose member-customers decide to invest the profits for social goals. Cooperatives compete in the market, but their internal organization is shielded to a degree from market forces. The German theorist Georg Draheim argued that cooperatives were simultaneously economic organizations and social groups.[99] Similarly, Holger Bonus states that cooperation is "a hybrid organizational mode blending market forces with elements of internal organization."[100] The emphasis on democratic control—whether it has always been developed fully or not—is important in order to differentiate cooperatives from many buying clubs that may give rebates or discounts but whose "members" in fact do not exercise any control. Cooperatives always have at least an official charter and mechanism through which members can choose the leadership of the cooperatives and exercise certain rights of recall, oversight, and initiative. Unlike business corporations, which have shareholders who theoretically can exercise some of these rights, but who possess more votes according to their number of shares, almost all cooperatives, since the days of Rochdale, have granted every member an equal vote.

Democratic procedures thus help differentiate cooperatives from the "cooperatives" started by business people in the nineteenth century, which were really commercialized buying clubs and were alternatives to both Socialist cooperatives and nonpartisan, but genuinely consumer-controlled cooperatives. Such "cooperatives" were sometimes parts of paternalist strategies by which employers sought to keep workers from participating in genuine working class organizations that might by allied with labor unions. In the 1880s and 1890s, the Flemish textile and harbor city of Ghent, Belgium, and the coalfields of the Nord-Pas-de-Calais in France were two of the most successful areas for cooperatives in continental Europe. Yet *Volksbelang* and the *Société Coopérative des Mineurs d'Anzin et de Denain* were the largest "cooperatives" in their regions. Members of these "cooperatives" might own "shares," but these shares only gave them the rights to earn dividends or take advantage of discounts. A small group of business people ran the organizations.[101]

Nonprofit status, that is, where profits are returned to members according the amount purchased or where the members can collectively decide to reinvest the profits, is a critical distinction. This has meant that owners, or a small group of managers or wealthy shareholders, do not have the right to dispose of the profits generated by a mass of customers. Tax-exempt status is critical to understanding the opposition to cooperatives and, for that matter, any other collective enterprise such as credit unions and mutual insurance societies. Nonprofit status has meant, in almost every country in almost every period, that cooperatives have been exempt from government taxes. (One important exception is Japan, where cooperatives pay a number of taxes.) As discussed above, this has always fueled opposition to cooperation from private retailers anytime the movement has had some success, for example, in Western and Central Europe in the interwar period and in Japan in the 1950s and 1960s.[102]

Generally cooperatives achieved relatively full freedom to operate and incorporate in the same era of legal liberalization in the mid- to late nineteenth century as did business corporations, labor unions, and political organizations. Already by their time of legal recognition, however, cooperatives could be hampered by government restrictions, which private retailers pushed to have applied to them.[103] Governments on their own could also restrict cooperatives' ability to expand, sell shares or bonds, open branches, or integrate production and distribution. These restrictions, however, were often the same or similar to those sometimes applied to department stores or chain stores. By themselves, the legal problems faced by cooperatives have not caused the movement's decline. It was only in combination with other trends that legal and political handicaps set the movement back.

We can also use the Industrial and Provident Societies Acts of 1893 in Great Britain as good examples for helping to define cooperatives. They established clearly that cooperatives were considered corporations, not partnerships. That is, the cooperatives continued to exist even though their officers and members changed, and the cooperative, not its individual members, was legally liable for its debts, infractions of the law, or other juridical difficulties.[104] Such laws, however, have also usually required that cooperatives not restrict their activities to members or restrict membership to certain groups, even though members can continue to exercise certain rights that nonmembers do not enjoy. The requirements to keep services open to all and to not restrict membership have usually been applied to prevent giving tax-exempt status to private clubs. In practice, cooperatives have almost always served largely their own members, or better, few nonmembers have patronized cooperatives. In 1919, less than 2 percent of the British cooperatives' business was estimated to be with nonmembers.[105] As Brett Fairbairn explains in his chapter in this volume, one variant of this, however, is Imperial Germany where consumer cooperatives were required to sell only to members. Cooperatives complained that anticooperative activists could harass them by reporting accidental sales to nonmembers or even entrapping salespeople. This provision was dropped under the Weimar govenment of the 1920s.[106]

Having defined cooperation more clearly, it is useful to examine the economic critique of it. Over the last century, observers have sometimes argued that cooperation is impractical, although the supposed reasons for this vary depending on observer, and the various reasons are often closely linked. First, cooperation, it has been argued, depends on alliance with or support for Socialist or other ideological working class movements. This supposedly inhibits cooperation from being able to make major decisions on its own or acting as a genuinely economic enterprise. Second, consumer cooperation, it is sometimes alleged, depends on small, local control, or decentralized operation. It thus cannot survive when capitalist consumer enterprises move, as they historically have in almost every industrialized country sooner or later, toward large-scale, multiregional operations. Third, in a somewhat related argument, cooperation, it has been claimed, is unable to amass large amounts of capital and work well with large economies of scale. Depending on the argument, this has been either because it is too dependent on local control, or because the Rochdalian commitment to returning some of the profits to members eliminates the possibility of capital accumulation. Fourth, cooperation allegedly depends on scarcity or a lack of competition due to oligopolistic, that is, quasi-monopolistic conditions, or government regulations. Where consumer items are scarce, poor quality, or high-priced or where consumers are constrained in their choices, cooperatives have something to offer by keeping costs down, concentrating on simple provisioning, or offering rebates. Where abundance, especially of food, is present, and consumers can be tempted to exercise taste, caprice, or impulse, cooperatives fail. Fifth, the dedication of cooperatives to democratic control is a fatal flaw. Once capitalist enterprise has sufficient capital and a free enough market in which to expand, cooperation lacks the central leadership to compete. Each of these criticisms is weaker than it appears, although the last three issues—use of capital, scarcity, and democratic control—point to three interrelated challenges that many, but by no means all, consumer cooperatives have failed to overcome. [107]

First, as pointed out earlier in the historical discussion, despite the close connections between socialism and cooperation, cooperation is not necessarily socialist, indeed, the majority of cooperative movements have not been socialist. Cooperation has not been statist; in many ways, it embodied private, free enterprise. The key differences—besides democratic control—between capitalism and cooperation have always been the distribution of profits, by a few under capitalist or by the collectivity under cooperation. Furthermore, that cooperation has been usually closely associated with socialism or other working class organization has not meant that cooperation has been radically distinct from the world of other private retailers. Private capitalist retailers and consumer cooperators have been part of the same milieu and borrowed ideas and techniques from each. In the early period of nineteenth century development of cooperatives, artisans and tradespeople formed cooperative buying ventures, exchanged credit, and tried to match production and consumption, i.e., a shoemaker might trade shoes for food from someone who did market gardening. In the late nineteenth and early twentieth centuries, cooperatives and private retailers sometimes collaborated. In exchange for discounts given to cooperative members by private retailers, cooperatives would recommend the retailers to their members.[108] Similarly, cooperatives innovated in offering self-serve retailing, which private retailers then adopted, while cooperatives copied some of the advertising and brand-name marketing of their competitors.

Second, cooperation did not suffer necessarily from failures to exploit economies of scale. Cooperatives were often pioneers in their size. While many economists believed cooperation was inherently incapable of dealing with large capital investments and economies of scale, the leading Belgian cooperatives were some of the largest commercial establishments in the country before the First World War. If they could pool their resources, cooperatives had the ability to invest in innovations. As Gabriella Hauch points out in her chapter in this volume, the first supermarket in Austria, opened in Linz in

1950, was part of the Austria cooperative network. In Britain, too, the first self-service supermarket was opened by the cooperatives, and for a time in the late 1950s, 90 percent of the self-service food outlets were parts of the cooperative movement.[109]

The real challenge for cooperation has been the integration of wholesale and retail, but this was a major problem for capitalist enterprises as well. Consumer cooperation emerged as a major force in the late nineteenth century at the same time as a host of cooperative economic institutions—agricultural cooperatives, credit unions, building societies, incorporated mutual insurance societies, and labor unions—and capitalist business institutions—limited liability corporations, cartels, and business federations. At the same time that corporations were forming to integrate suppliers of raw materials with final producers, the most successful federations of consumer cooperatives were doing much the same thing. The Austrian cooperative federation opened a milling operation rather than simply buy flour to make bread; the Belgian *Vooruit* cooperative built a textile mill and fishing fleet to supply its members with clothing and fish.

Cooperatives in almost all countries have tried, with varying degrees of success, to lower costs and increase their range of goods for sale by pooling their wholesale and distribution efforts. Cooperative warehousing and transportation was often critical to creating cooperatives that succeed in taking advantage of economies of scale. These same efforts, however, also led to criticisms that bureaucracy and a concern for capital accumulation were overtaking cooperation. This vertical integration was usually a later, second phase after the demise or downgrading of producers's cooperatives: cooperatives, or centralized federations of cooperatives set up manufacturing plants, fishing fleets, farms, and textile mills. The organization of production in these establishments has often been a hybrid of hierarchical management and worker rights. In other words, these production facilities were usually not cooperatives themselves. Italy's producers' cooperatives are an exception to this rule. Even today, the producers' cooperatives in Italy are about as important in the economy and in the cooperative movement as consumer cooperatives.

Third, consumer cooperation has shown the ability to amass large amounts of capital. Cooperators have not always shown the wisdom needed to invest capital most efficiently. In Belgium, Austria, Germany, and Scandinavia, the Labor Banks that flourished at various points in the twentieth century all had sizeable proportions of capital from cooperatives. The Danish and Swedish cooperative movements have always depended on reinvesting a proportion of their surplus into research, expansion, and attempts to cut costs.[110] In the late 1950s when British cooperators had to mobilize capital to face the immense challenges of supermarkets, chain and department stores, and American-style mass advertising, as Birchall points out, they still had a vast reserve of non-trade assets (amounting to 42 percent of their total assets), much locked away in safe investments outside of retailing. If the movement wanted it could mobilize all the capital it needed for development—around £100 million. (In 1990s U.S. dollars, this would be about a $1 billion US.) If more was needed the CWS could have borrowed against its very undervalued assets. The message was that the Cooperative Movement could finance a radical modernization program, if only it had the will to do so.[111]

The problem was how to use capital. Despite some innovative areas, the British cooperatives as a whole failed to invest in modernizing their stores or adding new ones, and as a result they fell behind their capitalist competitors. By 1985-1986, British co-ops had capital expenditures equal to only 3.3 percent of sales, while Sainsbury had 7.3 and Marks and Spencer had 4.3. As a result, they also only half to two-thirds the sales per employee that their competitors did.[112] Contrary to many outside perceptions, cooperatives have not been stymied by the need to give rebates to their members. Nor have the donations made by cooperatives been so large that capital accumulation or large-scale borrowing have been impossible. Rebates and the pressure to support other nonprofit organizations and social movements have been costly at times, but certainly no more wasteful than what has been done by the host of capitalist enterprises, which have gone bankrupt after having invested foolishly or gotten far too much into debt in attempts to expand. More typical have been cases like that of the British cooperatives that were not using capital the movement had accumulated in order to create efficiencies or integrate. Movements that did not make these mistakes, such as the Swiss, Scandinavians, and Japanese, have survived and thrived.

Fourth, scarcity or oligopolistic and regulated markets could be great advantages to cooperation, but these were not necessary to have cooperation succeed. Cooperatives could do well in the late twentieth century when food prices fell, although shifting to the kind of economy where food was not scarce or high-priced was a major challenge, which some failed to make. It is true that, originally, the scarcity of food, high prices, and adulterated products drove working people in nineteenth-century Europe and in twentieth-century Asia to create consumer cooperatives. Private capitalist retailers took advantage of limited markets to charge prices often for poor quality goods. Cooperatives would be more likely to provide food at reasonable costs because customers as members had an immediate voice in complaining about high prices and poor quality. It is no coincidence that in many European countries during and shortly after both World War I and World War II, when rationing was in force and goods were scarce, cooperatives did well. The greatest growth of consumer cooperation on record came in the huge influx of members in Britain and Germany during and immediately after World War I. Similarly, Japanese cooperatives have carved out a strong niche for themselves in the post-World War II era because many small retailers use government regulations to keep out competition and charge higher prices.[113] Nonetheless, cooperatives can adjust to a new situation of more competitive markets. Danish, Swedish, and Swiss cooperatives have succeeded by switching to higher quality goods, advertising more aggressively, and emphasizing service and consumer awareness. Despite the collapse of most of the German consumer cooperatives, the Dortmund-Kassel cooperative continued to do well into the 1990s by maintaining a high level of efficiency and close relations with its member-customers.[114]

It is the argument of most of the authors in this volume that the real challenge for consumer cooperation in the industrialized world has not been the movement's economic weaknesses but its obligation to confront the consumerist revolution. Cooperation's great crisis was adaption to changing times and tastes—providing a fuller range of goods and appealing to more tastes without giving up the advantages of low costs and democratic, consumer participation. Food had been the mainstay of cooperatives' business since the mid-nineteenth century. Cooperatives had difficulties in shifting into furniture, clothing, and household appliances. Of greater importance, as described more fully below, the nature of consumption as a whole changed. Whereas middle and upper classes since the late eighteenth century had indulged in conspicuous consumption and the vagaries of style and fashion, the mid-twentieth century saw working class people finally becoming enmeshed in consumer culture in an important way. The 1920s, with the explosion of advertising and entertainment, formed the critical watershed. People came out of the scarcity of the War ready to embrace a different attitude toward spending, debt, and the buying of the right good—not simply the cheapest good as a way to avoid debt or hunger. As a German cooperative leader noted in the late 1920s: "I have found that before the War, people were actually not as demanding in the choice of food as they are today. These increased demands have probably been created by the food problems which developed right after the War and in the inflation. In addition to this, people today probably place more value on quality."[115] By the 1930s, even as unemployment tore at countless workers' lives, the fall in the cost of living and, still more, the newly stoked appetite for consumer items created a new kind of retail economy. "In a decade of unparalled depression," wrote George Orwell in bewilderment, "the consumption of all cheap luxuries has increased." [116] The traditional goal of consumer cooperation, in other words, had been to take the great expansion of production that industrialization—workers' toil—had made possible and offer its bounties to the workers' family by selling inexpensive goods and by allowing the family to stretch its way. The key advantages of cooperation, it was assumed, were satisfying needs, selling inexpensively, and eschewing luxury and waste. All these assumptions became undermined during the interwar period.

The fundamental shift in thinking from the nineteenth to twentieth centuries, which caught consumer cooperation in midstream, was the move from production to consumption. Virtually every nineteenth-century economics textbook begins with production, every twentieth-century one with demand.

As noted earlier, cooperative thinkers had assumed that the vise of neo-classical economics helped justify consumer cooperatives because, in cooperatives, the customer or consumer had primary control. In fact, unbridled consumption turned out to be a vastly more complex power than cooperative activists had imagined. Cooperatives, with some important exceptions, found it difficult to reorient their goals from provisioning people cheaply—taking advantage of the fall in the cost of production—to meeting a variety of demands. Allowing workers to buy more on credit appeared to encourage reckless not thoughtful consumption. To attract and hold members in large numbers, cooperatives found themselves forced to offer clothing and household goods, which went rapidly in and out of fashion and whose inventory costs ate up cooperatives' jealously guarded reserves. [117]

The major shift away from food as the primary item of expenditure for the mass of the working population was one of the great threats to traditional consumer cooperation. As William Richardson pointed out in 1977,

> Food supply is the traditional business of the Co-operative Movement and for more than a century has represented the greater proportion of its sales and production. The Movement has been less successful in the supply of non-food products. [118]

As late as 1860, the typical British working class family spent 62 percent of its income on food. [119] The creation of a global grain market in the late nineteenth century drastically lowered prices and lowered the proportion of income spent on food. Nonetheless, as late as the Second World War consumer cooperation could concentrate on supplying food at inexpensive prices as its main line of business because food remained the major item of expenditure for the vast majority of lower-income people. In England, with probably the cheapest food prices in Europe because of lower tariffs and excellent transportation networks, between 1920 and 1938, the average proportion of income spent on food only fell from 50.7 percent to 46.6 percent. [120] After 1945, this level began to fall in Britain and Continental Western Europe alike and has continued to fall down to the present. By 1970, Western European households paid only 27.8 percent of their income on food, and this included a range of food items of higher quality and greater diversity than had been imaginable in 1945. [121] As recently as the 1920s, many retail shops and cooperatives alike stocked only 1,000 different items; by the 1970s, 4,000 to 8,000 items was common. [122] In many ways, the first wave of mass retailing in Western Europe after 1945 paralleled the earlier impact of chain stores in the United States in the 1920s and 1930s. Chains found ways to adapt themselves to working class neighborhoods and offered more choice and a wider array of goods than cooperatives or small shops had done.[123] Increasingly, profit margins on food shrank, food became a smaller proportion of retail trade, while private retail grocery chains made a substantial part of their profits from nonfood items. Traditional consumer cooperatives, outside Scandinavia and Japan at least, found it difficult to break into the nonfood sector and were caught with low profit margins in a very competitive market. One additional argument for the difficulty that consumer cooperation traditionally had in the United States was the relatively lower proportion of income spent on food.

Cooperatives could have expanded into the full-service food and nonfood sectors as did the largest private retail chains. In Britain, Austria, and Scandinavia, cooperatives were the leaders in the 1950s in opening self-service stores and supermarkets.[124] But many of the cooperative-run self-service stores were too small and their costs weighed down the few genuine supermarkets that cooperatives opened. The great decline of consumer cooperation in Western Europe came with the changes generated in working class life and mass retailing in the period of economic expansion of the 1960s. As Brett Fairbairn demonstrates in his chapter in this volume, in the early post-1945 era, German cooperatives competed well by adopting many of the features of private retailing, but most of them eventually collapsed due to financial mismanagment by 1990.[125] By the 1970s, supermarkets were predominantly a private chain phenomenon and were gaining rapidly on the cooperatives' share of the retail food trade.

More than scarcity or lack of capital, the connection between wholesale and retail was the crucial link in determining whether cooperation succeeded. Ironically, the earliest cooperators had seen the critical importance of this connection. Price-fixing and scarcity drove workers to create cooperatives that could sell at lower prices than what private retailers charged. Private distributors and wholesalers who added huge markups to food and goods were often the real enemy. "By-pass the middle man, go direct to the source of supply" was a common slogan.[126] Even when, by the late nineteenth century, production cooperatives proved difficult to sustain, consumer cooperatives tried to set up their own production or distribution facilities or at least to do a major share of their own wholesaling. By the 1930s, the mills and dairies of the British CWS provided 22 percent of the milk and 17 percent of the flour in England, while CWS tea plantations in South Asia made the CWS the world's largest distributor of tea.[127] During the twentieth century, however, cooperation—outside Scandinavia—failed to integrate vertically to create real economies of scale as did huge private manufacturers like Unilever and Proctor and Gamble and large retail chains such as Sainsbury in Britain, Aldi in Germany, Monoprix in France, and Delhaize in Belgium. At the peak of self-production in 1938-1939, the British cooperatives produced about one-third of their sales. After 1945, usually a quarter or less of their sales were purchased from their own manufacturers. Meanwhile, the over 30,000 cooperative retail outlets were often too small, divergent in clientele, and autonomous to bring about real economies of scale on the retail side. As one historian of English cooperation, William Richardson, described the situation in the 1960s,

> The Movement had so far failed to co-ordinate the enormous buying and manufacturing power of the retail and wholesale sides and wield it as a national marketing and sales promotion force. Fragmentation and local autonomy prevailed in almost every field of Co-operative trading at a time when private enterprise was marshaling its forces into specialized, nationally controlled units.[128]

The Scandinavian countries where cooperation managed to surmount these changes provide an instructive exception that proves the rule. As Niels Finn Christiansen shows in his chapter in this volume, the cooperative movement in Denmark is a successful economic and social movement that retained 17 percent of all retail trade, 25 percent of the food sales, and one-third of the food and beverage market in the 1980s.[129] The major growth of consumer cooperation took place among Danish farmers, and it was sustained by a strong network of local newspapers linked to the farmers political party. Farmers were important in the national organization of cooperation founded in 1896, and they were instrumental in founding dairy cooperatives. The alliance between farmers' cooperatives—both producers and consumers—and urban consumer cooperatives has allowed cooperation as a whole in Denmark to flourish. Consumer cooperation built up the capital reserves with which it could support the introduction of new products, respond to changing consumer tastes, and open bigger and more attractive stores. Similarly, the Norwegian and Swedish cooperative movements consolidated enough control over local cooperatives to lessen inefficiency and develop inexpensive wholesaling. In Norway in 1982, 25 percent of all retail trade was in cooperatives, while in Sweden in the 1980s cooperatives accounted for 7.4 percent of all private consumption.[130] In Japan, cooperatives, by one estimate, accounted for one-third of retail food trade.[131]

Fifth, democratic control of cooperation, although difficult to maintain, has not been a fatal flaw for the success of cooperatives. Indeed, there is evidence for the reverse. When cooperative movements neglected cultivating their grassroots membership and allowed democratic procedures to atrophy, the movements suffered economically as well. This does not mean that democratic procedures require literal control of the major decisions by members. Rather, leaders have to be accountable to members through elections, have to depend for their legitimacy on popular support, and, equally important, have to keep members informed of the organization's problems and activities. The best research for this comes from work done on farmers' cooperatives, but many of the lessons apply to the consumer sector as well. Agricultural cooperatives—groups that purchase equipment and market products together—have been most successful when they depend on a flexible amount of democracy in order to keep members committed to the organization and ensure the leadership has the legitimacy to act in the name of the members.[132] It is no coincidence that the cooperatives and national cooperative movements that have survived have been those with close contacts with their grassroots members. The Scandinavian cooperatives have long kept published periodicals to inform their members and have been sensitive to changing their policies to suit members' opinions. Japanese cooperatives, especially the famous Kobe cooperative, which is probably the largest single consumer cooperative in the world, organize many members into *han* groups that buy their products together. *Han* groups, largely made up of women, also sample goods together, hold study groups, and send representatives to larger assemblies. The result is a close relationship between local customers and the executives overseeing the entire cooperative.[133]

The history of consumer cooperatives, then, suggests that cooperatives could be competitive in economic terms. Many of the successful aspects of what has been seen as intrinsic to capitalist enterprise could be carried out in cooperatives—creation of large-scale organizations, higher levels of capitalization, and centralization. Cooperatives all struggled with how to maintain consumer participation and democratic recognition while still creating the degree of bureaucracy and centralization needed to compete. Cooperatives also contended with capitalism's hold on government policy, but sometimes they were just as vulnerable to petty bourgeois pressure through government policies that opposed cooperation not because it was anticapitalist but because it was successful at being large-scale.

This history also illuminates the ways that consumer cooperation's commercial strategies and responses have historically been shaped within cultural concerns. The consumer culture advocated and practiced within cooperative commerce differed in important ways from that of capitalist commerce, and where it overlapped (as was increasingly the case from the 1920s) capitalist consumer culture often proved more appealing to new generations of consumers. The culture of consumption articulated by and through consumer cooperation was one that expressed older notions of community, of collective responsibility, and of forms of sociability and leisure that were not necessarily commercially based. Brass bands, theaters, puppet shows, children's choruses, temperance teas, and, by the interwar period, vacation centers for collective leisure were among the many cooperative activities that drew upon working class cultures and communities. The ethos of cooperation emerged from communities in which scarcity rather than abundance informed patterns of purchasing and sociability. By the late nineteenth and into the twentieth centuries, this economy of scarcity, or at best of financial prudence, was in transition. The growth, however uneven, of real wages and the proliferation, especially in urban areas, of capitalist exchange networks and institutions of mass culture contributed to the breaking down of older patterns of working class life. The commercialized consumer culture of advertising, department stores, national brands, and chain stores fostered individualist acquisitiveness, not collective solidarity or prudence. New forms of sociability and leisure such as music halls, variety shows, vacations, and movies that emphasized individualist pleasures, were appealing and deemed "modern." [134]

The chapters in this volume highlight several areas in which cooperative commercial culture differed from that of capitalist commercial culture, and one aspect will serve here to underscore the different commercial cultures of cooperative and capitalist retailing. Throughout its history, consumer cooperation has advocated the role of commerce in fostering a "moral economy." While the meanings and emphases of this notion changed over time, there has been a persistent concern within the cooperative movement that commerce was more than profit-making, that commercial transactions should be part of larger ethical commitments, and that those commitments could lead to more just social and economic systems. We can see this perspective in the cooperative movement's understanding of the goods themselves.

From its origins until well into the twentieth century, cooperators situated goods within both a language and a set of practices that spoke to dualistic notions of "true" and "false" needs. Discussions of "needs" were a way cooperators projected an alternative to the kind of materialist, individualist, and profit-oriented consumerism being constructed by capitalist commerce, a consumerism that depended upon elastic notions of ever-expanding consumer needs and desires.[135] Cooperators believed that retailers' creation of needs was artificial, conspiratorial, and simply a search for profit. The kinds of goods sold in cooperative stores were meant to meet what cooperators considered "authentic" consumer needs, and in turn those of goods generally reflected what working people considered necessities and what they could afford—foodstuffs, household items, clothing, dry goods, and so forth. Well into the twentieth century, both workers and artisans continued to spend by far the largest share of their income on food (as much as 60 percent in the mid-nineteenth century),[136] and as noted above, foodstuffs were the mainstay of cooperative commerce. Whereas a vibrant capitalist consumer culture was becoming a reality for middle-class people in the nineteenth and early twentieth centuries, and was indeed an important aspect of the very definition of being middle class, for workers and artisans the commodities and leisure patterns associated with this culture were more visible than attainable. Working people might acquire extra clothing, a watch, some household items and rough furniture, and perhaps an inexpensive decorative item, but in general they rarely experienced enough of an increase in disposable income necessary for accessing the full range of available consumer goods and leisure activities. Hence, cooperatives tended to concentrate primarily on foodstuffs (groceries, baked goods, fresh meat, dairy products, and tea). Most also sold household items (lamps, dishes and glasses, etc.), school supplies, clothing, cloth and other dry goods, and shoes.[137] As Peter Gurney notes in this volume, cooperators focused on selling goods that were "honest," unlike overpriced or shoddy commodities or adulterated foodstuffs sold by small shopkeepers or the emerging capitalist chain stores. The demand by cooperators for unadulterated food at honest weights and measures reflected very real problems of commercial fraud in the era preceding self-service and prepackaging. It was widely acknowledged that foodstuffs such as flour and wine were adulterated, and consumers would find that their ground coffee contained roots and fruit pits. Cooperatives guaranteed honest weights and measures of foodstuffs, priding themselves on not weighting the scales and overcharging consumers. This can be seen in one widely disseminated pamphlet from the British cooperative movement that was translated into other languages, *Five Reasons for Joining a Cooperative*. In this pamphlet, a fictive worker explained why he favored cooperation: "I want no more adulteration or deception, or that which is part of the pursuit of profits. When I am my own merchant I will not seek to deceive myself. I want just prices and measure in the store so that justice and truth will be first realized in small things prior to being realized in larger things."[138] Similarly, even in the earliest days of Japanese consumer cooperation, writes Ruth Grubel, "the high quality of the products was seen as essential to the organization's success."[139]

Cooperatives also placed their commercial operations in critical counterpoint to what they considered to be another form of deceit, that of "false" luxury and seduction. While department stores and chain stores were experimenting with advertising strategies, concentrating on making stores appear as luxurious as possible, presenting goods in exotic and opulent displays to create new versions of mass spectacle, and fostering a dream world of magic and enchantment filled with objects of desire meant to enhance self-identities,[140] cooperatives consciously rejected these techniques. Until at least the twentieth century, cooperatives eschewed advertising, considering that it created "false" needs. Whereas department stores and chain stores were generally located on busy streets and had brightly lit and decorative window displays, cooperatives sought to represent their stores as modest and part of the neighborhood. A description of Parisian cooperatives prior to World War I, for example, noted that "Cooperatives whiten their store windows, certainly no laws oblige them to do this." Another observed that cooperatives were generally located on back streets, and that with an "affectation of austere purity," they often had unpolished glass. He went on, however, to describe the interior of a Parisian cooperative as bustling with activity, bright, pleasant, and decorated with prints, a bust of the Republic, and placards about meetings.[141] Cooperatives also persisted in not allowing credit within the stores, considering that it was a form of "temptation" for consumers, seducing them into buying goods that were not necessary. As Peder Aléx in his chapter on Sweden illustrates, credit had been seen as one of the great scourges of working-class life in the nineteenth century. Rather than offering credit, cooperatives encouraged workers to save and to take the dividends or bonuses from the cooperative at the end of the year as their reward.

A result of these perspectives was that consumer cooperatives were relatively slow to expand into a wide variety of goods, and cautious about the new merchandising techniques that were part of the "retailing revolution." However, by the interwar period, as incomes were rising and the products and pleasures of mass consumption were becoming more widely available, cooperators were forced to respond to the increasing pressure and competition from capitalist retailers—including fierce competition from the spread of five-and-dime stores modeled on Woolworths.[142] Central to the multiplication of sites to meet expanding "needs" was the conscious appeal by retailers to notions of ever-expanding individual "choice" in the selection of commodities. As cooperators realized that the future would be capitalist rather than cooperative, they began to rethink at least some of their commercial strategies and to stock a wider variety of goods, such as furniture, bicycles, and bedding, in order to compete commercially. As the smaller cooperatives merged into larger commercial enterprises after the First World War, the stores became much larger and began physically to resemble those of capitalist enterprises. Mimicking the layout of department stores and five-and-dime stores, cooperatives restructured their sales floors into departments. In Sweden the national movement opened its own architectural office in 1925 to design new, modern stores inspired by Bauhaus norms.

Consumer comparatives also shifted their position on advertising as a purveyor of "false needs." As advertising within capitalist retailing became increasingly pervasive and sophisticated, elaborating a new kind of commodity aesthetic, cooperators realized the necessity of responding to this challenge.[143] In France, for example, advocates of advertising began to argue that advertising did not create false needs, but that it was simply a form of consumer education. In 1922 the French movement established the National Office for Cooperative Advertising, and the advertisements it produced were barely distinguishable in their appeals and aesthetics from other commercial advertising.[144] Another advertising initiative concerned the use of a trademark brand. While many national cooperative movements had long had distinguishing logos (the wheat shaft in Britain, the clasped hands in France), by the 1920s the International Cooperative Alliance urged national organizations to adopt the more transnational and apolitical log COOP, which then was applied to product labels, posters, stationery, and to the signs on the outside of local cooperative stores. And yet, while the cooperative movement adjusted its commercial strategies to compete with capitalist commerce, it was not without ambiguity and a certain commitment to the movement's cultural heritage. As Peder Aléx notes in his chapter in this volume, the cooperative movement in Sweden remained very skeptical toward commercialism and mass consumer culture, viewing a profit-driven economy as manipulative and not geared toward satisfying human needs. He describes the ways that the movement began in the 1920s to address what those "needs" were through a systematic program of consumer education that emphasized the importance of product information, proper labeling of contents, healthful nutrition, and "good taste." The latter encompassed a wide range of concerns, including the importance of light, air, and cleanliness in the home, as well as household articles whose aesthetics reflected their functionality in contrast to cheap, mass-produced ones imitating aristocratic highly ornamented design.

The cooperative movement's commercial culture of a "moral economy" also consistently linked human "needs" to social and political concerns. As Peter Gurney notes in his chapter in this volume, the cooperative ethos did not view goods as autonomous icons, abstracted from history, but rather as enmeshed in discernable cycles of production, distribution, and consumption. Consumer cooperatives refused to carry products produced by sweated labor, and sought to educate consumers about the role of labor in the production of the goods themselves. Consumer cooperatives made genuine efforts to purchase goods produced under fair and just conditions of labor. As workers and artisans, cooperators understood that goods were products of labor, and consequently that control over the exchange of goods indirectly and directly controlled labor. As the cooperative movement grew, it was increasingly committed to strong wholesaling operations that could ensure high quality products ideally produced under its aegis. Cooperators sought an active role in restructuring production, arguing that capitalist production resulted in division of labor, low salaries, and shoddy adulterated products. They sought to forge a system whereby consumer cooperatives, organized in a national wholesale society, would command production (ideally based within producer cooperatives) and with fair and just labor practices. Cooperatives historically supported the rights of labor in other ways as well, hiring workers fired from their jobs for labor agitation, funding strikes and housing the children of workers on strike, and working to ensure fair labor practices within the cooperatives themselves. The cooperative movement's commitment to justice in the workplace has continued to the present. In her chapter in this volume, for example, Ruth Grubel describes how a large consumer cooperative in Japan imports its bananas from a worker-owned plantation in the Philippines that is committed to improving the lives of its workers. Cooperatives have also continued in their dedication to social justice. In her chapter, Gabriella Hauch notes that in the 1980s the Austrian cooperative movement made a point to purchase coffee from Nicaragua to support its efforts toward self-determination and to protest the American boycott; Austrian cooperators also attempted to enforce the boycott of South African products in cooperatives during the apartheid era. Co-op America, the umbrella organization for the consumer activist movement in the United States, has campaigned with some successes against corporationsthat rely on workers who labor in grossly inadequate working conditions in underdeveloped countries.[145] In these, and numerous other ways, cooperators continued to see commodities as mediators for just social and economic relations and commercial integrity.

Consumer needs and wants have been shaped by a variety of forces—rising individualism, the growth and stagnation of working-class movements, economic ideology, war and totalitarianism, generational shifts, and, finally, the changing techniques of advertising and capitalist marketing. In the discursive and material elaboration of the notion of "need," cooperators were essentially arguing that people "needed" honest retailing, an economy that provided meaningful labor and security, fair and just working conditions, a democratic political system that protected the interests of its citizens, and access to social and cultural activities. The ethos of consumer cooperation meant a focus not on the fetishistic aspects of commodities themselves, but on the individual and collective benefits of consumption. For cooperators, the goods themselves were then seen not only in terms of their roles in meeting authentic human needs, but also as building blocks for creating community and mutuality, and for enhancing a way of life. It is important, therefore, not to underestimate the power of cultural models of meanings of goods and consumption, both those that became dominant and those that represented alternative visions and practices. As the working-class movement and collective solidarities have waned in the face of rising standards of living, manipulation of "needs" and of commercialized mass culture, cooperation's moral economy based within commitments to democratic control, nonprofit commerce, consumer education, and economic justice, was eclipsed by an individualist culture of consumption. Cooperation remains a viable option, but the successful cases of consumer cooperation demonstrate that cooperation has had to respond continually to competitive pressures within capitalist societies and, frequently, to be allied with other social movements to remain viable and resist political opposition.

Gender and the Cooperative Movement

The consumer cooperative movement developed within an historical context that saw the emergence and consolidation of family economies wherein households were increasingly dependent upon the market for consumer goods and services. In working-class families, this meant negotiating an increasingly complex environment in which efforts to stretch meager family budgets and to make ends meet were vitally important for the maintenance of household economies.[146] While the household mode of production did not entirely disappear during the era of industrialization, the division of labor within house-holds by the late nineteenth century most often meant that husbands and unmarried children were family wage earners, while wives devoted most of their time to household management and child care. In part, this was due to the confluence of two ideologies: the ideology of domesticity and working-class ideologies of masculinity. In the latter, for example, male trade unionists often argued for the gendered notion of a "family wage" earned by men, which would be sufficient to enable women to remain at home. This belief, with its implicit asymmetry of labor, would ensure that men would be occupied with productive "public" labor and women with domestic tasks.[147] While a strict gendered division of labor within families was neither straightforward nor universally embraced, it was most often the case that the gendered division of labor within families meant that women were generally responsible for con-sumption and for managing the family budget. In working-class families, significant constraints on spending due to low wages, the vagaries of the labor market, and the dearth of discretionary monies meant that being the family "spender" required time and expertise, and women employed a variety of strategies to make ends meet. These included some nonmarket activities, such as remaking clothing, exchanges of services, etc., but also involved the use of pawnshops and elaborate credit arrangements with local shopkeepers.[148]

In this environment of often precarious consumption, consumer coopera-tives could exert tremendous appeal. In cooperatives, working-class consumers were assured of fair prices, unadulterated food, serviceable household items and clothing, and a cash dividend based on the amount of goods purchased. Also consumer cooperatives often provided a range of services that were helpful—mutual insurance, cooperative housing, low-cost banking, clothing clubs, and payments to members on the births of children. Consumer coopera-tives also offered a wide variety of appealing avenues for sociability, such as festivals, cafes, libraries, singing groups, brass bands, children's activities, travel opportunities, and other organized groups and events that often built upon older patterns of working-class leisure. The reinvestment of profits into a wide variety of social and educational activities that were often family oriented was a persistent commitment within the cooperative movement.

Cooperatives then, operated within a gendered social context. As a move-ment, cooperation's commercial success depended upon women as consumers and sought to ensure their loyalty to the store. This, combined with coopera-tion's radically egalitarian heritage within utopian socialism, as well as its on-going principles of mutuality and social justice, provided the possibility for women to claim entry into the life and governance of cooperatives, influence cooperative policies, and hence to share power.[149] In many countries in which the cooperative movement was active, several metaphors emerged to signal women's importance to the movement as well as gendered visions for the transformative potential of the movement as a whole. One of the most oft-evoked was that of their "basket power." As historian Gillian Scott describes it, "basket power" implied mobilizing a "democracy of working women" around their traditional activity of shopping. It signified the common identity of women cooperators as customers at the cooperative stores, and, especially in England, as members of the women's organization the Women's Co-operative Guild. English cooperator and President of the Guild, Margaret Llewelyn Davies, put it this way in 1931: "This peaceful revolution from autocratic Capitalism to democratic Cooperation is based on the women's Marketing Basket. Isolated in their own individual homes, it is through their common everyday interest as buyers that married working women have come together, and found their place in the labour world and national life."[150] The term also conveyed the potential for women, as consumers and cooperators, to create new opportunities for themselves within the cooperative movement—as policymakers, as agents of social transformation in the conditions of labor (both in cooperatives and in enterprises producing goods for cooperatives), and as a lever for setting agendas within the movement to address their special needs as women.[151] We learn from Peder Alex's chapter, in this volume, that this notion of the "woman with the basket" was invoked in Scandinavia to underscore women's power as consumers over production. He notes that as early as 1908, and particularly in the 1920s and 1930s, the Swedish cooperative press asserted that through their purchases, women claimed the economic power to influence the quality and quantity of goods produced. Basket power was thus economic power; as one Swedish cooperator put it rather grandiosely: "The housewife of today has the power of consumption in her hand, and this can steer the economy of a society. . . . Consumption is the base of production, and decides the direction and formation of the whole of economic life."[152] A related metaphor used to describe women's activities within the movement was that of "the home." Historian Dana Frank, in her work on cooperation in the United States, has described the ways that women cooperators used notions of the home to characterize the goals of cooperation and to guide their activities within the movement. For example, women cooperators in Seattle organized a separate lounge for women in one local cooperative, and designed it to be "homelike." They also invoked their roles as mothers when planning a social club to sponsor dances for single girls, and in starting a day-care center. And, they blended waged and unwaged work, market and nonmarket relations in the creation of the Women's Exchange, an independent dry goods department within the main cooperative store in downtown Seattle. Here they sold not only commercially produced goods, but also sewed new clothes and repaired old ones, thus bringing their home-based skills to bear within the market; the Women's Exchange also donated clothing to the needy, and in this way worked outside the market as well.[153] A third metaphor was that cooperation was, as French cooperator Alice Jouenne put it in 1911, "only the family enlarged." As such, she went on, women had the "place of honor and were its cornerstone."[154]

The cooperative movement also provided space for making political and social claims as women. One of the most important avenues for advancing women's issues were the groups of women cooperators that were founded within the movement from the 1880s on. By far the largest and most influential of these groups was the Women's Cooperative Guild in England, founded in 1883.[155] As this group demonstrated the benefits for women within the movement, cooperators in other countries followed suit in establishing groups of women cooperators, among them Scotland (1892), France (1903, and later one representing the socialist cooperatives in 1910), Ireland (1906), Holland (1907), Sweden (1907), and Germany (1912).[156] In 1921, the organizations of women cooperators united to form the International Co-operative Women's Guild, with members from twenty-seven countries in the early 1930s. The International Guild held regular meetings dominated by themes such as "The Family Wash," the legal cooperative status of women, and "whether the economic position of women should be best solved by State family allowances or factory work." The International Guild was also active in disarmament and peace activism in the interwar period.[157] Indeed, in many ways the International Cooperative Women's Guild was the international organization for working-class women in general in the interwar period, since the other major women's international organizations were overwhelmingly middle and upper class.[158]

While women's groups in other countries had varying degrees of success, the most powerful was the Women's Co-operative Guild in England. Its founding in 1883 signaled "the arrival of women as an organized force" within consumer cooperation.[159] After preliminary discussions among women cooperators, Alice Acland mentioned the idea of forming a women's organization in her "Women's Corner" column in the *Co-operative New* in February 1883. As one cooperator recalled, there were high hopes from the beginning for women in the Guild. Margaret Llewelyn Davies remembered that they "welcomed the prospect of women becoming members of Committees . . . it did good that women should take part in everything, and that the Guild, as an association of women, should take up all subjects in which women were concerned."[160] From seven members in April 1883, Guild membership grew to 30,000 by 1914, and reached 87,000 in 1939. Significantly, the Guild retained relative autonomy from the national administration of the Cooperative movement as a whole. Local branches of the Guild collected their own dues, managed their own affairs, and were associated regionally. Guild members elected a standing Central Committee, which held annual Congresses. Under the strong leadership of Margaret Llewelyn Davies (elected General Secretary in 1889), the Guild moved into citizenship work, including demands for women's suffrage, more egalitarian divorce laws, and maternity care. As political scientist Naomi Black notes, the Guild "used familiar social feminist arguments to derive public duties from domestic ones."[161] For example, from the 1890s, the Guild was an important source of support for women's suffrage. In the early years, Guild member Sarah Reddish was especially active in this regard. As President of the Guild in Bolton, she welcomed suffrage speakers to meetings of the Guild, and there they were "always certain of a sympathetic audience."[162] In 1901 Guildswomen presented a petition with 31,000 signatures of Yorkshire and Cheshire women textile workers in favor of suffrage to the House of Commons, and in 1904 launched their campaign for women's enfranchisement. The suffrage activities of the Guild were vested in the People's Suffrage Federation, a group composed of Labour and Liberal suffragists and within which Margaret Llewelyn Davies was especially active.[163] The Guild took up divorce reform in 1910 after it was invited to testify before a Royal Commission on Divorce and Matrimonial Causes. The Guild conducted an inquiry and found majority support among its members for reform, and in the process elicited a range of personal testimony about the injustices suffered by women within marriage.[164] The Guild also engaged in a vigorous campaign for government support of women's maternity needs that began in 1911. After concerted efforts, which included meeting of deputations from the Guild with government officials and the publication of letters from Guild members entitled *Maternity: Letters from Working Women* in 1915, the Guild helped to secure a maternity benefit under the National Insurance Act. Largely due to the Guild's efforts, the maternity benefit was paid to the women and not to husbands, given to both unemployed and employed women, and contained a provision for four weeks sick pay at childbirth for employed women. The Guild continued to press for, and won, the establishment of Municipal Maternity Centers for delivery as well as pre- and postnatal care.[165] The maternity campaign not only illustrates an important political effort by the Guild, but it reframed definitions of gender within the movement. Building upon Margaret Llewelyn Davies' belief that women's work within the home was productive labor, the Guild campaign conceived of maternity as work to be supported in its own right. As historian Linda Gordon noted of the *Maternity* letters: "The message of *Maternity* was . . . that maternity is labor, hard and dangerous labor, and that mothers deserve decent working conditions and the respect due to other workers, on the principle that only human labor produced civilization. Guild members frequently emphasized that they did not seek charity for mothers, but state-supported, pubic programs. They did not want pity, but their rights."[166] Thus, Guildswomen demanded public rights and benefits. not only as *consumers*, members of the cooperative movement, but as *producers* laboring as mothers.

The Guild also provided important conceptual and literal space for women's personal and collective empowerment. Finding time and energy for participating in Guild and cooperative activities—attending Guild meetings, presenting papers, reading works on cooperation and related subjects—was by no means an easy task for working-class women. And yet, as Virginia Woolf wrote, recalling her attendance at a Congress of the Guild as a "benevolent spectator" in 1913, "determination and resolution" were stamped on the faces of the speakers at the Congress, who argued "constructively and pugnaciously" on behalf of divorce, the vote, taxation of land values, the minimum wage, and the education of children over fourteen. On the other hand, while Woolf was impressed by how "the minds of working women were humming and their imaginations were awake," she remained skeptical. How, she queried, "could women whose hands were full of work, whose kitchens were thick with steam, who had neither education nor encouragement nor leisure remodel the world according to the ideas of working women?"[167]

But Guild members did find time to work for remodeling the world, and in the process they found their voices and remade themselves as well. In many ways, this was possible because the Guild became, in essence, a "collective room of their own." As Virginia Woolf noted, the Guild "gave them in the first place the rarest of all possessions—a room where they could sit down and think remote from boiling saucepans and crying children; and then that room became not merely a sitting room and a meeting place, but a workshop where, laying their heads together, they could remodel their houses, could remodel their lives, could beat out this reform and that."[168] Some of the most eloquent testimony to the effect of the Guild on women's lives can be found in *Life as We Have Known It*, a collection of letters and papers edited by Margaret Llewelyn Davies. Mrs. F. H. Smith, for example, who was the wife of a miner, wrote of how the Guild meetings uplifted her and helped her to carry on. Mrs. Scott, a felt hat worker, credited the Guild with obtaining more representation for women in positions of authority within the cooperative movement. She, along with other contributors to the collection, praised the Guild for enlarging her vision, providing her with new skills, and perhaps most importantly, for providing her with self-confidence:

> The Women's Co-operative Guild . . . has meant so much to the working woman, brought new visions and opened the doors and windows so that we may see the City Beautiful. Also it taught us to become articulate and able to ask for the things we need. For so many, although they have known the needs and desired a better system of society, have not been able to express themselves.[169]

Others spoke as well of their personal growth within the collective context of the Guild. A "Lancashire Guildswoman" asserted that "Each day my vision seemed to be widening, and my spirit felt that here was the very opportunity I had always been seeking but never put into words. I had longings and aspirations within myself which had never had an opportunity of realization. At the close of the meetings I felt as I imagine a War Horse must feel when he hears the beat of the drums." And, finally, a "London Guildswoman" summarized the effects of the Guild on working women cooperators when she noted that she felt "more and more what an immense power united action" could be, it gave her courage "to speak boldly." She stated that the Guild taught her and other women "to think on social questions they at one time would have passed over as outside their capacity. . . . They have certainly become less self-centered and more public spirited. In words which our members often use, 'it has brought us out.'"[170]

And yet, while the history of the Guild illustrates the possibilities within the cooperative movement for personal and collective empowerment and for rethinking gender definitions, there were limitations within the movement as a whole, in England and elsewhere, that blunted the radical potential of cooperation. Despite the efforts of many women within cooperation, the movement remained male-dominated, and the opportunities for broad-based institutionalized power for women were constrained by social conservatism. In part this derived from the family based divisions of labor and economic power that characterized members of cooperatives. While there were single working women who were active cooperators, most were married and financially dependent upon their husbands. As such, within the cooperative movement, as well as the trade union and socialist movements, the asssumptions of power tended to equate masculinity with "public" employment as wage earners, and femininity with "private" domestic labor as wage spenders. While there were women active in trade unionism and socialism, trade unions reenforced notions of its members as *producers*, and hence masculine; socialism by the late nineteenth century mobilized people as *citizens*, potential voters, and hence also masculine in an era when few women had the right to vote.

The particular situation of consumer cooperation as a public movement of consumers, and of cooperatives as market-based public institutions (albeit privately owned by its members) raised the possibility of a more egalitarian perspective on the ways gender could inform the meanings of consumer cooperation. Not only did the movement depend on women as consumers for its commercial success, but the theoretical foundations of the movement insisted upon the interrelationship and interdependence of production and consumption. A theoretical component of the harmony between production and consumption for the utopian socialists of the 1830s and 1840s was that neither production nor consumption was necessarily linked to masculinity or femininity. In their visions, men and women were both producers and consumers. These visions thus provided space for envisioning a broad range of possibilities for both men and women. For example, early statutes of the Rochdale Pioneers stipulated that women and men were to be equal members of cooperative societies. Yet, cooperators from the late nineteenth century reconfigured this earlier cooperative heritage by linking masculinity with both production and consumption and femininity for the most part only with consumption.

There were instances where a rhetoric of equality, and in some cases egalitarian practices, survived within the movement. Certain cooperatives, such as *La Fraternelle* in Saint-Claude (France), made a special point to insert in their statues that women were to have full membership privileges in the cooperative.[171] Cooperators consistently invoked the cooperative movement as a counter to the larger society in the rights and opportunities afforded to women, contrasting the relative egalitarianism of consumer cooperation with the lack of women's rights in society as a whole. For example, Achille Daudé-Bancel, a prominent French cooperator, noted "if cruel legislation forbids women to vote, it does not forbid them to administer cooperatives." Another cooperator, M. Tholozan, noted that "a cooperator is naturally won to the cause of women's emancipation." Noting the inequalities of women in the larger society, he asserted that "cooperators find all of this unjust, ridiculous, and wrong. . . . Cooperation/emancipation: these words rhyme and should never be separated."[172]

But, there were often gaps between rhetoric and practice. At all levels of the cooperative movement, from local cooperatives to the national and international organizations, men remained in most positions of power. In part this was because the general tendency within the movement was for one member of the family, generally the man, to own shares. This made it difficult for women to administer cooperatives since only shareholders could assume administrative positions. While there were women cooperators who were active in the administration of cooperatives, and who served on important committees within the movement, women in high positions of power within the movement remained exceptions rather than the rule. When women's demands, most often generated from within the women's organizations, challenged what some perceived to be the limits of cooperation's goals, the negative reactions reveal the limitations of cooperation's commitment to equality and social justice. For example, when the Women's Co-operative Guild's action on behalf of divorce reform in 1914 ran into criticism from Catholic cooperators, the Central Board of the British movement voted to rescind payment of the Guild's annual grant unless it agreed to give up divorce law reform and have other subsequent questions approved by the Board.[173] There were also objections when the Guild advocated access to contraception in 1924 and endorsed therapeutic abortions in 1934. When the Guild endorsed pacifism in the 1930s, a position that conflicted with the official policy of the Co-operative Party, the Party banned Guild members from lists of possible candidates for party elections. Even issues that would perhaps be seen as "appropriate" for women tended to be managed by the male leadership. In the 1920s in Great Britain, for example, there were heated discussions over campaigns and materials to educate newly enfranchised women about issues of cooperation in British elections. The Women's Cooperative Guild was not allowed to generate these materials, and the Guild in turn rejected the materials prepared by the Central Education Committee of the movement.[174]

It can be argued that cooperators' discussions about women's emancipation were less about women than a symbolic and propagandistic way to demonstrate the virtues of cooperation and to elicit women's support as family shoppers for the movement. In large part this was because of the movement's social conservatism regarding the proper roles of men and women, and hence of the gendering of production and consumption.[175] For example, a French cooperator noted in 1885 that he was a supporter of women's equal rights within cooperation, and that he was "overjoyed" to see women taking a more active role as speakers in meetings of cooperatives. He observed that women's participation offered "very clear and rapid perception of delicate situations that inevitably escape workers absorbed all day with machinery." The bifurcation of women from production was even more explicit when he noted that "women ought to be, for themselves, their husbands, and their children, the saintly delight of the home." This logic can be seen as well in Steven Leikin's chapter in this volume. Leikin's analysis of cooperation in Stoneham and Minneapolis reveals that male cooperators rarely provided opportunities for women to obtain places of power, and as skilled artisans, they also maintained sharp divisions between themselves and unskilled workers. Here as elsewhere, women's emancipation was understood in terms of emancipation from wage labor, the freedom to contribute to the cooperative cause as active consumers in terms of their roles as wives and mothers.

This construction of gender-ed identities within the movement can also be seen in the metaphoric uses of the term "family." Cooperator's discursive use of "family" was, as we have seen, quite complex. While it could signify women's domestic contributions to cooperation, it also served as a metaphor for a hierarchical, male-dominated system in which gender roles were relatively rigid. These family-based notions in turn had clear implications for internal movement politics and the distribution of power. Because men in families were legally and culturally dominant and responsible, men in the cooperative movement were cast as leaders within the movement itself. As Ellen Furlough notes in her chapter in this volume, the cooperative movement generally reinforced a social division that supported an idealized version of separate and complementary spheres for men and women. The prominent French cooperator Charles Gide, for example, stated in 1921: "The role of man is predominant in production, whereas in consumption it is the woman who is the most important. . . . The role of men is to produce wealth and that of women is to spend it. In the economic order, the attribute of a man is a tool, and that of a woman is a basket . . . production and consumption are not only the two poles of the economic world, but also of the small world of the household."[176] In the 1950s, a male German cooperative leader argued that cooperation was vital to women and that, therefore, "women should support cooperation." The idea that women should lead cooperation, or even have a significant share of the leadership, was not considered.[177] By the twentieth century, women were constructed within the movement as housewives and consumers. The theoretical and institutional thrust of the cooperative movement invoked women's "power" as consumers in order to secure their loyalty as shoppers to the cooperative stores, while denying the vast majority of women cooperators effective roles in the movement's leadership or administration.[178] In essence, this allowed male cooperators to preserve notions of strength and masculine authority within a movement concerned with consumption—a sphere potentially associated with femininity. The gender identification of femininity solely with consumption and masculinity with both production and consumption thus undermined the transformative potential of consumer cooperation since it imagined consumption as a separate women's activity without a link to production.

Strengthening this redefinition was the impact of the new social welfare policies introduced into Western societies in the interwar and early post-World War II eras. In many countries, leaders of both governments and social movements reacted to the trauma of the World Wars and the Great Depression by seeking to shore up families and securing the traditional security found in established gender roles. In Germany, the particularly severe social upheaval of the first half of the twentieth century reinforced the promises to treat women as members of families and consumers, and not open new roles for them. The brief period of experimentation in the early Weimar period of the 1920s did not lead to further change; indeed, the conservatism of the 1950s was in some ways a backlash against experimentation, which could be unsettling.[179] In Britain, social welfare came in during the 1930s linked with helping the male breadwinner, while in France the focus was on family allowances to keep up fertility and encourage child-rearing. In either case, however, the goal of pre-World War I reformers such as the leaders of the cooperative movement to transform society as a whole into a "cooperative republic" was side-tracked.[180]

It was within these constraints that women cooperators, notably within the Women's Cooperative Guild, attempted to build upon cooperation's egalitarian heritage and claim rights for women both within the cooperative movement and in the larger polity. They did so as consumers, and in some campaigns as mothers, but their efforts sought to expand those terms to include their rights as citizens and as producers. In essence, these women used the ideology of domesticity and reinterpreted it to claim an expended political and social vision. In the process they expanded their visions of their own personal capabilities, what we would now call a form of "consciousness raising," to make good on cooperation's ethos of self-help within a collective context. And yet, given the larger ideology of gender that prevailed, their efforts met with opposition and their impact on the movement as a whole was limited. A later image from the movement illustrates these limitations. In the late 1950s, the Federated Co-operatives Limited (FCL), the major cooperative organization in western Canada, created the position of "Donna Rochdale" to inform members about its products and policies. "Donna Rochdale" worked closely with the women's Guilds in the western Canadian provinces, and oversaw baking demonstrations and product surveys and testing.[181] As with "Betty Crocker" (although "Betty" was fictional and "Donna" a real person), "Donna Rochdale" was a persona with whom women homemakers could identify. Yet while she was a symbol of the knowledgeable female consumer, she was displaced from the male-dominated centers of power and decision making within the larger commercial institution.

The creation and replication of gendered identities within consumer cooperation, then, reveals the weight of conservatism within the movement. The relative stability of notions of sexual difference within consumer cooperation narrowed the possibilities for women's activism, and for the transformative potential of a feminist critique within consumer cooperation. The identifications of masculinity with production and of femininity with consumption were strikingly similar to those being constructed by capitalist commerce. While cooperation differed in important ways from capitalist consumerism, notably in its commitment to social control over consumption, an analysis of the ways that gender informed the cooperative movement calls into question the cooperative movement's claim to be an active counterexample to capitalist society.

Conclusion

This volume analyzes the variegated historical manifestations of Euro-American consumer cooperation with a collective eye toward complicating linear notions that European and American consumer economies, institutions, and cultures were necessarily and inevitably capitalist, individualistic, and apolitical. The history of consumer cooperation challenges all of these assumptions, and reveals that historical transitions to capitalist networks of exchange and distribution were not only contested but that strong and viable alternatives existed as well. The growth of Euro-American consumer economies and societies, we argue, must be seen as a conflicted process, one involving contests over institutional and discursive power.

The consumer cooperative movements of the past did not go on to fulfill their initial promise. Most countries' cooperative consumer movements failed to see how they could adapt their laudable goals to the growing individualism that capitalist consumption succeeded in reaching. Creating genuinely powerful organizations to confront private retail and opening themselves to the tremendous potential of their own women members also proved beyond most movements. Yet the movements' nonetheless impressive achievements and their struggle with capitalist conumer culture should remind us that the dominant economic patterns of any society have never evolved simply according to an abstract or inevitable process. Our habits of buying and selling are part of a created process, one with enormous consequences for justice, power, and equality. Consumption is not simply a category of activity. It is a classic example of how a stream of small, seemingly insignificant decisions by individuals, families, and institutions add up to momentous consequences. If people in industrialized societies in the twenty-first century are to confront the question of how just, equal, and democratic their economies are, they will certainly have to learn from the lessons of the conflicted history of consumer cooperation.

Notes

1. Some of the few recent English language studies done of consumer cooperation are Stephen Yeo, ed. *New Views of Co-operation* (London, 1988); Johnston Birchall, *Co-op: The People's Business* (Manchester, 1994); Johann Brazda and Robert Schediwy, eds., *Consumer Co-operatives in a Changing World* (Geneva, 1989).

2. Judith Williamson, *Consuming Passsions: The Dynamics of Popular Culture* (London, 1986); George P. Moschis, *Consumer Socialization: A Life-Cycle Perspective* (Lexington, Mass., 1987); Gary Cross, *Time and Money: The Making of Consumer Culture* (New York, 1993); Frank Mort, *Cultures of Consumption: Masculinities and Social Space in Late Twentieth-Century Britain* (London, 1996); Daniel Miller, ed., *Acknowledging Consumption: A Review of New Studies* (London, 1995); David Howes, ed., *Cross-Cultural Consumption: Global Markets, Local Realities* (London, 1996); Gary Cross, "Consumer History and Dilemmas of Working-Class History," *Labor History Review* 62 vol. 3 (1997): 261-74; and Peter Stearns, "Stages of Consumerism: Recent Work on the Issues of Periodization," *Journal of Modern History* 69 (March 1997): 102-17.

3. Mary Douglas and Baron Isherwood, *The World of Goods: Towards an Anthropology of Consumption* (London, 1996), 37.

4. See, for example, Leonard S. Woolf, *Socialism and Cooperation* (London, 1921); Louis DeBrouckère, *La Coopération, ses origines, sa nature, et ses grandes fonctions* (Brussels, 1927).

5. Jean Prudhommeaux, *Coopération et pacification* (Paris, 1904), 71.

6. Ernest Poisson, *The Co-operative Republic* (London, 1925), ix and 177. For an historical examination of this trend of thought, see B. Lancaster and P. Maguire, eds., *Towards the Co-operative Commonwealth* (Loughborough, 1996).

7. Dana Frank, *Purchasing Power: Consumer Organizing, Gender, and the Seattle Labor Movement, 1919-1929* (Cambridge, 1994).

8. For a brilliant analysis of the role of consumption in the constitution of class, in this case the nineteenth-century bourgeoisie, see Leora Auslander, *Taste and Power: Furnishing Modern France* (Berkeley, 1996).

9. Paul Glennie, "Consumption Within Historical Studies," ed. Miller, 167-84; Stearns, "Stages of Consumerism": 102-12; Neil McKendrick, John Brewer, and J. H. Plumb, *The Birth of a Consumer Society: The Commercialization of Eighteenth Century England* (Bloomington, 1982); John Brewer and Roy Porter, eds. *Consumption and the World of Goods* (London, 1993); and Laurence Fontaine, *History of Pedlars in Europe* (Durham, 1996).

10. This may correspond to "merchant capitalism," i.e., a greater proportion of the workforce engaged in being merchants, brokers, pedlars, financiers, and market people, Carole Shammas, *The Pre-industrial Consumer in England and America* (Oxford, 1990); Rudolf Braun, *Industrialisation and Everyday Life* (Cambridge, 1990); René Leboutte, *Reconversions de la main-d'oeuvre et transitions démographique. Les bassins industriels en le val de Liège XVIIe-XXe siècles* (Paris, 1988), 127-35; and Jan DeVries, *European Urbanization* (Cambridge, Mass., 1986).

11. Mine owners were particularly noted for paternalist labor practices. For a discussion of company "cooperatives" in France, see Ellen Furlough, *Consumer Cooperation in France: The Politics of Consumption, 1834-1930* (Ithaca, 1991), 40-41; and Donald Reid, *The Miners of Decazeville: A Genealogy of Deindustrialization* (Cambridge, Mass., 1985), 81-85.

12. I. J. Prothero, *Artisans and Politics* (Baton Rouge, 1979), 28-30, 232-38; Henry Pelling, *A History of British Trade Unionism*, 3rd ed. (London, 1976), 21; and Rudolf Rezsohazy, *Histoire du mouvement mutualiste chrétien en Belgique* (Paris, 1957), 70-94.

13. Peter Gurney, *Co-operative culture and the politics of consumption in England, 1870-1930* (Manchester, 1996), 12-13; Jennifer Tann, "Co-operative Corn Milling: Self-help During the Grain Crisis of the Napoleonic Wars," *Agricultural History Review* 28 (1980): 46-51; Ben Jones, *Co-operative Production* (Oxford, 1894), 170-174; and Bernard Moss, *The Origins of the French Labor Movement, 1830-1914* (Berkeley, 1976), 31-41. See also Andy Durr, "William King of Brighton: Co-operation's Prophet?" in Yeo, ed. *New Views*, 10-26.

14. As political theorist Jürgen Habermas has argued, it was within new social institutions generally associated with a new commercial culture—cafes, salons, publishing ventures, and the like, in which "public opinion" flourished and from which citizens could mount social and political critiques. Most studies of the emergence and consolidation of the public sphere have tended to emphasize its association with an emergent bourgeoisie and a critique of absolutism. On the (re)invention of "society," see Daniel Gordon, *Citizens without Sovereignty: Equality and Sociability in French Thought, 1670-1789* (Princeton, 1994); on the bourgeois public sphere, see Jurgen Habermas, *The Structural Transformation of the Public Sphere: An Inquiry into a Category of Bourgeois Society* (1962; reprint Cambridge, Mass., 1991).

15. Eric Hopkins, *Working-Class Self-Help in Nineteenth-Century England: Responses to Industrialisation* (New York, 1995), 9-24.

16. Barbara Taylor, *Eve and the New Jerusalem: Socialism and Feminism in the Nineteenth Century* (London, 1983); J. F. C. Harrison, *Robert Owen and the Owenites in Britain and America* (London, 1969); Hopkins, *Working-Class*, 185-201; and Brett

Fairbairn, *The Meaning of Rochdale: The Rochdale Pioneers and the Co-operative Principles* (Saskatoon, 1994), 2-4.

17. Paul Lambert, *Studies in the Social Philosophy of Co-operation* (Manchester, 1963), 42-59. This is a translation of *La doctrine cooperative* (Brussels, 1959).

18. Peter Gurney, "Labour's Great Arch: Cooperation and Cultural Revolution in Britain, 1795-1926," 136-38, in this volume. On Chartism and cooperation, see Robin Thornes, "Change and Continuity in the Development of Co-operation," in Yeo, ed. *New Views*, 27-51; and F. Hall and W. P. Watkins, *Co-operation: A Survey of the History, Principles, and Organisation of the Co-operative Movement in Great Britain and Ireland* (Manchester, 1934), 82-90.

19. Moss, *Origins*, 25-51; and Fairbairn, "The Rise and Fall of Consumer Cooperation in Germany," in this volume.

20. Charles Gide, *Fourier, précuseur de la coopération* (Paris, 1924); Jean Gaumont, *Histoire générale de la coopération en France* 2 vols. (Paris, 1924), I: 85-182; and Jonathan Beecher, *Charles Fourier: The Visionary and His World* (Berkeley, 1986), 328-29, 548.

21. While there are numerous studies of the Rochdale Pioneers, our discussion here is largely drawn from the excellent study by Fairbairn, *The Meaning of Rochdale*, 2-16. The quotation is from page 4. The classic studies are by George J. Holyoake, *Self-Help by the People: History of Co-operation in Rochdale* (1858) and *The History of Co-operation in England* (1875).

22. Fairbairn, *The Meaning of Rochdale*, 10-12. On the British wholesale societies, see J. Kinloch and J. Butt, *History of the Scottish Co-operative Wholesale Society Limited* (Glasgow, 1981) and Percy Redfern, *The Story of the CWS* (Manchester, 1938).

23. Fairbairn, "The Rise and Fall of Consumer Cooperation," in this volume, and International Cooperative Alliance, *Cooperation in the European Market Economies* (New York, 1967), 27.

24. Ian MacPherson, *Each for All: A History of the Co-operative Movement in English Canada, 1900-1945* (Toronto, 1979); and Brett Fairbairn, *Building a Dream: The Co-operative Retailing System in Western Canada, 1928-1988* (Saskatoon, 1989).

25. Fairbairn, *The Meaning of Rochdale*, 17-18; Ellis Cowling, *Co-operatives in America: Their Past, Present and Future* (New York, 1938); Emory S. Bogardus, "Cooperatives in United States," in *Dictionary of Cooperation* (New York, 1948).

26. Gabrielle Hauch, "From Self-Help to Konzern," in this volume, 6.

27. Furlough, *Cooperation in France*, 41-46.

28. Fairbairn, "Rise and Fall," in this volume, 27-28.

29. Diarmid Coffey, *The Cooperative Movement in Jugoslavia, Rumania and North Italy During and After the World War* (New York, 1922); and Aloysius Balawyder, ed. *Cooperative Movements in Eastern Europe* (Montclair, N.J., 1980).

30. John Earle, *The Italian Cooperative Movement: A Portrait of the Lega Nazionale delle Cooperative e Mutue* (London, 1986), 14-15.

31. Bertrand, *Histoire de la coopération*, 2:2622-23.

32. Earle, *The Italian Cooperative Movement*, 15.

33. John From Wilkinson, *The Friendly Society Movement: Its Origin, Rise, and Growth* (London, 1891); Marcel van der Linden, ed., *Social Security Mutualism: The Comparative History of Mutual Insurance Societies* (Bern, 1996).

34. Patrick Joyce, *Work, Society, and Politics: The Culture of the Factory in Later Victorian England* (New Brunswick, 1980), 289.

35. David F. Crew, *Town in the Ruhr: A Social History of Bochum, 1860-1914* (New York, 1979), 96-97.

36. E. J. Hobsbawm, "The Aristocracy of Labour Reconsidered," in his *Workers: Worlds of Labor* (New York, 1984), 239.

37. H. Faber, *Co-operation in Danish Agriculture* (London, 1931).

38. Michael Tracy, *Government and Agriculture in Western Europe 1880-1980*, 3rd ed. (New York, 1980), 102-3; and Leen van Molle, *Ieder voor Allen: De Belgische Boerenbond 1890-1990* (Leuven, 1990).

39. Balawyder, *Cooperative Movements in Eastern Europe*, 88-89.

40. Balawyder, 89-93.

41. Earle, 65. In the mid-1980s, the Catholic-inspired *Confederazione* claimed 4 million members, the Communist *Lega Nazionale* claimed 3.8 million, and another million or so cooperators belonged to other organizations.

42. Besides Leikin's essay in this volume, see Kim Voss, *The Making of American Exceptionalism: The Knights of Labor and Class Formation in the Nineteenth Century* (Ithaca, 1993), 84-101.

43. Joan Wallach Scott, *The Glassworkers of Carmaux* (Cambridge, Mass., 1974) tells the story of a successful worker-run cooperative enterprise, which gradually turned into a private business owned by the remaining ex-workers.

44. E. Ray Canterbery, *The Making of Economics*, 3rd ed. (Belmont, Calif., 1987), 97-142; and Michael Stewart, *Keynes and After*, 3rd ed. (New York, 1986), 30-46.

45. W. P. Watkins, *The International Co-operative Alliance, 1895-1970* (London, 1970), 49. The European countries represented at the first congress by delegates or observers were: Austria, Belgium, Denmark, France, Great Britain, Holland, Hungary, Italy, Rumania, Russia, Serbia, and Switzerland. There were also delegates from Australia, India, Argentina, and the USA. Representatives from Great Britain outnumbered all the rest (Watkins, 30). See also International Cooperative Alliance [ICA], *International Directory of the Co-operative Press* (London, 1909); ICA, *Bibliographie Coopérative Internationale* (London, 1906); and Hans Müller, "Die Genossenschaftliche Internationale," *Sozialistische Monatshefte* 14, no. 8 (April 1910): 471-82.

46. Gurney, *Co-operative culture*, 169-82.

47. Robert Stuart, *Marxism at Work: Ideology, Class, and French Socialism during the Third Republic* (Cambridge, 1992), 209-17.

48. Gerhard Huck, "Arbeiterkonsumverein und Verbraucherorganisation. Die Entwicklung der Konsumgenossenschaften im Ruhrgebiet 1860-1914," in *Fabrik, Familie, Feierabend: Beitrage zur Sozialgeschichte des Alltags im Industriezeitalter*, eds. Jurgen Reulecke and Wolfhard Weber (Wuppertal, 1978).

49. Watkins, *International Co-operative Alliance*, 85-86.

50. Sura Levine, "Politics and the Graphic Arts of the Belgian Avant-Garde," in *Les XX and the Belgian Avant-Garde*, ed. Stephen Goddard (Lawrence, 1992); and Paul Aron, *Les écrivains belges et le socialisme (1880-1913)* (Brussels, 1985), 70-100.

51. Emile Vandervelde, *La coopération neutre et la coopération socialiste* (Paris, 1913).

52. George Gaget, *Etude sur le mouvement coopératif en Belgique* (Toulouse, 1901); and Thomas Dawe, *A Co-operative Tour in Belgium and France* (Manchester, 1901).

53. Gurney, "Labor's Great Arch," in this volume.

54. Stephen Yeo, "Rival Clusters of Potential: Ways of Seeing Co-operation," in *New Views of Co-operation,* ed. Yeo, 7.

55. In Britain and Belgium, for example, the consumer cooperative movement had more members than did either the Labour or socialist parties or the trade union movement. Gurney, *Cooperative Culture,* 242; Strikwerda, "Alternative Visions," in this volume.

56. Gerald Feldman, *The Great Disorder* (Oxford, 1993), 60-77.

57. Elsie Terry Blanc, *Co-operative Movement in Russia* (New York, 1924), 209.

58. Gurney, *Co-operative culture,* 208-16.

59. Sidney Pollard, "The Founding of the Co-operative Party," in *Essays in Labour History, 1886-1923,* eds. Asa Briggs and John Saville (London, 1971); Tony Adams, "The Formation of the Co-coperative Party Reconsidered," *International Review of Social History,* [*IRSH*] 22 (1987), 48-68; Sidney Pollard, "The Co-operative Party—Reflections on a Re-Consideration," *IRSH,* 22 (1987), 168-173. Labour and the Co-operative Party began formal cooperation in Parliament in 1926. As recently as 1974, seventeen of the "Labour" MPs were actually Co-operative Party delegates. Donald K. Ross and David Langdon, "Business as Usual: Consumer Cooperatives in England," in Ralph Nader Task Force on European Cooperatives, *Making Change? Learning From Europe's Consumer Cooperatives* (Washington, D.C., 1985), 9.

60. Blanc, *Co-operative Movement,* 184-222. See also Eugene M. Kayden and Alexis N. Antsiferov, *The Cooperative Movement in Russia During the War* (New Haven, 1929); and Andrew J. Kress, *Introduction to the Cooperative Movement* (New York, 1941), 24-25.

61. Johann Brazda, "Germany," in *Consumer Cooperatives in a Changing World,* eds. Johann Brazda and Robert Scheidwy (Geneva, 1989), 160; Theodor Cassau, *The Consumers' Cooperative Movement in Germany* (New York, 1924), 96. Calculations of the membership of cooperatives is often difficult because many if not most cooperatives used family membership, in which only one member of the family, usually the adult male head of the household, was a member. Thus, it would be more accurate to say that 35 percent of the population in Britain in 1920 and 20 percent of the population of Germany in 1921 beleonged to families in which at least one family member belonged to a cooperative.

62. Feldman, *Great Disorder,* 171, 661.

63. *The Canadian Co-operator* 15, no. 6, (March 1924): 1, reproduced in Ian MacPherson, *Building and Protecting the Co-operative Movement: A Brief History of the Co-operative Union of Canada 1909-1084* (Ottawa, 1984), 74.

64. Norman Silber, *Test and Protect: The Influence of the Consumers' Union* (New York, 1983); and Colston E. Warne, *The Consumer Movement,* eds. Richard Morse and Florence Snyder (Manhattan, Kansas, 1993).

65. Ross and Langdon, "Business as Usual," 7.

66. Gary DeLoss, "Making Change: Consumer Cooperatives in Sweden," in *Making Change,* 66-68.

67. Birchall, *Co-op*, 117.

68. G. N. Ostergaard and A. H. Halsey, *Power in Co-operatives: A Study of the Internal Politics of British Retail Societies* (Oxford, 1965).

69. David Schoenbaum, *Hitler's Social Revolution: Class and Status in Nazi Germany, 1933-1939* (New York, 1966), 129-51.

70. Philip Nord, *Paris Shopkeepers and the Politics of Resentment* (Princeton, 1986); 406-89; Serge Jaumain, *Les petites commerçants belges face à la modernité* (Brussels, 1995).

71. Quoted in Neil Killingback, "Limits to Mutuality: Economic and Political Attacks on Co-operation During the 1920s and 1930s," in *New Views*, ed. Yeo, 207.

72. Heinz-Gerhard Haupt and Charlotte Niermann, "Bremen Shopkeepers in the Weimar Republic," in *Splintered Classes: Politics and the Lower Middle Classes in Interwar Europe*, ed. Rudy Koshar (New York, 1990), 60-64.

73. Adrian Lyttleton, *The Seizure of Power: Fascism in Italy 1919-1929*, 2nd ed. (Princeton, 1987), 38-71.

74. Carl Strikwerda, "Corporatism and the Lower Middle Classes: Interwar Belgium," in ed. Koshar, *Splintered Classes*, 227; and Heinrich A. Winkler, *Mittelstand, Demokratie, und Nationalsozialismus: Die politische Entwicklung von Handwerk und Kleinhandel in der Weimarer Republik* (Cologne, 1972), 190.

75. Hauch, "From Self-Help to Konzern," in this volume, 28; and Carl Strikwerda, "The Belgian Working Class and the Crisis of the 1930s," in *Chance und Illusion/Labor in Retreat*, eds. Helmut Gruber and Wolfgang Maderthaner (Vienna, 1988).

76. On Italy, Earle, *Italian Cooperative Movement*, 26-30; on Japan, Grubel, "Democratic Responses," in this volume, 5.

77. Philip Mause and Cheryl Wyman, "Falling Out of the Market: German Cooperatives," in *Making Change*, 119.

78. Hauch, "From Self-Help to Konzern," 30.

79. Richard Tomasson, *Sweden: Prototype of Modern Society* (New York, 1970), 35-45.

80. Meynaud excludes the cooperatives of the Soviet Bloc on the grounds that they were not true cooperatives.

81. Craig Cox, *Storefront Revolution: Food Co-ops and the Counterculture* (New Brunswick, 1994); and American Enterprise Institute, *The National Consumer Cooperative Bank Bill* (Washington, D.C., 1978).

82. Eberhard Dülfer, "Managerial Economics of Cooperatives," 587-92, and Jerker Nilsson, "Marketing Strategies of Co-operatives," 596-600, both in *International Handbook of Cooperative Organizations*, ed. Dülfer (Göttingen, 1994); and Will Greenlee, "Co-ops Can Help Small Businesses Compete With Chains," *Wilmington Star-News*, 29 June, 1997, 5E.

83. Robert Schediwy, "France," in Brazda and Schediwy, 686.

84. Joel Colton, *Leon Blum: Humanist in Politics*, 2nd ed. (Durham, 1987), 62.

85. Johann Brazda and Robert Schediwy, "Own Production, Consumer Cooperative," in *International Handbook*, ed., 669-70.

86. Franz Helm, *The Economics of Co-operative Enterprise* (London, 1968), 3.

87. Emory S. Bogardus, "Edward A. Filene," in *Dictionary of Cooperation*, 41.

88. Hans Münckner, "British-Indian Pattern of Cooperation," in *International Handbook*, 57-60.

89. Günter Vacek, "Japan," in Brazda and Schediwy, eds., *Consumer Cooperation*, 2:1026-35.

90. Dr. Fauquet, "La Service de la Coopération du Bureau international du Travail," in *Internationales Handwörterbuch des Genossenschaftswesens*, ed. T. Totomianz, (Berlin, 1928), 484-5.

91. S. C. Mehta, *Consumer Co-operation in India* (Delhi, 1964), 71.

92. Mohinder Singh, *Co-operatives in Asia* (New York, 1970); K. K. Taimni, *Consumers' Co-operatives in Third World Strategy for Development* (Poona, 1978); and Samuel O. Adeyeye, *The Co-operative Movement in Nigeria* (Gottingen, 1978). Ironically, while the ICA after the Second World War excluded many cooperatives from Communist countries as government organizations and disputes between Western and Communist movements were a major problem for the ICA, the international Communist movement still claimed the cooperative movements in Asia and Africa as part of the anti-imperialist struggle as itself. V. Maslennikov, *The Co-operative Movement in Asia and Africa* (Moscow, 1983), 196-204.

93. Birchall, *Co-op*, 199.

94. Henk Thomas and Chris Logan, *Mondragon: An Economic Analysis* (London, 1982); and Sharryn Kasmir, *The Myth of Mondragón: Cooperatives, Politics, and Working-Class Life in a Basque Town* (Albany, 1996). Kasmir criticizes Mondragon because it is not fully cooperative in its structure, but her book still contains a great deal of informative material on the cooperative aspects of Mondragon.

95. Piero Ammirato, *La Lega: The Making of a Successful Cooperative Network* (Aldershot, 1996).

96. K. K. Taimni, "Rural Cooperatives in Asia: Perspectives and Challenges," in *Asia's Rural Cooperatives*, ed. K. K. Taimni (Boulder, 1994).

97. Robert Tomsho, "Costly Funerals Spur A Co-op Movement to Hold Down Bills," *Wall Street Journal*, November 12, 1996, A1, A5; and *Co-op America Quarterly*; "And You Don't Have to Worry About Parking: Car-Sharing Is Catching On in German Cities," *The Week in Germany*, May 9, 1997, 6.

98. Ralph Nader, preface, *Making Change*, vi.

99. George Draheim, *Die Genossenschaft als Unternchmungstyp.* (Göttingen, 1962), 16-18.

100. Holger Bonus, "The Cooperative Association as a Business Enterprise: A Study in the Economics of Transactions," *Journal of Institutional and Theoretical Economics* 142, no. 2 (June 1986), 335. Bonus outlines Draheim's ideas and, while drawing most of his evidence from cooperative associations of small businesses, provides a theory that can apply to consumer cooperatives as well.

101. Carl Strikwerda, *A House Divided: Catholics, Socialists, and Flemish Nationalists in Nineteenth-Century Belgium* (Lanham, 1997), 124, 232; Furlough, *Consumer Cooperation*, 187.

102. Gunther Vacek, "The Consumer Cooperatives in Japan," in Brazda and Schediwy, 1049-54.

103. Nord, *Davis Shopkeepers*, 406-89.

104. Appendix V, "Principal Provisions of the Industrial and Provident Societies Acts," Hall and Watkins, *Co-operation*, 387-89.

105. Killingback, "Limits," 212.

106. Fairbairn, "Rise and Fall," in this volume, 34.

107. On the problems caused by ideology, especially Marxism, Georges DeLeener and Emile James, *Le probleme de la consommation* (Brussels, 1937), 142-4, and David Miller, "Consumption as the Vanguard of History," in *Acknowledging Consumption*, 38. On the handicap of small size, Helm, 130-40. On the problems of capital accumulation, Brazca and Schediwy, "Own Production, Consumer Co-operation," in *International Handbook*, ed. Duffler, 669-70 and Richard Heflebower, *Cooperatives and Mutuals in the Market System* (Madison, 1980), 123-31. On cooperation as dependent on scarcity or regulation, Werner Sombart, "Kapitalismus und Genossenschaftswesen," *Internationales Handwörterbuch*, ed. Totomianz, 537; Walter Hesselbach, *Public, Trade Union and Cooperative Enterprise in Germany: the Commonweal Idea* (London, 1976), 129-43; and Heflebower, *Cooperatives*, 127-31. Although sympathetic to the principle of democratic control, Ostergaard and Halsey, *Power in Co-operatives* richly details the problems of democracy.

108. Fairbairn, "Rise and Fall," in this volume, 18; Strikwerda, *A House Divided*, 179.

109. Hauch, "From Self-Help to Konzern," in this voume, 21; Franz Muller, "Consumer Co-operation in Great Britain," 77.

110. Clemens Pedersen, ed., *The Danish Co-operative Movement* (Copenhagen, 1977), 89; David Thompson, "Good Intentions: The French Cooperative Movement," in *Making Change*, 152-53; and Gary DeLoss, "Making Change: Consumer Cooperatives in Sweden," in *Making Change*, 65-69

111. Birchall, *Co-op*, 153.

112. FransMuller, "The Consumer Co-operatives in Great Britain," Brarda and Schediwy, 115-17.

113. Grubel, "Democractic Responses," in this volume, 30.

114. Brazda, "Germany," 217-18.

115. Quoted in Feldman, *Great Disorder*, 850.

116. George Orwell, *The Road to Wigan Pier* (London, 1938), 79.

117. Ben Fine, "From Political Economy to Consumption," in *Acknowledging Consumption*, ed. Miller, 185-89.

118. William Richardson, *The CWS in War and Peace 1938-1976* (Manchester, 1977), 66-67.

119. Charles Feinstein, "Changes in Nominal Wages, the cost of living, and real wages in the United Kingdom over two centuries, 1780-1990," *Labour's Reward: Real Wages and Economic Change in 19th and 20th-Century Europe*, eds. P. Scholliers and V. Zamagni (Aldershot, 1995), 22.

120. Birchall, *Co-op*, 124.

121. European Communities, *Our Farming Future* (Brussels, 1993), 28. This applies to the six original Common Market countries. By 1990, in the now expanded European Community of 12 countries, the percentage had fallen to 21.6.

122. Hesselbach, *Public*, 55.

123. Lizabeth Cohen, *Making a New Deal: Industrial Workers in Chicago, 1919-1939* (Cambridge, 1990), 101-20; Ben Fine and Eileen Leopold, *The World of Consumption* (London, 1993), 162-93.

124. Hauch, "From Self-Help to Konzern," in this volume, 40; Muller, "Consumer Co-opratives,", 77.

125. Fairbairn, "Rise and Fall," in this volume, 36.

126. Richardson, *CWS*, 46.

127. Birchall, *Co-op*, 127.

128. Richardson, *CWS*, 199.

129. Christiansen, "Cooperation in Denmark," in this volume, 28; Donald K. Ross and David Langdon, "The Other Side of the Coin: Consumer Cooperatives in Denmark," in *Making Change*; O. Boekgaard, "The Consumer Society, the Retail Trade, and the Co-op," in *The Danish Co-operative Movement*, ed. Clemens Pedersen (Copenhagen, 1977).

130. Donald K. Ross and David Langdon, "A Way of Life: Consumer Cooperatives in Norway," 54-57 and Gary DeLoss, "Making Change: Consumer Cooperatives in Sweden," 63-90, both in *Making Change*.

131. John Clammen, "Aesthetics of the Self," *Livestyle Shopping: the Subject of Consumption*, ed. Rob Shields (London, 1992), 202-03.

132. Tushaar Shah, *Catalyzing Co-operation: Design of Self-Governing Organisations* (London, 1996), 43-45.

133. Grubel, "Democratic Responses to State-Led Capitalism in the Consumer Cooperatives in Japan,"in this volume; Hidekazu Nomura, "Consumer Co-operatives in Japan," *Kyoto University Economic Review* 56, no. 2 (October 1986): 11-7; Vacek, 1061-65.

134. See, for example, Leo Charney and Vanessa R. Schwartz, eds., *Cinema and the Invention of Modern Life* (Berkeley, 1995); Michael Denning, "Mass Culture and the Working Class, 1914-1970," *International Labor and Working-Class History*, no. 37 (Spring 1990): 2-31; Frederic Jameson, "Pleasure: A Political Issue," in *Formations of Pleasure*, (Boston, 1983), 1-14; Cross, *Time and Money* and Gary Cross, ed. *Worktowners at Blackpool: Mass-Observation and Popular Leisure in the 1930's* (London, 1990), John K. Walton, *The English Seaside Resort: A Social History, 1750-1914* (Leicester, 1983) and "Towns and Consumerism, 1840-1950," in *The Cambridge Urban History of Britain*, vol. 3 ed. M. J. Daunton (forthcoming); Alain Corbin, ed. *L'Avènement des Loisirs, 1850-1960* (Paris: Aubier, 1995).

135. For an introduction to general themes and practices of capitalist consumer culture, see Brewer and Porter, eds., *Consumption and the World of Goods*; John Benson, *The Rise of Consumer Society in Britain, 1880-1980* (London, 1994); Cross, *Time and Money*; Neil Harris, *Cultural Excursions: Marketing Appetites and Cultural Tastes in Modern America* (Chicago, 1990); Fine and Leopold, *The World of Consumption*; Richard Wightman Fox and T. J. Jackson Lears, eds., *The Culture of Consumption* (New York, 1983); Celia Lury, *Consumer Culture* (New Brunswick, 1996); and Mike Featherstone, *Consumer Culture and Postmodernism* (London, 1991).

136. David Grigg, *The Transformation of Agriculture in the West* (Oxford, 1992), 66-70. See also note 119.

137. This inventory in from *L'Union d'Amiens* (France) in 1903. Furlough, *Consumer Cooperation in France*, 137.

138. *Five Reasons for Joining a Cooperative*, reprinted in Pierre Brizon and Ernest Poisson, *La Coopération* (Paris, 1913), 20-22.

139. Grubel, "Democratic Responses," in this volume, 13.

140. See Susan Buck-Morss, *The Dialectics of Seeing: Walter Benjamin and the Arcades Project* (Cambridge, 1989); Rachel Bowlby, *Shopping with Freud* (London, 1993); David Chaney, "The Department Store as Cultural Form," *Theory, Culture, and Society* 3 (1983): 22-31; and Shields, ed., *Lifestyle Shopping: The Subject of Consumption*. The literature on department stores has become quite extensive. For good introductions see Hrant Pasdermadjian, *The Department Store: Its Origins, Evolution, and Economics* (London, 1954) and William Lancaster, *The Department Store: A Social History* (London, 1995). For department stores in particular geographical areas, see United States—Susan Porter Benson, *Counter Cultures: Saleswomen, Managers, and Customers in American Department Stores, 1890-1940* (Urbana, 1986); William Leach, *Land of Desire: Merchants, Power, and the Rise of a New American Culture* (New York, 1993); France—Michael B. Miller, *The Bon Marché: Bourgeois Culture an the Department Store, 1869-1920* (Princeton, 1981); François Faraut, *Histoire de la Belle Jardinière* (Paris, 1996); Britain—Alison Adburgham, *Shops and Shopping, 1800-1914* (London, 1989); Sean Callery, *Harrods, Knightsbridge: The Story of Society's Favorite Store* (London, 1991); Erika Rappaport, "The West End and Women's Pleasure: Gender and Commercial Culture in London, 1860-1914" (Ph.D. diss., Rutgers University, 1993); Germany—Paul Gohre, *Das Warenhaus* (Frankfurt am main, 1907); Asia/Australia—Kerrie L. MacPherson, ed. *Asian Department Stores* (Honolulu, 1998); Gail Reekie, *Temptation: Sex, Selling, and the Department Store* (Sydney, 1993).

141. Louis Héliès, *La Bellevilloise, 1887-1912: Son historique* (Paris, 1912), 10 and Joseph Cernesson, "Les sociétés coopératives de consommation," *Revue des deux Mondes* 5 (15 October 1908): 899-907.

142. On these retailing developments, see Roger Picard, *Formes et méthods nouvelles des entreprises commerciales* (Paris, 1936) and Ellen Furlough, "Selling the American Way in Interwar France: Prix Uniques and the Salon des Arts Ménagers," *Journal of Social History*, 26/3 (Spring 1993): 491-519. See also Hamish W. Fraser, *The Coming of the Mass Market, 1850-1914* (Hamden, Conn., 1981) and Susan Strasser, *Satisfaction Guaranteed: The Making of the American Mass Market* (New York, 1989).

143. On the history of advertising, see Thomas Richards, *The Commodity Culture of Victorian England: Advertising and Spectacle, 1851-1914* (Stanford, 1990); Marc Martin, *Trois Siècles de Publicité en France* (Paris, 1992); Roland Marchand, *Advertising the American Dream: Making Way for Modernity, 1920-1940* (Berkeley, 1985); and James Twitchell, *ADCULT USA: The Triumph of Advertising in American Culture* (New York, 1996). On commodity aesthetics, see W. F. Haug, *Critique of Commodity Aesthetics: Appearance, Sexuality and Advertising in Capitalist Society* (Minneapolis, 1986) and *Commodity Aesthetics, Ideology and Culture* (New York, 1987).

144. For a more extensive discussion and examples of cooperative advertisements from the 1920s, see Furlough, *Consumer Cooperation in France*, 270-73.

145. "Special Issue Against Sweatshop Labor," *Co-op American Quarterly*, no. 46, Summer, 1998.

146. Melanie Tebbutt, *Making Ends Meet: Pawnbroking and Working-Class Credit* (New York, 1983); Joan W. Scott and Louise A. Tilly, *Women, Work, and Family* (New York, 1978), 176-77; and Victoria de Grazia, with Ellen Furlough, eds., *The Sex of Things: Gender and Consumption in Historical Perspective*, (Berkeley, 1996), 159-61.

147. Michelle Perrot, "L'éloge de la ménagère dans le discours des ouvriers français du dix-neuvième siècle," *Romantisme* 13-14 (1976): 105-21; Gita Sen, "The sexual division of labour and the working class family: towards a conceptual synthesis of class relations and the subordination of women," *Review of Radical Political Economics* 12 (1980): 76-86; and Lawrence Glickman, "Inventing the 'American Standard of Living': Gender, Race, and Working-Class Identity, 1880-1925," *Labor History* 34, nos. 2-3 (spring-summer 1993): 221-235.

148. See Elizabeth Roberts, "Women as Housewives and Managers," ch. 4 in *A Women's Place: An Oral History of Working-Class Women, 1890-1940* (Oxford and New York, 1984), and Susan Porter Benson, "Living on the Margin: Working-Class Marriages and Family Survival Strategies in the United States, 1919-1941," in de Grazia, *The Sex of Things*, 212-43. See also Martin Pugh, "Women, Food, and Politics, 1880-1930," *History Today*, 41 (March 1991).

149. Barbara Taylor, *Eve and the New Jerusalem: Socialism and Feminism in the Nineteenth Century* (New York, 1983); Claire Goldberg Moses, *French Feminism in the Nineteenth Century* (Albany, 1984); Helga Grubitzsch, "Women's Projects and Co-operatives in France at the Beginning of the Nineteenth Century," *Women's Studies International Forum* 8/4 (1985): 279-286; and Susan K. Grogan, *French Socialism and Sexual Difference: Women and the New Society, 1803-44* (London, 1992).

150. Margaret Llewelyn Davies, ed., *Life as We Have Known It* (New York, 1975), x-xi.

151. Gillian Scott, "Basket Power and Market Forces: The Women's Co-operative Guild, 1883-1920," in *Women and Market Societies: Crisis and Opportunity*, eds. Barbara Einhorn and Elleen Yeo (Aldershot, 1995), 34-35.

152. Axel Gjöres, "Kvinnan med korgen," *Konsumentbladet* (1926), 20. Cited in Peder Aléx, "Swedish Consumer Cooperation as an Educational Endeavor," in this volume.

153. Dana Frank, *Purchasing Power: Consumer Organizing, Gender, and the Seattle Labor Movement* (New York, 1994), 56-59.

154. Alice Jouenne, *La femme et la coopération* (Paris, 1911), 1-2.

155. On the Women's Co-operative Guild, see Gillian Scott, *Feminism and the Politics of Working Women: The Women's Co-operative Guild, 1880s to the Second World War* (London, 1998); Jean Gaffin and David Thoms, *Caring and Sharing: The Centenary History of the Co-operative Women's Guild* (Manchester, 1983); Margaret Llewelyn Davies, *The Women's Co-operative Guild* (Kerksby Lonsdale, 1904); and Catherine Webb, *The Woman with the Basket: The Story of the Women's Co-operative Guild* (Manchester, 1927).

156. Honora Enfield, "Women's Work for Cooperation," *Review of International Cooperation* 22 (August 1929): 293-95.

157. Davies, *Life*, xiii.

158. Leila Rupp, *Worlds of Women: The Making of an International Women's Movement* (Princeton, 1997), 37-53; Francoise Baulier, "Femmes et organisations feminines dans l'Alliance Cooperative Internationale," *Communante's*, 74 (1985), 10-40.

159. Scott, "Basket Power," 32

160. Davies, *The Women's Co-operative Guild*, 32.

161. Naomi Black, *Social Feminism* (Ithaca, 1989), 118.

162. Jill Liddington and Jill Norris, *One Hand Tied Behind Us: The Rise of the Women's Suffrage Movement* (London, 1984), 136.

163. Rochelle Mains, "Meanings of Motherhood: The Women's Cooperative Guild and the Maternity Campaign" (Brown University, Literature and Society Honors Thesis, 1982), 22 and Black, *Social Feminism*, 129.

164. Scott, "Basket Power," 36-37.

165. Linda Gordon, "Introduction," *Maternity: Letters from Working Women*, ed. Margaret Llewelyn Davies, 2nd ed. (New York, 1978), v-xii, and Mains, "Meanings of Motherhood."

166. Gordon, "Introduction," xii.

167. Virginia Woolf, "Introductory Letter to Margaret Llewelyn Davies," in Davies, *Life*, xv-xxxix.

168. Woolf, "Introductory Letter," xxxv-xxxvi.

169. Davies, *Life*, 101.

170. Davies, *Life*, 132 and 140-41.

171. Furlough, *Consumer Cooperation*, 159.

172. *L'Union Coopérative*, 15 November 1910; *Bulletin Mensuel . . . de Levallois-Perret* (France), July 1900.

173. The Central Board argued that individual members did not necessarily object to divorce law reform, but rather to its inclusion as an issue under the banner of the cooperative movement. The grant was only restored in 1918, after married women received the vote in England and the Board was eager to have women's support for the newly formed Co-operative Party. Scott, "Basket Power," 36-41.

174. Black, *Social Feminism*, 121 and 137.

175. A fuller discussion of the material that follows can be found in Furlough, *Consumer Cooperation in France*, 199-224.

176. Charles Gide, "La consommation," *Revue de Métaphysique et de Morale*, April-June 1921.

177. Fairbairn, "Rise and Fall," in this volume, 40-41.

178. The examples of this attitude are legion. For one example, see the work by Belgian cooperator Victor Serwy, *La Coopération et la Femme: Vade mecum de la Propaganadiste Coopératrice* (Ghent, 1924).

179. Katherine Pence, "Labours of Consumption: Gendered Consumers in Post-War East and West German Reconstruction," in *Gender Relations in German History: Power, Agency, and Experience from the Sixteenth to the Twentieth Century*, eds. Lynn Abrams and Elizabeth Harvey (Durham, 1997), 214-35; Robert G. Moeller, *Protecting Motherhood: Women and the Family in the Politics of Postwar West Germany* (Berkeley, 1993).

180. Susan Pedersen, *Family, Dependence, and the Origins of the Welfare State: Britain and France, 1914-1945* (Cambridge, 1993), 292-411; John Benson, *The Working Class in Britain, 1850-1939* (London, 1989), 51-154.

181. Brett Fairbairn, *Building a Dream: The Co-operative Retailing System in Western Canada, 1928-198* (Saskatoon, 1989), 159.

Chapter 2

"Alternative Visions" and Working-Class Culture: The Political Economy of Consumer Cooperation in Belgium, 1860-1980

Carl Strikwerda

One of the central problems in understanding the rise of industrial society is weighing the conflicting pulls of economic individualism and communal solidarity. On the one hand, modern capitalism depended on individuals and economic enterprises competing with each other and on breaking up old communities whose traditions and regulations restricted innovation. Rising incomes, advertising, name-brands, and urban transportation promised the mass of people the chance of becoming individualized consumers. By picking and choosing between products and retailers, they could, in theory, map their own economic destiny. On the other hand, modern industrialism also made possible the construction of new, much larger categories—by weakening old loyalties, producing enormous resources, congregating people into cities, and organizing vast new bureaucracies. Economic individualism in the face of this capitalist power could mean less freedom, not more. In reaction to capitalism's de-stabilizing power, many individuals tried to create new forms of solidarity to protect themselves from economic insecurity. In the midst of the tremendous changes set off by industrialization, many workers, farmers, and middle-class people tried to form alternative visions of modern economic society from that offered by individualist, competitive capitalism. These alternative cooperative visions were often prompted by the argument that capitalism, while dependent on economic individualism for its growth, was also denying people genuine individualism. Wage earners in large enterprises and consumers, as members of impersonal categories, were only superficially economic individuals. They had to take the jobs and buy the products that capitalism offered. Only through acting cooperatively, according to these alternative visions, could ordinary people benefit from the technological achievements of capitalism without suffering its depersonalizing and authoritarian effects. The particular balance that societies have decided to strike between individualism and community has often been one of the most crucial decisions defining them in the twentieth century. Around issues such as labor laws, the control of credit, hours of being open, right-to-work, and monopolies, Western societies have struggled to meet the competing demands of individuals, families, and social groups.

In the area of consumption, capitalism, on balance, seems to have triumphed in creating economic individualism. Yet one must ask whether different forms of economic organization could have succeeded. After all, industrialization also resulted in the creation of groups that have checked individualism, for example, labor unions, farmers' associations, chambers of commerce, and social movements. Even in the area of consumerism, advertisers have increasingly depended on identifying individuals in groups: retirees, teenagers, or women. Could consumers not band together more naturally to advance their own interests in buying goods? Some countries, particularly Sweden, have organized a strong cooperative retailing sector.[1]

Moreover, the spread of individualized consumption—individuals buying retail goods from private businesses for most of their needs—should not obscure the long struggle waged by cooperative consumer institutions in many Western countries to carve out a sector for themselves. Consumer cooperation has been one of the most important attempts to create an alternative vision of modern economic organization, to form, in Gramsci's terms, a basis for a counter-hegemony to the hegemony of capitalism. The struggles waged by these institutions can tell us a great deal about why and how our contemporary economic system evolved, as well as give us clues as to whether further modifications in that system are possible. In addition, the history of Western consumer cooperation may provide some insights for those concerned with developments in the newly developing parts of the world today, where consumer cooperation is experiencing its greatest growth at present.

This chapter will examine the rise and, less extensively, the decline of consumer cooperation in Belgium.[2] Belgium provides an interesting test case for examining the fate of consumer cooperation. Both a strong spirit of association and a vibrant economic individualism have flourished there. The second country in the world to industrialize, Belgium also is a virtual laboratory of subgroups. In a territory the size of the state of Maryland, two languages, Dutch and French, are spoken, and a wide diversity of economic activities occur—textiles, coal and steel, intensive farming, one of the world's largest ports, and white-collar commerce. This diversity allows for an examination of consumer cooperation in a variety of settings. In particular, the heavy industrialization of Belgium helped create a powerful socialist movement, which included most of the country's consumer cooperatives. Belgian consumer cooperation, in fact, became the prime example, for most observers in the early twentieth century, of how together socialism as a political movement and consumer cooperation as an economic movement could forge an alliance that strengthened them both.

I will argue that, in Belgium, consumer cooperation did not suffer from some of the flaws that have commonly been attributed to the movement. It has been frequently argued that consumer cooperatives suffer from a failure to enjoy economies of scale, a lack of capital, and a vulnerability to more aggressive private competitors. Belgian cooperatives, however, were among the first large retailers; some of them created their own bank, which was listed on the Brussels Stock Exchange; and, ironically, in many ways it was the small private retailers, not large establishments, which undercut the cooperatives. Consumer cooperation has also been criticized, at times, because it supposedly could succeed only in a regulated economy. Again, ironically, in Belgium, cooperation grew during a period of little government intervention and stagnated when government regulation controlled retailing.

Belgium also provides evidence for another commonly cited problem for cooperatives, that they have been weakened by ideological leadership. Along with socialism, Belgium also had a strong social Catholic movement in which cooperatives were less important than in the socialist camp but still played a large role. Yet the support of political parties or social movements strengthened as much as weakened the Belgian cooperatives. Instead, I will argue that Belgian cooperatives succeeded as much as they did, initially, because they had the support of ideological movements. Nor, as argued below, is it true that the division between socialist and Catholic cooperation weakened Belgian cooperation. The major problems that hampered cooperation lay more often within each movement, not caused by the existence of rival movements. The cooperatives did face a difficult challenge in adapting to the transformations in working-class culture. But this was not an insurmountable task, if the cooperatives acted vigorously and if the political economy of the society had not put obstacles in the way of the cooperatives. When they ceased to grow as fast as the rest of the economy, it was because powerful interest groups, in part through state policies, worked against them and because the ideological movements themselves made some critical decisions that hurt the cooperatives. In many ways, the conflict over the creation of the welfare state in the 1920s and 1930s realigned the interest groups and ideological movements in Belgium. Through state action, small private retailers obtained advantages denied to cooperatives; the socialist and Catholic movements that had previously supported cooperatives began focusing on other ways to help their members. Rather than the consumer cooperatives being doomed by any intrinsic economic or political factors, in other words, it was the battles they lost over control of working-class culture that fatally weakened them.

To tell this story, we will look at the origins of consumer cooperation in nineteenth-century Belgium, at the crucial battles of the interwar period, and at the decline of consumer cooperation during World War II and the postwar era. Finally, the Belgian experience of consumer cooperation can be examined to derive some lessons for what it may reveal about how capitalist consumerism has developed in Western Europe.

The Origins of Consumer Cooperation

Consumer cooperatives began in Belgium in the late nineteenth century because private retailers had a difficult time meeting the demands of a growing industrial, urban population. A variety of other methods supplied the needs the retail sector failed to meet. In the southern, French-speaking factory town of Verviers, which was the center of woolen textile production, many women supplemented their husbands' wages by preparing small quantities of food and household items and selling them to city dwellers who did not have time to produce them.[3] A wide variety of "company stores" flourished, at which workers bought necessities from employers. Some of these were created to control workers, but they were prevalent even in towns where competition might be expected. This suggests that the lack of a developed retail sector also prompted employers to create them.[4] Even in an industrial city such as Seraing, which had approximately 30,000 people in 1870, workers formed informal buying clubs, "*groupes économiques*," to buy food and goods in large quantities more cheaply.[5]

Private retailing failed to meet some of these needs for a variety of reasons. Shopkeepers in established urban centers hesitated to move to the raw new industrial areas. Capital tended to go to heavy industry, rather than to commerce. Setting up shop was legally free to anyone after the French Revolution, but it did require purchasing a license, or *patente*, which was beyond the reach of many workers. Wages in Belgium, as well, were low, much lower than in Britain or the Netherlands. Securing a profit margin in industrial towns subject to periodic unemployment required real ingenuity and stamina. Small retailers often had to extend credit to their customers, a practice that lowered profits and brought many to bankruptcy in hard times.[6]

Consequently, workers were attracted to the news of British cooperatives that filtered through the trade links which Belgium enjoyed with the island in the textile and metallurgical trades.[7] Ideas and news about cooperation may have also been transmitted through cultural contacts between British and Belgian upper and middle classes as well.[8] In addition, the influence of French Utopian Socialists such as Fourier and Cabet may have also encouraged notions of experimenting with new forms of solidarity.[9]

Although there were a few scattered attempts to form cooperatives in the 1850s and early 1860s, the real beginning of consumer cooperation in Belgium came during the First International, 1866 to 1876. The International had a large impact on Belgium, possibly larger than on any other European country.

Perhaps as many as 250,000 workers at one time or another belonged to one of the short-lived organizations that affiliated with or was in contact with the International.[10] The militants in the International encouraged a wide variety of organizations for workers—newspapers, labor unions, political clubs, and cooperatives both for production and consumption. Indeed, one of the reasons for the International's failure, besides repression, was that it involved itself in too many activities and spread itself too thinly. One act of the government that helped cooperatives may have been in response to the demands of workers in the International: in 1873, the liberal Catholic government eased the requirements for forming cooperatives and gave these institutions many of the same rights as business corporations.

Most of the cooperatives fostered by the International in the industrial areas failed by the late 1870s. There was a lack of experienced leaders, and once the economic downturn of the 1870s hit, most cooperatives went under. The reaction to the International, nonetheless, shaped the future of cooperation in at least one region. To prevent workers from joining consumer cooperatives, industrialists in the iron and coal region of Liège created stores that they dubbed "cooperatives." Most of these appear to have been rebaptized company stores, which now had some form of association linking customers together and offered more generous discounts. Real control usually remained in the hands of businessmen or their appointees.[11] Until just before World War I, genuine customer-controlled cooperatives were less successful in Liège than in other industrialized areas of Belgium. Instead, a kind of "business cooperation," large discount houses run by businessmen, flourished.[12]

The real breakthrough for consumer cooperation came in Ghent, a Dutch-speaking textile and harbor town in the northern part of Belgium. In 1873, a group of textile workers, mostly skilled weavers who belonged to the International, founded a cooperative bakery, the *Vrije Bakkers* (the Free Bakers). Unlike the cooperative ventures elsewhere, this one survived and even prospered during the 1870s. Ghent, one of the homes of the industrial revolution on the continent, had a long-established, native working class. Ghent workers enjoyed a rich associational life, which provided a foundation for cooperation that other industrial centers probably lacked. After the decline of the International, the Ghent militants switched their allegiances from Proudhian or Utopian socialism to a more Marxist or "collectivist" socialism. The cooperative became one of the member organizations in the Flemish Socialist Party, founded in 1878.[13] Surprisingly, the cooperative began a practice, which many later cooperatives copied, of not extending credit for routine purchases. Though this may have kept some customers away initially, it also kept the cooperative solvent and allowed it build up financial reserves. Low prices appear to have compensated for the demand to purchase bread in cash.[14] Success for the cooperative soon brought a crisis that, again, became a typical turning point for many later cooperatives. Some of its leaders wanted to cut ties to the socialist party and turn it into a nonpartisan, more business-like operation. As a result, in 1880, a group of committed socialists left and started a number of other cooperatives.

One of these, *Vooruit* (Forward), became the most influential cooperative in Belgium and one of the most famous in Europe. *Vooruit* became the core of the socialist movement in Ghent by utilizing success in the commercial sphere to create a host of other institutions. The profits and liquid financial reserves of *Vooruit* spawned a mutual insurance company, a labor union movement, the local socialist political party, a publishing house, and, for a time, a set of manufacturing firms and a bank. The first step in *Vooruit*'s success was the decision by its leaders to buy new Borbeck ovens, which could produce larger amounts of bread more cheaply. At the same time, they decided not to lower the price of bread as much as they could, but rather to give coupons back to each member of the cooperative according to how many loaves they purchased. The coupons, of course, could only be redeemed by purchasing more items from the cooperative. This way, the cooperative avoided selling bread on credit, but gave customers the appearance of generous discounts. Since coupons could be used for items other than bread, it encouraged members of *Vooruit* to patronize the cooperative for clothing and household goods, areas where it usually had a harder time competing with private retailers. Most important, the profits from the bakery gave *Vooruit* large financial resources. With these, it offered a generous program of free bread to the families of members who were sick, unemployed, on strike, or who had gone through a family transition such as a death in the household or the birth of a child. The financial reserves also allowed it to purchase new buildings and to continue to expand its size and to enter new lines of operation. In 1881, *Vooruit* sold 2,000 loaves of bread; in 1899, it sold 200,000, with the price having been dropped over 40 percent.[15] By 1900, the cooperative had 7,000 members. In a city with a population of 200,000, over 30,000 people belonged to families that were members of *Vooruit*.[16] The importance of *Vooruit* was sealed by the creation of a daily newspaper of the same name in 1884, which quickly became the socialist newspaper for the Dutch-speaking population in Belgium and one of the largest Flemish publications of any political stripe. Until World War I, among the Flemish population all over Belgium "*Vooruiters*" served as a synonym for socialist.

The Socialist Model and Its Weaknesses

Socialist consumer cooperatives, usually modeled on *Vooruit*, soon spread to the capital, Brussels, to the mining region in Hainaut in central southern Belgium, and to a number of smaller Flemish towns that had populations of textile factory workers.[17] The *Maison du Peuple* in Brussels by the 1890s came to be the largest consumer cooperative in the country, with some 20,000 members in 1900. Both *Le Progrès* of Jolimont, in the region in Hainaut known as the Centre, with 17,000 members and *De Werker* of Antwerp with 10,000 also grew to be larger than *Vooruit*.[18] In many ways, nonetheless, *Vooruit* served as a model for most of the socialist cooperatives in that they tried to copy the way it encouraged a whole range of associations and activities around it. Like *Vooruit*, many of the cooperatives offered local socialist labor unions meeting places on their premises, created mutual insurance societies, and organized women's clubs, festivals, a Socialist Young Guard, and a host of other groups. Typically, all these groups together formed the socialist party in each town or local area. Of critical importance for both socialism and cooperation was the practice whereby almost all socialist cooperatives regularly donated 2 or so percent of their profits to the party. Most of them also made loans to socialist organizations. Anseele, in an oft-quoted phrase, described the cooperatives as the "milkcows of the party." Critics of socialism claimed that the cooperatives acted simply as businesses whose profits went to politicians, not businessmen. Consumer cooperation, then, served both practical and symbolic functions. The cooperative provided a place to meet and financial reserves; it also acted as a manifestation of socialist goals, a concrete symbol of the worker-controlled society that was to come. One consumer cooperative in the small coal mining town of Flemalle-Grande near Liège, an area that was frequently the scene of violent strikes, was even built with bars over the windows so that strikers could flee to the cooperative building to protect themselves from the attacks of the police.[19]

Understandably, this creation of a socialist community around consumer cooperation provoked a large amount of comment by observers and the admiration of many supporters of cooperation or socialism in other countries.[20] The Belgian model of a "marriage" between socialism and cooperation came to mean this symbiosis of the two movements.[21] This was a striking contrast to the situation in many other countries where the two movements opposed each other or went their separate ways. In the United States and Denmark, orthodox Marxist socialists worried that consumer cooperation could deflect workers from more fundamental political and economic concerns. In Britain and France, consumer cooperation was very often apolitical, and some of its supporters even saw it as an antidote to socialism. The success of the Belgian socialists in bringing cooperation and Socialism together can be seen in the way they dominated consumer cooperation in the country. Before World War I, probably 80 percent of all cooperators belonged to socialist cooperatives; perhaps 90 percent of all cooperatives were socialist ones.

The Belgian combination of socialism and cooperation may have had an international effect as well. The migration of Flemish workers from Belgium into northern France, for example, also brought a large influence of Belgian socialism. Even though the leader of the French Socialists in the north was Jules Guesde, an orthodox Marxist who opposed consumer cooperation, the movement there came to resemble the Belgian one. The large cooperatives of Lille and Roubaix, in fact, either began with Belgian help or looked to the Belgians as a model.[22] Similarly, Emile Vandervelde, the longtime head of the Belgian Socialist party and chairman of the Second International, in several publications with a European-wide audience, vigorously opposed allowing consumer cooperatives to be independent of the Socialist party.[23] At the other extreme, the influential French anarcho-syndicalist writer Georges Sorel denounced the Belgian cooperatives as "*économats*," cheap food stores run for a profit.[24]

Unsurprisingly perhaps, the Belgian socialists themselves portrayed their movement as deeply rooted in consumer cooperation. Ironically, even left-wing critics of the socialist party helped perpetuate the idea that the Belgian socialist movement was deeply dependent on consumer cooperation. Dissident socialists such as Hendrik DeMan and Louis DeBrouckère in 1911 blamed the emphasis on consumer cooperation for what they saw as the movement's reformist, bourgeois quality.[25] During the post-1968 era, radicals saw socialist consumer cooperation as part of the movement's original sin of "economism." [26] Even the party's official centennial history, published in 1985, accepted the virtual equation of cooperation and socialism in the movement's early days, describing what is called "*le socialisme coopératif*."[27]

This view of the importance of consumer cooperation for Belgian socialism, I believe, can easily be exaggerated. Consumer cooperatives were more important for the political support they gave the socialist party than for their economic impact. Socialist consumer cooperation in Belgium never came to develop the position that it did in Scandinavia; indeed by the 1970s, it was virtually dead. One can explain this decline, despite the picture of success portrayed for the pre-world War I period, only by taking a closer look at the socialist cooperatives. Belgian sources, especially the socialist ones, rarely try to measure the movement's real impact or to assess its weaknesses, as well as its undeniable strengths. Fortunately some French and British sources help arrive at a more objective analysis. Arriving at a more accurate perspective of the cooperatives' position before 1914, furthermore, helps in understanding the transformations that they eventually underwent in the interwar and post-World War II periods.

Even though the socialist cooperatives provided important resources for the party, their members made up only a small part of the population and not even a majority of the socialist supporters. In 1908, the socialist federation of cooperatives had 127,000 cooperators in its member institutions. The pioneering British sociologist B. Seebohm Rowntree estimated that this represented only 1.8 percent of the Belgian population. In England and Wales, in 1904, by contrast, 5.6 percent of the population belonged to cooperatives. Even adding in the Belgians who belonged to nonsocialist cooperatives and to socialist cooperatives that did not belong to the federation would probably not raise the figure to more than 2.5 percent. The Belgian cooperatives, according to Rowntree, sold on average 10 pounds, 11 shillings per member, the English and Welsh 39 pounds, 4 shillings.[28] Even taking account of British prices being much higher than Belgium's would leave the English cooperatives selling approximately two and a half times as much per member as the Belgian ones. The 127,000 cooperative members in the socialist federation in 1908 must be compared to the 467,000 votes that the socialist party received in the 1900 elections and to the approximately 600,000 it won in 1912.[29]

The strength of the social Catholic movement did not cause the weaknesses of Belgian socialist consumer cooperation. Belgian social Catholics were remarkably successful in organizing many lower- and middle-class people and opposing socialism.[30] After universal male suffrage went into effect in 1894 (although socialists were hurt by plural votes given to the middle and upper class), the Catholic party routinely dominated national elections. Social Catholics organized workers into clubs, mutual insurance societies, and, by 1914, proportionately, the most successful religious labor union movement in Europe. In 1913, there were 126,745 socialist unionists and 102,177 Catholic labor unionists.[31] Yet, in part because of the opposition of Catholic shopkeepers, social Catholics were much slower to create Catholic consumer cooperatives. Before 1895, there were almost none. By 1914, there were at most 30,000 Catholic consumer cooperators.[32] Furthermore, these Catholic cooperatives seem to have had even lower sales per member than did the socialist cooperatives. And, most significantly, there was no correlation between the strength of socialist consumer cooperation and that of Catholic consumer cooperation. Socialist cooperation was strong in Ghent, home of *Vooruit*, and in Brussels, home of *La Maison du Peoples*, where Catholics organized two of their strongest cooperatives, *Het Volk* and *Le Bon Pain Bruxellois*. Socialists cooperation was very weak in many of coalmining areas of southern, French-speaking Belgium, where the socialist party won as much as 50 percent of the votes in three-way races against Catholics and Liberals, and where Catholic cooperation had little support.[33]

Socialist consumer cooperation, too, remained cut off from other kinds of cooperation in Belgium. The large network of agricultural cooperatives, united in the *Boerenbond* or Farmers' League, was organized by Catholics who opposed the socialists. These cooperatives helped farmers sell their produce and livestock, borrow to modernize their equipment, and, in some cases, buy consumer items. Like the rural cooperatives in Denmark and some other countries, the *Boerenbond* cooperatives eventually helped Belgium switch from cereals to dairying, truck farming, and livestock. Neither politically nor economically, however, did they work with the socialist cooperatives to create an alternative to private enterprise.[34] Similarly, unlike Britain or Germany, there were few "building societies." What few there were usually organized as nonpartisan associations and had no ties to the socialists.[35] The scarcity of building societies in Belgium resulted from the low rents, which are about half of those of Britain, and, as will be discussed below, from the government's policy of encouraging workers from the countryside and small towns to commute to the big cities.[36]

Despite Belgium's generally *laissez-faire* tradition, government policy in the late nineteenth century created an unfavorable environment for consumer cooperatives.[37] Once the socialists had begun to organize successfully, the Catholic government yielded to the demands of lower-middle-class leaders and, in 1891, imposed the *patente*, the obligatory retailing license, on cooperatives. Property and most other local taxes also fell on cooperatives. At the same time, small business that had no employees other than family members went virtually untaxed.[38] National and local governments also began subsidizing both agricultural cooperatives, like the *Boerenbond*, and mutual insurance societies, which were and are extremely important in Belgium. Consumer cooperatives, by contrast, did not receive subsidies.[39]

The government's policy to slow urbanization may not seem as directly aimed at cooperatives, but, in fact, it had a tremendous effect. To the world's densest railway network, the government in the late nineteenth century added a large system of tramways or interurbans and reduced workmen's tickets on the railroads. As a consequence, thousands of workers commuted to the big cities to work, rather than moving there permanently. The result was a peculiarly decentralized growth of smaller towns and cities, rather than metropolises, despite Belgium being one of the most densely populated countries in the world. It was difficult to establish a successful consumer cooperative outside the larger towns because cooperatives relied on economies of scale to offer cheaper prices than private retailers.

The concentration of socialist cooperation in the large cities, nonetheless, points to both the limits and the real achievement of the movement. In the pre-World War I era, successful socialist cooperatives were disproportionately in the large cities. In 1908, the socialist federation of cooperatives had 162 member cooperatives, with a total of 127,000 cooperators belonging to them. The four largest cooperatives—the *Maison du peuple*, *Le Progrés*, *De Werker*, and *Vooruit*—together had 55,000 members, accounting for over 43 percent of the total number in the federation. These four cooperatives were in four of the country's five largest urban areas. In other words, while these four giants averaged well over 10,000 members, the other 158 cooperatives in the federation averaged less than 500.[40] In some small towns, socialist consumer cooperatives grew up quickly and then languished for years. In many of the small coal mining turns around Liège, for example, many cooperatives founded in the Socialist movement's early days in the 1880s were about the same size or had even shrunk in membership twenty years later.[41]

The Achievements of Socialist Cooperation

The achievements of socialist consumer cooperatives in their heyday before World War I fell into three areas: economies of scale, mutual insurance and capital formation, and, finally, the creation of a political community.

Where they were able to reach a large urban clientele, the socialist cooperatives pioneered mass consumer distribution in Belgium. *Vooruit, Le Progrés,* and the Brussels *Maison du peuple* each had hundreds of employees; the *Maison* had dozens of branches, warehouses, and production shops scattered over the region of Brussels and was the largest bakery in the country. The socialist cooperatives were still heavily dependent, it is true, on the sale of bread, which had been their starting point. In the early 1900s, bread still accounted for 40 percent of *Vooruit*'s sales, 50 percent of the *Maison*'s.[42] Their range of goods and number of branches were nonetheless impressive. Only one private retailer—Delhaize, which appropriately is still the country's largest grocer—appears to have operated as extensively. The successful nonsocialist consumer cooperatives depended on the same economies of scale as the socialists, except that they operated more as limited liability companies. One of the largest Catholic cooperatives, *Volksbelang* (People's Interest) in Ghent, was virtually run by a group of businessmen. Clients in these kinds of cooperatives might receive bonuses for their purchases, but they usually had no other rights or benefits as members unless they owned stock.[43] It is striking that the nonsocialist cooperatives, in fact, almost only succeeded where they were very large: *Volksbelang* had 8,500 members, another Catholic cooperative near Charleroi claimed 9,000, and the one large Liberal cooperative, in Antwerp, had 11,000. There were only a few other nonsocialist cooperatives, almost all of whom had under 1,000 members, which survived. The one large urban area that socialist cooperation did not penetrate before 1914, Liège, is the exception that proves the rule: the old company store "cooperatives," run by businessmen, copied the methods of the socialist consumer cooperatives elsewhere in Belgium and succeeded by expanding their clientele into the thousands.[44]

Although not the largest cooperative, *Vooruit* had by far the biggest impact in creating economic institutions in areas outside of consumer sales. Its contribution deserves, therefore, to be treated separately. In Belgium, as in other countries, producers' cooperatives had generally failed, despite the attempts of liberal reformers, socialists, and progressive Catholics alike. *Vooruit*, like other consumer cooperatives and many labor unions, experimented with producers' cooperatives, but after 1900 began setting up its own production facilities as profit-sharing, commercial operations. It concentrated on cotton-spinning, the major industry in Flanders, but soon expanded into weaving, garments-making, and furniture. By the 1920s, the industrial operations had over 1,000 workers, but in addition there were shipping and construction operations.[45] In 1913, Edouard Anseele, the administrator of *Vooruit*, led the Ghent Socialists to cap this empire with the creation of a socialist-owned "Labor Bank," *Bank van de Arbeid/Banque du Travail*, whose shares were traded on the Brussels Stock Exchange. The Labor Bank held the funds of many cooperatives and labor unions and, in turn, loaned to them. This economic system was fated to crash in the Great Depression, but while it lasted it demonstrated the immense economic potential of cooperation. One institution started by *Vooruit* that had longer-lasting impact was its mutual insurance society, the *Bond Moyson*. In the 1890s already, *Moyson* insured almost all the member families in *Vooruit*, whereas in most other cooperatives insurance for a long time trailed consumption in importance.[46] Influenced by the example of Ghent, the socialist movement in 1907 created a national insurance society, *La prevovance social*. By 1910, it had 96,000 members; by 1913, over 125,000. The impressive potential of cooperative-run insurance could been seen in *La prevovance* tripling its incoming premiums between 1909 and 1912.[47]

Besides pioneering in economies of scale and in encouraging mutual insurance, the socialist consumer cooperatives made an important contribution toward creating an alternative society. By making membership tied to further purchases and to participation in running the institution, the cooperatives tried to make a statement to working-class families about the value of economic inter-dependence. Some foreign observers saw this as a striking contrast to the British cooperatives, for example, which they feared encouraged workers to buy merely out of self-interest. The Belgians tried, too, to influence workers' ideas about themselves and their community. The cooperatives carved out a space for workers to learn new skills of administration, new ideas about society and politics, and new possible ways to organize themselves. Cooperatives hosted visiting labor union organizers, socialist gymnastic teams, and political candidates. The whole network of socialist institutions in Ghent, which was based on *Vooruit*, was described by observers as a "Socialist citadel" and as a "Socialist state within the state." In Brussels, the *Maison du peuple* sponsored a particularly innovative workers' education program, complete with workers' tours of art exhibits and lectures by artists, scientists, and foreign scholars.[48] In these areas of cultural influence, education, and propaganda, even the small socialist cooperatives could have an influence that ran far beyond their size or apparent economic impact. The 150 or so cooperatives that had less than 500 members before World War I might appear insignificant. Yet almost every area where the socialist movement grew after World War I in union membership, vote totals, or insurance society membership was an area where the cooperatives had first penetrated before the war.

Cooperation in Transition: The Interwar Period

During the interwar period, consumer cooperation in Belgium appeared on the surface to expand and, in a sense, to build on the pre-War foundations. Yet, the Depression dealt severe blows to the cooperatives, and, by the end of the 1930s, the movement had begun to slip more to the margins of the consumer economy. Just as important, the government, the socialists, and the lower middle class had forged new alliances, which hampered the cooperatives.

The total number of cooperators grew in an impressive fashion immediately after World War I and kept pace with the population thereafter until the 1940s. In 1924, 378,143 people belonged to consumer cooperatives, representing 5.1 percent of the population; by 1938, the hard times of the Depression had raised this number to 578,056, 7.1 percent of the population.[49] (Socialist cooperators in 1924 numbered 270,000 or 3.6 percent.) Since membership was almost always restricted to heads of households, one can multiply the number of members by four to estimate the total population served. Thus, approximately a quarter of the population had some direct contact with the cooperative movement during the interwar movement.

Cooperation also became much more centralized. By 1925, the socialist federation had reduced the number of cooperatives from over 200 to only sixty; by the 1930s, it fell to forty. On the surface, at least in the area of administration, the Socialists appeared to have solved some of the pre-World War I problems created by excessive localism. In 1924, the various production facilities of the cooperatives joined to form a centralized *Société Générale Coopérative*. Besides the "Prevoyance Sociale" insurance company, the socialist movement also created a national pharmacy cooperative and a savings bank.[50] The production facilities set up by *Vooruit* before the war remained separate enterprises from the rest of the cooperative movement, but the Labor Bank that financed them held funds of many of the socialist consumer cooperatives. Most of the Catholic cooperatives that were genuinely worker-controlled formed a national federation, as did the nonpartisan or neutral cooperatives.

In many ways, the alternative vision of a cooperative economy remained alive and well among the socialists in the interwar period. For a time, in the 1920s, socialist leaders could view cooperation as part of their multifaceted strategy to transform the economy. Together with workers' control of production through factory councils, cooperation could gradually accumulate consumers' capital and increasingly push aside the private sector. Louis DeBrouckère, the former dissident who was given the chair in cooperative studies at the Université libre de Bruxelles, envisioned cooperation growing with the rest of the socialist movement toward the "Cooperative Republic."[51] The socialist labor unions increased their membership almost fourfold, from 136,000 to

600,000, between 1913 and 1922, while the socialist party became nearly the largest party in parliament. If the movement as a whole continued to grow, and cooperatives could expand proportionately, at a certain point the size and concentration of the nonprofit sector could give it financial power great enough to effect changes in the entire economy.

This dream remained unfilled. The most devastating blow that the socialist cooperatives received came from the Great Depression, which caused coopera-tors to withdraw their savings, reduce their purchases, and call on the coopera-tives' provisions for unemployed members in more massive numbers than had ever been intended. In 1930, the savings bank run by the socialist federation appeared near to collapse and was taken over by the Labor Bank. By 1934, the Labor Bank itself had to close its doors, despite the Socialist party's attempts to get the government to rescue it. At the same time, the bank set up by the Flemish Catholic farmers, the *Boerenbond*, which had become probably the second largest in the country, also went bankrupt. The collapse of the Labor Bank was a catastrophe for almost all socialist cooperatives, who either had their own funds in the bank or were deeply involved in joint operations with other cooperatives dependent on the Bank. To save the cooperatives, the government granted them a large loan. In return, they gave up their activity in savings and consumer credit, and a new socialist credit union, under much stricter government controls, took over handling many workers' savings. Not until 1956 did the socialist cooperatives finish paying back the loan to the government.[52]

The difficulties encountered by consumer cooperation in the interwar period, however, went deeper than the Great Depression. The buying habits of the mass of Belgian consumers did not become more oriented for cooperatives even when the number of cooperative members grew. At the same time, the socialist movement as a whole did not help change the attitudes of these consumers, and a powerful expansion of capitalist consumerism put the whole cooperative movement on the defensive. Many cooperative members appear to have purchased only a small part of their consumer expenditures at the cooper-ative, and cooperatives still represented a small part of the whole economy. In 1930, cooperative sales represented only 3.24 percent of total sales, and this had even shrunk to 3.15 by 1938.[53] The cooperatives that grew the most in the interwar period were Catholic or nonpartisan ones that had lower sales per member than did the socialist. The number of socialist cooperative members grew only 12 percent between 1924 and 1938, from 270,189 to 305,673. The Catholic cooperators, meanwhile, grew from 20,813 to 110,673, yet in 1938 they purchased only two-thirds as much per member from their cooperatives as did their socialist counterparts.[54]

The cul-de-sac in which the socialist cooperatives found themselves reflected, in part, the difficulties of the movement as a whole, after the explo-sive growth of the immediate post-World War I years. Although union membership and socialist voting had increased tremendously between 1918 and 1922, this growth had come in the industrial areas where the movement had been active already before the war. The shift in political consciousness and the retreat of conservativism after the war, in other words, brought in workers in the older industrial areas who had been acquainted with socialism but had hesitated joining. Yet the industries in these areas—textiles, coal, iron, and steel—grew more slowly in the 1920s and 1930s than did chemicals, electronics, commerce, white-collar business, and small machine-building. These growth industries tended to be located in other areas, particularly Flanders, where Catholic organizations were strong and where socialism had difficulty penetrating. Between 1924 and 1938, socialist unions grew barely 10 percent, while Catholic unions more than doubled in size.[55] The close association of consumer cooperation and socialism, which had been a source of strength in the heroic years before the War, proved a handicap in some ways. The cooperative movement had difficulty growing because socialism failed to grow. The weaknesses of socialist cooperatives before the War could be overlooked because the movement as a whole was optimistic that future growth would overcome these problems. In the more competitive, anxious 1930s, the alternative vision of a cooperative economy had to be judged on its concrete achievements. In particular, the socialist cooperative movement, like the socialist labor unions and the party, did a poor job involving women in its leadership. In the 1930s, socialist women activists launched some bitter attacks on the traditionalism of the socialist movement, but the tough economic times were not conducive to changing the attitudes of the leadership. By and large, socialists and cooperators of all types during the Great Depression jettisoned the goal of a larger vision and concentrated on simply trying to keep cooperatives alive.

At the same time, however, consumer cooperation itself, in contrast to the pre-World War I era, had difficulty bringing people into socialism. This seems to have indicated a shift within working-class families to which cooperatives found it awkward to adjust. According to one economist studying consumption, for many people socialist cooperatives remained identified solely with providing cheap food to industrial workers, rather than with offering a variety of goods to consumers of all walks of life.[56] During the 1930s, socialist cooperatives managed to hold their own in food sales, but saw their share of sales in the area of furniture and household items fall almost by a third.[57] Meanwhile, the number of small retailers in Belgium exploded in the interwar period: from approximately 200,000 retailers in 1910, the number grew to 231,000 in 1930, an increase of 15 percent in twenty years; by 1937, the number had grown to 291,000, an increase of 26 percent in only seven years.[58] Many of these retailers, of course, barely squeezed out a living by employing only family members and making very small profits. Nonetheless, it seems clear that many of these small private retailers did better than the cooperatives in selling the range of new or more available goods unleashed in the interwar years—radios, record players, automobiles, margarine, electric lamps, and clothes made with synthetic fibers. Even though many of these retailers complained about fierce competition, in fact, the strongest of them appear to have adjusted better to the new, more individualistic culture emerging in the interwar years. Advertising, buying on credit, a diversity of brands—all of these were tempting to working-class consumers, but were not aspects of commerce at which the cooperatives had excelled.

Commerce and the Rise of Interest Group Politics

The other crucial development of the interwar era was the rise of a militant lower middle class, in which organizations of small retailers formed the core. As in other Western European countries, the gains of organized labor after World War I and the power of big business and finance made small business-people feel that they had lost the attention of government and the rest of society. Since previously the lower-middle-class had largely been content to follow the lead of the upper-middle-class leaders of the Catholic and Liberal parties, small retailers had to build new organizations before they could hope to exert some influence. By 1932, a group of lower-middle-class organizations came together in a *Union nationale des classes moyennes*, which claimed 100,000 members. The enormous challenge of meeting the Depression meant that the established political parties did little in the early 1930s to satisfy lower middle class demands. In 1936, many shopkeepers' organizations, grouped in a radical *Eenheidsfront van de Middenstand*, cooperated in elections with a new proto-fascist party called *Rex*, which won 11.5 percent of the vote.[59]

In reaction to the rising anger of the lower middle class, especially as manifested in votes for *Rex*, the government took a whole range of actions to protect small business, actions that also limited the sphere of consumer cooperatives.[60] In 1937, stronger regulations came down against civil servants managing their own businesses on the side. Civil servants were expressly forbidden for the first time from holding a job in the management of consumer cooperatives. Even the wives of civil servants could not hold such a job. On January 13, 1937, in what became known as the "padlock law," the government froze all diversified stores above a certain size: five employees in cities of over 100,000, three in smaller towns. The Ministry of Economic Affairs from now on controlled whether or not these stores could be opened, be enlarged, or add new lines. This law was strengthened in 1938 when large stores were also forbidden to manage another retailer's activity.[61] The law, in effect, made all diversified retail businesses subject to government control, while giving free entry to small, family owned stores. There were only a half-dozen towns over 100,000, so the effective limit on stores free of government control was three employees—the maximum number of employees for almost all family owned retailers. Not surprisingly, perhaps, the "padlock law" was closely followed by Nazi Germany, which had tried to reward its lower-middle-class supporters with similar controls.[62] The new relationship of the lower middle class was sealed by the government's creation of credit institutions, which loaned money to stave off bankruptcies. Organizations of retailers even helped name the managers of the credit institutions.[63]

Why did the socialists, who were part of the coalition governments from 1934 on, go along with the special privileges given to the lower-middle-class shopkeepers who had been their competitors for almost 50 years? First, the government loan to the cooperatives after the collapse of the Labor Bank weakened the socialists' bargaining position. They could hardly argue that state intervention to help a beleaguered economic sector was inappropriate when they asked for assistance themselves. Second, the entire position of the consumer cooperatives within the socialist camp had changed from the heroic days before World War I. From being the center of a unified movement, the cooperatives were now increasingly shunted aside by other kinds of socialist organizations. Up to 1914, the labor unions had fewer members than did the consumer cooperatives. By 1938, the 540,000 unionists far outnumbered the 305,000 cooperators. The unions were even less willing to support the cooperatives since the unions, too, had lost a large part of their funds in the collapse of the Labor Bank. After a huge strike wave in June 1936, almost simultaneous with the Popular Front strikes in France, the labor unions won important concessions from employers and the government. Their focus shifted from a socialist-led transformation of society to negotiations with employers, governments, and their erstwhile rivals, the Catholic labor unions.[64]

The new socialist leaders of the 1930s accelerated the cooperatives' loss of position within the movement. From 1933 on, Hendrik DeMan led the socialists in trying to recruit middle-class support for an expansionary economic program. DeMan's "Labor Plan," which embodied his program and which the party adopted, did not even mention the cooperatives. DeMan had been one of Weimar Germany's leading socialist theorists before returning to his native Belgium. He had long argued, in works such as *The Psychology of Socialism*, that Marxism's reliance on the working class had to be transcended. As a government minister in the coalition governments, DeMan apparently supported most of the actions taken on behalf of the lower middle class; he was finance minister when the new credit arrangements were created.[65]

Third, the socialists accepted the government's accommodation with small-scale commerce because they themselves had affinities with that approach to retailing. The socialist cooperatives had made their initial impact before World War I by exploiting economies of scale, and they had greatly centralized the movement in the 1920s. Yet an important part of the socialist movement remained attached to the neighborhood store, the *"magasin de quartier,"* even if it was a cooperative.[66] As pointed out earlier, prior to World War I, the cooperative movement had been extremely decentralized, with many small, even tiny cooperatives. Officially, centralization after World War I brought the number of cooperatives to forty, and of these, nine had 85 percent of the members and ten did 90 percent of sales. Nonetheless, in 1939, there were 1,139 branches. Given the small size of their total sales, many of these branches could not be justified. Many of these branches were, in reality, the old small cooperatives under a new name. Even when they had a small membership, they remained alive because they represented one of the centers of the local socialist movement. Many centralized cooperatives, in other words, during the 1920s had amalgamated the older, tiny cooperatives together without changing their role.[67] The smaller cooperatives hesitated to challenge the private retailers, too, because they often bought nonfood items wholesale from the same distributors. These wholesale and distribution arrangements depended on custom as much as business, yet, because food prices were low, these arrangements provided one of the few sources of profits.[68] Indeed, the cooperatives found themselves so squeezed by the Depression that they appear to have done little to reduce retail prices. Between 1929 and 1933, wholesale prices dropped 42 percent, while retail prices fell only 17 percent.[69] Yet cooperatives and private retailers were widely reported to follow similar pricing policies.[70] One economist believed that the real failure of the cooperatives was that, except for the few giants, they never tackled the problem of distribution and tried to radically shorten the distance between producers and consumers.[71] In this area, the gulf between the Catholic-controlled *Boerenbond* in agriculture and the largely socialist urban consumer cooperation may have been particularly important. In Denmark, for example, urban consumer cooperation were linked more directly to rural producers cooperatives and were thus more able to keep down prices. In Belgium, because rural cooperation was overwhelmingly Catholic—organized in the *Boerenbond*—the socialist consumer cooperatives found it difficult to link producers and consumers more directly.

Decline and Heritage: World War II to the Present

The occupation of Belgium by the Nazis during the war hit the cooperatives extremely hard, harder even than German occupation in the First World War. The cooperatives had difficulty using the transportation system, fought constant battles with the occupying authorities, and, most of all, found the black market siphoning off goods at an astonishing rate. The price of coffee, for example, went up 100-fold.[72] From a long-term perspective, however, the war only accelerated earlier trends. The socialist cooperatives remained confined to older industrial areas, and even though non-socialist cooperation grew it did not significantly alter the low sales recorded by the movement. Between 1945 and 1949, during the reconstruction after the war, membership in the Catholic cooperatives grew threefold, while the socialist membership doubled.[73] The total percentage of sales in cooperative hands, meanwhile, had fallen sharply: from 3.15 percent of consumer sales in 1938 to only 2.07 in 1950.[74] Cooperatives continued to rely heavily on selling food, rather than on marketing consumer goods. At the same time, the padlock law severely limited any expansion or merging of retail outlets by either cooperatives or private business.

During the 1950s, a new climate of opinion emerged among political and business leaders in Belgium, which helped hasten the weakening of the cooperatives' last hold on the consumer economy. Belgian economic growth lagged behind that of its Western European neighbors, except Britain, which had the slowest growing economy in Western Europe. Especially with the opening of the Common Market, or European Economic Community, in 1957, the key way to recharge the Belgian economy appeared to be inviting in foreign investment. Low costs, including lower wages, and a larger labor pool, leaders hoped, would help attract foreign investment. Yet it appeared to be clear that the retail sector employed a disproportionate amount of labor and had a low level of productivity. Retail prices were artificially high due to the inordinate number of small stores and the failure to develop an efficient distribution system.[75] Neither the labor union movement nor business leaders were willing to allow the consumer sector to remain unchanged.

In 1958, the government finally lifted the padlock law and the cooperatives, like the small retailers, had to contend with a wave of mass market retailing. The large supermarket and department store chains could take advantage of a set of trends that undermined the cooperatives. Nonfood consumption grew twice as fast as food consumption in the 1960s. Between 1956 and 1968, the number of food stores decreased by one-third, while the average size of stores doubled. Rooted in a neighborhood, the small branch cooperative, like the small store, had difficulty competing when the number of cars tripled in a little over a decade.[76] (To put Belgian developments in perspective for a foreign audience, it helps to note that Sarma, Belgium's second largest retailer, was taken over by J.C. Penney's, one of the four largest retail chains in the United States.) Briefly, the socialist and Catholic cooperative federations discussed a joint mass marketing effort with French and Belgian retail chains, but the philosophies of the cooperatives and private companies were too incompatible for the venture to succeed. By the 1980s, only a handful of consumer cooperatives still operated in Belgium. It is indicative of the political situation in which consumer cooperation found itself enmeshed that the one area where cooperatives still do well is pharmacies. Already in the 1880s, cooperatives had found selling medicines a small but profitable activity and this continues even today. Yet pharmacy is one of the most heavily protected of trades in Belgium: obtaining a license is a virtual permit to reap monopoly profits. As late as the 1980s, even plastic bandages and aspirin could only be purchased from pharmacies, and the government faced enormous pressure from insurers and consumers to weaken pharmacies' privileges.[77]

Consumer cooperation in Belgium, however, has given birth to some significant social and economic movements, which still flourish. Like the labor unions, insurance began under the wing of the socialist consumer cooperatives and has long ago taken off on its own. *La Prévoyance sociale* now insures one out of every six Belgians. One of the very largest Belgian insurance companies, it has a long tradition of encouraging preventive medicine and continues to be run as a nonprofit institution. The savings bank, known as CODEP, set up in the 1930s out of the ruin of the Labor Bank continues as well. Equally important is the consumer movement, which grew out of the membership in the consumer cooperatives. As the interest-group and social welfare state begun in the 1930s became more elaborate, the cooperatives succeeded in winning a place for consumers in the political system. In 1948, consumer representatives joined the Central Economic Council, charged with national planning. In 1956, they, along with the largely Catholic family leagues, served on the national Advisory Commission on Prices.[78] This consumerist movement has grown and become, along with the socialist insurance society, the chief contribution of consumer cooperation to contemporary Belgium.

In conclusion, the history of Belgian cooperation offers some significant lessons. For a time, the socialist cooperatives seemed to capture both the communal longing of many individuals in a capitalist society and the need to serve these individuals economically by competing with private business in providing goods inexpensively. The socialist ideology of a cooperative economy provided the inspiration for the consumer cooperative movement. Yet when the cooperatives tended to serve only the political or communitarian needs of workers who identified with socialism, they lost the opportunity to reach a broader audience and to create a viable alternative to private business. The ideological and the business sides of socialist cooperation thus are difficult to separate. When the movement as a whole had a vital mission, before World War I, it managed to pioneer more in business methods and at the same time to adapt to the needs of consumers. When the movement lost its forward motion in the interest-group politics of the 1930s, cooperation, too, failed to innovate. Continual adaption to consumer needs and desires was central, yet the padlock law and the decentralized urbanization pattern in Belgium in the twentieth century kept the cooperatives in a holding pattern in which they failed to change. By 1958, when the padlock law ended and Belgium entered the Common Market, it was too late to innovate successfully. There was always in Belgium, nonetheless, significant potential for alternatives to private commerce. The success of the *Boerenbond* and *Le prévovance sociale*, both of which continue today, demonstrates what could perhaps be accomplished. If consumer cooperation and similar movements can still accomplish something in contemporary economies it may be that they would have to find ways to appeal to individuals' desires both to choose freely between options and to find ways to band together in forms of community. The legacy of Belgian cooperation may be the tremendous potential that such appeals can have, as well as the difficult challenge that combining individuality and community can be.

Notes

1. Marquis Childs, *Sweden: The Middle Way* (New York, 1938); Gosta Esping-Anderson, *Politics Against Markets: The Social Democratic Road to Power* (Princeton, 1982); and Peder Aléx's article in this collection, "Swedish Consumer Cooperation as an Educational Endeavor."

2. For a useful overview, Jean Puissant, "L'historiographie de la coopération en Belgique" and his "La coopération en Belgique. Tentative d'evaluation globale," both in *Belgisch Tijdschrift voor Nieuwste Geschiedenis/Revue belge d'histoire contemporaine* 22, 1-2 (1991). On Belgian politics and society as a whole in the formative period of Cooperation, see Carl Strikwerda, *A House Divided: Catholics, Socialists, and Flemish Nationalists in Nineteenth Century Belgium* (London, 1997).

3. George Alter, *Family and the Female Life Course: Verviers 1840-1848* (Madison, 1988), 105-10.

4. Commission du travail, *Proces-verbaux du commission du travail* 7 vols. (Bruxelles, 1887), I:655, II:174.

5. Victor Serwy, *Histoire du cooperation en Belgique*, 4 vols. (Bruxelles, 1942-1946).

6. J. J. Boddewyn, *Belgian Policy Toward Retailing since 1789* (East Lansing, 1978), 12-16; and Joel Mokyr, *Industrialization in the Low Countries 1790-1850* (New Haven, 1975), 189.

7. Belgium bought much of its more advanced textile machinery from Britain and ties in the metallurgical trades were close enough that British workers sent emissaries to Belgium to ensure that strikebreakers not come to Britain from Belgium: *De Vier Getouwen* (Gent, 1892), 1-2; Denise DeWeerdt, *Belgisch Socialisme op zoek naar zijn eigen vorm. 1866-1872* (Antwerpen, 1970), 72-78.

8. Perhaps to avoid complete absorption into French culture, there was a kind of minor craze for things British in mid-nineteenth century Belgium: liberals and conservatives in the Belgian parliament called themselves "Whigs" and "Tories," and even a working-class newspaper quoted Gladstone: *De Lichtstraal*, 9 November 1889, 3.

9. Avanti [pseud.] *Een terugblik. Proeve eeener geschiedenis der Gentsche Socialistische Arbeidersbeweging gedurende de XIXe eeuw* (Ghent, 1909), 14; Louis Bertrand, *Histoire de la cooperation en Belgique*, 2 vols. (Brussels, 1900), I:169-395.

10. DeWeerdt, *Op zoek*, passim.

11. Serwy, *Histoire*, 2:301-304

12. George Gaget, *Etude sur le mouvement cooperatif en Belgique* (Toulouse, 1901), 76.

13. Avanti, *En terugblik*, 325-36; and Paul de Witte, *De Geschiedenis van Vooruit* (Ghent, 1898) 100-106.

14. Gaget, *Eutde*, 32.

15. Thomas Dawe, *A Co-operative Tour in Belgium and France* (Manchester, 1901), 10.

16. Louis Varlez, "La fédération ouvrière gantoise," *Le musee social*, Janvier 1899, 38.

17. Louis Bertrand, one of the founders of the Brussels' *Maison du peuple*, cited *Vooruit* more often than his own cooperative as an example in a pamphlet advocating cooperation: *La cooperation. Ses advantages—son avenir* (Brussels, 1888).

18. Bertrand, *Histoire*, 2:356, 395.

19. Joseph Bondas, *Histoire anecdotique au mouvement ouvrier au pays de Liège* (Liège, 1955), 158.

20. *Vooruit* was even known to cooperators in the United States: Albert Sonnichsen, "A Baker and What He Baked," *The Outlook* [The Co-operative League of America] December 27, 1913; and Emory S. Bogardus, *Dictionary of Cooperation* (New York and Chicago, 1948), 60, 97.

21. The image of a "marriage" was that of Edouward Anseele, "Socialism and Cooperation," in *Modern Socialism*, ed. R. C. K. Ensor (London, 1907), 285-86.

22. Ellen Furlough, "The Politics of Consumption: The Consumer Cooperative in France, 1834-1930," Ph.D. diss., Brown University, 1987, 179; and Jean Gaumont, *Histoire générale de la cooperation en France*, 2 vols. (Paris, 1924), 2:274.

23. Emile Vandervelde, *La coopération neutre et la coopération socialiste* (Paris, 1913). This book was based on articles that Vandervelde wrote; the book appeared in Dutch and German as well as in French. For a favorable German view of Belgian Socialist cooperation, see W. Kulemann, *Die Genossenschaftsbewegung*, 2 vols. (Berlin, 1922), 1:161-65, 2:207, 216.

24. *Introduction à l'économie moderne*, 168, cited by Kulemann, *Genossenschaftsbewegung*, 1:163.

25. The hostility of the party to their criticism was such that DeMan and DeBrouckère had to publish their work in Germany: *Die Arbeiterbewegung in Belgien* (Stuttgart, 1911), a reprint of their articles in *Die Neue Zeit*.

26. Marcel Liebman, *Les sociolistes belges, 1855-1914* (Brussels, 1979); and Andre Mommen, *die Belgische Werkledenpartij, 1880-1914* (Ghent, 1980). For another attempt to analyze the movement's past, see Carl Strikwerda, "The Paradoxes of Urbanization: Belgian Socialism and Society in the *belle epoque*," *Urban History Yearbook 1989*, 82-96.

27. Guy Qaden and Robert Ramaekers, "Le Socialisme Coopératif," in *1885/1985, Du parti ouvrier au parti socialiste* (Brussels, 1985). Similarly, Pussant, "La coopération," while noting in passing that many Socialist cooperatives were small accepts the traditional pictures of the Socialist cooperation before the First World War as a largely successful movement.

28. B. Seebohm Rowntree, *Land and Labour: Lessons from Belgium* (London, 1911), 407.

29. H. Balthazar, "Verkiezingresultaten," in *Geschiedenis van de Socialistische arbeidersbeweging in Belgie* (Antwerp, 1960), 596. Estimating the Socialist votes in 1912 is difficult because many candidates ran on coalition tickets with Liberals.

30. See Strikwerda, *A House*, 213-80; Carl Strikwerda, "A Resurgent Religion: The Rise of Catholic Social Movements in Nineteenth Century Belgian Cities," in *European Religion in the Age of Great Cities*, ed. Hugh McLeod (London, 1995).

31. Strikwerda, *A House*, 348.

32. Bertrand, *Historie*, 2:600-18; Rowntree, *Land and Labour*, 408.

33. Strikwerda, *A House*, 177-205.

34. Leen Van Molle, *Leder Voor Allen: De Belgische Boerenbond 1890-1990* (Leuven, 1990); Abel Varzim, *Le Boerenbond Belge* (Paris, 1934); and E. J. Ross, *Belgian Rural Cooperation* (Milwaukee, 1940).

35. Rowntree, *Land and Labour*, 453, 457.

36. Ernest Mahaim, *Les abonnements d'ouvriers* (Brussels, 1910).

37. B. S. Chlepener, *Cent ans d'Histoire Sociale en Belgique* (Brussels, 1958), 55-65.

38. Dame, *Co-operative Tour*, 10; Rowntree, *Land and Labour*, 327.

39. Rowntree, *Land and Labour*, 336.

40. Numbers calculated from Bertrand, *Histoire*, vol. 2. Rowntree using slightly different statistics arrives at a similar result: the seven largest cooperatives, he estimated, did half the business done by the cooperatives in the Socialist federation, 407.

41. Bertrand, *Histoire*, 2:434-38. *Les Artisans reunies* of the Hologne-aux-Pierres, where the Socialist party and miners' unions were active though not always successful, saw its membership go from 203 when it was founded in 1886 to 110 in 1900.

42. Rowntree, *Land and Labour*, 408-9.

43. Gaget, *Etude*, 46-47.

44. Gaget, *Etude*, 76.

45. G. Vanschoenbeek, "En toch draait ze! Het verhaal van de kooperatieve wererij van Vooruit te Gent, 1903-1910," *BTNG/RBHC* 22, nos. 1-2 (1991); Pol Hannick, *Geschiedenis der Socialistische Naamloze Vennootschap "Vereenigde Spinnerijen en Weverijen"* (Ghent, 1929) 75; and E. Souter, *Le systeme de Gand. Essai sur les sociétés ouvrieres en Belgique* (Lille, 1935).

46. Raf van Lerberge, *De Geschiedenis van Bond Movson* (Ghent, 1978).

47. *De Metaalbewerker*, Oogst, 1910, 8. See also, J. Dockx, "De Prevoyance Sociale' als typevoorbeeld van een socialistische verzekeringscooperatie," *BTNG/RBHC* 2, nos. 1-2 (1991).

48. Jules van den Heuvel, *Une citadelle socialiste. Le Vooruit de Gand* (Paris, 1897); Jules Destree and Emile Vandervelde, *Le Socialisme en Belgique* (Paris, 1903), 373-82, 395-403. On the relation between Socialism and the arts in Brussels, see Donald Drew Egbert, *Social Radicalism and the Arts* (New York, 1970), 603-18; and Eugenia Herbert, *The Artist and Social Reform in France and Belgium 1885-1898* (New Haven, 1961).

49. Calculated from Emile Dutilleul, "The Co-operatives," *The Annals of the American Academy of Political and Social Science* 247 (1946): 63; and B. R. Mitchell, *European Historical Statistics 1750-1970* (New York, 1975), 3.

50. H. Legros, "La structures de la coopération socialiste, 1900-1940," *BTNG/RBHC* 22:1-2 (1991): 73-127.

51. *La coopération: ses origines-sa nature-ses grandes fonctions* (Brussels, 1926).

52. Mieke Claeys-van Hegendoren *25 Jaar Belgisch Socialisme* (Antwerp, 1967), 327-31; and B. S. Chlepner, *Belgian Banking and Banking Theory* (Washington, D.C., 1943), 71-72.

53. Richard Evely, "Patterns of Consumption and Cooperative Trade: 5. Belgium," *Review of International Cooperation* 46, no. 10 (October 1953): 249.

54. Calculated from Dutilleul, "Co-operatives," Table I, 63.

55. Jan Dhondt, et al. "L'influence de la crise sur les mouvements ouvriers en Belgique," *Mouvements Ouvriers et Depression Economique de 1929 à 1939* (Assen, 1966); and Carl Strikwerda, "The Belgian Working Class and the Crisis of the 1930s," in *Chance und Illusion/Labor in Retreat. Studien uber der Krise der Sozialdemokratie in der Zwischenkriegzeit/Studies on Social Democracy in the Interwar period* (Vienna, 1988), 279-304.

56. Georges De Leener, *La distribution des Marchandises* (Brussels, 1934), 294.

57. Evely, "Patterns," Table VIII, 249.

58. "Le commerce de detail," [Banque Nationale de Belgique] *Bulletin* 13, (1938): 511; Boddewyn, 35.

59. Arthur Wauters, "Les classes moyennes devant la crise," *Revue du travail* 8, no. 34 (1933): 944-45; and Etienne Verhoeyen and Frank Uytterhaegen, *De Kreeft met de Zwarte Scharen. 50 Jaar Rechts en Uiterste Rechts in België* (Ghent, 1981), 140-41.

60. Most of the literature on commerce and the lower middle class in the interwar era in Belgium does not make a connection between the government's action and the danger that the lower middle class would turn to fascism. I argue this position more fully in "Corporatism and the Belgian Lower Middle Class," in *Splintered Classes: The European Lower Middle Classes in the Age of Fascism*, ed. Rudy Koshar (New York, 1990).

61. Boddewyn, *Belgian Policy*, 49-54. There were also attempts to impose higher taxes on cooperatives and to limit their membership to low-income individuals, *People's Yearbook 1939* (Manchester and Glasgow, 1939), 219.

62. Heinrich August Winkler, *Mittelstand Demokratie und Nationalsozialismus* (Koln, 1972), 190. David Schoenbaum, *Hitler's Social Revolution* (Garden City, N.Y., 1966), 4-6, 128-43, provides important useful background to this issue.

63. L.-Th. Leger, "Les institutions de crédit d'état pour les classes moyennes en Belgique," *Revue economique internationale* août (1938) 264-98; Raoul Miry, "Beschouwingen over Middenstandskrediet," *Bulletin* 13, (10 avril, 1938); and Chlepner, *Belgian Banking*, 141-42, 150-54.

64. Monica DeVriendt and Yvan VanDenBerghe, *De Algemene Werkstaking van 1936* (Hasselt, 1967); Strikwerda, "The Belgian Working Class"; and Mieke Claeys-VanHaegendoren, *25 Jaar Belgische Socialisme* (Antwerp, 1967), esp. 365-67.

65. Henri DeMan, *Planned Socialism: the Plan du Travail of the Belgian Labour Party* (London, 1935); Henri DeMan, *Corporatisme et Socialisme* (Paris, 1935); and Erik Hansen, "Depression Decade Crisis: Social Democracy and Planisme in Belgium and the Netherlands," *Journal of Contemporary History* 16, 1981. DeMan's emphasis on economic planning has been seen as a primary source for French fascism, Zeev

Sternhell, *Ni droite, ni gauche: L'ideologie fasciste en France* (Paris, 1983), 136-232. DeMan did collaborate with the Nazis in 1940-1941.

66. Quaden and Raemaekers, "Socialisme Coopératif," 114.

67. International Cooperative Alliance, 35-36.

68. DeLeener, *La distribution*, 220.

69. M. J. VanderGucht, "Les tendances actuelles du commerce de détail," *Bulletin*, 11 (1936): 290.

70. DeLeener, *La distribution*, 282-83.

71. Emile James, in Georges DeLeener and Emile James, *Le problèm de consommation* (Brussels, 1938), 143-44.

72. Dutilleul, "Co-operatives," 64-66; and Fernand Baudhuin, *L'économie belge sous l'occupation 1940-1944* (Brussels, 1945), 244, 318-322.

73. International Cooperative Alliance, *International Cooperation 1937-1949* (London, 1953), 36-40.

74. Evely, "Patterns," 249.

75. Boddewyn, *Belgian Policy*, 81-82; and Jacques Van Offelen, *Deux ans de politique* (Brussels, 1956), esp. 57-61. Van Offelen was the highest ranking civil servant in the Ministry of Economic Affairs and his pamphlet was published by the Liberal Party.

76. Boddewyn, *Belgian Policy*, 165-67.

77. Quaden and Ramaekers, "Socialisme Coopératif," 114-15. About a third of the private pharmacies in Belgium went on strike in 1980 to protest government attempts to weaken their monopoly.

78. Quaden and Ramaekers, "Socialisme Coopératif," 113-15; and Boddewyn, *Belgian Policy*, 158.

Chapter 3

The Citizen Producer: The Rise and Fall of Working-Class Cooperatives in the United States

Steven Leikin

In the long-running debate over the exceptionalism of the American working class historians and social scientists have asked why the United States, unlike its European counterparts, failed to develop a large Socialist movement or working-class party.[1] Rarely in this debate have scholars compared the role of cooperation in the evolution of working-class movements in the United States and Europe. Yet in the countries taken as models of working-class activism—Britain, Germany, Belgium, and Scandinavia—cooperatives were critical to the success of Socialist and working-class movements. Indeed, cooperative movements were sometimes larger than unions or parties and often provided vital support to these institutions.

In the United States, according to recent scholarship, a labor movement similarly inclined toward cooperation emerged in the immediate post-Civil War years. Organized as the Knights of Labor this movement was a broadly based collection of trade and labor unions as well as cooperatives. In both the European movements and the Knights of Labor, producers' cooperatives were initially as important if not more important than consumer cooperatives. While European activists gradually neglected producers' cooperatives when capital costs proved too daunting and then turned toward consumer organizing, the American labor movement lost its enthusiasm for cooperation as a broad strategy for change after the Knights of Labor failed in the late 1880s. When the labor movement reorganized as the American Federation of Labor it specifically rejected labor reform of this kind. Thus, in order to understand fully the unique trajectory of the American labor movement, it is crucial to examine the role of both producers' and consumers' cooperation in its development. Such an examination will also help explain why the American consumer cooperative movement that grew up later in the Progressive era was quite different than its European counterparts in having few ties to organized labor.

The involvement of American workers in cooperative production and consumption has long remained an underexamined area of American labor history. Yet over the course of the nineteenth century wage-earning men and women established thousands of cooperative stores, workshops, and factories in the United States. For nearly sixty years trade unionists and short-hour advocates spoke of cooperation as an essential element of labor reform. Indeed, cooperation rested at the heart of the labor movement's social vision and under the auspices of trade unions, citywide trade assemblies and, in its most advanced form, the Knights of Labor, the cooperative became a working-class tool and model for a more just economy.[2]

What did this movement, dismissed by historians as backward and hopelessly utopian, mean to American workers? Unlike the early nineteenth century utopian socialists who developed detailed plans of social reconstruction, cooperators often began their enterprises with only a vague formula for self-help and a nebulous vision of workplace democracy.[3] Paradoxically, it is in this vagueness that the meaning of cooperation can be discerned. Within a loosely defined concept of worker ownership labor reformers created a variety of competing visions of a more just economy. In fact, skilled trade unionists, less-skilled laborers, and women workers constructed their own definitions of fraternity, mutuality, and democracy under the rubric of cooperation. This form of self-help was part of a larger struggle among wage earners to assess their democratic experience, ascertain how they would exercise their rights in the economic world, and determine who among them would function as the legitimate laborers and citizens in American society.

This article will examine the ideals of nineteenth-century cooperators and the rise of cooperative labor reform from the 1830s to the decline of the Knights of Labor. By comparing two local case studies of successful cooperative movements, as well as drawing on some significant examples from other locales, this article will show how cooperative production and consumption provided workers with a means to stabilize their communities and build the labor movement. It will also suggest the reasons for cooperation's failure in the late 1880s and its impact on the labor movement and future cooperative efforts.

Ideals and Origins

Most organized workers in nineteenth-century America considered cooperation to be an appropriate and practical alternative to what they called "competitive capitalism." They deemed it appropriate because it emerged from the very familiar milieu of the skilled laborer. Fused within the cooperative ideal were the craftsman's panoply of beliefs and practices including the labor theory of value, the pride and manly independence of craft work, and the skilled workers' commitment to the collective responsibility of trade unionism. Cooperation provided a skilled worker with the ready means not only to implement his craft ethos but to resolve the dilemmas of shop floor conflict by furnishing steady employment and providing reasonably priced goods.[4]

Moreover, the practicality of cooperation seemed self-evident. Not only could retail businesses and many trades still be entered into with relatively small investments of capital and compete with "privately" owned firms,[5] but a postmillenialist tendency among labor reformers predisposed them to a belief in the efficacy of their own reform measures. The world, they surmised, could be changed with relative ease and the success of cooperation depended merely upon the participants' willingness to sacrifice the necessary funds, time, and energy. Labor reformers believed that their own will would make or break their efforts to control the market economy. If they failed, they had no one to blame but themselves.[6]

Cooperation also appealed to the ideals of independence and virtue deeply rooted in the political psyche of the American worker, a complex of ideals that historians have called working-class republicanism. A leading spokesman for cooperation, John Samuel, expressed this well when he contended in the 1860s that:

> The principles of Co-operation are more in harmony with the principles of our form of government than our present social system. Our social system in many things is at variance with our political institutions. The relation of Employer & Employed is not the normal condition of Freemen. Superiority & Inferiority is implied in the relation. . . . Co-operation supersedes this relation and places men just where the Declaration of Independence was designed to place them—equal—& with equal rights to liberty & the pursuit of happiness.[7]

In a cooperative a member was freed from the strictures of "wage slavery" and could stand as an independent citizen. He could, in theory, determine his own wages and hence receive the full value of his labor. In a democratically run cooperative the participant created a republic in miniature where no member, with his vote and his stake in the enterprise, could be forced to suffer the economic or political influence of another.[8]

The ideals of working-class republicanism, however, posed a number of problems for cooperators. First, these ideals did not provide a plan nor define to any meaningful degree how cooperatives should be organized. Workers established their businesses without a blueprint to negotiate the demands of the marketplace. When difficult questions arose concerning the legitimacy of profits, the role of unions, the privileges of skilled labor, and the desirability of market competition, cooperators experimented and at times fought among themselves. Second, the ideals of working-class republicanism, as other historians have noted, coexisted with the hierarchies of gender and skill.[9] These inequalities contradicted the ostensibly democratic ethos of cooperation and women and less-skilled workers challenged male cooperators to expand their notions of citizenship and independence. If cooperatives were to succeed, or the ideals of working-class republicanism assume concrete form, these issues would have to be resolved.

During the 1830s cooperation first appeared, according to historian Bruce Laurie, as "a major tactical departure" for the fledgling labor movement. Anticipating an endless battle with employers over wages and working conditions, the National Trades' Union of 1836 recommended cooperation as a permanent solution to strikes, speculation, and the dilution of craft skills. In 1845 another group of reform-minded mechanics established the Working Men's Protective Union in Boston, a network of cooperatively owned stores and buying clubs. Two years later wage earners had organized 40 Protective Union associations in the industrial areas of Vermont, Maine, New Hampshire, and eastern Massachusetts. By the late 1850s thousands of members from communities scattered through New England, New York, and Canada sold basic provisions and groceries in over 800 Union "divisions." [10]

In addition to these efforts, a small number of skilled workers established cooperative factories and workshops during the 1840s and 1850s. Cordwainers in Lynn, Pittsburgh, and New York City; molders in Ohio, Pennsylvania, and West Virginia; tailors in Boston; and bakers, shirt sewers, and hat finishers in New York City set up workshops. Wilhelm Weitling and the cooperative movement in Germany inspired German tailors and cabinet makers in New York City to do the same. [11]

The movement of the 1830s, the Protective Unions and the scattered efforts of craftsmen did not survive the economic and political turmoil of the antebellum years. The Panic of 1837 drained the resources and the will of the first American labor movement and destroyed its cooperative experiments. Later the Protective Unions fell victim to internal discord, competition from other retail establishments and the disruption of the Civil War. The fledgling efforts of craftsmen to produce cooperatively also collapsed from economic decline and wartime disorder. [12]

The ideals of cooperation, however, continued to resonate with American workers as the labor movement reemerged in the 1860s. Cooperation, in fact, captured the imagination of postwar labor leaders. When a group of English immigrants established an insignificant storefront enterprise in Philadelphia, the Union Cooperative Association No. 1, they attracted as members such leading notables in the labor movement as William Sylvis, President of the Iron Molders' Union, Jonathan Fincher, the labor reform newspaper editor, and John Samuel, union activist, cooperator, and future Knights of Labor executive. The Union Cooperative Association, one of the first Rochdale cooperatives in America, was just the kind of working-class institution these men hoped would become commonplace among their constituencies. [13]

Knowledge of the Rochdale method spread among organized workers and by 1863 cooperation in this new and more practical form emerged as a force in the American labor movement.[14] Under the Rochdale system a cooperative store would sell its shares to a member but allow the stockholder only one vote regardless of the number of shares held. The shares would entitle him or her to a fixed dividend of no more than 5 percent on the investment. Stores sold all goods for cash at market prices with the profits returned to members in proportion to their purchases.[15] John Samuel estimated that one hundred cooperative stores, many operating under Rochdale principles, opened for business during the decade of the Civil War. In the 1870s, the Sovereigns of Industry, a reform organization advocating the establishment of cooperative stores and factories, adopted the Rochdale system and its 280 local councils in New England and 170 in the Middle and Central states each had a purchasing club or store. A decade later the Knights of Labor supplanted the Sovereigns and operated an unknown number of consumer cooperatives possibly totaling in the thousands.[16]

The wage earners who promoted Rochdale stores were in most cases the same workers who championed producer cooperatives and they often advanced retail stores as a means to accumulate capital for production.[17] In the two decades following the Civil War they came largely from the ranks of shoeworkers, molders, miners, carpenters, machinists, clothing workers, cigar makers, and printers. Between 1866 and 1876 shoeworkers operated at least forty factories and molders at least thirty-six foundries. Both trades established cooperative stores. In addition, bakers, coach-makers, collar-makers, ship-wrights, nailers, ship carpenters and caulkers, glassblowers, hatters, boiler-makers, plumbers, and iron-rollers organized cooperative workshops. A total of at least five hundred cooperative workshops and factories opened for business in the twenty-five years following the Civil War. Two hundred and ninety of these producer establishments commenced business between 1884 and 1888.[18]

Despite the support of important leaders in the labor movement, national and regional trade unions launched very few cooperative enterprises. In large part this reflected the realities of working-class life. The world of the nineteenth-century worker was centered in the local community and cooperatives took their form and substance from the experience of workers in their locales. The ideological significance and meaning of cooperation would emerge from workers assembling their own institutions within their own social and economic milieus.

The men and women who built cooperatives were reconstructing their communities along new lines. They had, however, no uniform vision of the good life nor of the proper parameters of their own power and authority. They held up a democratic ideal originating in the craftsman's republican ethos but one that also concealed the divisive hierarchies of gender and skill. How they would reconcile this divisiveness with cooperation's democratic promise was the product of their day-to-day decisions within the context of their community life.

The Cooperative Shoeworkers of Stoneham

In one small shoe manufacturing city, Stoneham, Massachusetts, shoeworkers built a variety of successful cooperative institutions in the post-Civil War years. These men and women were convinced they had accomplished something unique, and one resident laster described Stoneham as ". . . the only place in the world where co-operation has succeeded. . . ."[19] They had, in fact, over the course of fifteen years established two cooperative stores, four steam-powered shoe factories, and a stitching workshop.[20] At their moment of greatest success in 1885, 15 percent of the 1,228 shoeworkers of Stoneham worked in cooperative shoe factories.[21]

These cooperators also formed a vital segment of the city's population. They were well organized initially in both branches of the shoeworkers' union, the Knights and Daughters of St. Crispin, active in reform party politics and a force of some significance in the city. Their names appeared on the roles of local churches, voluntary associations such as the Grand Army of the Republic, the International Organization of Odd Fellows, fire departments, and temperance societies, as well as labor reform organizations, the Democratic and Republican parties, and trade unions. They functioned alongside an often sympathetic middle class as their names surfaced in the transcripts of town meetings and as they filled, or ran for almost all of Stoneham's offices. Four were sent to the Massachusetts General Court to represent Middlesex County and many others participated in their election. When conflict arose in the workplaces of Stoneham they took leading positions in the formation of strike committees or offered relief to strikers. In the 1880s they joined with the Knights of Labor in large numbers and avidly pursued third-party politics.[22]

Well ensconced in the institutions that defined the city, the men who established the first cooperatives in 1873 had a set of interests that marked them off as particularly concerned with community institutions. They were older, more often married, and more frequently the heads of households with more children than other shoeworkers, and many had been geographically mobile before they settled into the city. These workers sought stability for themselves and their families as they labored in an industry subject to on-going technological change and an economy characterized by severe cyclical fluctuations.[23]

The cooperators of Stoneham achieved this stability for a time as they ran their shops all year around, paid themselves relatively high wages, and purchased property. They were remarkably successful in fulfilling cooperation's principle commitment to pay workers the full value of their product. Indeed, other shoeworkers used the wages paid in these factories as a measure of what their employers were capable of paying. The cooperators also created within their factories a relaxed environment and exercised little discipline on the shop floor. As the architects of their own workplace they were not in the business to discipline, punish, or deprive themselves of work.[24]

In addition, the cooperators established through and around their places of work a rather close-knit social world undivided, in all but one instance, by ethnic differences. It was possible to find cooperators, after a day's work, serving dinner in their shop with the cooperators from other shops in attendance. On weekends they might go on outings and in the evenings stage musical entertainments. When baseball fever surged through the city, cooperators formed teams and competed against one another. The integrity of the working-class community was reinforced by the relationships these shoeworkers formed in and around their own shops.[25]

As a consequence of their community activities the cooperators reached for a familiar organizational model to structure their own institutions. When shoeworkers established Stoneham's first cooperative factory in 1873 they organized themselves as they had in voluntary associations and town meetings, first by electing their officers through popular vote. The cooperators then mimicked the procedure of the city's town meetings with a nearly obsessive concern with democratic process. So meticulously did they observe democratic procedures that it was not unusual to find shareholders voting in order to vote on whether or not a vote should proceed, all to approve some minor action of the board of directors.[26]

These cooperators created a new community based on their own democratically organized enterprises deeply rooted in their craft and trade union traditions, democratic values, and local experience. Their efforts, however, had very real limitations. All of the cooperatives hired nonmember and often less-skilled workers as employees and paid them a wage. These workers, unlike their employers, would never have an equal say in how the factories should function. In one cooperative non-native-born Americans were unwelcome as members. The same factory's directors readily abandoned their commitment to the labor movement when such a commitment threatened the profits of their enterprise. In 1885 they precipitated a strike among their own member and nonmember workers by defying a demand of the Knights of Labor to distribute wages on a weekly rather than monthly basis. In all the cooperative shoe factories women, even as shareholding members, were restricted to the stitching rooms, a position long established by the sexual division of labor in the industry.[27]

Cooperation was an expression, in other words, of the male skilled worker's democratic ideals as well as his hierarchical and exclusionary impulses. Indeed, cooperators sought to stabilize the workplace, community, and the family by preserving the skilled male worker as the primary family breadwinner. Male cooperators apparently believed that through their store, advertised in Stoneham as the "family peacemaker," and the cooperative factory they could earn a wage sufficient to accomplish this end.[28]

Yet the democratic and participatory nature of cooperative life could not be so easily contained. In 1873 the local assembly of the Daughters of St. Crispin had enthusiastically supported Stoneham's first cooperative shoe factory and donated a wax thread machine to the cause.[29] By the mid-1880s, however, a number of women workers who had purchased shares in Stoneham's cooperatives formulated their own vision of cooperative democracy.[30] They used their position as stockholders to demand equal treatment and to expand their control in the workshop. In 1886, the agent of one shoe cooperative in Stoneham complained bitterly of female stockholders in the stitching room:

> They are carried away, he said, by the idea that as stockholders they should
> be permitted to do as they please; and they are too independent. In the stitch-
> ing room it is desirable, to economize machinery, to have stitchers change off,
> doing one kind of work a part of the day, and something else at other times.
> If they are stockholders young women object.[31]

To the dismay of this foreman, working women in the stitching room acted like skilled working-men and refused to allow a supervisor to direct and speed up their labor. These women forcibly widened the parameters of cooperation to include themselves. In fact, several Stoneham women, all members of the Knights of Labor, had already opened a cooperative stitching shop, which they ran on their own.[32]

This tendency among women in Stoneham to fashion cooperation to meet their own needs was evident in the Knights' national organization as well as in other local assemblies. The national spokesperson for women in the Knights of Labor, Leonora Barry, regarded cooperation as particularly useful. In her report to the General Assembly in 1887 she recommended that the Order "turn [its] whole undivided attention to the forming of productive and distributive co-operative enterprises,"[33] in order to alleviate the most egregious conditions under which women worked. In a number of cities including Chicago, Indianapolis, and St. Louis, women clothing workers established cooperatives under the aegis of the Knights. In two of these cooperatives female members made a special point of placing women on their boards of directors and inserting in their constitutions, with no small symbolic import, "she" instead of the standard "he."[34]

More significantly, as women entered the labor movement in greater numbers activists recast the gendered basis of the cooperative vision. Rather than basing their ideals on what they considered the coercive manly values of independent skilled labor, some influential labor reformers located cooperative principles in what they considered the "feminine" virtues of mutual aid and voluntarism. Cooperators confronted with the needs of a diverse constituency redefined their ideals in more inclusive terms. Mutual aid voluntarily exercised appealed directly to a much broader cross section of workers than the "manly independence" of craft work.[35]

The gendered distinction between coercive and voluntaristic cooperation was raised most tellingly during the Knights' national debate over a large-scale plan for social reconstruction introduced in 1884 by Henry Sharpe, secretary of the Knights' cooperative board. He proposed the establishment of a "Cooperative Guild," a vast bureaucratic organization that would parallel the Knights' national structure and manage a network of cooperative stores and factories. The Guild, supported by a compulsory tax on all members, would ultimately supplant the market economy with its own structure for buying, selling, and producing goods controlled within the Knights hierarchy. Advocates of feminine voluntarism denounced the coercive and manly elements of the Guild, i.e., the tax that supported it and its centralized structure. The membership defeated the proposal. The majority of Knights were unwilling to hand over to some powerful bureaucracy the very local control that made cooperation attractive.[36]

Meanwhile members of the Knights of Labor recognized the possibility for some form of systematic cooperation. Given the potential purchasing power of the organization's membership, activists appealed to fellow Knights to assist one another by purchasing shares in cooperative businesses and buying cooperatively produced goods. This appeared in a small way in Belleville, Illinois, where miners established a cooperative coal mine, in part, by selling shares to members in nearby St. Louis. The St. Louis Knights then opened a cooperative coal yard of their own to sell the coal. The Knights of Raleigh, North Carolina, raised the necessary capital to establish a cooperative tobacco company by selling one dollar shares to over one thousand local assemblies in the Order. They had promised to deposit a fixed percentage of the profits into the Knights' central cooperative fund. In New York, District Assembly 49 setup a network of cooperatives by selling shares that accrued no interest at all. Shareholders might have expected employment in one of their enterprises but received nothing directly from their investment.[37]

The cooperators of Stoneham participated in this national debate and recognized the need for mutual aid as they struggled to survive in a competitive and turbulent market. In fact, by the mid-1880s when market changes adversely affected the shoe industry, they turned to the national Knights of Labor for help. The city's delegate to the Knights' 1886 General Assembly, John Best, sat on the Committee of Cooperation and voted to implement a central tax to fund local cooperatives. The General Assembly decided to allocate $40,000 annually for cooperation but failed to implement the plan as the national organization rapidly deteriorated.[38]

The collapse of the Knights of Labor over the next few years left Stoneham's cooperators on their own. Now they had only their experience of community, the complex interactions of workers and worker-businessmen, shopkeepers, professionals, and small and large employers, to guide them. They had achieved power, respectability, and independence within this community and they believed that through politics, unions, and cooperatives the will of their community would prevail over the willful behavior of individual men.

The cooperators' belief in their own power and position was not enough to guarantee success. In fact the independence and power they had achieved within the city diminished their capacity to innovate and confront threats to their cooperative institutions. It was as if the very alliances that made their place in the community viable narrowed their choices. Having worked with and gained the sympathy of shopkeepers and professionals, the cooperators shied away from anything that would threaten the position of manufacturers in the city. Their goal, now that they had achieved republican independence, was not to control the town but to become legitimate and respected elements within it.

One alternative they might have pursued, the pooling of resources among the cooperatives, would have provided some protection from the volatility of the market. Three of the four cooperative shoe factories sold their products in the western states and all four had drummers competing with one another for sales.[39] If they had jointly marketed their goods they would have saved money and effort. They never thought, though, in greater terms than their own businesses and never once turned to each other to join their productive or marketing efforts together. So instead of threatening their fellow townsmen with a coordinated effort or an expansive cooperative vision, Stoneham's workers allowed their cooperatives to fail. None of the cooperatives survived into the 1890s. In the end, their integration into the city, and their actual power, immobilized them as their dream of cooperative control lapsed into a defensive trade unionism.[40]

The Cooperative Coopers of Minneapolis

In Minneapolis, Minnesota, barrel makers established a formidable network of cooperatives and built a labor movement that in some respects resembled Stoneham's efforts. The Minneapolis cooperators were skilled workers who remade their communities in order to stabilize their lives and establish their own vision of equity. The coopers, however, lived and worked in a very different environment from that experienced by Stoneham's workers and they created a very different solution to the problems they faced as cooperators. Indeed, they redefined the boundaries of what cooperatives could accomplish and what cooperators could do. At the same time they fought over the meaning of cooperation and their conflicts contributed to the decline and failure of the Knights of Labor in Minneapolis.

Minneapolis was settled in the mid-nineteenth century and grew rapidly over the next few decades into a major urban area of well over 100,000 inhabitants. It grew rapidly, in part, because of its expanding primary industry, flour milling. Located at the hub of the Northwestern railroad systems, the city became a principle distribution point for the surrounding territories and states. This region supplied wheat to a new world market, and Minneapolis' central location guaranteed that it would become the largest wheat receiving market in America. By 1886, Minneapolis boasted of twenty-six mills producing 35,000 barrels of flour a day. Alongside the mills grew a smaller but bustling barrel industry necessary to the packing, storing, and shipping of flour. The skilled coopers who made these barrels would become the region's preeminent cooperators.[41]

During the late 1860s the coopers of Minneapolis organized as a union under the auspices of the International Workingmen's Association. Their union, along with a strong demand for barrels, insured steady work and good pay. These favorable conditions, however, attracted a surplus workforce that overwhelmed the city's labor market and allowed the "boss" coopers, as the owners of the shops were called, to reduce wages and ultimately destroy the union. At this juncture a handful of barrel makers organized the first successful cooperative barrel company in Minneapolis, a long-lasting business employing at one point as many as 120 working members. Their bylaws, written in 1874, provided the model for at least eleven other barrel shops whose success, in turn, inspired a cooperative store, a painter's cooperative, a worker-owned cigar factory, a shirt company, and a cooperative laundry.[42]

Cooperative activity grew in the 1880s along with the power and prestige of the Knights of Labor. By 1886 seven barrel cooperatives engaged in over one million dollars worth of business and employed 321 journeymen-owners out of 600 to 700 barrel makers in the city. Around 40 percent of these cooperators were native born craftsmen, while the rest, in the words of a contemporary observer, were ". . . a mixed multitude of Swedes, Norwegians, Irish, Germans, [and] Italians. . . ." Actually as many as one-fourth of the cooperators were Scandinavian and another fifth German.[43]

The enthusiasm of the Knights and the barrel makers for cooperative enterprises spread throughout the city. Local assemblies debated the virtues of cooperation and the issue was discussed at the weekly meetings of the city's Trade and Labor Assembly.[44] The coopers, who were highly skilled and independent workers, led this effort in defense of their craft skills and as a justifiable extension of their artisanal culture.[45]

Like their counterparts in Stoneham, the coopers searched for permanence of place as they created democratically organized cooperatives. Over time they devised a network of institutions to ensure steady work and the preservation of their craft. At the same time they built homes around their factories. In 1886, the typical cooperator was a married home owner living in the immediate vicinity of his workshop.[46]

The coopers' political experience differed, however, from Stoneham's shoeworkers. While they participated in a number of political contests and succeeded in electing one of their own to the state legislature, their connections with the machinations of government were remote. In 1887 John Lamb, a leading Knight appointed to head the State Bureau of Labor Statistics, recommended that workers maintain a safe distance from the state. An advocate of cooperation he advised wage earners to ". . . not ask the state to do for us anything we can do for ourselves." At the same time, the secretary-treasurer of the Knights' statewide District Assembly 79 criticized the "planting of political chestnuts" and argued that political reform could only be accomplished through social and industrial change.[47] Apparently the coopers and the Knights had little faith in politics as they turned to the reformative power of cooperative enterprise.

The problems, however, that the coopers faced were far greater than what the shop or cooperative store could resolve, and this is where a comparison with Stoneham is most instructive. As in Stoneham, these problems were built into the limitations of cooperative production and working-class republicanism. Forming a business, the cooperators believed, was the quickest and easiest way to banish the boss from the shop and to extend democracy to the workplace,[48] but it could not guarantee a job. The market for barrels, based on a highly competitive contract system, was driving prices down and pushing many coopers out of the business. Under this system barrel companies would arrange with a mill to supply a set number of barrels at a given price. Always suspicious that other companies might underbid them, the boss coopers and cooperators would lower prices in order to secure their contracts. Wage reductions would follow and the barrel factories would enter a ruinous bout of competition.[49] In addition, the industry entered a period of stagnation during the mid-1880s as flour mills slowly converted to the use of canvas sacks. Compounding these problems, the barrel companies had mechanized and competitive pressures had forced the cooperative shops to install machinery and reduce their workforces.[50] In order to deal with this the leaders of the Knights in Minneapolis, cooperative advocates all, developed a plan the likes of which would never have crossed the minds of Stoneham's cooperators. Having created independent communities with no apparent cross-class alliances, they had no fears of middle-class opprobrium. Community loyalties did not hold them back. The cooperators of Minneapolis were free to innovate.

In 1887, disillusioned with the ineffectiveness of strikes, the Knights' District Assembly 79 devised an alternative plan that would transform the cooperage business in Minneapolis. The assembly proposed that all barrel companies form an organization under the auspices of the Knights of Labor. The agreement they hammered out created a "pool" of barrel factories and gave the District Assembly the power to oversee the work of all shops, determine how much a shop was to produce, how many workers were to produce it, and at what price it was to be sold. The Knights of Minneapolis had gone beyond the single cooperative as a solution to the labor problem.[51]

At first, all but two of the cooperative shops agreed to join the "pool," and one of those recalcitrant factories soon agreed to follow suit. As in Stoneham the year before, a minority of cooperators seemed to divorce their interests from those of the labor movement. In Minneapolis the situation clearly exposed the limitations of working-class republicanism as a guide to cooperation. The barrel makers who refused to join the pool, members of the North Star Cooperative Barrel Co., never admitted to betraying the principles of cooperation or their obligations as trade unionists. Cooperation offered them the opportunity for independence, stability, and democratic participation. No rules, however, explicitly defined their obligations to other cooperative firms. So the members of the North Star chose to define their obligations narrowly. If joining the pool would force the North Star to share business, denying its members the maximum benefits of cooperation, then they would refuse to participate. They were acting, so they argued, as any properly run business concern should act. To do otherwise would be a disservice to their own members. Even after the Knights expelled them as "scabs" from the local assembly, they insisted on their innocence and their good standing as union members. The millers, of course, vehemently opposed the pool. They added to the confusion by attempting to lure barrel manufacturers away with lucrative contracts and threats. That they failed for even a short while to attract other companies was a tribute to the power of the Knights in Minneapolis.[52]

By the mid-1880s, the coopers' pool was one small element of a comprehensive plan for cooperative reform devised by the leaders of the Knights of Labor.[53] Their plan consisted of three distinct strategies. First, the Knights were to open cooperative stores; second, establish factories; and third, settle agricultural and industrial colonies. Indeed they implemented all three approaches with varying degrees of success.

In 1885, the coopers experimented with the consumer strategy when they established a grocery based on Rochdale principles. Two years later the leaders of District Assembly 79 laid plans for a central cooperative wholesale "depot." The depot was to channel cooperatively produced goods to farmers and the farmers' produce to industrial cooperators. Established by the Knights in 1888, the depot was expected to lead to a widespread network of production and exchange.[54]

The next step, cooperative production, was also a reality and its over-whelming success among Minneapolis' coopers had a profound impact on the labor movement.[55] In fact, it encouraged a more grandiose idea to circulate. That idea, the founding of a cooperative colony, captivated the imagination of the Knights' leadership.[56] A colony offered a voluntarist solution to class conflict and one that the Knights could hold up as a model for others to emulate. According to one leader of the Knights:

> If we can succeed in firmly establishing one colony, with home industries, established on home land, and protected by home exchange, with home money, under associated home government, we will have done more to solve the industrial question, than have the books of all the writers and talk of all the orators of the past hundred years.[57]

A practical demonstration, they believed, would make believers of men.[58]

The coopers and their leaders viewed the ruinous competition afflicting their industry in the moral terms of working-class republicanism, and they saw themselves, the political sovereigns, as the principle agents of change. To achieve social progress they had first to reform themselves and join together to institute the practical "gospel of Christ" through cooperation.[59] In 1887 the coopers believed in their right to change the conditions of their work lives and when they put their pooling arrangement into effect they had no qualms about controlling all barrel making in the city.

Yet their attempt to remake the cooperage industry confronted formidable and ultimately insurmountable obstacles. The pooling agreement was probably the most vulnerable of their strategies that they could never enforce over the long term. Though they would try numerous times during the next few years, all such agreements were sabotaged by the noncooperative shops.[60] In addition, the resistance of the North Star cooperative to the pool in 1887 created such acrimony within the Knights that the local assembly lost much of its legitimacy and most of its members. At the same time long-term changes were undermining the cooperators' collective strength. The mechanization of barrel making challenged the very nature of the cooperatives and compelled them to reduce their memberships, buy out shareholders, and hire nonmembers to run the machines. Undermining their own skill, the coopers eliminated one principle reason for their own cooperation, the maintenance of a craft tradition. At the same time the millers conversion to the use of canvas sacks eliminated any growth in demand for barrels. Under these pressures the cooperatives fought a losing battle.

Other cooperative efforts by the Minneapolis Knights proved equally evanescent. The cooperative colony and the cooperative store disappeared not long after their formation. However, the single most important cause of the failure of cooperation in Minneapolis was the Knights' organizational decline after 1886. Without the Knights' power, both locally and nationally, to bind working people together, Minneapolis' workers had little inclination to maintain a commitment to cooperative community. In fact the ideals of working-class republicanism never defined the precise characteristics of that community and under conditions of decline the artisanal ethos that inspired the coopers now constrained their imaginations. They continued to restrict membership in their cooperatives to fully apprenticed craftsmen at a time when such artisans were a dying breed. Rather than admit machine operators as shareholders, the cooperators hired them only as wage laborers. As a consequence the coopers became employers and their shops slowly lost their cooperative identities. At the end of the century three cooperatives still produced barrels but with the industry in decline, the members had lost much of their spirit.[61]

For a moment in the 1880s, the coopers of Minneapolis could justify their domination of an entire industry. As craft workers they carried with them an independence, pride, and trade union tradition that, combined with their desire for stability and community, sustained their cooperative activism. But it was as relatively isolated members of an expanding urban environment that they joined a broad-based labor movement and acted to transform their industry. The Knights' power galvanized the coopers and their leadership broadened the barrel makers' vision of feasible reform. When conflict among competing cooperators generated discord in the coopers' local assembly and the national labor movement collapsed in the late 1880s, the coopers reverted to a strategy of craft exclusionism. For these craftsmen cooperation lost its visionary appeal and became their last defense against the unskilled.

Conclusion

The cooperative stores and factories established by wage earners in the late nineteenth century were basic building blocks of the labor movement. The leaders and rank and file of trade unions and the Knights of Labor considered cooperation a practical alternative to the instability of "competitive" capitalism capable of satisfying workers' immediate needs for necessities and steady employment. Cooperation's ultimate goal to supersede the wage system and competition, however, was not so easily defined or accomplished. As cooperators attempted to remake their communities, they drew upon a republican vision rooted in the craft and trade union traditions that they often understood only in the vaguest moral terms. Through their experiments these practical utopians attempted to clarify their place as workers in an industrializing republic. They tested the very boundaries of their republican vision and the meaning of democracy in a rapidly changing economic world.

To complicate matters the cooperative experience was riddled with contradictions. Profoundly democratic, male cooperators often fought to preserve
their own advantages over women and less-skilled workers, as in Stoneham
and Minneapolis, respectively. Only under the influence of subordinate workers
themselves or leaders of the Knights of Labor did reformers recast their vision
and widen the acceptable boundaries of democratic participation. At the same
time the voluntary and local cooperation championed by the Order could not
survive the demands of the market without some form of outside assistance.
If cooperators were to maintain stability and create community they required
resources far greater than their single shops could provide. They found no easy
solutions to the problems of cooperatives in a market economy. [62]

Cooperators, however, established a new level of mutualism that the
Knights of Labor could support through its local and national organizations.
This commitment to resolve the problems of wage labor could not outlast the
Knights. When the Order began its rapid decline in the late 1880s, the working-class phase of cooperation in the United States came to an end. Some
individual cooperators made their way into various socialist organizations, but
the labor movement as a whole abandoned what it now defined as a hopelessly
utopian endeavor. Discouraged and disillusioned, cooperators rethought their
assumptions, reconciled themselves to the practical gains of trade unionism and
buried their vision of the independent producer citizen with the close of the
nineteenth century. The American labor movement was well along its path to
exceptionalism.

Notes

1. The literature on American exceptionalism includes the following: Kim Voss,
*The Making of American Exceptionalism: The Knights of Labor and Class Formation
in the Nineteenth Century* (Ithaca, 1993); John M. Laslett and Seymour Martin Lipset,
eds., *Failure of a Dream: Essays in the History of American Socialism* (Berkeley,
1984); Sean Wilentz, "Against Exceptionalism: Class Consciousness and the American
Labor Movement, 1790-1920," *International Labor and Working Class History* 26
(1984); Eric Foner, "Why is There No Socialism in America?" *History Workshop* 17
(1984); Byron E. Shafer, ed., *Is America Different? A New Look at American
Exceptionalism* (Oxford, 1991); Seymour Martin Lipset, *American Exceptionalism: A
Double-Edged Sword* (New York, 1996); and Rick Halpern and Jonathan Morris, eds.,
American Exceptionalism?: US Working-Class Formation in an International Context
(New York, 1997).

2. This article is adapted from, Steve Leikin, "The Practical Utopians: Cooperation
and the American Labor Movement, 1860-1890" (Ph.D. diss. University of California,
Berkeley, 1992).

3. For surveys of communitarian experiments in nineteenth-century United States, see Edward K. Spann, *Brotherly Tomorrows: Movements for a Cooperative Society in America, 1820-1920* (New York, 1989); and Carl J. Guarneri, *The Utopian Alternative: Fourierism in Nineteenth-Century America* (Ithaca, 1991). For a standard work see, Arthur Bestor, *Backwoods Utopias: The Sectarian Origins and the Owenite Phase of Communitarian Socialism in America: 1663-1829* (Philadelphia, 1950, 1970).

4. For a general discussion of the origins of cooperative ideals, see Leikin, "The Practical Utopians," chapters 1 and 3.

5. Bruce Laurie and Mark Schmitz, "Manufacture and Productivity: The Making of an Industrial Base, Philadelphia, 1850-1880," in *Philadelphia: Work, Space, Family, and Group Experience in the 19th Century*, ed. Theodore Hershberg (Oxford, 1981), 86-88.

6. Leikin, "The Practical Utopians," chapter 3. The influence of religion on the labor movement in this period has been dealt with by Herbert Gutman, "Protestantism and the American Labor Movement: The Christian Spirit in the Gilded Age," in *Work, Culture and Society in Industrializing America* (Oxford, 1966), 79-118; and Ken Fones-Wolf, *Trade Union Gospel: Christianity and Labor in Industrial Philadelphia, 1865-1915* (Philadelphia, 1989).

7. John Samuel, Untitled Cooperative Address, circa 1866, John Samuel Papers, Reel 3, Microfilm edition, Wisconsin State Historical Society.

8. Leikin, "The Practical Utopians," chapter 3. The literature on republicanism and the American working class has burgeoned in recent years. The most relevant works are: Sean Wilentz, *Chants Democratic: New York City and the Rise of the American Working Class, 1788-1850* (New York, 1984); Leon Fink, *Workingmen's Democracy: The Knights of Labor and American Politics* (Urbana, 1983); Leon Fink, "Looking Backward: Reflections on Workers' Culture and Certain Conceptual Dilemmas within Labor History," in *Perspectives on American Labor History: The Problems of Synthesis*, eds. J. Carroll Moody and Alice Kessler-Harris (DeKalb, 1989); and Richard Oestreicher, "Terence V. Powderly, the Knights of Labor, and Artisanal Republicanism," in *Labor Leaders in America*, eds. Melvyn Dubofsky and Warren Van Tine (Urbana, 1987).

9. See Eva Baron, ed., *Work Engendered: Toward a New History of American Labor* (Ithaca, 1991).

10. Bruce Laurie, *Artisans into Workers: Labor in Nineteenth Century America* (New York, 1989), 89-91; Joseph G. Knapp, *The Rise of American Cooperative Enterprise: 1620-1920* (U.S.A., 1969), 10; John R. Commons, ed., *A Documentary History of American Industrial Society*, 11 vols. (Cleveland, 1910-1911), 5:58-59, 328, 368; Clare Horner, "Producers' Co-operatives in the United States, 1865-1890," (Ph.D. diss. University of Pittsburgh, 1978), 22; Edwin Charles Rozwenc, "Cooperatives Come to America: The History of the Protective Union Store Movement, 1845-1867," (Ph.D. diss. Columbia University, 1941), 27-29, 33, 39, 116; Norman Ware, *The Industrial Worker, 1840-1860* (New York, 1964), 187-192; and George McNeill, ed., *The Labor Movement: The Problem of To-day* (New York, 1886), 99-101.

11. Horner, "Producers' Cooperatives," 26-30; Norman Ware, *The Industrial Worker*, 194; Wilentz, *Chants Democratic*, 366-369.

12. Laurie, *Artisans*, 89-91; Horner, "Producers' Cooperatives," 22, 29-30; Rozwenc, "Cooperatives," 98-104.

13. For the membership of the Union Cooperative Association, see UCA-Minutes, Vol. 1, 1 December 1864, 2 May 1865; UCA-Minutes, Vol. 2, 10 April 1866, 18 October 1866, Thomas Phillips Papers, Wisconsin State Historical Society; "Good News From Delaware," *Fincher's Trades' Review*, 10 December 1864, 6; "Cooperation in Philadelphia," *Fincher's Trades' Review*, 27 January 1866, 68; and Leikin, "The Practical Utopians," chapter 2; The location and date of the first Rochdale cooperative in the United States is unknown. Thomas Phillips of the Union Cooperative Association and Thomas Sellers of the Lawrence (Massachusetts) Cooperative Association each claimed their respective institutions as the first American cooperatives to base their operations on the Rochdale model. See Clifton Yearley, "Thomas Phillips, A Yorkshire Shoemaker in Philadelphia," *Pennsylvania Magazine of History and Biography* 79 (April 1955): 178-79; see also, "Philadelphia Union Co-operation, No. 1," *Fincher's Trades' Review*, 6 May 1865, 91 and "Reply to 'Worker,'" *Fincher's Trades' Review*, 20 May 1865, 99; This is also discussed in Irwin Yellowitz, *Industrialization and the American Labor Movement, 1850-1900* (Port Washington, N.Y., 1977).

14. *New York Tribune*, 11 October 1858; Thomas Phillips, "Biography of Thomas Phillips," Cooperative Associations Papers, Box 1, Folder 4a, Wisconsin State Historical Society; *Fincher's Trades' Review*, 28 November 1863, 104; 5 November 1864, 90, 91; 19 November 1864, 99; *K.O.S.C. Monthly Journal*, January 1873, 105-14, Knights of St. Crispin Papers, Miscellaneous Holdings, Wisconsin State Historical Society. The Rochdale experience was mentioned often in *Fincher's Trades' Review*, *The Daily Evening Voice*, *The Sovereigns of Industry Bulletin*, and the *Iron Molders Journal*.

15. See Johnston Birchall, *Co-op: The People's Business* (Manchester, 1994), 49-64; George Jacob Holyoake, *Self-help by the People. History of Co-operation in Rochdale* (London, [1858]), 16, 46.

16. Manuscript headed, "Written while in Fincher's office between 1865-6," Notebooks, Vols. 13-16, Notes on Cooperation, John Samuel Papers Microfilm Reel No. 3, reel p. 848; see also Massachusetts State Bureau of Statistics of Labor, "Cooperation," *Annual Report of 1875, Part V*, 55-61; "Statements of Co-operative Associations, Certified to Secretary of Commonwealth as Organized Under Chapter 290, Acts of 1866," *Pamphlets in American History*, Cooperative Societies # 134; Edward Bemis, "Cooperation in New England," in *History of Cooperation in the United States*, ed. Herbert B. Adams (Baltimore, 1888), 26-32, 53, 66, 78-79, 127, 128; James Ford, *Co-operation in New England, Urban and Rural* (New York, 1913), 22. A complete history of the Sovereigns of Industry has yet to be written, though some details of its development can be found in John Commons, *History of Labour in the United States*, Vol. 2 (New York, 1918), 171-175; Edwin M. Chamberlin, *The Sovereigns of Industry* (Westport, 1976, originally 1875), 123-60; Franklin H. Giddings, "Co-operation," in *The Labor Movement: The Problem of Today*, 515; James Ford, *Co-operation in New England*, 21-28; Philip Foner, *History of the Labor Movement in the United States From Colonial Times to the Founding of the American Federation of Labor* (New York, 1978), 475-76; Horner, "Producers' Cooperatives," 32-34. The number of cooperative stores initiated by the Knights of Labor cannot be precisely determined. That "many" of the thousands of local assemblies operated stores is claimed by Ellis Cowling, *Co-operatives in America: Their Past, Present and Future* (New York, 1943), 93.

17. See Leikin, "The Practical Utopians," chapter 2.

18. Scattered evidence suggests that the Machinists and Blacksmiths and the Carpenters and Joiners unions were the most active in establishing cooperative stores in the mid-1860s; see *Fincher's Trades' Review*, 23 January 1864, 16 April 1864, 14 January 1865, 18 February 1865, 29 April 1865, 24 February 1866. When trades' assemblies organized stores a wide range of unions participated, see *Fincher's Trades' Review*, 26 November 1864 on Cincinnati. According to the statistics provided by Clare Horner, pp. 229-242, the trades most active in cooperative industries between 1865 and 1875 were (from most to least active) shoe making, iron molding, clothing manufacturing, machine shops, cigar making, and printing; John Commons, *History of Labour in the United States*, Vol. 1, 111; Joseph G. Knapp, *The Rise of American Cooperative Enterprise*, 32; *American Workman*, 2 October 1869, 5; Leikin, "The Practical Utopians," chapter 2.

19. "Cooperation in Stoneham," *Stoneham Independent*, 2 January 1886, reprinted from the *Boston Sunday Globe*.

20. A group of approximately 50 curriers organized a cooperative currying company in 1886 and sold subscriptions to stock totaling $10,000.00. No evidence exists of the company actually opening for business. *Stoneham Independent*, 31 July 1886.

21. Leikin, "The Practical Utopians," chapter 5.

22. Ibid.

23. Ibid. This analysis is based in part on data found on 47 members of the Stoneham Cooperative Boot and Shoe Company (there were approximately 60 members in all). The data come from the federal census from Middlesex County 1870 and 1880, the *Valuation of the Town of Stoneham and State, County, and Town Tax*, from 1867 to 1889; and information gathered from the *Stoneham Amateur* and *Stoneham Independent* and "Records of the Stoneham Cooperative Shoe Company, from 1872-1889," Stoneham Historical Society.

24. Leikin, "The Practical Utopians," chapter five; "Records of the Stoneham Cooperative Boot and Shoe Company," Stoneham Historical Society; Martha Coons, "Section Two: Factories and Workers in the Nineteenth Century," in *Stoneham Massachusetts: A Shoe Town* (Stoneham, MA, 1981), 91.

25. Massachusetts Bureau of Statistics of Labor, *Annual Report of 1886*, 216, 220. The Stoneham and Middlesex cooperatives both had native born American, Irish, and Canadian members; *Stoneham Independent*: "Base Ball," 10 July 1875; 4 January 1879; "Factory Warming," 1 February 1879; 24 April 1880; 29 May 1880; "Local News," 30 October 1880; "Social Gatherings," 18 December 1880; "The Stoneham Co-operative Supper," 8 January 1881; "Surprises," 29 January 1881; "Local," 12 March 1881; "Local," 1 July 1881; "Local," 24 June 1882; "Silver Wedding," 5 May 1883; "A Foreman Surprised," 12 February 1887.

26. "Records of the Stoneham Co-operative Boot and Shoe Company," 17; *Stoneham Independent*: "Installation," 18 July 1874; "Installation," 9 January 1875; "C.T.A.S." 10 February 1877; "Adjourned Town Meeting," *Stoneham Independent*, 3 March 1875; Leikin, chapter 5.

27. Leikin, "The Practical Utopians," chapter 5.

28. *Stoneham Directory 1886*, 151.

29. "Records of the Stoneham Co-operative Boot and Shoe Company," 1, 18, 39; Coons, 91.

30. Massachusetts Bureau of Statistics of Labor, *Annual Report of 1886*, 216-26.

31. Ibid., 229; Also quoted in Coons, "Section Two," 93.

32. "Reports of District Master Workmen," *Journal of United Labor*, 8 October 1884, 760.

33. Knights of Labor, *Proceedings of the Eleventh Regular Session, 1887*, 1582.

34. The Our Girl's Cooperative Clothing Company of Chicago and the Martha Washington K. of L. Co-operative Overall Association of Indianapolis made a special point of the fact that women would control their companies. "Our Girls' Co-operative Clothing Mfg. Co. of Chicago Illinois," *Pamphlets in American History*, Cooperative Societies #161; "Rules and Regulations of the Jewel Co-operative Knitting Co. of St. Louis, Mo." Pamphlets in American History, Cooperative Societies #111; "By-Laws of M.W.C.A." *Pamphlets in American History*, Cooperative Societies #140; Horner, "Producers' Cooperatives," 91-92.

35. Leikin, "Practical Utopians," chapter 3.

36. Ibid., chapters 3 and 4.

37. Ibid., chapter 4.

38. Ibid., chapters 4 and 5.

39. Massachusetts Bureau of Statistics of Labor, *Annual Report of 1886*, 216-22.

40. In 1889 the Lasters' Protective Union still existed in Stoneham and had some former cooperators as supporters. "The Campfire of the Stoneham Lasters' Protective Union," *Stoneham Independent*, 13 April 1889.

41. Joseph Stipanovich, *City of Lakes: An Illustrated History of Minneapolis* (Windsor Publications, 1982), 9; *The Statistics of the Population of the United States from the Ninth Census by Francis A. Walker*, Vol. I (Washington, 1872), 178; *Statistics of the Population of the United States from the Tenth Census (June 1, 1880)* (Washington), 226; Albert Shaw, "Cooperation in the Northwest," in *History of Cooperation in the United States*, 199-202.

42. Shaw, "Cooperation," 203-30, 240, 263-66, 268, 274; "Coopers' Chips," *Northwestern Miller*, 14 August 1885.

43. G. O. Virtue, "The Co-operative Coopers of Minneapolis," *The Quarterly Journal of Economics* 19 (August 1905), 537; Shaw, 217, 220-23, 225; "Cooperation," *Journal of United Labor* (July 1886), 2164. These are rough estimates of the cooperators' ethnic makeup derived from Shaw, 217, 220-23, 225.

44. George B. Engberg, "The Knights of Labor in Minnesota," *Minnesota History* 22 (December 1941), 375; Shaw, 302.

45. See for example, *Second Biennial Report of the [Wisconsin] Bureau of Labor and Industrial Statistics, 1885-1886, Madison, Wisconsin* (Democrat Printing Co., State Printers, 1886) 187-88.

46. "By-Laws of the Hennepin County Barrel Co. with Articles of Incorporation, Co-operative Laws of 1870 & Amendments," (Minneapolis, 1886), *Pamphlets in American History*, Co-operative Societies #99, 1-12; Shaw, "Cooperation," 203, 207, 216, 217, 220, 222, 225, 226, 228, 249, 253.

47. Shaw, "Cooperation," 238; Engberg, "Knights of Labor," 384-88; Knights of Labor, *Record of Proceedings of the Twentieth Regular Meeting of D.A. 79, K. of L. held at St. Paul, Minnesota, July 17, 1887*, John P. McGaughey Papers, Minnesota Historical Society, 26.

48. *Twentieth Regular Meeting of D.A. 79*, 59.

49. *First Biennial Report of the Bureau of labor Statistics of the State of Minnesota for the two years ending December 31, 1887-8*, 225.

50. Virtue, "Co-operative Coopers," 530-32; Shaw, "Cooperatives," 231, 215, 216, 219, 221; *First Biennial Report—Minnesota*, 225.

51. Shaw, "Cooperatives," 232-34; *First Biennial Report—Minnesota*, 225; Knights of Labor, *Record of Proceedings of the Fifth Quarterly Meeting of D.A. 79, K. of L. Held at Mankato, Minnesota, January 16, 1887* (Thos. A. Clark & Co.), 17, 18, 20, 26, 34-35; Knights of Labor, *Twentieth Regular Meeting of D.A. 79*, 36, 40, 42-43.

52. See the weekly column "Coopers' Chips" in the *Northwestern Miller*, 3, 10, 17 June 1887; 8, 15, 22 July 1887; 12, 19, 26 August 1887; 2, 9, 16, 23, 30 September 1887; *Twentieth Regular Meeting of D.A. 79*, 44, 46-47; Knights of Labor, *Record of Proceedings of the Twenty-First Regular Meeting of D. A. 79, K. of L. Held at Minneapolis, Minnesota, January 15, 1888*, 29-30, 32, Terence Powderly Papers.

53. *Twentieth Regular Meeting of D.A. 79*, 8, 26.

54. Knights of Labor, Address of the Chairman of the Special Committee on Co-operation appointed at the Mankato Session, *Twentieth Regular Meeting of D.A. 79*, 59-64; Knights of Labor, Report of the Committee on Co-operation and Education, *Twentieth Regular Meeting of D.A. 79*, 70; Knights of Labor, *Twenty-First Regular Meeting of D.A. 79*, 5-11; Knights of Labor, Report of the District Treasurer, *Twenty-First Regular Meeting of D.A. 79*, 23; Knights of Labor, Report of the Secretary-Treasurer, Knights of Labor, *Record of Proceedings of the Twenty-Third Regular Meeting of D.A. 79, K. of L. held at Minneapolis, Minnesota, January 20, 1889*, 14-19, Terence Powderly Papers; Shaw, 263.

55. J. S. Rankin, "Hard Times: Their Cause and Cure," 45, *Pamphlets in American Socialism* #290.

56. J. P. McGaughey, "Land as a Basis for Co-operative Labor," *Journal of United Labor*, 1198, John Samuel Papers, Box 5, Newspaper Clippings; Shaw, "Cooperatives," 244, 248; *First Biennial Report—Minnesota*, 240-42.

57. *Twentieth Regular Meeting of D.A. 79*, 9.

58. Rankin, "Hard Times," 47.

59. Ibid., 35, 4.

60. William Argus to E. W. Bemis, August 25, and September 15, 1896, Wisconsin State Historical Society Labor Collection, Misc. Biographies and Papers, Box 2 Bemis Papers, Folder Bemis Papers; *Northwestern Miller*, 30 September 1887, 20 July 1888; Virtue, "Co-operative Coopers," 529-40.

61. There is no record of the agricultural colony after 1888; *Northwestern Miller*, 4 January 1889; G. O. Virtue, "The End of the Cooperative Coopers," *Quarterly Journal of Economics* 46 (May 1932): 541-45.

62. On the failure of cooperatives, see Zelda F. Gamson and Henry M. Levin, "Obstacles to the Survival of Democratic Workplaces," in *Worker Cooperatives in America*, eds. Robert Jackall and Henry M. Levin (Berkeley, 1984), 219-244; and Joan Scott, *The Glassworkers of Carmaux: French Craftsmen and Political Action in a Nineteenth-Century City* (Cambridge, 1974).

Chapter 4

From Cooperative Commonwealth to Cooperative Democracy: The American Cooperative Ideal, 1880-1940

Kathleen Donohue

In the late nineteenth and early twentieth centuries, a number of American and European intellectuals, concerned by the social and economic upheaval wrought by industrialization, turned to cooperation. Both groups saw cooperation as an economic system that would not only mitigate the worst effects of industrialization but that could also usher in the "good society." Yet when it came to identifying precisely what those effects were or even defining what exactly constituted the "good society," American and European intellectuals found much less common ground. Indeed, what is striking about the various attempts by American intellectuals to construct a theory of cooperation is the extent to which their attempts were influenced by an American intellectual tradition.

Just how powerful that intellectual tradition could be becomes apparent when one examines the ideas of the major American cooperative theorists of the late nineteenth and early twentieth centuries. As Richard T. Ely, Albert Sonnichsen, James Peter Warbasse, and Horace Kallen each constructed their cooperative theories, all relied heavily on an American political language rooted in republican and liberal notions of a "good society." All stressed the democratic, individualistic, and voluntaristic nature of cooperation, key concepts in American political theory. All suggested that a cooperative order would be free from class conflict, an attractive feature to individuals steeped in an intellectual tradition that tended to minimize if not completely ignore issues of class. Three of the theorists suggested that cooperation offered an alternative to an activist state, thereby tapping into the growing concern in the early twentieth century that increasing state and federal power violated a basic tenet of both republican and liberal political theory—the importance of a limited government. And finally, while only two theorists explicitly identified cooperation as a system firmly rooted in private property, all were careful to avoid presenting cooperation as an ideology that would socialize private property.[1]

That American cooperative theorists—and in the case of Sonnichsen and Warbasse, cooperative activists—who came from a variety of backgrounds, lived at different times, and had diverse political agendas could achieve such a consensus is itself striking. What is even more striking, however, is the extent to which these theorists maintained such a consensus at a time when cooperative theory was undergoing a major transformation. On both sides of the Atlantic cooperative theorists were coming to see not producer but consumer cooperatives as the foundation of a cooperative order. But while European thinkers turned to consumer cooperatives because they saw them as a more effective weapon in the working-class struggle against capitalism, American thinkers embraced consumer cooperation because it offered them a better means of attaining a classless, democratic, and individualistic political order.

Richard T. Ely was probably the most influential American intellectual to turn to cooperation. As a professor of economics at Johns Hopkins and later at the University of Wisconsin, he established a reputation not only as one of the foremost scholars of the day but also as a dedicated social activist. Ely published numerous books and articles, including one of the more widely used economics textbooks of the late nineteenth and early twentieth centuries, and was a founding member of the American Economic Association. He was also a vocal supporter of the labor movement, a position that almost cost him his professorship at the University of Wisconsin. And he helped to shape the progressive public policy of Wisconsin.[2]

Ely's political ideas were shaped in part by his exposure, while a graduate student in Germany, to the ideas of the so-called *Kathedersozialisten*, German academics who advocated a mildly socialistic program to correct the ills of a modern industrial society. The socialist influence was evident in Ely's conviction that the most serious problem caused by industrialization was the emergence of two hostile classes. It was also evident in his belief that the solution required not only "abolishing a distinct capitalist class of employers" but also uniting "labor and capital in the same hands, the hands of the actual workers." Finally, it was evident in his call for an expansion of the powers of the state.[3]

Ely, however, was no Marxist. His strong protestant convictions made him unwilling to embrace a doctrine that rejected religion. And his roots in a republican and liberal intellectual tradition made him uncomfortable with the idea of class conflict, never mind class warfare. Indeed, his greatest fear was that the widening gulf separating rich and poor would increase the appeal of such dangerous ideologies as revolutionary socialism and even anarchism. Unless something could be done to "keep alive the unity of civilization among us," he warned in *Labor Movement in America* (1886), "our future downfall will be inevitable."[4]

That something was cooperation.[5] It promised to abolish class conflict without class war, relying instead on "voluntary association" to transform the "present industrial society" into a cooperative commonwealth based on the Christian doctrines of "human brotherhood" and "love thy neighbor."[6] In cooperation Ely's republican and liberal heritage, his protestant convictions, and his socialist leanings found a common meeting ground.

When Ely advocated a cooperative order, he meant one organized around producer not consumer cooperatives. Only producer cooperatives, he insisted, could eliminate class conflict, because they alone could replace the two hostile categories of employers and employees with one category, that of independent producers. Once all members of society were independent producers, then class conflict would cease to exist because classes would cease to exist. As for consumer cooperatives—Ely dismissed them as little more than cheap stores. They might teach the worker "thrift and frugality" and provide him with "an opportunity to invest his savings." They might even offer the worker an education in cooperative principles.[7] But they were not, in his view, capable of eliminating class conflict.

While Ely was quick to grasp that the implications of producer cooperatives extended far beyond their existence as individual profit-making enterprises, he failed to perceive similar implications with consumer cooperatives. In an industrialized economy, however, the consumer identity had a far greater theoretical potential to transcend class than did the producer identity. The problem with the producer identity was that by the late nineteenth century it had long ceased to be a universal category. While it may have been possible in a preindustrial or early industrial economy to label most members of society producers, the complexity of a mature industrial economy dominated by large corporations called such an all-inclusive definition of producer into question. Should industrialists be classified as producers or parasites? What about corporate managers or investment bankers? The alternative to an all-inclusive and ultimately obsolete definition of the producer was to define that category more narrowly. Marxists, for example, adopted such an approach, reserving the producer label for wage workers. But the more exclusive the definition of producer, the more likely such a definition would carry with it connotations of class conflict.

The consumer identity, by contrast, was an all-inclusive identity. And it was an identity that became more rather than less relevant as the economy industrialized. It was, thus, an identity that had the same theoretical potential to transcend class in an industrial economy that the producer identity had possessed in a preindustrial era.

Ely, however, found it difficult to embrace the consumer identity, a difficulty he shared with many an American intellectual.[8] And he was unwilling to adopt a class-based definition of the producer identity with its implicit class conflict. Producer cooperation provided him with a third alternative. It allowed him to define producer as an all-inclusive category. It might promise to solve the problems of an industrial society by recreating the preindustrial world of small, independent producers, but at least that world would be free of class conflict.

By the late nineteenth century producer cooperation had come under siege. At the forefront of this assault were European thinkers who suggested that while producer cooperatives might be attractive ideologically, they were not successful. If an economy dominated by small, independent producers had given way to an industrialized order dominated by huge corporations, then the time had come to place cooperation within that order.

While this intellectual shift occurred in cooperative circles across Europe, it was the British experience that had the greatest influence on American cooperative thought.[9] From the earliest days when Rochdale had set the standard for consumer cooperation, American cooperators had turned to British cooperation as a model, both at the practical and the theoretical levels.[10] It was, therefore, not surprising that a British theoretical work, Beatrice Potter's *The Co-Operative Movement in Great Britain* (1891), should first suggest to American cooperative thinkers the radical potential of consumer cooperatives.

Potter's book had a profound—though somewhat delayed—impact on American cooperative thought. American cooperators hailed the work as "roadbreaking," the "original philosophic analysis of the Consumers' Cooperative Movement," with critical implications for the development of cooperative thought. Horace Kallen summed up the high esteem in which Potter's book was held when he wrote: "[It] had been to the movement from its publication what the first edition of Mill's *Principles of Political Economy* was to the order of free capitalist enterprise."[11] While such descriptions might overstate Potter's influence on cooperative theory in general, they give some indication of her influence on American cooperative thought.

Like earlier British cooperative thinkers, Potter saw cooperation as a way to improve the existence of society's producers. But she departed from traditional British thought by rejecting producer cooperation. In the modern industrial world, she argued, such cooperatives had little hope of success. At best, these cooperatives were anachronistic, attempting to return society to an earlier stage in which production was organized around small workshops. At worst producer cooperatives were little better than their capitalist competitors, exploiting worker and consumer alike. "For it is self-evident," Potter wrote, "that all Associations of Producers whether they be capitalists buying labour, or labourers buying capital, or a co-partnership between the two, are directly opposed in their interest to the interest of the community. They are, and must always remain, profit-seekers—intent on securing a large margin between the cost of production and the price given." In either case, producer cooperatives had proved thoroughly unsuccessful in correcting the evils of a competitive, capitalist system.[12]

In discrediting producer cooperatives Potter had effectively brought one of the major tenets of American cooperative thought into question: the notion that consumer cooperatives were only a means to producer cooperatives. If producer cooperatives ceased to be a goal, could consumer cooperatives—only a means to that goal—be of any value? And even more specifically, if consumer cooperatives *could* exist in their own right, could they be integrated as effectively into a working-class ideology as producer cooperatives had been? Earlier nineteenth-century cooperative thinkers such as Ely had believed that the answer to those questions must be "no." Potter answered both questions in the affirmative.

Since "the state of society in which the individual producer owns alike the instrument and the product of his labour is past praying for," Potter argued that workers had to "regain collectively" what they had lost individually. Labor had already taken the first step toward a collective assault by organizing in trade unions. But trade unions could only address those problems caused by capitalist manipulation of the production process. Capitalist manipulation of the distribution process was beyond their control. In an industrialized economy, however, exploitation in the marketplace was as significant as exploitation in the workplace. Only if the working class organized both as consumers and as producers, Potter argued, could it transform the existing capitalist system based on profit into an industrial democracy based on "representative selfgovernment [in] the commercial and manufacturing enterprise of the country."[13] On the distributive front, members of the working class could use their consumer cooperatives to "pierce monopoly prices and uncover fraudulent quality until the fund known as profit—the entire surplus between the act of buying and the act of selling—is distributed directly or indirectly throughout the whole community." The cooperatives could also frustrate capitalist attempts to recoup through higher prices income lost because of wage increases. Through their trade unions, workers could prevent capitalists from reducing wages on the basis of the declining cost of living permitted by the cooperative store.[14]

According to Potter, the transforming power of consumer cooperation was not limited to the distributive arena. It could also play a role in shaping the production process. Cooperative consumers could have a positive impact on working conditions by maintaining adequate working conditions in their own factories.[15] And they could force the introduction of such conditions throughout England by refusing to carry "sweated products" in the cooperative stores and by boycotting any manufacturer whose factory did not maintain an acceptable labor standard. Thus, Potter argued, consumer cooperation would be one of the levers with which to "secure sovereign power in industry as in politics," the other, of course, being the trade union. Only by organizing on two fronts, as consumers *and* as producers, could labor hope to correct the economic imbalances brought on by industrialization.[16]

Potter's approach to cooperation, in effect, turned Ely's version on its head.[17] Ely had stressed the radical potential of producer cooperation while minimizing that of consumer cooperation. According to Potter, however, producer cooperatives, dependent upon competition and profit, were firmly entrenched in the capitalist system. It was consumer cooperation that offered the real alternative to capitalist economics. It relied on "democratic control" rather than competition to lower prices and raise quality. And it replaced a system dependent upon individual profit with one in which "each man and woman would work, not for personal subsistence or personal gain, but for the whole community." In short, not producer but consumer cooperatives would be instrumental in forming "out of the present state of industrial war a great Republic of Industry firmly based on the Co-operative principle of 'all for each and each for all.'"[18]

Ultimately, Potter and Ely differed in their attitudes toward cooperation because they held different views on the social and political order that should and could evolve. Both saw labor as the primary victim of industrial capitalism and both looked to cooperation to introduce a more equitable order. For Ely that could best be done by eliminating class conflict. As far as he was concerned, producer cooperatives, by eliminating class itself, could do just that. Potter, however, believed that class struggle was inherent in the modern industrial order. The appeal of consumer cooperation for Potter was that it offered the working class a way to win that struggle.

Potter's book did not have an immediate impact on American cooperative practice, in part because cooperation had fallen into general disfavor in the United States by the turn of the century. It was not that Americans had suddenly come to terms with an industrial America. Instead, they chose to place their faith in programs far removed from cooperation. The collapse of the Knights of Labor discredited cooperatives in labor circles. Their successor, the American Federation of Labor, placed its emphasis on "pure and simple" unionism and for several decades counselled against cooperative ventures.[19] The failure of the Farmers' Alliance movement meant that even in rural areas, where cooperatives were most accepted, cooperation ceased to be the vibrant force it had once been.[20] As for middle-class reformers? Most of them were riding the wave of progressivism, placing their faith in an active government and a dynamic presidency.

Cooperatives, however, did not completely disappear during these years. Farmers continued to patronize those cooperatives that survived the collapse of the Farmers' Alliance. And in the industrial areas working-class immigrants who had had experience with cooperation in their homelands, established cooperative stores.[21] But if consumer cooperation survived in those years, it was not so much because of its radical potential as because of its ability to reduce the cost of living.

In the teens cooperation began once again to attract attention on the American side of the Atlantic. A decade and a half of progressivism had failed to eliminate the negative aspects of an industrialized, capitalist order. And it was becoming ever clearer that the socialist road was not one the American people were willing to travel. A number of middle-class intellectuals once again suggested that cooperation might offer a more "American" road to a "just and democratic" society.

The new era in consumer organization officially began in 1916 with the founding by James Peter Warbasse of the Co-operative League of the United States, a national umbrella organization that would coordinate cooperative efforts throughout the United States.[22] It was not Warbasse, however, but Albert Sonnichsen, a secretary of the Co-operative League, who first attempted to integrate the consumer-orientation of European cooperative thought into an American theoretical framework. Sonnichsen, the son of the Danish Counsel to San Francisco, had spent his early years as a foreign correspondent, in the process encountering a variety of radical ideas. While he flirted with a number of them, he eventually decided that consumers' cooperation as a distinct ideology offered the best hope for regenerating society.[23]

As Sonnichsen constructed his theory of cooperation, he relied heavily on the work of Beatrice Potter (Webb), embracing much of her cooperative worldview. Like her, he believed that the only solution to labor's problems in a modern industrial order was for "*all* the workers together, as a mass, [to] combine, and own and control collectively *all* the machinery of production."[24] But Sonnichsen parted company with Potter over the issue of how that collectively was to be achieved and administered.

According to Potter it was imperative that cooperation and trade unionism join forces, functioning as two arms of one movement. Only together could they secure for their members "the unearned income now received by other classes." In Potter's view, however, trade unionism and cooperation had their limitations. They were incapable of effecting the final step in a real social transformation—the creation of a social democratic order. As she saw it, the only way of completing the process that cooperation and trade unionism had begun was through political action. Only the state, she argued, through taxation of upper- and middle-class incomes as well as "compulsory acquisition" of key industries, could add "the social production of wealth" to "the communal administration and control," thereby establishing a truly democratic society.[25]

Sonnichsen, by contrast, rejected the notion that cooperation could only be effective in conjunction with trade unionism.[26] And he denied that it was merely the first step on the road to a social democracy. Far from being a tool at the service of revolutionary or political socialism, it was an alternative to them, "an anti-capitalist, revolutionary movement, aiming toward a radical social reconstruction based on an all-inclusive collectivism." True, the two ideologies shared certain similarities. Like socialism, consumer cooperation objected to the inequities within the capitalist system; it recognized that so-called democracy under any government within such a system was a mere illusion; it placed the blame for the problems brought by industrialization at the door of private profit; and finally, like socialism it sought a classless democratic society.[27] But beyond these similarities there were real differences.

The primary difference was one of means. Potter insisted that only political action could create a democratic order.[28] Sonnichsen, favoring economic action, disagreed. A new social order, he insisted, could not be legislated into existence, "a fact which the Socialists refuse to recognize."[29] Only through competition with private enterprise—in short, through an "evolutionary process"—would cooperation "acquire supreme power and take the place of capitalism."[30] But the shortcomings of political action extended beyond its inability to create a viable order. According to Sonnichsen, political action would prove equally incapable of establishing a democratic order. Any state, even a Socialist one, imposed its will from above. Cooperation, by contrast, rooted all social authority in the individual and the group. Furthermore, the state's authority extended to all members of society while cooperation was voluntaristic, "opposed to the idea of conscription." Quintessentially democratic, it could best be characterized, Sonnichsen decided, not as Socialism but as "Anarchism rationalized."[31]

While Sonnichsen was eager to distinguish cooperation from socialism, he was nevertheless determined to establish its labor credentials. To do so, he found it necessary to broaden the definition of labor to such an extent that the term took on a completely new meaning. He decided that labor included everyone who lived on a wage or a salary. Thus, individuals were considered capitalists or workers not on the basis of how wealthy they were or where their political allegiances lay but on how they made their money—through labor, be it mental or physical or through return on invested capital, be it profits, rents, or interest. Under such a scheme, an admiral would be classified as a laborer while a pushcart peddler would not. The former lives "by effort," the latter "by speculative trade." If only those who lived off private profit were excluded from the ranks of labor, then a cooperative system that eliminated private profit would eventually bring all of society into the ranks of labor. It would, in essence, be nothing more than the "workers, organized as consumers."

The difference between Sonnichsen's and Potter's attempts to establish the labor credentials of the consumer identity highlights the extent to which the American intellectual tradition shaped the American cooperative worldview. Potter's consumer was a class-based identity. It represented that part of the worker that was exploited by the capitalists in the marketplace.[32] For Potter, class conflict was an integral part of an industrialized society and consumer cooperation was one of the working-class weapons in that conflict.

By contrast, Sonnichsen's approach to cooperation was one that attempted to minimize class conflict. Like Ely, he was drawn to cooperation in his search for a universal, all-inclusive category around which to organize society. Ely had found that category in an obsolete version of the producer identity. Sonnichsen found it in the consumer identity. As far as Sonnichsen was concerned, class conflict would not exist in a system dedicated to the consumer's interests because "consumers are not a class."[33] Ely and Sonnichsen were worlds apart in much of their approach yet both had sought to eliminate class conflict not by granting victory to one class or another, as did Potter, but by defining "class" out of existence.

Rooting a social order in a consumer identity carried with it certain philosophical obstacles. It was clear why producers were entitled to share in social wealth. They, after all, had helped to create it. It was not so clear however by what right consumers consumed. Sonnichsen, in part, attempted to justify philosophically his substitution of the consumer for the producer by identifying "consumption as the chief end of society, labor being merely a means to that end." But he found his most compelling argument in that sacrosanct icon of American politics, "democracy." Only when consumption was elevated over production, Sonnichsen maintained, could "a true democracy find a uniform foundation, for it is the one interest which we all have in common, and to very nearly the same degree." Potter had envisioned a system in which the workers represented the consumers' interest; Sonnichsen flipped Potter's vision on its head, calling for a system in which the consumers represented the workers' interests. In so doing he expanded Potter's collectivism of the people as workers into a collectivism of "the people as a whole."[34]

By revising European cooperative thought Sonnichsen had created a theoretical system that might hold some appeal for an American audience. He had given a nation in which ideologies rooted in class conflict had never enjoyed much success, an ideology that eliminated class conflict by defining it out of existence. He had devised a stateless system for a people who had traditionally distrusted an activist state. And for a nation obsessed with the idea of individual liberty he had formulated a political philosophy that merged Thomas Jefferson with Michael Bakunin.

> I realize that there will be no little protest on the part of most Americans against an attempt to prove affinity between Thomas Jefferson [and] Michael Bakunin. But this is common between them: each instinctively recognizes the superiority of the individual over the State; while Lasalle and Marx raise the State above the individual. Jefferson would have authority initiate from below, mounting upward. Marx would concentrate it in a center radiating outward and downward. Jefferson was a democrat. Marx, at best was only a republican.[35]

James Peter Warbasse, the author of *Co-operative Democracy*, was as determined as Sonnichsen to depict cooperation as an American form of radicalism. But while Sonnichsen was a sophisticated theoretician, Warbasse

was more of a popularizer. As he attempted to convert his readers to cooperation, he showed little regard for theoretical consistency, borrowing freely from
a variety of philosophical schools, ranging from radical to progressive liberalism. The result was a book that presented cooperation as a system of thought
that was utopian as well as scientific, as an ideology both allied with and
opposed to the labor movement, and as an economic system based on property,
self interest, and individualism but still the antithesis of capitalism. Despite his
eclectic approach and his limited theoretical skills Warbasse, nevertheless, left
his mark on cooperative thought, in part because he was the foremost American cooperator of his day but also because he was more committed than any
of his predecessors to establishing cooperation's credentials as a consumer
ideology.

Warbasse epitomized the progressive-era social reformer. A descendant of
a pre-Revolutionary War family and independently wealthy, he nevertheless
took up a career in medicine and devoted much of his time to treating the New
York City poor. Eventually, he decided that piecemeal efforts were ineffective.
"Palliative work, [he] came to realize, though temporarily of aid to the individual, solves no problem." It merely makes it "easier for *other* people to be
poor."[36] Warbasse concluded that only a complete transformation of the economic system could eradicate poverty. In 1918 he gave up his career in medicine to devote himself full time to the Cooperative League of the United
States.

Warbasse's education in cooperative ideas was a European one. He had
first encountered cooperation while studying in Germany around the turn of the
century and he had been a regular participant at the International Cooperative
Alliance conventions. By 1905 the International Cooperative Alliance had
committed itself to what it called a "revolutionary" vision of consumer cooperation, demanding the peaceful destruction of the existing industrial order and
the creation of a new social order that would emerge as the people organized
as consumers.[37]

What Warbasse took from European cooperative theory was a willingness
to root cooperation in the consumer. What he did not take from European
cooperative theory was a definition of consumer as a member of the working
class. Workers, he insisted, made up only a part of the social category of
consumer. While he was not unsympathetic to the needs of labor, he was more
sensitive than most Europeans and indeed American cooperative theoreticians
had been to the ways in which labor interests conflicted with those of consumers.[38] Workers, he acknowledged, were exploited. But so too were consumers.
And because the latter was a larger group, their interests should take precedence. If workers would subsume their producer identity within their consumer
identity, then they too could come out from under capitalist oppression.

Not surprisingly, Warbasse's exclusive focus on consumer identity influenced his definition of the "good society." Any real transformation of society,

he insisted, would require that a system designed for profit be replaced by one devoted to the manufacture of beautiful things for use. Working-class activism could never effect such a transformation because it only sought to increase labor's share of society's wealth. Those labor activists who called for reform wanted "wages—and more wages to the limit." And those who called for revolution "would only superficially change one set of bosses for another." Neither group, however, sought to change either "the purpose of industry" or "the motive of production." Neither demanded "the production of better goods" or the eradication of the profit motive.[39]

More than his predecessors Warbasse appreciated the extent to which the existing system exploited consumers. Earlier thinkers had seen profit as something taken from the worker either in the workplace through low wages or in the marketplace through high prices. They had turned to cooperation as a way to "stop this leak in the middle."[40] Warbasse, however, saw profit as something "confiscated" not from the worker but the consumer "in the form of excess charges." It was generated through planned scarcity as manufacturers curtailed production to keep prices and profits high. It was augmented through advertising the sole purpose of which was to get consumers to purchase things they neither wanted nor needed and the costs of which were passed on to the consumer. Such ploys had little to do with denying workers the fruits of their labor. They were explicitly and exclusively forms of consumer exploitation.[41]

Warbasse warned that the negative effects of organizing society around the producer extended beyond the exploitation of the consumer. In such a society those most closely identified with production would exert more control than those who were not. Because production was a male-dominated activity, such a society would be a male-dominated one. Because women only achieved anything near equality with men in the home, only an ideology that was rooted in the home could improve the status of women. Cooperation, Warbasse insisted, was just that because it was rooted in "the home and the family," rather than in "the workshop and the worker."[42]

Warbasse was not only intent upon establishing cooperation as an ideology that would eliminate all social conflict, be it the conflict between men and women or the conflict between classes. He was also committed to showing how cooperation offered a voluntary, nonpolitical alternative to the coercive state.[43] Like Sonnichsen, Warbasse rejected Potter's fusion of socialism and cooperation.[44] In Warbasse's view, any state, be it capitalist or socialist, was a coercive organization. How could it be anything else? The very idea of a state had its roots in the attempts of the privileged classes to control the masses. Those who controlled the state were not the people but "those who control the property and industries." Inevitably, the state sided with the "propertied" and the "privileged," protecting them "against the demands of the unpropertied and unprivileged." Therefore, Warbasse concluded, it was useless to try to gain political control without first gaining economic control. An economic movement, cooperation could secure control where control really mattered.[45]

The role of the state in the creation of a cooperative order had been an issue long under debate on both sides of the Atlantic. Some thinkers such as Richard T. Ely and Edward Bellamy in the United States and Ferdinand Lasalle and Sidney and Beatrice Webb in Europe, believed that the inequalities rampant in the capitalist system could only be offset by a strong state. Widely accepted in Europe, the statist version of cooperative thought was a short-lived phenomenon on the American side of the Atlantic, primarily a response to the laissez-faire policies that characterized late-nineteenth-century American politics. Indeed, most Americans who turned to cooperation did so precisely because it was a system that had the potential to transform society without relying on the power of the state.

Americans, however, were not alone in their appreciation of cooperation's antistatist potential. Anarchist Petr Kropotkin, for example, had stressed that potential in his highly influential work, *Mutual Aid*. According to Kropotkin, human relations were dominated by two opposing currents, mutual aid and "the self-assertion of the individual." Mutual aid had been at the core of most evolutionary progress and was a critical element in the progress of humanity. Self-assertion of the individual, on the other hand, retarded human progress except when that self-assertion was on behalf of society as a whole. The problem with the state, according to Kropotkin, was that it created and fostered animosities which discouraged the true human propensity for cooperative interaction.[46]

Warbasse found Kropotkin's ideas appealing. Indeed, his understanding of anarchism was shaped predominantly by *Mutual Aid*. Ultimately, however, he failed to grasp Kropotkin's argument. For Kropotkin anarchism was the antithesis of individualism. Communistic rather than individualistic, it was an ideology in which the interests of all *always* took precedence over the interests of the individual.[47] For Warbasse, by contrast, anarchism was an ideology in which the interests of the individual took precedence over the group—so much so that it promised to "protect minorities from the oppression of majorities." As for the state—the problem with it, Warbasse believed, was not that it fostered animosities, thereby discouraging cooperation, but that it squashed individual liberty.[48]

It is not particularly surprising that Warbasse defended anarchism. Its antistatist impulse was consistent with his own concerns about expanded government. What is surprising is that an advocate of a cooperative order would stress the individualistic aspects of anarchism rather than the communal ones. For Warbasse, the "good society" might be cooperative but it was also individualistic.

Warbasse had to engage in some intellectual gymnastics to establish cooperation as a system that "exhalts the individual." The real intellectual challenge, however, was his attempt to establish it as a system based on private property. He did so by suggesting that the cooperative did not own the property of its members. It merely administered it. Individual cooperators, however, retained full ownership. Warbasse might admire Petr Kropotkin, but his intellectual debt to John Locke was the more apparent one.

Warbasse justified his defense of private over socialized property by arguing that not private property but its misuse—"its use in an unsocial way"—was at the root of exploitation. Public ownership was no more immune from "unsocial" use than private ownership, and perhaps less so in that it reduced the people, "to a propertyless mass...dependent upon the benefactions of a great impersonal machine, called the government." [49] Far from representing the interests of the people, public ownership under any system of government represented the interests of the state. "I am a citizen of the corporation, the city of New York," Warbasse explained:

> but as a citizen I do not know how much I own of the buildings, stores, and automobiles of the city of New York, nor can I sell my share. The reason is simple enough: I do not own any property of the city of New York. That property belongs to a great impersonal machine called the municipality, which taxes me severely, permits me to use certain of its property, and is run entirely by a vast bureaucracy of officials not one of whom I ever voted for and not one of whom represents me. I should consequently say that this so-called public ownership is far removed from me as a citizen. It is, indeed, a very different property relationship from that which exists between my cooperative society and myself.[50]

Warbasse's description of cooperation as a system dedicated to liberty, private property, and the minimalist state, was the most "American" version to date. It was a version soon superseded by that of Horace Kallen.[51] Kallen was a philosophy professor of some renown at the New School for Social Research, an institution that became a haven for a number of iconoclast thinkers. Like some of his colleagues at the New School, Kallen had had somewhat of a turbulent academic career. In 1905 he had lost his position at Princeton because of his atheism. In 1919 he had been fired from the University of Wisconsin for his defense of pacifism during the First World War.

Kallen's approach to philosophy was similar to that of his more famous contemporary, John Dewey. Like Dewey, he believed that philosophy had an important role to play in the transformation of society. It was a discipline that had long focused on the question of what constituted the "good society." For Kallen, such a society was one that promoted such fundamental concepts of American political theory as democracy, individualism, and freedom.[52]

Like Dewey, Kallen was also a pragmatist. Convinced that the best principles were not those with the longest tradition but those that worked, he was more than willing to challenge existing institutions and beliefs once they ceased to promote "the good society." Kallen's pragmatism, for example, prompted him to challenge the melting-pot theory, a theory to which almost all Americans subscribed. As far as Kallen was concerned, however, that theory was no longer consistent with such basic American concepts as democracy and individualism and should, therefore, be replaced. It was for this reason that he advocated multiethnic cultural pluralism, one of the first American thinkers to do so.[53]

Kallen's pragmatism also played a role in his turn to cooperation. Once he had become convinced that the existing economic organization was no longer capable of accomplishing the goals for which it had been designed, it was inevitable that he would seek an alternative. He illustrated the disjuncture between the existing economy's operation and its goals by recounting a story from Oliver Goldsmith's *Vicar of Wakefield*. The vicar's son, it seemed, had purchased some razors that proved to be completely useless as shaving instruments. When the vicar's son tried to return them, however, the vendor denied ever having claimed the razors were any good for shaving. Well, the vicar's son wanted to know, for what then were the razors made, if not for shaving. Why, to sell, was the vendor's response.[54]

For Kallen the story captured the very essence of a perverted capitalism. Capitalism had initially, he suggested, been an economic system dedicated to the needs of the consumer. Indeed, Adam Smith had suggested that consumption was "the sole end and purpose of all production." During industrialization, however, the obsession with profits came to dominate all other aspects of the economy. A system that had once held out the promise of abundance began fostering scarcity. Kallen concluded that consumption, once the end, had become nothing more than a means, "a servant of production."[55]

Kallen was quick to suggest that the problem was not capitalism, but its perversion. As industrialization had progressed "the sacred 'law' of supply and demand [had been] manipulated, not obeyed," resulting in monopolies and rigid prices. But in its pure form, capitalism remained a highly effective economic system, "adjust[ing] prices and production to changing demands." As for the traditional targets of economic radicalism—price, profit, and private property—in much the same way that Warbasse defended private property, Kallen located the problem in the abuses not the uses of these three "pillars of capitalism." In themselves they were not tools of exploitation but highly effective economic mechanisms. Indeed, they were the foundation not just of capitalism but of any economy of abundance. A cooperative economy would rest on them as firmly as the existing economy did.[56]

But if an economy rested on the three "pillars of capitalism"—private property, the profit motive, and the price system—then was it not a capitalist economy? According to Kallen, it was. Consumer cooperation, he decided, was not so much an alternative to capitalism as a variation on it. He predicted that as a variation it would not replace capitalism so much as displace it, "as the automobile displaced the horse, the electric light, the lamp; scientific medicine, old wives' remedies; not by attacking and harming the competitor, but by doing this work in a better way, a shorter time, at a smaller cost, in greater freedom, and thus superseding him as one species of the same genus of plant or animal supersedes another."[57] There would be no need for revolutions, no necessity for drastic upheavals.

Given the corporate economy of the 1930s and the less-than-successful New Deal forays into economic planning, it is not difficult to see how Kallen could claim that consumer cooperation was the real inheritor of the Smithian world view. Capitalism, as Adam Smith had envisioned it, was a system that would foster abundance through competition among equals each following their own self-interest through free trade.[58] But in the depression economy it was difficult to find evidence of abundance, competition, equality, or free trade. Cooperation, however—or, at least, the version that Kallen described—incorporated each of these concepts and thus seemed to offer the best means of returning capitalism to its true origins. "Anarchism, rationalized" had been transformed into "Adam Smith, rationalized."

Having established Adam Smith as the father of cooperative economics, Kallen next attempted to establish the political paternity of John Locke. Surveying American political history Kallen identified what he called an "American philosophy of life." It was a philosophy embodied in the Declaration of Independence, whose dominant themes were such Lockean concepts as the "inalienable right to life, liberty and the pursuit of happiness," equality, the social contract, and voluntary association. All these concepts, Kallen maintained, were consummatory in nature. Thus, he argued, the founding principles of the United States of America could best be fostered in an economy organized around the consumer rather than the producer. In such an economy, all members shared the same identity and were thus equal. Such an economy, furthermore, was one that was dedicated to abundance, a necessary prerequisite for a free society. Organizing the economy around the producer, by contrast, resulted in scarcity, inequality, and conflict. In addition, a consumer-oriented political economy would be a self-governed one since self-government was "the historic principle of consumers; to be governed by others the historic burden of producers." Finally such a political economy would foster individualism, because it fostered democratic rule and equality, two important conditions for the existence of individualism.[59]

If a consumer economy promoted the ideals of American politics, a consumer economy based on cooperation did so only that much more. In fact, Kallen concluded, the American goal of a classless society could best be achieved through cooperation since "a classless society is necessarily a voluntary association—ie an association based on consent—of individuals in which each enjoys equal liberty." "The economic organization of liberty," consumer cooperation offered the surest way to embody "the ideals of Jefferson and

Lincoln in the times of Edison and Einstein."[60] Like Sonnichsen before him, Kallen appreciated the value of evoking American political icons in his attempt to convert an American audience to cooperation.

Kallen had made cooperation a philosophy more American than the Declaration of Independence and more capitalist than Adam Smith. In so doing he nullified its power as a form of activism. Identified so closely with American values, cooperation ceased to offer an alternative to the dominant political culture. And Kallen's insistence that the emergence of a cooperative economy was inevitable transformed cooperation into the ultimate laissez-faire ideology. If the cooperative consumer society was as inevitable as Kallen maintained, then consumers need not agitate on its behalf. Consumer activism could, in essence, become consumer passivism.

That cooperative theory in the United States became increasingly conservative in the late nineteenth and early twentieth centuries should come as no surprise. When American cooperative theorists turned to a European form of radicalism for an American audience, they found it necessary to emphasize the extent to which that radicalism was compatible with basic American principles. But the more successfully they rooted cooperation in an American political language, the more likely it was that cooperative theory would cease to represent a radical alternative to the existing system. True, it might not advocate the same means as the existing system but, at least theoretically, it championed the same ends. And so doing it became conservative in the most literal sense of that word, dedicated to conserving the most cherished of American political principles.

Notes

1. The classic discussion of American exceptionalism is Louis Hartz, *The Liberal Tradition in America* (New York, 1955). Dorothy Ross parts company with Hartz arguing that not only liberal ideas but also protestant and republican ones shaped American exceptionalism. See Dorothy Ross, *The Origins of American Social Science* (Cambridge, 1991). Michael Kazin traces the impact of an American political language in *The Populist Persuasion* (New York, 1995).

2. Ross, *The Origins of American Social Science*, 98-122 and "Socialism and American Liberalism: Academic Social Thought in the 1880s," *Perspectives in American History*, 11 (1977-8); Leon Fink, *In Search of the Working Class: Essays in American Labor History and Political Culture* (Urbana, 1994); James T. Kloppenberg, *Uncertain Victory: Social Democracy and Progressivism in European and American Thought, 1870-1920* (New York, 1986), esp. 207-12. On Wisconsin progressivism see David P. Thelen, *The New Citizenship: Origins of Progressivism in Wisconsin, 1885-1900* (Columbia, 1972).

3. Richard T. Ely, *The Labor Movement in America* (New York: Thomas Y. Crowell & Co., 1886), ix, 6.

4. Ely, *The Labor Movement in America*, 61, 113-114, 217-19, 286-94.

5. Ely was not the only intellectual to turn to cooperation as a solution to the problems caused by industrialization. Other late-nineteenth-century intellectuals who were drawn to cooperative ideas of one sort or another included Edward Bellamy, Laurence Gronlund, Horace Greeley, Edward W. Bemis, and Henry Demarest Lloyd.

6. Ely, *The Labor Movement in America*, 3-6, 77-78.

7. *Ibid.*, 97, 136-38, 147, 169-73, 185, 205-7, 296, 311-13, 325-26, 331.

8. The literature on the impact on political thought of puritan and republican aversions to luxury is immense. See, for example, J. E. Crowley, *This Sheba, Self* (Baltimore, 1974), 3-4, 34-36, 45, 76, 95, 102-10, 128; Drew McCoy, *The Elusive Republic* (Chapel Hill, 1980), 7-11, 16-26, 67-78, 236-37; Gordon S. Wood, *The Creation of the American Republic, 1776-1787* (Chapel Hill, 1969), 47, 52-53, 64-65, 108-18, 419-24; and John Sekora, *Luxury: The Concept in Western Thought, Eden to Smollett* (Baltimore, 1977).

9. Several immigrant groups brought with them their own national versions of cooperation to this country. Finns and Bohemians were especially active cooperators. See Carl Ross, *The Finn Factor in American Labor, Culture and Society* (New York Mills, Minn., 1980). African Americans also turned to cooperation. Their efforts were influenced both by African culture and slave experiences. See W. E. B. Du Bois, *Economic Co-operation Among Negro Americans* (Atlanta, 1907).

10. In the early nineteenth century Americans were influenced by Frenchman Charles Fourier as well as Englishman Robert Owen. By the 1860s, however, the Rochdale model began attracting converts, and British influence rose steadily after that. The Knights of Labor, for example, sought British advice and guidance with some frequency if the correspondence of John Samuel, Executive Secretary for the General Cooperative Board of the K of L, is any indication. John Samuel Papers (microfilm edition, 1976), State Historical Society of Wisconsin. Carl J. Guarneri, *The Utopian Alternative: Fourierism in Nineteenth-century America* (Ithaca, N.Y., 1991); Ronald G. Walters, *American Reformers: 1815-1860* (New York, 1978), 39-75; and Edward K. Spann, *Brotherly Tomorrows: Movements for a Cooperative Society in America, 1820-1920* (New York, 1989).

11. Foreword by E. R. Bowen in Beatrice Webb, *The Discovery of the Consumer* (New York, 1930). Introduction by John Graham Brooks in Albert Sonnichsen *Consumer's Cooperation* (New York, 1919), vi; Sonnichsen, *Consumers' Cooperation*, 44-45, 77-78, 175, 196; Horace Kallen, *The Decline and Rise of the Consumer* (New York, 1936), 182.

12. Beatrice Potter, *The Co-operative Movement in Great Britain* (London, 1891), 156, 167-68.

13. Potter, *The Co-operative Movement in Great Britain*, 168-69, 218.

14. Potter's merging of cooperation with trade unionism effectively silenced the Lasallean objection to consumer cooperatives, namely that such cooperatives could never lead to lasting change because any reduction in price that they facilitated would inevitably lead to a reduction in wages.

15. By the late nineteenth century British cooperatives had become involved in the manufacture of a number of goods carried by the cooperative stores. Such consumer cooperative factories were a far cry from the producer cooperatives of old. Producer cooperatives had been shops owned and managed by workers. Consumer cooperative factories were factories owned and managed by consumers.

16. Potter, *The Co-operative Movement in Great Britain*, 193-203.

17. Despite certain crucial differences, Ely and Potter (the future Beatrice Webb) shared much intellectual ground. See Kloppenberg, *Uncertain Victory*, 209; and Ross, "Socialism and American Liberalism," 35-37.

18. Potter, *The Co-operative Movement in Great Britain*, 204-6, 221.

19. The AFL did come out in favor of consumer cooperatives in the World War I period. See, for example, Colston Estey Warne, *Consumers' Cooperative Movement in Illinois* (Chicago, 1926); and Dana Frank, *Purchasing Power: Consumer Organizing, Gender, and the Seattle Labor Movement, 1919-1929* (Cambridge, 1994).

20. On agrarian cooperation and the populist movement, see Lawrence Goodwyn, *The Populist Moment: A Short History of the Agrarian Revolt in America* (Oxford, 1978).

21. In 1908 Bohemians organized a society at Dillonvale and in 1909 the Finnish immigrants established a store at Waukegan Illinois, each of which became a nucleus of a successful cooperative movement. Kallen, *The Decline and Rise of the Consumer*, 263.

22. By 1924, 333 societies with total membership of 50,000 and an annual business of almost $15,000,000 were affiliated with the League. Warbasse defined the League's duties as follows: "it collected all possible information concerning Co-operation in the United States; made surveys of failures and successes; published information; gave advice; standardized methods; created definite policies of action; prepared by-laws for societies; drafted bills to be introduced in legislative bodies; promoted favorable legislation; sent out advisors to societies; provided lectures; prepared study courses; conducted a school; published books, pamphlets, and periodicals; and in every way possible promoted practical Cooperation." James Peter Warbasse, *Co-operative Democracy* (New York, 1923), 437.

23. Kallen, *The Decline and Rise of the Consumer*, 252.

24. Sonnichsen, *Consumer's Cooperation*, 54.

25. Beatrice Potter, *The Co-operative Movement in Great Britain*, 202, 227, 238.

26. Albert Sonnichsen, *Consumer's Cooperation*, 211-12.

27. *Ibid.*, 185-86.

28. Potter, *The Co-operative Movement in Great Britain*, 190.

29. Sonnichsen did not reject all political action. He believed that cooperators would have to enter politics to defend themselves against restrictive legislation. He also believed that governmental regulation of industry and in particular of working conditions would be critical for the emergence of a cooperative democracy. Without such regulation cooperative attempts to upgrade labor conditions would prove a serious handicap in the competitive market. Only if private enterprise were forced through legislation to bear the cost of adequate working conditions in its factories could the two meet as equals in the marketplace. Sonnichsen, *Consumer's Cooperation*, 186-97.

30. As Potter saw it, the existing system had failed because competition had proved ineffective not only in guaranteeing economic equity and a democratic order but also in preventing waste and fraud. Sonnichsen, however, did not see the problem as the failure of a competitive system so much as the failure of a system to be competitive. Competition, in his view, was the only guarantee of a democratic order. Sonnichsen, *Consumer's Cooperation*, 193-99; Potter, *The Co-operative Movement in Great Britain*, 190.

31. Sonnichsen, *Consumer's Cooperation*, 192-93, 199, 203.

32. Potter, *The Co-operative Movement in Great Britain*, 239-40.

33. Sonnichsen, *Consumer's Cooperation*, 187.

34. *Ibid.*, 212-15.

35. *Ibid.*, 203.

36. Warbasse, *Co-operative Democracy*, viii, 41.

37. The Alliance had been established in 1896 as an international federation of cooperatives. It held semiregular meetings to which national cooperative organizations sent delegates. By establishing such an international framework for cooperation, the Alliance facilitated the exchange of cooperative ideas among the member nations. Sonnichsen, *Consumers' Cooperation*, 82-84.

38. *Ibid.*, 289-93.

39. *Ibid.*, 8, vii-ix, 268-72, 281, 295, 311.

40. Sonnichsen, *Consumer's Cooperation*, 211-12.

41. Warbasse, *Co-operative Democracy*, 57, 235.

42. Warbasse, *Co-operative Democracy*, viii, 309.

43. *Ibid.*, vii, 13.

44. Potter had seen the state as nothing more than an association of consumers and thus did not consider it a threat to democratic society. Potter, *The Co-operative Movement in Great Britain*, 229-32.

45. Warbasse, *Co-operative Democracy*, vii-ix, 114-16, 268-72, 281, 295, 311.

46. Peter Kropotkin, *Mutual Aid* (New York, 1902), xvi-xvii, 293-300.

47. Warbasse, *Co-operative Democracy*, 370-71.

48. Warbasse, *Co-operative Democracy*, 367-68.

49. *Ibid.*, 126-32.

50. *Ibid.*, 131-32.

51. In the twenties interest in consumer cooperatives once again declined. As prices fell and consumers found themselves with access to easy credit, consumption inequities ceased to be a concern for much of the population. By 1928 only 138 cooperative societies were still affiliated with the League although these did represent a combined membership of 77,843. Only in the farming regions, where twenties "prosperity" failed to make itself felt did interest in cooperative enterprises continue. But as "twenties prosperity" gave way to the Great Depression large numbers of Americans again became interested in issues of consumption, and consumer cooperation was once more on the rise. Ellis Cowling, *Co-operatives in America: Their Past, Present and Future* (New York, 1938), 110; Florence E. Parker, "Consumers' Cooperation in the United States" *The Annuals of the American Academy of Political and Social Science* (May 1937): 98-99.

52. See, for example, Horace Kallen *Culture and Democracy in the United States* (New York, 1924), *Individualism: An American Way of Life* (New York, 1933) and *A Free Society* (New York, 1934).

53. Kallen, *Culture and Democracy in the United States.*

54. Kallen, *The Decline and Rise of the Consumer,* 50.

55. Kallen, *The Decline and Rise of the Consumer,* vii-xi, 12-13, 268-72, 281, 295, 311. Adam Smith quoted on p. 22.

56. *Ibid.,* xii, 52-54, 70, 86-87, 108.

57. *Ibid.,* ix-xii, 12-13, 23, 66, 331, 351, 405, 414.

58. *Ibid.,* 51.

59. *Ibid.,* viii-xiii, 12-14, 202-6.

60. *Ibid.,* xiii, 99, 422, 443.

Chapter 5

Labor's Great Arch: Cooperation and Cultural Revolution in Britain, 1795-1926

Peter Gurney

Political and Cultural Revolution

Historians have either ignored or largely misunderstood the important attempts made by British consumer cooperation to construct an alternative social and economic order. Preferring to label the movement "reformist" in an a priori manner, they have traditionally concentrated on labor's political challenge, which eventually found institutional form in the trade-union-sponsored Labour Representation Committee and soon after in the Labour Party. The significance of workers' attempts to construct a different way of life this side of the revolution—and consumer cooperation played a vital role here—continue to be seriously underestimated, and no full-length scholarly study of the movement has appeared since G. D. H. Cole's centenary history was published at the end of World War II.[1]

The distinction between political and cultural revolution—that is between profound transformations on the level of the state and the generation of alternative social and economic forms within civil society—provides a useful way of situating cooperative development in Britain in the late nineteenth and early twentieth centuries.[2] Cultural revolution cannot be understood as a single event but nor should it be regarded as a necessarily peaceful strategy that presupposes an easy accommodation with capitalism; it is not "evolution" in the dominant late-nineteenth-century sense of the term. Cultural revolution is a process, embedded in modes of behavior and social practice, involving the development of new modes of signification as well as new modes of production and consumption—these processes are inseparable. All this takes time, experience, struggle, memory. Cooperation can indeed be read as a form of cultural revolution, a transformation that was faltering and uneven but very different in conception and practice to ideologies that emphasised *the* revolutionary moment. British cooperators, I shall argue below, moved beyond "trade union consciousness," not by means of a vanguard party or an elite of

Webbian experts, but by utilizing and extending what cooperators termed the "art of association." As Ross McKibbin's work suggests, in Britain the cultural revolution represented by working-class associations, generally, preceeded and over-determined the political revolution before World War I.[3] What we need to consider then are the ways in which the political and cultural revolutions have interacted in both supportive and antagonistic ways as this dialectic could provide a much more illuminating explanatory framework than the tired antinomy between reform and revolution.

This essay contends that cooperators in late-nineteenth-, early-twentieth-century Britain attempted to build a bridge, materially and ideologically, between the competitive present and the cooperative future. The great arch metaphor is taken from E. P. Thompson's seminal essay, "The Peculiarities of the English" (1965). Thompson used this metaphor to describe the gradual construction of bourgeois civilization in England since the sixteenth century. More recently this notion has been brilliantly elaborated by Phillip Corrigan and Derek Sayer. The making of bourgeois civilization has always been contested as the authors explain.

> It is only through the struggles of the subordinated that the tyranny of social forms and practices . . . can be recognised for the fetters on the liberation of human capacities they are. It is only in such struggles that emancipatory social forms . . . are discovered. These, too, do not fall from the sky.[4]

The social forms that this chapter analyses did not fall from the sky but were actively created, tested, and changed. I intend to explore, very schematically, a part of the other side of the process of bourgeois state formation, an absence recognized by Corrigan and Sayer in their work. What follows is not an exhaustive treatment but an *argument* about the significance of cooperative culture. A wide repertoire of collective cultural forms were employed and developed by cooperators whose desires and ambitions have been effaced by what Thompson once famously referred to as "the enormous condescension of posterity." Consumer cooperation offered, then, an alternative economy and culture, a new mode of production and consumption, and a way of life based on the idea of community. For many British cooperators, cooperation was a great arch that bridged the capitalist and socialist worlds.

Genealogy

The cooperative movement grew out of the critique of an increasingly individualistic, market-orientated, and competitive mode of production and consumption in eighteenth-century England. In a tantalizing aside, E. P. Thompson once alluded to the continuities between early and later phases of cooperative history. According to Thompson, the "moral economy of the crowd" did not expire overnight but was "picked up by the early co-operative flour mills, by some Owenite socialists, and it lingered on for years somewhere in the bowels of the Co-operative Wholesale Society."[5] I shall return to the moral economy theme later. The flour mills Thompson referred to were established by the urban poor in various localities from at least the mid-eighteenth century; the dockyard workers of Woolwich and Chatham founded cooperative mills as early as 1760.[6] Maxine Berg has pointed to the lack of scholarly interest in these forms noting that "we know virtually nothing of the place of artisan structures or of cooperative alternatives in industrialization."[7] Bread of course was the staple diet of the common people and the conflicts that arose over its production, distribution, and exchange had often been intense during the eighteenth century. It is hardly surprising then that early efforts were made in this area.

A highly successful mill was established by workers in Hull in 1795 (a year of acute agricultural distress), which was given the appropriate title of the Hull Anti-Mill Co-operative Society. This mill and similar ventures in other ports (Whitby, Sheerness, and Devonport for example) were established by working people to provide cheap, unadulterated bread and liberation from the fraudulent practices of local millers and shopkeepers. In Hull the number of original members of the society was 1,435 and each subscribed 1s.1d. per week for four weeks, then 6d. per week for a further four weeks. The cooperators also received donations from the local gentry to the tune of about £350; with the French Revolution troubling their peace of mind the latter were happy to support an association they hoped would encourage social harmony and loyalist sentiment. The Anti-Mill was so successful that local millers indicted the society as a nuisance in 1810; the following year a Yorkshire jury "considered poverty a still greater nuisance" found in its favour. By 1891 the society had over 5,000 members and had sold £37,000 worth of flour during the preceding year.[8]

The early nineteenth century was punctuated by various phases of co-operative development, by waves of experimentation in collective associational forms invented and adapted for particular purposes. Many of these experiments were short-lived. Framework knitters in Nottingham in 1818, for example, founded a producers cooperative in an effort to cut out big hosiers and middlemen. The venture failed within a few months owing to weak organisation and lack of funds, and the workers resorted to strike action.[9] Social historians have recovered some of this rich history in recent years, especially in relation to the Owenite movement; we know a good deal about early Owenite cooperative stores and labour exchanges.[10] Importantly during this phase "co-operation" and "socialism" were synonymous terms. Cooperative stores were seen as a practical route to "Community" by George Mudie as early as 1821. In 1828 Dr William King published the *Co-operator* in which he promulgated a similar strategy. According to this journal some 300 co-operative trading associations had been established by 1830. The Owenite stores indicated that successful working-class associations could be built in the sphere of consumption and profits accumulated and later ploughed back into production. This mode of social transformation was preferable to and more practical than Owen's mixture of millenarianism and philanthropic patronage. In many localities these associations were forerunners of later cooperative stores. [11]

So too were those stores established by local Chartist groups in the late 1830s and early 1840s, about which we know much less. Owenism, especially on the theoretical level, tended to eschew the political sphere and regarded political agitation as diversionary. In contrast, Chartism prioritised this arena and sought to creatively relate the economic, political, and social. Chartist strategy—as outlined in the "Ulterior Measures" recommended by the Chartist Convention in 1839—consisted of an imaginative mixture of direct and indirect, "short" and "long," revolutionary tactics aimed at undermining the state. These included the establishment of a people's militia, the "Sacred Month" or general strike, as well as "exclusive dealing"—only trading with shopkeepers sympathetic to the democratic cause. The latter rapidly led to the formation of Chartist cooperative stores, again seen as a way of building a way out of the competitive world but this time closely connected to the question of state power. Here is the local Chartist leader James Sweet advocating cooperation in the pages of the *Nottingham Review* in 1840:

> To you who are of the slave class, who have no part in the constitution—to you who know and feel the miseries of the poor, who wish to be free in reality and not in name only—who wish your homes to be comfortable, your wives happy and your children educated—who wish to labour and enjoy the fruits thereof—I would point out a large part of your duty which you have too long neglected, and urge you to adopt it (exclusive dealing) without delay, and overthrow the tyranny that oppresses you and redeem your class from slavery, want and woe.[12]

Chartists thus regarded consumption as an intensely political sphere. The working-class domestic economy was usually controlled by women and they were particularly active in this crucial phase of cooperative development. [13]

The 1830s and 1840s was marked by moments of acute confrontation between an increasingly interventionist capitalist state and an organised working class. Chartist cooperation took on greater importance after the failure of direct, insurrectionary tactics in 1839. The defeat of the general strike of 1842 and the subsequent show trial of Chartist leaders forced the lesson home further and also set the parameters for a visibly modern system of labor relations and working-class association. Strict divisions were drawn between economic, social, and political activity during the trial; subsequently trades

unions could only legitimately pursue the former. After this date direct confrontation with the state became less prominent within working-class
transformative ideology and practice. Labor's political and cultural revolution
was fractured as the conquest of state power seemed less and less feasible.[14]

An increasing amount of associational activity was channelled into economic and social solutions to the inequality and oppression engendered by
competition: Chartist decline and cooperative success was synchronous in
many localities.[15] Importantly, working-class cooperators colluded in the
separation of spheres sketched above. The original rules of the Rochdale
Pioneers (1844) emphasized that politics should be kept out of cooperation and
despite the mythology it was this feature of the Rochdale model that was truly
innovative, not the discovery of the dividend.[16] In context such collusion was
understandable, though the repercussions were profound. Thus the "short"
revolution (on the level of politics and the state) and the "long" revolution
(building collective, social forms, constructing labor's great arch) were deliberately separated and named—described as legitimate or illegitimate —after a
series of violent social conflicts by the capitalist state during this period.

The modus vivendi among the English bourgeoisie, organized labor, and
the state was clearly symbolised by the Industrial and Provident Societies Act
of 1852. Drawn up mainly by the Christian Socialist J. M. Ludlow, who was
keen to "humanise" and regulate the new urban "masses", the Act was vigorously supported by liberal intellectuals such as J. S. Mill.[17] It simultaneously
conferred certain privileges and set certain limitations on co-operative practice.
The early stores had been bedevilled by their uncertain legal position and
officials frequently defrauded societies causing insolvency and sometimes ruin.
The 1852 Act placed cooperative societies in a similar position to Friendly
Societies, which meant that their funds were now protected against fraud.
Societies were forbidden, however, to engage in banking, mining, or wholesaling or to hold land. In 1855 the Act was amended making land-owning legitimate but disallowing expenditure on education. Limited liability and the right
to establish a wholesale society was not granted until 1862.[18]

Despite this protracted struggle and partial incorporation, cooperation
remained a threatening presence. Though they were often critical, revolutionary
Chartists like Ernest Jones and G. J. Harney continued to recognize the potential of cooperative forms. In the early 1850s, they urged cooperators to once
again connect their project with the political, short revolution.[19] This was also
Marx's advice in the *Inaugural Address of the Working Men's International
Association* (1864). He warmly praised cooperation claiming that it represented
a victory for the "political economy of labour" over the "political economy of
capital." Marx looked forward to a time when the capitalist mode of production would be replaced by a cooperative or associated mode of production and
opined: "The value of these great social experiments cannot be over-rated."

However, the immediate task was to foster cooperation "by national means," which involved the conquest of political power by the working classes.[20]

That Marx was not the only commentator to grasp this potential for the practical success of cooperation was clearly apparent by this time. Between the late nineteenth and early twentieth centuries the cooperative movement continued to grow at a remarkable pace and the statistics may be briefly noted. In 1881 there were 971 distributive societies in Britain with a membership of 547,000. Profits were divided among members according to the value of their purchases and redistributed as dividend or "divi," and a percentage was reserved for educational and recreational purposes. Profits were divided between members according to the value of goods purchased during a quarter; membership was conferred by the ownership of a £1 share, which could be bought with accumulated dividend. Stores were run democratically—members had the same voting rights regardless of the number of shares held. Education and recreation were arranged by elected educational committees, which regularly held delegate meetings throughout the country. Women were particularly active in these areas and in 1883 set up their own independent organization, the Women's Co-operative Guild (WCG), a body that could claim over 30,000 members—mostly working-class married women—by the First World War. Most local societies were members of the English or Scottish Co-operative Wholesale Societies (established in 1863 and 1868, respectively), subscribed to these bodies according to the size of their membership, and elected the boards of management. In 1883 the annual net sales of the English CWS amounted to over £4.5 million. The Co-operative Union, the movement's central, federal organization, furnished legal advice, published literature and propaganda, promoted cooperative education, and organized the Annual Congresses, held every spring from 1869. By 1920 there were 1,379 distributive stores in Britain with over 4.5 million members. The annual sales of the English CWS that year was over £105 million, making it one of the largest enterprises of its kind in the world.[21] The movement's visibility in the late Victorian and Edwardian periods contrasts vividly with its marginalization by recent historians: the numerous stores in working-class neighborhoods; the elaborate central emporia with their libraries, concert halls, and reading rooms in the centres of northern towns; and the boot and shoe, soap and jam, biscuit and hosiery factories made the cooperative movement a central feature of the urban landscape. The significance and meaning of this phenomenon were widely debated, for had not all this been achieved without the help or intervention of either experts or capitalists?

Moral Economy

The statistics were certainly impressive but financial success also made it possible for cooperators to build within the movement an alternative and sometimes oppositional culture or way of life, a rich and complex "signifying system."[22] Consumers' cooperation was frequently denounced for its "materialism" by middle-class observers in the nineteenth century—the Christian Socialist Thomas Hughes called it the "guts gospel" for example—and this charge has been rehearsed by many historians since.[23] A consideration of the content and meaning of cooperative culture will serve to challenge such simplistic formulations.

It would be misleading to separate the materialistic from the idealistic unproblematically, for the practice, ritual, and symbolism of cooperative trading itself helped constitute cooperative culture. As J. T. W. Mitchell, the late-nineteenth-century Chairman of the English CWS put it, "There was no culture that could surpass the culture of the co-operative store."[24] Shopping at and then becoming a member of the store was the most important point of entry to this culture. CWS goods were emblazoned with the wheatsheaf design, which represented the power of association. The dividend met many practical needs and its regular quarterly or half-yearly distribution—the "divi day"—punctuated the annual cycle of working-class community life. An anonymous contributor to the *Failsworth Co-operative Messenger* in 1913 recommended cooperation thus:

> I thank the day I became a co-operator. I have been a widow for fifteen years, and had to earn my own living, and thankful that I have my 'divi' to draw at the quarters' end—it pays for coal. . . . The advice of my mother, a staunch co-operator, who died at the age of ninety-one, was 'keep true to the store and the store will keep true to you.'[25]

Working-class women, who frequently had to negotiate a narrow path between scarcity and survival, made up an ardent rank and file. The dividend was often used for major purchases—coal, clothes, furniture, holidays. The usefulness of this form became part of the common sense, which helped working-class families make ends meet.

According to many local and national cooperative activists the project of the movement was to moralize economic relations. As Edward Jackson explained in his history of the Bristol Society, "the extension of the cooperative method induces a great moral awakening among the shareholders . . ."[26] This was the crucial difference between the capitalist joint-stock form of collective ownership, where shares meant individual power, and the democratic, cooperative form. Jackson linked nineteenth-century cooperation, because of this moral dimension, to the medieval guilds. He proposed that the medieval idea of industry, underpined by the teachings of the Church, was "essentially moral," and that the idea that there was a value-free domain called the economy, where moral sensibilities could be suspended, was at that time unknown. Jackson described the workings of the local tailors guild that regulated competition and provided sickness benefits and concluded, "the Co-operative movement of today sets out to exhibit the same spirit of fraternity . . ."[27] The movement sought to abolish profit and regulate fairly the relationship between buyer and seller, producer and consumer. The isolation of the economy as a neutral sphere, as Jackson well understood, was a major intellectual and practical achievement for capitalism, theorized most famously of course by Adam Smith in the *Wealth of Nations* in 1776.[28]

So cooperators attempted to rework this category by posing moral questions and utilizing a moral vocabulary. In a sense CWS cocoa, Holyoake boots and Pelaw soap were the "concrete form" in which the "intellectual and moral reform" effected by cooperation presented itself.[29] Cooperative trade and cooperative goods were "honest," unlike the adulterated, overpriced, or shoddy commodities competition generated. The success of competitive commodities, it was argued, depended increasingly on advertising, a form of legalised fraud and trickery. The advertising industry was revolutionized and professionalized in the 1880s and 1890s in conditions of large-scale capitalism, as Raymond Williams has observed.[30] J. T. W. Mitchell agreed that cooperators should be well-informed about cooperative productions but hoped cooperators would avoid advertising, a mode that he once called, "the Barnum wickedness of the competitive world."[31]

Outside commentators sometimes drew attention to these differences. In his revised *History of Socialism* (1900), the antistate socialist Thomas Kirkup sounded this warning to the movement's detractors:

> it should also be said that many of the objections raised by the critics of the movement are really due to the fact that they do not understand its real nature, and imagine that they find old things where really they meet only old names.[32]

Seven years later, the editor of the *Wheatsheaf* contrasted the terms used in capitalist and cooperative enterprise:

> The word 'director' is associated with the autocracy of capital, with mastership; while to speak of a 'shareholder' is to bring to the mind an image of a mere investor anxious only for his dividends. It is different with 'member'; that word stands for a man who, so far from having taken shares in a speculative profit-making company, has entered an industrial brotherhood which aims at abolishing the system of profit-making altogether.[33]

We may note once again the moral language employed, though the editor's apologetics were somewhat misleading; cooperation also had "directors" and "shareholders," as well as individuals whose fundamental motivation was the "divi" and we must be careful not to simply conflate the opinions of local and national activists with those of the majority membership. Nevertheless, the "old names"—and Kirkup's observation was incisive here—did not correspond exactly to the "old things," the practices and morality of industrial capitalism. For cooperation sought to replace this system with a new moral economy, an associated mode of consumption and production that was different from the paternalist model that had existed before the triumph of the "free" market and bourgeois individualism, but similar in the sense that the ultimate ambition was to reintegrate the economy into the common social life of the people.

Cultures of Cooperation

This moral sensibility infused the movement: cooperative recreation it was hoped would communicate these modes of thought and feeling. A wide range of social activities were organized around the nexus of the store. The repertoire of forms included tea parties and soirées, exhibitions of cooperative productions, festivals, choirs, galas, field days and outings, demonstrations and marches—here is the British equivalent of the the cultural construction that characterized the Social Democratic Party in Germany before World War I. Cooperative social life provided a sense of belonging, a collective identity that valued all members as equals. Cooperative culture attempted to remake social relations, not on the morrow of the revolution, but in a present itself seen from its other side.[34]

The commonest form of recreational activity was the tea party or soirée, which had been used by Chartists and Owenites in the 1840s.[35] At these meetings, usually held during the winter months, food and nonalcoholic refreshment was served to members and their guests, followed by music and dance. The meal was often optional in an effort to reduce cost and maximize participation. The ban on alcohol was important; these events were family based and offered an alternative to the male-dominated culture of the pub. They became very popular from mid-century onwards. G. J. Holyoake described the tea parties organized by the Leeds Society in the mid-1860s.

Not liking the prevailing system of trade-puffing and advertisements, and yet needing publicity for the business carried on, a series of tea meetings were devised in various parts of the town, and a free ticket was given to all members who applied for them. Thus a great number of the members were brought together, when a new social feeling and better knowledge of the society were the results. The number of members who partook of these teas was 2,500.[36]

The tea party served as an alternative to developing forms of capitalist advertising and simultaneously constructed "a new social feeling" based on equality and fellowship—at least this was the ideal. By the early 1870s these events were a regular feature of working-class life, especially in Lancashire and Yorkshire. A lecture on cooperation was invariably sandwiched between musical entertainment in an effort to increase membership. Local societies subsidized socials from their educational funds and the Educational Committees organized both education and recreation. As James Clay noted in his history of the Coventry Society, the intention was to provide both education and "the means of social life."[37] In cooperative discourse the keyword "social" carried strong Owenite resonances; Owenite lecturers had been known as "Social Missionaries" in the 1840s. The word suggested warm, mutualistic relationships and carried an emphatic rejection of individualist forms of ownership and pleasure.[38]

Cooperative exhibitions also served to proselytize the message. Exhibitions of industrial goods had enjoyed great popularity among working people long before the Great Exhibition of 1851. They had been organized by Mechanics Institutes in the 1830s in an attempt to create better taste in the lower orders and triumphantly display products of English skill and industry.[39] Local cooperators made increasing use of this cultural form from the 1870s, though with different intent—an exhibition featured as part of the Derby Society's jubilee celebrations in 1900, for example. It was held in the Drill Hall, which had a capacity of 4,000 and included fustian from Hebden Bridge, hosiery from Leicester, clothing from Kettering, and cutlery from Sheffield. The hall was decorated with numerous banners and the "great names of co-operative heroes." Speeches were given followed by music from the Derby Co-operative Choral Society and Orchestra. The proceedings rounded off with "an exhibition of the cinematograph and limelight views of co-operative production and prominent advocates of co-operation."[40]

Exhibitions were indices of material success and served to promote cooperative production, but they also signified the necessity for working-class independence. Utopian readings of these events multiplied in the years before the First World War. In 1913 the historian of the Cainscross Society drew the following lesson from an exhibition held in the mid-1890s:

> Up to this time local co-operators, while long familiar with a shop or store as
> a centre of Co-operative distribution had no conception that the working
> classes owned mills, factories, and all the instruments of production.[41]

At an exhibition held in the Oldham Co-operative Hall around the same time, J. T. Taylor, Chairman of the Educational Committee, declared that:

if Co-operation must be the success which its founders desired it should be, not only must they distribute that which was produced, but they must produce that which was distributed. The promoters of that exhibition wished to make it an object lesson in the study of co-operation. [42]

Goods from twenty-five societies were displayed and the hall was decorated with banners, mottoes, and flags. Exhibitions like these were "crystal palaces" for working people. These spectacles, however, did not reify the goods as autonomous icons abstracted from history, but simultaneously celebrated and situated them within a cycle of working-class production, distribution, and consumption. [43]

The movement constructed and articulated a specific cooperative identity then, one which expressed a commitment to inclusive, democratic, and collective cultural forms, self-provided by the working class. The enthusiasm for music is instructive here. An editorial in the *News* in 1884 entitled "Music for the Millions" advocated the establishment of groups for musical practice, linked to the stores. Sol-fa classes and glee clubs were regarded as especially important for young members because they encouraged indigenous talent, which would render expenditure on outside vocalists unnecessary. [44] Again cost was an important consideration. It was much cheaper to train working-class people to sing, especially using the sol-fa method perfected in the mid-nineteenth century, than it was to provide large numbers of instruments. By 1904 seventeen societies in Lancashire and Yorkshire were members of the North West Choral Association, which helped establish singing classes for adults and children. [45] At one of the Association's meetings in 1914 (it now had thirty-six member societies) held in the Bolton Co-operative Hall, Mr Fairbrother underlined the utopian function of harmonic singing: "Co-operation receives a great impetus from the musical side of its work . . . They wanted co-operative festivals to be the prophets preparing the way for the Co-operative Commonwealth." [46] There was a great deal of local talent and societies often staged their own productions of Handel's *Messiah* or Haydn's *Creation* and competed, often successfully, in national music festivals. [47] Moreover, such cultural activity could easily be turned to more overtly political ends; concerts were sometimes staged to raise funds for workers engaged in conflict. The London branch of the Co-operative Printing Society, for example, held a concert for employees in March 1901. The aim was to raise money for the locked-out Penrhyn Quarrymen of South Wales. [48] The Pendleton Society's brass band performed on the town's streets in the early months of 1913 and collected money for striking miners. [49]

Cooperators also took to the streets to proclaim the cooperative gospel. Demonstrations were held to celebrate the opening of a new branch store, a hall or some other large investment. At these moments working people took control of public territory with a display of self-confidence and pride. In 1900 a demonstration took place in south east London, organised by the Royal Arsenal Co-operative Society, to commemorate the construction of the Bostal housing estate, or the "Co-operative town" as *Comradeship* described it. (Roads were named after Owen and Holyoake.) Fifty vans and carts drawn by about eighty horses proceeded from the Central Stores in Woolich to the estate to erect a memorial tablet. The route took them through the principal streets of Woolwich, Charlton, and Plumstead and they arrived at the estate at 4 p.m. after two hours. Thousands were then entertained by a brass band. Celebrations continued into the evening at the Drill Hall, where about 2,000 people sat down to a tea and concert.[50] Events like these were particularly suitable for children and most societies also held outdoor galas and special Children's Days in the summer months from the late nineteenth century, which included singing, refreshments, games, and sports.

Such events contrasted with militaristic rituals of state and populist displays of community belonging orchestrated by paternalistic capitalist employers, such as factory celebrations or competitive exhibitions.[51] Co-operators sometimes made this point explicitly. In 1902 the *Wheatsheaf* described a demonstration in Accrington in which over 6,000 children participated. Marching six-deep and carrying the society's banners, the procession was almost a mile in length. Girls dressed in white were garlanded with flowers and two bands played along the route. The correspondent noted:

> Scarlet coats, gleaming helmets and glittering bayonets may look pretty in a procession, but they are too closely connected with violence and destruction to commend themselves to all. A cheerful and prettier sight, speaking only of cheerful industry and mutual help, was afforded by the demonstration recently promoted by the Educational Department and the Women's Guild at Accrington.[52]

The recent experience of the Boer War undoubtedly made such oppositions clearer. These demonstrations had a carnivalesque atmosphere and dramatised that in fact as well as in imagination the world was being turned upside down by cooperation.

Cooperative values and practices were inscribed in the social life of the movement but they were also communicated explicitly. The repertoire of educational forms employed was extensive and included the cooperative press, libraries and reading rooms, and lectures and classes; late-nineteenth-century co-operators were as committed to education as Owenites had been in earlier decades. Again, inclusivity and informality were key features and this was important, particularly to working-class housewives.[53] Spare time to attend lectures or classes was a rare luxury for women whose domestic labour often took up the whole day. Mrs Wrigley, who joined the Oldham Society in the mid-1870s, later recalled: "What I have read has been Guild and Co-operative literature and newspapers, for I have learnt a great deal through newspapers."[54]

The national publications were the *Co-operative News* (weekly from 1871), the *Wheatsheaf* (monthly from 1896), a photo-journal, *Millgate Monthly* (from 1905), and *Our Circle*, a children's paper (monthly from 1907). The circulation of the *News* disappointed the hopes of many and only topped the 100,000 mark at the end of World War I.[55] The *Wheatsheaf*, which was intended to serve local interests and publicise the Wholesale's productions, had a much wider circulation, 0.5 million by 1918.[56] Many societies also produced their own monthly or quarterly records from the 1870s. In 1916 there were 32 local records with a monthly circulation of 212,000.[57] The free distribution of these records accounted for a large proportion of local societies' educational expenditure. If we add to these publications the plethora of cooperative pamphlets and books we can begin to appreciate the key role the printed word played in cooperative culture.

Cooperative libraries were a central feature of educational provision. Perhaps the most famous was the one opened by the Rochdale Pioneers in 1849. Built up from donations at first, by 1870 a library of 7,000 volumes was housed in the Central Store. In 1876 the library held 12,000 volumes and had a circulating reference section; fiction and literature were the largest categories making up a total of 3,900 volumes, though history and biography were also popular. The central newsroom supplied twenty-seven daily and fifty-five weekly papers in the mid-1870s. By 1887 the movement spent £23,256 per annum on educational grants and over half this figure went to provide reading rooms and libraries, which stocked a total of 200,000 volumes.[58] The Oldham Society, for example, had a central library in 1895 of 18,800 volumes, which boasted a popular Ladies Room. The society also supported twenty newsrooms, established at branch stores in working-class neighbourhoods, which were supplied with a total of 787 papers each week.[59] Such initiatives helped secure the future progress of cooperation, for as Savage's work on Preston has ably demonstrated, the success of the movement was intimately connected to its rootedness in working-class neighbourhoods.[60] A central store in the middle of town with an impressive library and well-stocked reading rooms was all very well as a showcase, but the movement also had to reach working-class people where they lived if it was to become part of the texture of social and cultural life. The survey carried out by the "Special Committee of Enquiry on Education," which reported to the 1897 Congress, revealed that out of 296 societies, 376 reading rooms were maintained by 95 societies and 131 societies supported libraries with a total stock of nearly 350,000 volumes. The total annual cost of this provision was £16,600.[61]

The movement also developed formal and systematic instruction in cooperative classes. These were commenced in 1883 but the real growth in this area occurred from the turn of the century. In the 1902-1903 session 1,664 adults attended classes and by 1914 the number had risen to 5,176. Subjects included bookkeeping and accounting, cooperative history and theory, economics, and citizenship. The largest expansion in this area was in classes for junior co-operators, organised by the WCG from the late 1880s. The movement produced a textbook for children in 1903 entitled *Our Story*, written by Isa Nicholson. By 1911 it had sold 61,000 copies. It was republished for the ninth time that year in a penny illustrated edition that ran to 250,000 copies.[62] This text related in simple prose the horrors of industrialisation, Owen's role, the revolution effected by the Pioneers, and the progress of the modern movement. Fred Abbotts, a Walsall cooperator who attended these classes before the First World War and later went on to be a class teacher, has recalled this experience.

> There (in the class) we were given a book to read. It was a sort of text-book for junior classes called *Our Story* by Nicholson. You read the childish version of the Rochdale Pioneers, and of course I used to know the thing off by heart almost, and I became very interested in the educational side.[63]

How many other working-class children were inspired in this way can only be guessed at, but the strength of the movement in the interwar years may have been due in part to this initiative. By 1914 16,777 children attended classes in junior cooperation.[64]

Why was education so important to cooperators? First, because they were as critical of inequalities in the consumption and production of knowledge as they were of inequalities in the consumption and production of material goods. In 1876 J. T. W. Mitchell declared:

> co-operators believed education to be one of the best elements in their system. They not only wanted to make money, but they desired to make themselves into men and women, and to cultivate their minds. By education they could make themselves equal to the highest and noblest in the land. Why should the children of any of those whom he saw before him have an inferior education to the Queen upon the throne. (Hear, hear). Working people and their children ought to possess as great a share of the luxuries of this world as any nobleman that breathed . . .[65]

Mitchell argued that cooperators should not accept a second-rate education but should strive to "supply an education that was equal to any that could be got at any of the universities either in Oxford or Cambridge." Logie Barrow's concept of a "democratic epistemology" is useful here. In his work on plebeian spiritualism in nineteenth-century England, Barrow argues that particular spiritualist and medical discourses depended on democratic theories of knowledge. Such theories were open, privileged empiricism, encouraged suspicion toward established intellectuals and professions and were often in conflict with increasingly dominant elitist epistemologies. [66] Cooperative knowledge was open to all as we have seen and no democratic epistemologist could have been more empirical or suspicious of outside intellectuals than J. T. W. Mitchell. [67] Cooperative truths could be easily summarized and cooperative knowledge performed a demystifying function, further characteristics of a democratic epistemology according to Barrow.

Second, as Mitchell clearly understood, working-class knowledge depended on association; theory was of little use unless it was linked to a liberating practice: intellectual and material liberation were intertwined in the cooperative project. As the American radical H. D. Lloyd observed after a tour of Britain in 1897: "At a very early period in the movement, co-operation set before itself the task of becoming mentally independent as being quite as important as that of becoming independent in its groceries."[68] Cooperative education, it was thought, depended on and also facilitated successful association because it strengthened affective bonds between members. The relationship between cooperative education and association was symbiotic; co-operative knowledge was more than the accumulation of certain ideas and facts, it implied a particular sensibility, one which emphasized humanity's social nature. Holyoake repeatedly articulated this idea.

> The education fund created by the Pioneers was to prepare members for 'companionship'. They did not require classical, scientific and historical knowledge in order to sell oatmeal and candles. It was the social education which goes before and after which they had primary need.[69]

The movement's local and national leadership shared Holyoake's belief that the "art of association" had to be based on alternative values and an altruistic psychology—character formation was a common preoccupation. Employing a typically religious idiom at the Leicester Congress in 1877, Mitchell explicitly linked cooperative education to social transformation:

> let them promote the diffusion of that knowledge and the boon of education which would extinguish superstition and jealousy, and they would have that bond of united interest which no power on earth could break asunder—they could free themselves from the toil and misery which oppressed them; they could make for themselves a heaven upon earth. (Cheers)[70]

In fine, cooperators believed in and supported education because they regarded it, as had the Owenites, as the motor for social and economic change.

Third, cooperators recognised that this type of education would not be provided by private capital or the state. Indeed cooperative initiatives in this field had often been directly prohibited by law. As I noted above, the movement gained legal recognition in 1852, but in 1856 the Industrial and Provident Societies Act was amended, making expenditure on recreation and education illegal.[71] The repercussions were considerable. After 1852 the Rochdale Pioneers had revised their rules in light of the new Act and included the provision of 2 percent of profits for educational purposes. Many other societies, especially those established after this date, copied these rules in toto.[72] The amendment of 1856 meant that many societies were therefore breaking the law. The Failsworth Society, for example, registered its rules in 1859 and included a clause relating to instruction and recreation. Mr Tidd Pratt, the Registrar of Friendly Societies, struck out this clause because of its technical illegality. Although this restriction was lifted by an Act of 1862, the Failsworth Society did not make a grant again for these purposes until 1868.[73] The same thing happened to the York Society, established in 1858. This setback was more serious; the society made no provision following Tidd Pratt's veto until 1899.[74] Most societies, however, simply ignored the law. In his history of the Pioneers, Holyoake described the newsroom, library, and mutual improvement class maintained by the society throughout the 1850s, regardless of the hostile legislation.[75] Recognition from the state carried certain protections, but also attempted to limit and contain working-class association. At a conference in 1888, the Reading cooperator W. T. Carter put the matter very bluntly when he pointed out: "They would never get a proper system of education until the working classes took it out of the hands of the State, and under their own management."[76]

Cooperative culture had to compete with capitalist forms of business, learning, and pleasure. In the field of recreation the major alternative attractions in this period were the pub, the betting shop, and the music hall. Competitive forms of education were purveyed by state schools and the capitalist press. Co-operators critiqued these forms, attempted to transform working-class manners and morals in radical ways, and provided an alternative to the showy delights held out by leisure entrepreneurs: "In recreation, as well as in business, we should be pioneers and reformers," ran an editorial in the News in 1903.[77] To see this intervention as part of a generalized "culture of consolation," that helped defuse and contain revolutionary potential is very unhelpful.[78] Co-operative recreation was certainly rational, designed to be "of a fairly high tone" which would "elevate and purify," and thus strengthen association.[79] The cooperative press, in the main, was didactic and serious, a world away from Newnes's penny Tit-Bits or Northcliff's Answers. The problem, of course, was that many working people could not live up to such demanding ideals all the time and continued to desire the consolation of drink, bawdy humor and romantic novels. Occasionally this led some of the movement's leaders to lose patience with those members of the working class who continued to be seduced by the lure of the music hall or the yellow press.[80] This response stemmed not from a desire for respectability, but was a corollary of co-operators' utopianism. For those like Thomas Tweddell, vice president of the CWS, cooperative culture brought nearer and prefigured a time when "the whole community" would constitute the movement—"then Socialism will be triumphant."[81]

Utopianism

This ambition deserves further consideration. In his *Co-operative Production* (1894), Ben Jones admitted that the Owenite community ideal was no longer feasible but maintained that cooperators followed

> the philosophy advocated in the Brighton tracts of 1828-9; which was, to begin with what they could do, however small, and gradually go on from this, until they co-operated for everything. When this is accomplished we shall, though it may not be in the form usually understood, then have a co-operative community. [82]

Jones reached back to the old language of community to describe the ultimate aim. The notion that it was possible to sidestep capitalism had been proved unfeasible in the 1840s; the system had to be contested and unmade in the streets and neighborhoods where people lived and worked. Community had to be built from the bottom up.

Commenting on the debate between "individualism" and "collectivism" from the 1880s, Stefan Collini has written that, "In the immense literature which was thus generated, the older Utopian tradition was largely eclipsed by the newly-important State Socialism."[83] In the cooperative movement, however, this tradition and the language of community persisted. At the National Cooperative Festival in 1907 William Openshaw of the CWS observed:

> Almost every variety of the necessaries of life was now co-operatively produced, but co-operators had a long way to go before they reached the end they had in view, viz., to become a practically self-supporting and self-employing community, co-extensive with the limits of the civilised world.[84]

This neo-Owenite discourse pervaded the movement. Catherine Webb published an article on "The 'Community' Idea" in the *Millgate Monthly* that year. She described the work of the Owenite feminist Mary Hennell, agreed that cooperators should control the land but recognized that moving out of the urban environment was no longer viable:

> It seems to me that today, in the building up of a co-operative community, we are not called upon to separate ourselves wholly from the social common life of the people. Indeed we cannot if we would.[85]

She went on to argue that the community impulse was stronger now than it had been in Owen's day because of the accumulation of cooperative capital, the existence of trained working-class men and women, and the legal right to associate. What was required was the proper application of these resources, to "carry co-operation forward from a 'movement' to a 'commonwealth.'"

Though it is difficult to reconstruct exactly when the term entered cooperative discourse, by the turn of the century the eventual goal was commonly described as the "Co-operative Commonwealth." Writing in the late 1930s, W. H. Brown noted the general purchase this term now had in the movement and stated that he had been able to trace it to an address given by Dr. Garth Wilkinson, the spiritualist homeopath, to members of the St. John's Wood Cooperative Society in London in 1866.[86] The American Marxist, Laurence Gronlund, entitled his vision of a postrevolution society, *The Co-operative Commonwealth*, in 1886 and this usage is better known.[87] Officials of the CWS frequently imagined such a future. At the Leigh Society's jubilee celebrations in 1907, George Thorpe explained:

> when they went to purchase at their society, they supported purity of articles, shorter hours of labour, and higher renumeration, and the ultimate result would be that they would have a co-operative commonwealth in which the people would own the instruments of production and the capital, and use that capital in the production of their own goods and of the necessaries and conveniences of life. . . .[88]

CWS leaders, from the days of Mitchell, had often been the prophets of universalized cooperation; individuals like Lander, Maxwell, Openshaw, Tweddell, and Thorpe continued to disseminate the message, though they now had a new term for this project. Miles Parker, also a CWS official, opened new buildings for the Birkenhead Society in 1909 and offered the following advice:

> Co-operators needed to husband all their financial resources, so that they might secure for themselves the instruments of labour, which hitherto had been monopolised by the capitalists. But there were great financial forces against them, and it was only by standing shoulder to shoulder that they would succeed in obtaining the real co-operative commonwealth, in which all the necessaries of life would be made secure as well as every provision for old age. (Applause)[89]

Cooperators cited the success of the CWS as material proof that this was a perfectly rational utopia.[90] The editor of the local record of the Burnley Society reflected on the progress of this institution in 1912 and believed that it presaged the time "when everything we need may be supplied through co-operative channels." This would realize the movement's original ambition, which was to establish "the ideals of the Co-operative Commonwealth in our midst."[91]

To portray the CWS purely as the bearer of Owenite ideology and practice would be oversimplistic. The community idea and the Co-operative Commonwealth coexisted with a strong collectivist impulse, which threatened to undermine the more libertarian aspirations. It would be surprising if this were not the case as the CWS had to take advantage of economies of scale if it was to compete successfully with capitalist companies, and the problem of the democratic control of such a huge organization was immense. William Lander, for example, embraced "collectivism" whole-heartedly before World War I; Percy Redfern, the official historian of the CWS, described himself as a "collectivist" in 1910.[92] It was by no means certain that the communitarian impulse would triumph over the collectivist for different currents competed within the movement. Cooperation had to struggle with its own project and against hostile outside alternatives simultaneously.

It is also difficult to quantify the prevalence of the desire for a Co-operative Commonwealth in this period. Nevertheless, universalistic aims were commonly articulated and should not be marginalized as merely rhetorical. Critical outside observers recognized this. Kirkup believed that the movement represented "a new society rising in the midst of the old."[93] The Russian anarchist, Peter Kropotkin, who had detailed knowledge of the movement, emphasised that many cooperative ideologues believed that cooperation led "mankind to a higher harmonic stage of economical relations," and argued that:

> it is not possible to stay in some of the strongholds of co-operation in the North without realising that the great number of the rank-and-file hold the same opinion. Most of them would lose interest in the movement if that faith were gone.[94]

In the discourse sketched above the keyword "Commonwealth" appealed to co-operators because it carried the meaning, from the early seventeenth century at least, of a society in which supreme power was vested in the democratic will of the people. Coupling it to "co-operative" conferred an antistatist orientation, which had been subordinated within the Commonwealth established during the English revolution in 1649.[95] Within this teleological framework "co-operation" signified a transition phase between capitalism and the Co-operative Commonwealth.

During the First World War this imagined utopia became more concrete. In 1916 the editor of the *Plymouth Co-operative Record* articulated this hope in a local context. T. W. Mercer saw illimitable possibilities around the corner:

> As our trade increases in volume the General Committee will be emboldened to add department to department and store to store, to undertake new services

and enter new industries, until the society broadens into a self-supporting, self-sufficing co-operative community.[96]

In the same year the Co-operative Survey Committee presented a report to Congress that looked forward to the speedy establishment of a Co-operative Commonwealth. Mercer rejoiced at the decision to widen the objects of the Co-operative Union and give prominence to this notion; all member organizations from this time had to accept this declaration of principle—recognition and authorization from above of a desire long-articulated within the movement.[97] The Walsall cooperator, Fred Abbotts, was profoundly affected by the ferment engendered by the war. Abbotts had no sense of cooperation as a total alternative to capitalism until he returned from the trenches, started a local branch of the Co-operative Party, joined the International Co-operative Alliance, and saw how cooperation was spreading throughout the world. Reflecting on the widespread desire for social transformation he remarked: "At the end of his (Bonner's) book is a chapter on the Co-operative Commonwealth. Now all that sounds ridiculous today, but it wasn't ridiculous then. . . . There was that kind of looking forward, something better. . . ."[98]

Contradictions

I have argued that cooperative culture in Britain represented a vital component of labor's great arch and have consequently stressed the movement's positive contribution against the grain of historiographical orthodoxy. We are left with an obvious though no less important question: given all the activity, commitment, and ambition, what happened to the dream of the Co-operative Commonwealth? This is a complex question and in the remainder of this essay I can only suggest some possible lines of enquiry and explanation. In general my discussion of cooperative praxis has been necessarily simplified and one-sided. The historical reality was far more contradictory, and an adequate critique and assessment must address these tensions.

Cooperators thought that social transformation depended on the gradual and peaceful expansion of the movement until capitalism was unmade and replaced by the Co-operative Commonwealth. The agency for change was the forms and practices of voluntary association that would sweep away the old world, as capitalism had replaced feudalism. However, prioritizing consumption within this strategy conferred mixed blessings. In the cooperative ideology of the majority movement understanding and transforming capitalist relations of production were subordinated to the transformation of exchange relations. Moreover, the language of community tended to conceal difference within as well as outside the movement.[99] The saliency given to the role played by particular forms of class conflict—namely violent confrontation with the state or the capitalist class—was also seriously curtailed. Indeed co-operators, like earlier utopian socialists, tended to regard class conflict negatively and usually emphasised class collaboration rather than the leading role of the working class.[100] This ideology of consumption conferred certain benefits and should not be regarded as inherently counterrevolutionary. Inclusivity and universality were real strengths—everyone in principle was a consumer—but sometimes obscured the fact that cooperation was a working-class association, which was in conflict with the ideas and practices of other classes and within which intraclass struggles were being waged.[101]

These disabling weaknesses found various expression. The movement's attitude to industrial action was often ambivalent, at least at the national level; strikes, it was widely believed, wasted valuable funds that could be put to much better use. The violent character of the labor unrest which preceeded the First World War, was frequently lamented in the cooperative press.[102] Moreover, the position and status of labor within cooperative enterprises often left a lot to be desired. Wages were hardly generous in the stores or the productive works. As William Paine, the Fabian socialist, observed in *Shop Slavery and Emancipation* (1912), many societies only paid managers 28s a week, as for the salesman: "His hours under the co-operative system are a little better, and his wages a little worse. The difference to him is merely the difference of the hand that holds the pincers."[103] Despite J. T. W. Mitchell's belief that "there was no higher form of co-operative production in the world than that carried on by the Wholesale Society," workers in CWS factories often disagreed and strikes were not uncommon.[104] As noted above, some of the Wholesale's ideologists were tending to drift away from association toward collectivism and this latter project, the doctrine of leading state socialists before World War I, promised no democratic reordering of heads and hands, but would leave intact the productive relations of large-scale capitalist industry. An uncritical acceptance, even celebration, of the division of labor and mechanization was characteristic of this mentality.[105]

Such contradictions exacerbated divisions within the developing labour movement. Cooperators were slow to break with Gladstonian Liberalism and side decisively with the Labour-socialist cause, although on the surface at least they shared a similar vision. Many factors were involved, not least the pull of local political traditions and loyalties. However, though they frequently courted the movement, leading socialists showed little understanding of or sympathy for cooperative aims. They quite rightly criticized cooperation for its failure to reach large sections of the poor who found it materially impossible to engage in association but simultaneously marginalized the movement's impressive achievements. The solution to the problem of the transition was best sought, they argued, on the terrain of the state. According to Ramsay MacDonald in *Socialism and Society* (1905), the Rochdale Pioneers had modelled cooperation "on the organisation of existing society. The rest was ornament. . . ." He maintained that cooperation undermined class unity because it reinforced divisions within the proletariat and inculcated the "capitalist frame of mind."[106] Fifteen years later MacDonald prophesied that the movement was destined to become merely "a function in the industrial State."[107] Other Labour and socialist leaders including Henry Champion, Harry Quelch, Harry Snell, the Webbs, Philip Snowdon, and Keir Hardie (but not, significantly, Tom Mann) shared this negative assessment. The prioritization of the state in Labour-socialist discourse was a real stumbling block to friendly relations and joint action at the national level, though the available evidence suggests that the picture was more diverse and complex within particular localities.[108] Cooperators were generally very suspicious of statist modes of social transformation and this attitude can no longer be simply dismissed as evidence of reformism.

Finally, and most importantly, the gender politics of the movement were highly ambiguous; there were major differences between the New Moral World envisaged by late-nineteenth-century cooperators and the Owenite's utopian vision. The family form was problematized within Owenism, which treated class and gender oppression as inextricably entwined. Cooperative ideologues, however, tended to obscure or conveniently forget Owen's critique of the family.[109] Women played a vital part in cooperative culture, indeed unlike trade unions or political associations, this was one of the defining features of the movement. It was generally admitted that without the support of women the stores would have failed miserably—consumption unlike production was regarded as woman's proper sphere. Cooperative women, however, did not have their own autonomous voice until the WCG was formed in 1883 and they had to constantly struggle, before and after this date, against prejudice from many male cooperators who believed that women's involvement should be confined to shopping at the stores and helping at social events.[110]

Organizing around consumption, through families, brought many positive benefits for working-class women, especially wives and mothers who had a large measure of control over the family budget. Cooperation was one of the strongest arenas for women's politicization, for their personal and collective empowerment as consumers and many thousands gained invaluable experience of democratic practice and public speaking and debate within the Guild.[111] Nevertheless, women exercised little formal control over the movement, as Margaret Llewelyn Davies was keen to point out when she became president of the Guild in 1907. Noting that open membership had only been secured in a few societies, she concluded:

> Men are in possession (of most societies) and mostly prefer to remain so. The existence of women is continually overlooked, much prejudice exists against women as women, and the lack of encouragement and sympathy given to their

aspirations towards social service have a dispiriting and paralysing effect on them.[112]

According to Llewelyn Davies, patriarchal attitudes were the "chief obstacle" to female activity. She stressed that women were recognized as capable of "making tea and singing songs," but were discouraged from addressing meetings though their experience "would be better suited to convert an audience of working women than a man's string of figures about CWS sales!"[113]

An awareness of the internal factors that worked against the realisation of the Co-operative Commonwealth must not blind us to the fact that there were very powerful external forces ranged against the movement. In many ways this situation worsened during the late nineteenth and early twentieth centuries. Private capital had threatened the movement from its inception and most societies had had to suffer boycotts and fight trade wars at some time in their history. The attack was nationally coordinated in 1902 with the formation of at least 14 Traders' Defence Associations. Although Crossick has argued that the "campaign died away in inactivity,"[114] it could be argued that this challenge was met and defeated by the movement. Private shopkeepers demanded that the state alter the income tax liability of cooperatives, which effectively meant taxing the surplus or dividend. The consequences for the movement would have been disastrous and this issue continued to be a focus of further struggles, from the end of the First World War through to the early 1930s.[115]

The rapid development of consumer capitalism and the concomitant system of modern advertising during this period represented a more profound challenge in the long run. What Mathias has referred to as the "retailing revolution" could be described as a counterrevolution that undermined the foundations of the Co-operative Commonwealth. Multiple shops started to appear from the 1870s and capitalist entrepreneurs began to make huge profits in the sphere of consumption. Thomas Lipton, for example, opened his first shop in Glasgow in 1871. Twenty years later there were more than 100 branches throughout the country employing over 5,000 people. When shares were offered to the public in 1898—total capital issued was £2.5m.—Lipton claimed to own over 400 shops and to employ 10,000 people around the world. Profits had risen from £68,000 in 1890 to £176,000 in 1897. Lipton had witnessed the power of advertising on an early trip to America and adopted an elaborate mode of persuasion and publicity in Britain. By the 1890s advertising expenditure had reached £40,000 annually.[116] These trends gathered increasing momentum from the turn of the century. Indeed this sector of the economy later provided one of the major sources of recovery for British capitalism in the depression years of the 1930s.[117]

Containment

Although powerful socioeconomic forces and the internal problematic of the ideology of consumption conspired against cooperative ambition, during the First World War real opportunities began to open up as the politics of food moved center stage. Initially the state treated the movement with disdain and ignored repeated demands for rationing. Cooperators were also excluded from the mechanisms of food control that were established, including local food committees.[118] This exclusion was particularly galling because the number of cooperators rapidly expanded during the war—from 3,054,000 in 1914 to 4,131,000 by 1919. This represented an average annual percentage increase of 6.2 percent compared to a rate of 3.6 percent during the six years preceding the war. Over 10 percent of the total retail sales of food and household goods were sold by Co-operative societies by 1918.[119] Activists reasoned that if any organization had the right to speak for working-class consumers it was the cooperative movement yet they had been deliberately denied a voice. Moreover, capitalist interests clamoured more vociferously than ever for the taxation of co-operative "profits."[120] The jubilee historians of the Coventry Society sketched a rather apocalyptic scenario in 1917.

> Observers of public events will have noticed the gathering of forces for another assault on the Co-operative position. The State's need of money is deemed to have provided the enemy with a favourable opportunity, and anti-co-operators are promulgating their doctrines under the thin disguise of 'Patriotism.' . . . Co-operators must actively prepare to defeat once and for all a powerful 'combine' of would-be spoilators.[121]

Faced with this hostility, cooperators, along with other sections of the labor movement, moved to the left. A "fusion of forces"—the coordination of trade unionism, cooperation, and Labour politics—was frequently advocated during this phase. The formal separation of political and economic domains, which had been codified during the mid-nineteenth century and that, as McKibbin has argued, underpinned the ideology of free trade in late Victorian and early Edwardian England, was becoming increasingly anachronistic and untenable.[122] The war dissolved the divide between economics and politics, at least temporarily, and the movement formally entered politics in 1917, establishing the Co-operative Party two years later.[123] The pressing fear—as the Coventry historians made clear—was that burgeoning monopoly capitalist interests, particularly within the sphere of consumption, might link up with a partisan state and then attack cooperation. Thus direct political action was now regarded as vital in order to protect the movement.

By the end of the war the Coalition Government headed by Lloyd George was deeply concerned about the possibility of a "fusion of forces." Consequently the cooperative movement was kept under surveillance from 1917 and the Home Office sometimes drew the Cabinet's attention to its progress in the weekly intelligence summary, the "Reports on Revolutionary Organisations."[124] The real test came in 1919. At the end of the war the miners, inspired by syndicalist ideas and the success of the Russian Revolution and strengthened by the formation of the Triple Alliance with railwaymen and dockworkers in 1914, demanded the nationalization of the mines. Lloyd George initiated the Sankey Commission to stall for time and on the eve of publication of the Commission's Interim Report in March, voiced his fears in a letter to Bonar Law:

> The miners I happen to know, are relying upon the Co-operative stores to feed them. The great co-operative supplies are outside the mining areas. They ought not to be removed. Once the strike begins it is imperative that the state should win. Failure to do so would inevitably lead to a soviet Republic.[125]

Although we may admit that that these remarks were somewhat histrionic, there was some cause for alarm. If separated and differentiated forms of working-class association united in struggle, the idea and existence of the state could be seriously challenged.[126] Labour's political revolution, buttressed by the material and ideological resources of its cultural revolution, could at last become a real possibility. Lloyd George probably intuited this.

In the event, the delaying tactics proved successful, though the situation remained highly volatile throughout the early 1920s. According to the liberal historian, C. L. Mowat, there existed "the makings of a civil war" at this time.[127] Faced with determined opposition and weakened by the onset of postwar depression, the Triple Alliance collapsed on "Black Friday" in April 1921 and the threat of a general strike was temporarily averted. The miners battled on alone, heavily dependent on the cooperative movement for material support. After the failure of this strike, relations between the cooperative and Trade Union movements steadily deteriorated. In 1925 it was estimated that during the 1921 miner's strike, the movement had given £526,322 to members of cooperative societies, £82,395 in loans and goods to the value of £639,962. These figures did not compare favorably with the sums forwarded to unions during the general strike in 1926, and the worsening relations between the movements was partly due to the fact that many miners' unions still owed co-ops money—about £200,000 in total in 1926. The situation got so bad that during the general strike Ernest Bevin ignored repeated deputations and stubbornly insisted that cooperative employees, like their fellow workers employed in capitalist concerns, stop work for the duration of the strike. He told the CWS that they "should go to the Government for assistance" over transport problems, though cooperative supplies were needed to feed striking communities.[128] Ironically, a corporatist labor leader like Bevin could by this time be almost as unsympathetic and antagonistic as Lloyd George had been during an earlier moment of crisis. Clearly the "fusion of forces," much to the relief of the British state, was no longer on the agenda.

Attempts to use the state to protect the interests of working-class consumers also failed in the 1920s. The Co-operative Party put up eleven candidates in the General Election of 1922 and four were elected.[129] Headed by A. V. Alexander, the cooperative group in the Commons maintained that "profiteering" was symptomatic of the rise of trusts and price-fixing associations; regulation was the only solution. Alexander was made parliamentary secretary to the Board of Trade in the Labour Government of 1924 but the fall of the government in October scotched hopes of intervention. The price of food and the issue of profiteering played a vital role in the General Election that followed. In a campaign designed to appeal particularly to those women and unorganized working-class voters enfranchised only six years before, the Conservative leader Stanley Baldwin repeatedly emphasised the rise in prices since 1918, blamed Labour for failing to deal with the problem, and promised an investigation: "There is no subject I am more eager to attack," he assured the electorate.[130] After the Conservative victory Baldwin made good his promise and set up a Royal Commission on Food Prices.

The commission, chaired by Sir Auckland Geddes, examined ninety representatives from the food trades. A number of leading cooperators were interviewed in January 1925, including Alexander himself who was badgered by Geddes for nearly a whole day. Geddes refused to recognize the difference between "profit" and "surplus," "consumer" and "member," and insisted that "you are really indistinguishable . . . from any big capitalist trust."[131] A few days later Lord Vesty and Sir Edmund Vesty were interviewed. Archetypal profiteers, the Vesty brothers controlled the Union Cold Storage Company Ltd., which by 1925 owned over 2,300 shops, cattle ranches, and meat works in South America, Australia; and New Zealand; cold stores throughout the United Kingdom, and a fleet of refrigerated steamers. Geddes immediately accepted the claim that they were making minimal profits and when more searching questions were asked forced the commission to take the rest of the evidence in private.[132]

The commission's report, published at the beginning of May 1925, held few surprises and completely exonerated big capitalists like the Vestys: "we do not bring any accusation of dishonest trading or of profiteering against dealers in wheat, flour, bread or meat," declared the commissioners in the preamble.[133] The only concrete proposal was for the establishment of a Food Council that would be a purely advisory body. Reviewing the report the *Co-operative News* once again underlined the need for state regulation of monopolies. As Alexander's Trust and Combines Bill had been blocked in the Commons in February, there now seemed very little hope that any effective legislation would be seriously considered by Parliament.[134] When the members of the Food Council were announced in the summer the story degenerated into farce, the chairman Lord Bradbury openly admitting that "his main qualification for the post was that he knew nothing about the subject."[135] Alexander made another unsuccessful attempt to introduce a Consumers' Bill after the second Labour Government was elected in 1929. At the annual conference of the Co-operative Party the following year, Fred Hayward argued that the modern trust had reinvented the practices of regrating, engrossing, and forstalling. He went on to draw the following contrast:

> Public opinion and the State a few hundred years ago regarded the 'cornering' of the people's requirements for personal advantage as a crime and a disgrace, and the person convicted thereof might well be lucky if he only had to sit in the pillory as the target for amusement, abuse and garbage. Today the person or persons who agree to hold up commodities until they can exact their own prices and conditions are not regarded by the State as criminals. Some people think them clever and call them 'captains of industry', and they are more likely to find a resting place in the House of Lords than in the public pillory.[136]

Aware that it was unlikely that cooperation would defeat consumer capitalists like the Vestys alone, Hayward once more emphasized the need for state regulation of the market. However, by this time it was clear that the best that could be hoped for was that the state would not actively persecute the co-operative movement, and only lukewarm support for the rights of the consumer could be expected from the Labour Party. The prospects were not encouraging.

The growth of monopolies continued apace during this period, a sign of the so-called rationalization of British industry. In manufacturing the share of the largest 100 firms of total net output rose from 16 percent in 1909 to 24 percent in 1935. In distribution the tendency was even more pronounced; multiples, department stores, and co-ops between them accounted for 10-13 percent of total retail sales in 1900 and this had risen to 33-39 percent by 1950. However, the co-ops' share of this market declined from about 1920-1921, even for food, the mainstay of its business.[137] Amalgamation was most marked in the food industry, which impinged directly on the co-op. The merger of the Margarine Union and Lever Brothers to create Unilever in 1929 is the best known example here. This company now dominated the "systems of provision"—in Fine and Leopold's terms—for a number of key commodities. The circuit of production, distribution, marketing, and consumption of soap, for example, could now be organised from the palm oil plantations of the Congo right through to the Maypole, Home and Colonial and Liptons stores that had been swallowed up in the merger.[138] Both Labour and Conservative politicians alike, to the dismay of cooperators, tended to accept such developments as inevitable if not positively beneficial.[139]

In this context, and not surprisingly perhaps, the cooperative movement turned in on itself, became more defensive and cautious. Relations between co-operation and the other wings of the Labour movement were to remain important, though strained, before and after World War II, a theme that would repay detailed investigation.[140] Nevertheless—and this has been one of the key concerns in this chapter—Percy Redfern's words went largely unheeded after the debacles of the 1920s: "We need to live in the movement, but not to bury ourselves in it," he cautioned in 1914.[141] The moral economy of cooperation no doubt lingered on within many local communities during the interwar years and beyond but young working-class consumers were increasingly attracted to the delights and diversions of an expanding mass culture, which narrowed their role to that of passive reception.[142] Co-operators understandably became more introspective and the culture of co-operation, though still an alternative culture, lost much of its oppositional edge.

Notes

1. G. D. H. Cole, *A Century of Co-operation* (Manchester, 1945). There have been exceptions, notably the influential article by Sydney Pollard, "Nineteenth Century Co-operation: From Community-Building to Shopkeeping," in *Essays in Labour History Vol I*, Asa Briggs and John Saville, eds., (London, 1960). This essay probably hindered historical research in the field though as it argued strongly for the deradicalization of the movement after 1844. In the 1970s much energy was expanded in an attempt to flesh out the theory of the labour aristocracy and within this framework cooperators were seen as quintessential labor aristocrats who had accepted the horizons set by the capitalist social order. The most important titles included John Foster, *Class Struggle and the Industrial Revolution* (London, 1974); Robert Grey, *The Labour Aristocracy in Victorian Edinburgh* (Oxford, 1976); Trygve Tholfsen, *Working-Class Radicalism in Mid-Victorian England* (London, 1976); and Geoffrey Crossick, *An Artisan Elite in Victorian Society: Kentish London 1840-1880* (London, 1978). There are a number of internal general histories of the movement but these tend to be bland and celebratory. See, for example, Arnold Bonner, *British Co-operation* (Manchester, 1961); Jean Gaffin and David Thoms, *Caring and Sharing. The Centenary History of the Co-operative Women's Guild* (Manchester, 1983); and Johnston Birchall, *Co-op. The people's business* (Manchester, 1994). There is a useful chapter on consumer cooperation in W. H. Fraser, *The Coming of the Mass Market 1850-1914* (London, 1981). John Benson, however, in *The Rise of Consumer Society in Britain, 1880-1980* (London, 1994) almost completely ignores the movement. Two excellent local studies and a collection of essays have begun to address this absence: Bill Lancaster, *Radicalism, Co-operation and Socialism: Leicester working-class politics, 1860-1906* (Leicester, 1987); Mike Savage, *The Dynamics of Working-Class Politics. The Labour Movement in Preston, 1880-1940* (Cambridge, 1987); Stephen Yeo, ed., *New Views of Co-operation* (London, 1988). See

also my monograph, *Co-operative culture and the politics of consumption in England, 1870-1930* (Manchester, 1996).

2. I have taken this distinction from V. I. Lenin's essays, "On Co-operation", in *Collected Works*, Vol. 33 (Moscow, 1966), 471-75. Just before his death, Lenin asserted that in Russia "the political and social revolution preceded the cultural revolution, that very cultural revolution which nevertheless now confronts us." He argued that cooperative associations, especially among the peasantry, were the solution to this problem and declared: "given social ownership of the means of production, given the class victory of the proletariat over the bourgeoisie, the system of civilised co-operators is the system of socialism." For a useful commentary, see Charles Bettleheim, *Class Struggles in the USSR. First period: 1917-1923* (Brighton, 1976), 487-90.

3. See especially his essay, "Why was there no Marxism in Britain?", in *The Ideologies of Class. Social Relations in Britain 1880-1950* (Oxford, 1990), 38.

4. Phillip Corrigan and Derek Sayer, *The Great Arch. English State Formation as Cultural Revolution* (Oxford, 1985), 204-5.

5. E. P. Thompson, "The Moral Economy of the English Crowd in the Eighteenth Century," *Past and Present* 50 (1971), 89.

6. Percy Redfern, *The New History of the C.W.S.* (Manchester, 1938), 6.

7. Maxine Berg, *The Age of Manufactures. Industry, innovation and work in Britain 1700-1820* (London, 1985), 87. See also Charles Sabel and Jonathon Zeitlin, "Historical Alternatives to Mass Production," *Past and Present* 108, 1985.

8. Ben Jones, *Co-operative Production* (Oxford, 1894), 170-74.

9. Roy Church, *Economic and Social Change in a Midland Town. Victorian Nottingham 1815-1900* (London, 1966), 47.

10. See, for example, the work of J. F. C. Harrison, *Robert Owen and the Owenites in Britain and America* (London, 1969) and Barbara Taylor, *Eve and the New Jerusalem* (London, 1983).

11. See R. C. N. Thornes, "The Early Development of the Co-operative Movement in West Yorkshire, 1827-1863" (Unpublished D.Phil. thesis, University of Sussex 1984), 1-12.

12. F. W. Leeman, *Co-operation in Nottingham. A History of 100 Years of Nottingham Co-operative Society Limited* (Nottingham, 1963), 13-14. Sweet, secretary of the Nottingham Chartists, was quoting from Robert Lowery's pamphlet, *Address to the Fathers and Mothers, Sons and Daughters of the Working Classes, on the system of exclusive dealing and the formation of Joint Stock Provision Companies* (Newcastle-upon-Tyne, 1839). There is a useful treatment of Chartist cooperation in Thornes, "The Early Development of the Co-operative Movement," chapter 6.

13. For women and exclusive dealing, see *Northern Star*, 8 December 1838; 22 December 1838; 1 June 1839; 27 July 1839; 5 October 1839.

14. For the significance of the 1842 strike, see Mick Jenkins, *The General Strike of 1842* (London, 1980).

15. As some recent work makes clear. See Kate Tiller, "Late Chartism: Halifax 1847-1858," in *The Chartist Experience*, Dorothy Thompson and James Epstein, eds., (London, 1982), 328-33; Neville Kirk, *The Growth of Working-Class Reformism in Mid-Victorian England* (London, 1985), 143.

16. G. J. Holyoake's early propagandist work, *Self-Help by the People: History of Co-operation in Rochdale* (London, 1858) traced the origins of the modern movement to Rochdale though he himself recognized that the "divi" did not originate there. See his general text, *The History of Co-operation Vol I* (1875, London, 1906), 278-9.

17. For Christian Socialist connections, see John Saville, "The Christian Socialists of 1848," in *Democracy and the Labour Movement*, John Saville, ed., (London, 1954); Torben Christensen, *Origin and History of Christian Socialism, 1848-54* (Aarhus: Universitetsjorlaget, 1962); N. C. Masterman, *J. M. Ludlow. The Builder of Christian Socialism* (Cambridge, 1963); and Philip Backstrom, *Christian Socialism and Co-operation in Victorian England* (London, 1974).

18. For the changing legal status of cooperation see G. J. Holyoake, *The History of Co-operation*, 289-93; Ben Jones, *Co-operative Production*, 11-15; Cole, *A Century of Co-operation*, 114-26.

19. For Jones and Harney's views, see Thornes, "The Early Development of the Co-operative Movement," 255-73.

20. Karl Marx and Friedrich Engels, *Articles on Britain* (Moscow, 1971), 343-44.

21. These figures are taken from Cole, *A Century of Co-operation*, 371; Redfern, *New History*, 532-33.

22. For the distinction between alternative and oppositional culture, see Raymond Williams, "Base and Superstructure in Marxist Cultural Theory," in *Problems in Materialism and Culture* (London, 1980), 42; and for culture as a signifying system, see the same author's *Culture* (Glasgow, 1981), 13.

23. See especially Philip Backstrom, *Christian Socialism*; Paul Johnson, *Saving and Spending. The Working-class Economy in Britain 1870-1939* (Oxford, 1985).

24. At a public meeting in Dundee, reported in the *Co-operative News*, 1 October 1881, 659.

25. *Failsworth Co-operative Messenger*, June 1913, 150. For another good example of the uses of the "divi" see Fred Pickles, *Jubilee History of the Bridge End (Todmorden) Co-operative Society Limited. From 1847 to 1901* (Manchester, 1902), 115.

26. Edward Jackson, *A Study in Democracy; being an account of the rise and progress of Industrial Co-operation in Bristol* (Bristol, 1911), 441.

27. *Ibid.*, 5. See also Thomas Readshaw, *Jubilee History of the Bishop Auckland Industrial Co-operative Flour and Provision Society Ltd. from 1860-1910* (Manchester, 1910), 364; see also Pickles, *Jubilee History of the Bridge End (Todmorden) Co-operative Society Limited*, 78.

28. Thompson, "The Moral Economy of the English Crowd," 89.

29. See Quentin Hoare and George Nowell-Smith, eds., *Selections from the Prison Notebooks of Antonio Gramsci* (London, 1971), 133.

30. Raymond Williams, "Advertising the Magic System," in *Problems in Materialism and Culture*, 179.

31. At a quarterly meeting of the CWS reported in the *Co-operative News*, 11 December 1880, 809.

32. Thomas Kirkup, *A History of Socialism* (London, 1900), 352.

33. *Wheatsheaf,* October 1907, 50.

34. On the culture of the German Social Democratic Party, see Günther Roth, *The Social Democrats in Imperial Germany: A Study in Working Class Isolation and National Integration* (Totowa, N.J., 1963); Vernon Lidtke, *The Alternative Culture* (Oxford, 1985). The last phrase in this paragraph is taken from Jean Paul Sartre's *Search for a Method* (New York, 1968), 160.

35. See Eileen Yeo, "Culture and Constraint," in *Popular Culture and Class Conflict*, Eileen and Stephen Yeo, eds., (Brighton, 1981), 168.

36. G. J. Holyoake, *Leeds Industrial Co-operative Society Ltd., 1847-1897* (Manchester, 1897), 77.

37. W. H. Oliver et. al., *Jubilee History of Coventry Perseverance Society, 1867-1917* (Coventry, 1917), 310.

38. For the changing and contested meanings of "social" see Raymond Williams, *Keywords* (Glasgow, 1976), 238-9.

39. See Toshio Kusamitsu, "Great Exhibitions before 1851," *History Workshop Journal* 9 (1980). For the involvement of Owenites in some Mechanics Institute exhibitions, see Edward Royle, "Mechanics Institutes and the Working Classes," *The Historical Journal* 12 (1971).

40. *Labour Co-partneship*, August 1900, 133.

41. Bramwell Hudson, *History of Co-operation in Cainscross & District: a souvenir in commemoration of the Jubilee of Cainscross and Ebley Co-operative Society, 1863-1913* (Manchester, 1913), 106.

42. *Oldham Co-operative Record*, May 1894, 9.

43. See Thomas Richards, *The Commodity Culture of Victorian England. Advertising and Spectacle, 1851-1914* (London, 1991). I owe this point to Ellen Furlough.

44. *Co-operative News*, 28 June 1884, 594-5. For the importance of music in working-class culture, particularly in Yorkshire in this period, see David Russell, *Popular Music in England, 1840-1914* (Manchester, 1987).

45. *Co-operative News*, 18 March 1905, 313. A Midland Sectional Choral Association was founded the same year; see *ibid.*, 25 July 1914, 962, and Duncan McInnes, *Co-operative Education and the Sectional Choral Association* (Manchester, 1914).

46. *Co-operative News*, 28 Feb. 1914, 276. The meeting was entertained by the Bury Society's juvenile choir with such items as, "Comrades' Song of Hope."

47. See, for example, *Failsworth Co-operative Messenger*, December 1910, 289; *Co-operative News*, 27 May 1905, 606.

48. *Labour Co-partnership*, April 1901, 62.

49. *Pendleton Co-operative Record*, July 1912, 12; May 1913, 11.

50. *Comradeship*, November 1900, 107-9.

51. For these events, see Patrick Joyce, *Work, Society and Politics* (Brighton, 1980), ch. 5; J. M. MacKenzie, *Propaganda and Empire. The Manipulation of British Public Opinion, 1880-1940* (Manchester, 1984).

52. *Wheatsheaf*, August 1902, 17.

53. For radical education and informality in the early nineteenth century, see Richard Johnson, "'Really Useful Knowledge': radical education and Working-Class Culture, 1790-1848", in *Working-Class Culture. Studies in history and theory*, Jon Clark, Chas Critcher, and Richard Johnson, eds., (London, 1979), 79-80, 83-4.

54. Margaret Llewelyn-Davies, ed., *Life As We Have Known It* (1930, London, 1977), 66. From 1876 until his death in 1898 the *News* was edited by Samuel Bamford who pursued a tolerant, nonpartisan policy and provided an invaluable platform for women in the paper from 1883. Catherine Webb described him as, "a man of wide-sympathies and far-seeing co-operative judgement," who backed the "Women's Corner" against considerable opposition from the Newspaper Board, which was in the main, "dominated by male prejudices." Catherine Webb, *The Woman with the Basket: the Story of the Women's Co-operative Guild* (Manchester, 1927), 175. For women and cooperative education, see also June Purvis, "Working-class Women and Adult Education in Nineteenth Century Britain," *History of Education* 3 (1980), 206-11.

55. See *Co-operative Congress Report*, 1919, 137. The *News* replaced Henry Pitman's *Co-operator* and Holyoake's *Social Economist*, which had insufficiently covered the field in the 1860s. For the background to the establishment of the *News*, see Lloyd Jones' paper in the *Co-operative Congress Report*, 1870; W. M. Bamford, *Our Fifty Years, 1871-1921* (Manchester: Co-operative Printing Society, 1921); Fred Hall, *The History of the Co-operative Printing Society, 1869-1919* (Manchester, 1919).

56. *Co-operative Congress Report*, 1919, 137.

57. *Co-operative Congress Report*, 1916, 100. For a detailed study based on *Comradeship*, the local record of the Royal Arsenal Co-operative Society (London), see John Attfield's valuable *With Light of Knowledge* (London, 1981).

58. See *Co-operative News*, 10 January 1891, 30.

59. *Oldham Co-operative Record*, April 1895, 11.

60. Savage, *The Dynamics of Working-Class Politics*, 127-29. On the regional growth of cooperation, see also Martin Purvis, "The development of co-operative retailing in England and Wales, 1851-1901: a geographical study," *Journal of Historical Geography* 16/3 1990, 314-31; *idem*, "Co-operative retailing in Britain," in *The evolution of retail systems, c.1800-1914*, John Benson and Gareth Shaw, eds., (Leicester, 1992); John K. Walton, "Co-operation in Lancashire, 1844-1914," *North West Labour History* 19 (1994/5), 115-25.

61. Report of the Central Board to Congress, *Co-operative News*, 12 June 1897, 654 (figures refer to expenditure in 1895).

62. Publication figures from the *Co-operative News*, 8 April 1911, 437.

63. Interviewed by the author at Roe Green, Manchester, April 1986.

64. Fred Hall, *The Co-ordination and Extension of Co-operative Education* (Manchester, 1914), 21.

65. *Co-operative News*, 22 January 1876, 44.

66. Logie Barrow, *Independent Spirits. Spiritualism and English Plebeians 1850-1910* (London, 1986), 146-9.

67. See, for example, his remarks in the *Co-operative News*, 10 September 1887, 906.

68. H. D. Lloyd, *Labour Co-partnership* (New York, 1898), 148.

69. G. J. Holyoake, *Essentials of Co-operative Education* (Manchester, 1898), 7.

70. *Co-operative News*, 7 April 1877, 162. For more on Mitchell's ideology, see Stephen Yeo, *Who was J. T. W. Mitchell?* (Manchester, 1995).

71. See Cole, *A Century of Co-operation*, 118-21; Catherine Webb, *The Woman with the Basket*, 205-6.

72. Cole, *A Century of Co-operation*, 85-86; Fred Hall and W. P. Watkins, *Co-operation. A Survey of the History, Principles and Organisation of the Co-operative Movement in Great Britain and Ireland* (Manchester, 1937), 166.

73. J. F. Ogden, *Failsworth Industrial Co-operative Society Ltd: jubilee history 1859-1909* (Manchester, 1909), 53.

74. G. Briggs, *Jubilee History of the York Equitable Industrial Society Ltd* (Manchester, 1909), 237.

75. Holyoake, *Self-Help by the People*, 50-1.

76. *Co-operative News*, 12 May 1888, 442.

77. *Ibid.*, 12 September 1903, 1112.

78. This term was used by Gareth Stedman Jones in his influential article, "Working-Class Culture and Working-Class Politics in London, 1870-1900: Notes on the remaking of a working class," in *Languages of Class* (Cambridge, 1983).

79. See, for example, the editorials in the *Co-operative News*, 4 November 1882, 748; 12 July 1884, 639. For an excellent study of the development of rational recreation in the nineteenth century, see Peter Bailey, *Leisure and Class in Victorian England* (London, 1978).

80. I explore this issue more fully in *Co-operative culture and the politics of consumption.*

81. *CWS Annual* (Manchester, 1908), 145.

82. Ben Jones, *Co-operative Production*, 737. See also his description of "complete co-operation" on p. 143. Jones noted the existence of a small anarcho-socialist group called the Bolton Co-operative Commonwealth Society (established in 1890) in this text. J. C. Gray had written to Jones describing this "communistic society" composed of "socialists, followers of Gronlund and Bellamy." They worked in the evenings with tools bought from a common fund and aimed to establish a "Commonwealth."

83. Stefan Collini, *Liberalism and Sociology: L. T. Hobhouse and political argument in England 1880-1914* (Cambridge, 1979), 33.

84. *Labour Co-partnership*, September 1907, 137.

85. *Millgate Monthly*, November 1908, 91.

86. See W. H. Brown, *The Co-operative Manager. Being the Silver Jubilee History, 1912-1937, of the National Co-operative Manager's Association* (Manchester, 1937), 60.

87. Ironically Gronlund was an anti-cooperator who saw no role for cooperation in the making of the future socialist state.

88. *Co-operative News*, 31 August 1907, 1067.

89. *Ibid.*, 3 July 1909, 877.

90. For the notion of a rational utopia, see Patrick Wright, *On Living in an Old Country* (London, 1985), 255-6.

91. *Burnley Co-operative Record*, August 1912, 5-6.

92. See Lander's remarks in the *Co-operative News*, 12 December 1908, 1508; on Redfern, see John Saville and Joyce Bellamy, *Dictionary of Labour Biography Vol. I* (London, 1972), 280-82. For the relationship between cooperation and collectivism, see Stephen Yeo, "Notes on Three Socialisms, mainly in late-nineteenth and early-twentieth-century Britain," in *Socialism and the Intelligentsia*, Carl Levy, ed., (London, 1987); for collectivism and the Labour Party, see Bill Schwarz and Martin Durham, "'A safe and

sane labourism': socialism and the state. 1910-24", in *Crises in the British State 1880-1930*, Mary Langan and Bill Schwarz, eds., (London, 1985).

93. Kirkup, *A History of Socialism*, 389.

94. Peter Kropotkin, *Mutual Aid; A Factor of Evolution* (1902, London, 1910), 271-2.

95. See Christopher Hill, *The World Turned Upside Down* (London, 1972).

96. *Plymouth Co-operative Record*, January 1916, 2. See also June 1916, 195.

97. *Ibid.*, July 1916, 225-7. *Co-operative Congress Report* 1916.

98. Interviewed Roe Green, April 1986.

99. Williams noted that the major problem with the keyword "community" was that it tended to efface or conceal difference. See *Politics and Letters: Interviews with New Left Review* (London, 1979), 119.

100. Gareth Stedman Jones, "Utopian Socialism Reconsidered," in *People's History and Socialist Theory*, Raphael Samuel, ed., (London, 1981), 141; Noel Thompson, *The People's Science* (Cambridge, 1984).

101. *Co-operative Congress Report*, 1885, 3; *Co-operative Congress Report*, 1899, 151; *Co-operative Congress Report*, 1910, 34.

102. See *Co-operative News*, 12 November 1910, 1470; 23 March 1912, 362; 30 March 1912, 384; *Wheatsheaf*, May 1912, 161-2; June 1912, 177.

103. William Paine, *Shop Slavery and Emancipation. A Revolutionary Appeal to the Educated Young Men of the Middle Class* (London, 1912), 50. By 1900 there were approximately 80,000 cooperative employees and this had risen to 150,000 by 1914; about half of these were employed in distributive stores. The WCG, critical of the existence of "sweated labour" within the movement since the early 1890s, joined forces with the Amalgamated Union of Co-operative Employees (the AUCE was formed 1895) in 1905 to campaign for a minimum wage for cooperative employees. A wage of 24s per week for males over 21 and 17s for females over 20 was eventually recommended by the Newcastle Congress in 1909, but local societies and the CWS were slow to implement these rates. For this campaign, see Cole, *A Century of Co-operation*, 336-38, 339-41. Pressure from the AUCE during World War I eventually improved pay and conditions. See the Independent Labour Party report, *The Co-operative Movement and Socialism* (London, 1928), 29-30.

104. *Co-operative News*, 19 June 1886, 581. For strikes in co-op factories, see *Co-operative News*, 19 June 1886, 581; 11 December 1886, 1214-16; 12 March 1887, 245-47; Ben Jones, *Co-operative Production*, 228-30; Percy Redfern, *The Story of the C.W.S.* (Manchester, 1913), 172-73, 263-66, 281-82; *idem, New History*, 260-71, 414-16, *passim*. The issue of labour relations is explored in detail by Jayne Southern in, "The Co-operative Movement in the North West of England 1919-1939" (Ph.D thesis, University of Lancaster, 1996).

105. Jones, *Co-operative Production*, 747. This tendency helps explain why profit-sharing in CWS works was ardently advocated by Christian Socialists like E. V. Neale and old Owenites like G. J. Holyoake in the late nineteenth century. Backstrom, *Christian Socialism*, uncritically rehearses the arguments of profit-sharing "individualists" and as this way of seeing has hindered a proper appreciation of the majority movement I have deliberately avoided the debate in this chapter. For a provocative alternative to

Backstrom see R. Schatz, "Co-operative Production and the Ideology of Co-operation in England 1870-1895" unpublished ms., University of Pittsburgh, 1973.

106. James Ramsay MacDonald, *Socialism and Society* (1905), in *Ramsay MacDonald's Political Writings*, Bernard Barker, ed., (London, 1972), 65.

107. Ramsay MacDonald, *Parliament and Democracy* (1920), in Barker, *Ramsay MacDonald's Political Writings*, 256.

108. See Lancaster's work on the relationship between the ILP and cooperators in Leicester in, *Radicalism, Co-operation and Socialism*, chapter 10; Stephen Yeo, *Religion and Voluntary Organisations in Crisis* (London, 1976). On working-class hostility to the state, see Pat Thane, "The Working Class and State 'Welfare' in Britain, 1880-1914," *The Historical Journal* 4 (1984). For a more detailed consideration of these themes, see my *Co-operative culture and the politics of consumption*, chapter 7.

109. See G. J. Holyoake's comments in, *Sixty Years of an Agitators' Life* (London, 1893), 81. For another good example of Holyoake's partial deformation of Owen, see his speech at the commemoration ceremony at Owen's grave, reported in the *Co-operative News*, 12 July 1902. For the original Owenite critique of gender relations and the family, see Barbara Taylor, *Eve and the New Jerusalem*.

110. For two excellent, albeit extreme, examples of male hostility, see William Marcroft, *The Inner Circle of Family Life* (Manchester, 1886); W. J. Douse, *The True Remedy for Poverty!* (Nottingham, 1895).

111. See Margaret Llewelyn Davies, *The Women's Co-operative Guild, 1883-1904* (Kirkby Lonsdale, 1904), 155-56.

112. *Co-operative News*, 29 June 1907, 789.

113. By 1904 a total of 238 women from 108 societies in the Co-op Union sat on educational committees. See Cole, *A Century of Co-operation*, 225. For press coverage of the election of a woman onto a management committee—a rare occurrence—see *Co-operative News*, 4 April 1914, 444; and for a report of the first woman manager, see *ibid.*, 9 February 1918, 118. Gillian Scott's *Feminism, Femininity and the Politics of Working Women. The Women's Co-operative Guild, 1880s-WWII* (London, forthcoming 1998) is a long overdue scholarly critique of this important organization.

114. Geoffrey Crossick, "Shopkeepers and the State in Britain, 1870-1914," in *Shopkeepers and Master Artisans in Nineteenth Century Europe*, Geoffrey Crossick and Georg Haupt, eds., (London, 1984), 249. See also Michael Winstanley, *The Shopkeeper's World 1830-1914* (Manchester, 1983). For an excellent study of a local trade war see C. L. Laker, "Co-operators and Private Traders in Preston, 1870-1902" (MA thesis, University of Lancaster 1981).

115. For continuing conflicts over taxation, see Neil Killingback, "Limits to Mutuality: Economic and Political Attacks on Co-operation During the 1920s and 1930s," in *New Views*, Stephen Yeo, ed. After a fierce campaign waged by businessmen and large sections of the press, cooperative reserves, rather than "surplus," were made subject to taxation by the National Government in 1933, but the effect was not financially crippling.

116. Peter Mathias, *Retailing Revolution: A History of Multiple Retailing in the Food Trades* (London, 1967), 41-43, 100-113.

117. See D. H. Aldcroft, *The Inter-War Economy: Britain, 1919-1939* (London, 1970).

118. On food control, see L. M. Barnett, *British Food Policy During the First World War* (London, 1985)

119. Cole, *A Century of Co-operation*, 371; J. B. Jeffreys, *Retail Trading in Britain 1850-1950* (Cambridge, 1954), 58.

120. As well as a resurrected Traders' Defence League, the movement had also to deal with price-fixing coordinated by the Proprietary Articles Traders' Association. The PATA represented the producers of branded and highly advertized goods like patent medicines, toilet preparations, and baby foods and effectively boycotted the movement. For details, see *Co-operative Congress Report*, 1920, 509-10; *Co-operative Congress Report*, 1923, 90; *Co-operative Congress Report*, 1930, 447; J. B. Jeffreys, *Retail Trading in Britain*, 53-54; B. S. Yamey, ed., *Resale Price Maintenance* (London, 1966).

121. Oliver et. al., *Jubilee History of Coventry Perseverance Society*, 396.

122. McKibbin, *The Ideologies of Class*, 31-2.

123. See Sidney Pollard, "The Foundation of the Co-operative Party," in *Essays in Labour History Vol II*, Asa Briggs and John Saville, eds., (London, 1967). Pollard argued that this development was a gradual process that had been in train since the turn of the century. The "traditional" stress in cooperative historiography on the role of the war in radicalizing the movement is restated by Tony Adams in, "The Formation of the Co-operative Party Reconsidered," *International Review of Social History* (1987): 1. For earlier attempts to create a "fusion of forces," see *Co-operative News*, 8 February 1913 p. 164; 15 February 1913, 202; Ross McKibbin, *The Evolution of the Labour Party, 1910-1924* (Oxford, 1974), 43-47.

124. Patrick Maguire, "Co-operation and Crisis: Government, Co-operation and Politics 1917-22," *New Views*, in Stephen Yeo, ed., 194.

125. Quoted by Chris Wrigley in, *Lloyd George and the challenge of Labour, the post-war coalition, 1918-1922* (Hemel Hempstead, 1990), 160. As Wrigley notes (on p. 164) Lloyd George also recommended the seizure of motor lorries belonging to cooperative societies to ensure that miners would not be fed.

126. See Corrigan and Sayer, *The Great Arch*, 179. On this theme, see also Keith Burgess, *The Challenge of Labour. Shaping British Society 1850-1930* (London, 1980) chapters 5 and 6.

127. C. L. Mowat, *Britain Between the Wars* (London: Methuen, 1956), 121.

128. See J. Stevens, "The Coal-mining Lockout of 1926, with particular reference to the Co-operative Movement and the Poor Law" (Ph.D thesis, University of Sheffield, 1984), 139, 179, 208, 214, 233, 244.

129. Cole, *A Century of Co-operation*, 321; T. F. Carbery, *Consumers in Politics* (Manchester, 1969).

130. *Times*, 16 October 1924, 8; 21 October 1924, 10.

131. *First Report of the Royal Commission on Food Prices*, [Cmd. 2390] Vol II, Minutes of Evidence, 1925, 182. Alexander launched a damning attack on trusts in a pamphlet published in February entitled *Is Co-operation a Social Menace?* (Manchester, 1925), 16-17.

132. *First Report of the Royal Commission on Food Prices*, 220.

133. *Ibid.*, Vol. I, 2.

134. *Co-operative News*, 16 May 1925, 10; 30 May 1925, 8; *Hansard's*, 17 February 1925, 878-82; *Co-operative Congress Report*, 1926, 90, 440.

135. *Times*, 29 July 1925, 11.

136. Fred Hayward, *The Co-operative Boycott* (Manchester, 1930), 3. See also W. E. Snell in the *C.W.S. Annual* (Manchester, 1890), 210.

137. Barry Supple, ed., *Essays in British Business History* (Oxford, 1977), 20; Jefferys, *Retail Trading in Britain*, 73.

138. Ben Fine and Ellen Leopold, *The World of Consumption* (London, 1993), 20-35; Charles Wilson, *The History of Unilever*, Vol. 2 (London, 1954), 301-99; Mathias, *Retailing Revolution*, 258-97.

139. See Sidney Pollard, *The Development of the British Economy 1914-1967* (London, 1969), 168-72; Leslie Hannah, *The Rise of the Corporate Economy* (London, 1976), 47-50.

140. The movement was represented on the National Council of Labour from 1927 but was not properly consulted by the Labour Party even on issues that directly affected its future. This lack of coordination and sympathy is nicely symbolised by the nationalisation of the cooperative colliery at Shilbottle by the Labour government after World War II. See Leeman, *Co-operation in Nottingham*, 162-64. A study of the contemporary cooperative movement concludes that "co-operators today see the goal of the movement as one of survival. The movement should, it is argued, be aimed at Consumer Protection providing a good, efficient service to members, and providing within distribution an alternative alongside capitalist enterprise. Wider, more socialistic aims, such as replacing the capitalist system, attract little or no support." R. Donnelly, "Goal Displacements and the British Co-operative Movement" (Ph.D thesis, University of Strathclyde, 1980), v-vi.

141. Percy Redfern, *Co-operation For All* (Manchester, 1914), 118.

142. See David Fowler, *The First Teenagers? The Lifestyles of Young Wage-earners in Interwar Britain* (London, 1995). For the continuing importance of cooperation, see the autobiography by Linda McCullough Thew, *The Pit Village and the Store. The Portrait of a Mining Past* (London, 1985).

Chapter 6

French Consumer Cooperation, 1885-1930: From the "Third Pillar" of Socialism to "A Movement for All Consumers"

Ellen Furlough

> In the immense social war which places classes against each other in all countries—proletarians against proprietors, workers against capitalists, governed against government—cooperation furnishes for the numerous armies of the exploited one of its arms for combat, one of its means for struggie, one of the instruments for inevitable victory.[1]

> Politics divides men, cooperation unites them . . . cooperation is above political or religious discussions and observes the strictest neutrality.[2]

In the quotations above, French cooperators expressed different visions of the roles and meanings of consumer cooperation. The first was written by socialist cooperators just before World War I, when the cooperative movement in France saw itself as a vital part of the labor movement and as an economic and political alternative to capitalist consumerism. The second quote was written in the late 1920s, when the consumer cooperative movement represented itself as a politically independent regulator of capitalist consumerism rather than its alternative. How did cooperation challenge and differ from capitalist modes of consumption? What was the movement's relationship to the French labor movement and in what ways did that relationship influence cooperation's self-representation as an alternative to capitalist consumption? How did the French cooperative movement transform itself into a "movement for all consumers" that would complement consumer capitalism and remain politically "neutral"? This essay situates the French consumer cooperative movement at the confluence of labor militancy and emergent consumerism, and explores the importance of that intersection for the history of consumer cooperation, and to a lesser extent, for the histories of the labor movement and of French consumerism. I will first briefly discuss the cooperative movement in general, then turn to an analysis of socialist consumer cooperation as the major carrier for an alternative consumer culture that bridged working-class culture and political mobilization. I will then suggest some limits to the radical vision of consumer cooperation and implications of the revisioning of consumer cooperation in the 1920s.

French Consumer Cooperation as an Alternative to Capitalist Consumerism

While there had been consumer cooperatives in France since the 1830s, it was not until 1885 that French cooperators founded a national organization, the Cooperative Union (*Union coopérative*).[3] The national organization attempted to standardize cooperative ideology and practices. By the end of the 1880s, after the ascendancy of Charles Gide and his followers to leadership in the Cooperative Union, the movement defined cooperation as an economic and social "third way" to both capitalism and socialism.[4] The three major positions of this "third way" were the belief that consumption was the vehicle for correcting the worst abuses of capitalism and achieving selected socialist goals; advocacy of the "Cooperative Republic" as an inherently superior counterpoint to capitalist commerce, and strict political neutrality. Members of the Cooperative Union considered the capitalist economic system to be in an anarchic state, and blamed the unregulated disequilibrium between production and consumption. Their position was that consumers could restore order by associating their economic strength to implement justice, fairness, and harmony in all aspects of production as well as distribution. Gide called for a total and peaceful social and economic transformation subordinating production to consumer needs. His plan was to "completely overturn" the current capitalist economic order for a Cooperative Republic where overproduction, industrial crises, and unemployment would not exist since consumers would produce only what was necessary in exact proportion to their needs. All conflict would then disappear: "we are all consumers, we will henceforth be our own sellers, bankers, entrepreneurs. The working class will have realized its goal of acquiring ownership of the means of production, stores, machines, factories, the land, and the mines."[5] Unlike socialism, with its theoretical base in conflict, cooperators believed that change would come through persuasion and the moral and edifying example of cooperative activity.

In line with the larger goal of a cooperative republic, with its harmonious conflict-free solution to the "social question," the Cooperative Union believed that individual cooperatives should be "small republics" whose specific practices would embody cooperative ideology. Cooperators believed that the commercial strategies and techniques of local cooperatives were different from those of other commercial forms, and indeed that cooperative commerce offered a positive alternative to emergent capitalist consumerism.

During the period when cooperators were organizing the movement on a national level, French distributive institutions were in the midst of a "retailing revolution." Alongside older (and still dominant) small shopkeepers, newer department stores and chain stores were expanding their market shares, revolutionizing retailing structures, and producing meanings about commodities and consuming.[6] Both were large capitalist enterprises that aggressively sought new markets, focused on generating new "needs," and pioneered modern merchandising techniques. Both were carriers of structures and values that came to characterize modern consumerism: capitalist, individualist, materialist, and acquisitive. Department stores were pioneers in the arts of enhancing and contextualizing commodities by using exotic backdrops, lighting techniques, and the placement of numerous objects of connote abundance. Cooperatives, in contrast, were collective rather than capitalist, democratic and social rather than individualist. They linked human "needs" to social and political issues and used merchandising techniques that were focused not on the commodities themselves but on the individual and collective benefits of consumption.

Cooperatives and chain stores were especially competitive during the period prior to World War I, and there were important similarities between the two forms. For example, they sold a similar range of goods: foodstuffs, wine and spirits, coal, small-scale household items (*articles de ménage*), hardware, ready-made clothing, shoes, hats, and occasional items such as toys, paper goods, and school supplies.[7] They also tended to draw consumers from a similar socioeconomic base of workers, artisans, and the petit-bourgeoisie. Both cooperatives and chains grew rapidly in late nineteenth and early twentieth century France, although initially consumer cooperatives were more prevalent than chain stores. In 1906, for example, it was estimated that there were twenty-two chains with 1,792 stores. In 1906-1907, there were more consumer cooperatives (2,166 or 2,301) than capitalist chains (1,792) in France.[8] This contest among forms of retailing was not, however, simply a struggle between commercial forms over market share. It was instead an ideological clash over different visions of market culture and over the meanings and usages of consumption. A comparison of their different commercial strategies and accompanying ideological assumptions demonstrates the ways in which cooperators sought to create an alternative to capitalist commerce. These differences can be traced through commercial strategies and techniques such as profits, shares, management, and ideological assumptions.

A primary goal of capitalist commerce was to constantly enlarge the enterprise's capital base and to generate profits. Chain stores, like department stores, then returned those profits to shareholders in proportion to the number of shares owned. Generally, a small number of people owned multiple shares. Chains concentrated ownership and purchases in a central establishment (called the *maison mère*) then decentralized sales through dispersed branches. Professional managers managed branch stores of chains, and they were paid a percentage of the store's profits. These managers generally deposited a sum of money with the parent establishment to cover any deficit in operations. Thus the ultimate responsibility for the financial success or failure of each branch store rested with the manager.[9]

Ideologically, capitalist chain stores were important carriers to the French provinces of the same implicit value system as department stores. Central to the strategies of chain stores was the presentation of goods in such as way as to create individual desire for the commodities, a technique borrowed from department store displays. The stores used signifiers of luxury such as elegantly arranged display windows filled with goods that were increasingly less expensive due to mass production. A contemporary noted: "The stores are often installed with great luxuriousness. The cooperatives, to the contrary, are very simple. Chain stores influence the psychology of the buyer, they attract and fascinate." Another commented that the chain stores and their illustrated catalogues "diffused temptation in the countryside."[10] Not only was the physical appearance of the chain store purposely seductive, but the stores pioneered other technologies of temptation. One of the most successful was the system of rewarding individual purchases with small stamps redeemable for objects from the store or chosen from a catalogue. All of these developments focused attention on commodities, and produced meanings about those commodities linking them to individual welfare and status.

In the contest over forms and ideologies of commerce, consumer cooperation advocated an alternative to capitalist retailing. French cooperators used the "Rochdale System," a commercial strategy borrowed from the British cooperative movement. Cooperatives did not consider themselves to be profit-making enterprises. Indeed, they eschewed profit: "the genre of commerce that we repudiate is that which has no other goal than the realization of large profits, it manipulates and falsifies products necessary for life."[11] Cooperators' attempts to distance themselves from capitalist commerce was also evident in their use of alternative terms—they used *trop perçu* (overcharge) for the dividend and *repartition* (distribution) rather than sale. Dividends were returned to members of the cooperative proportionate to their consumption, and monies remaining after payment of the *trop perçu* were then used for "social works" such as monetary gifts following births and deaths, or educational purposes. Membership in a cooperative involved the purchase of a share, but unlike capitalist enterprises, cooperatives limited the number of shares per person.[12] Another difference between cooperatives and capitalist enterprises was that each member had one vote in the general assemblies no matter the number of shares. Cooperatives resisted the tendency to hire professional managers. Instead, committees of members, elected democratically, and for limited periods of time, managed cooperatives. Thus, the ultimate responsibility for the success or failure of the store rested with the members, and the governing assumption was that cooperation was a democratic institution.

Cooperatives also resisted, and indeed explicitly rejected, the use of advertising, which they considered to be deceitful. Cooperators castigated all commercial practices that sought "only to please, to flatter with luxury in all its forms."[13] While department and chain stores were located on busy streets and had brightly lit and decorative store windows, cooperatives were often located on back streets and had unpolished or whitened glass windows.[14] Cooperators sought to construct commercial institutions that were focused on human concerns as opposed to what they considered to be the deceptive materialist ones of capitalist retailing. Cooperators viewed the creation of needs by retailers as artificial and conspiratorial—simply a search for profit. Cooperators viewed commodities socially and politically, as mediators for just social relationships and commercial integrity rather than a way to fulfill endless individual desires. Not only did cooperators conceptualize retailing as an alternative to capitalist commerce, but they viewed consumption as a vital avenue for molding an alternative social and economic order.

The kind of alternative social and economic order differed, however, between two factions of cooperators—those of the Cooperative Union and more radical socialist cooperators. The political alignments of consumer cooperation are crucial for understanding the different interpretations of the meanings and usages of consumer cooperation. These political alignments were especially important in the late nineteenth century, a time of rising working-class militancy and the growth in numbers and power of trade unions and socialist parties. The Cooperative Union, despite its claim of political neutrality, was politically entangled with the social and political theory known as solidarism.

Many republicans embraced Solidarism in the late nineteenth century. Like the cooperators of the Cooperative Union, solidarists positioned themselves as a third way "between classical political economy and socialist systems."[15] Solidarists stressed social interdependence and mutual obligations. They envisioned a stable social order being achieved through government aid and commitment to social reform combined with a vast web of voluntary associations and institutions. In essence, solidarists wished to buttress the social order by overcoming the worst abuses of capitalism, thereby forging national unity and undercutting the appeals of socialism.[16] There were strong links between national cooperative leaders, notably Charles Gide and Charles Robert, and solidarist leaders and institutions. Cooperative movement literature and political positions were closely aligned with solidarist principles. This connection served to legitimize a view of cooperation that emphasized class conciliation rather than class conflict, and that believed that the most effective solution to the "social question" was through networks of associations that emphasized individualism while acknowledging collective responsibilities. The Cooperative Union's alignment with solidarism highlights its political position, despite claims of neutrality. Indeed "neutrality" was most often invoked during times of labor militancy when member cooperatives and individual cooperators were discouraged from participating in strikes, trade unionism or socialist politics. By the late nineteenth century, the Cooperative Union's stress on peaceful social change and refusal to endorse strikes or support political socialism was actually quite political. The "Cooperative Republic," a "third way" between capitalism and socialism, obviated a political commitment to the militant socialism of the late nineteenth century. This political stance embedded the Cooperative Union within the broader tendency of republicanism of this period to claim and construct a centrist position politically and economically, to fuse a Republican synthesis countering conservative monarchism and the growing strength of the socialist left.

Socialist Consumer Cooperation as the "Third Pillar" of Socialism

Socialist cooperators rejected what they considered to be the "reformist" politics of the Cooperative Union and formed their own national organization, the Socialist Cooperative Exchange (*Bourse des coopératives socialistes*) in 1895. While individual socialists had long been members of consumer cooperatives, socialism as a political movement came to be entangled with consumer cooperation only during the general acceleration of labor militancy from the late 1880s and 1890s. The close alignment of one wing of the cooperative movement with socialism and trade unionism heightened the radical possibilities of consumer cooperation and galvanized and financially sustained the labor movement. By the early 1900s, socialist consumer cooperation was considered one of the three interrelated and complementary aspects of the organized working-class movement, one of the "three pillars of socialism" along with trade unions and political socialism.[17] Socialist cooperatives were the fastest growing segment of the French cooperative movement, and socialist cooperatives were generally the largest and wealthiest cooperatives (and working-class institutions) in France. The organization of socialist cooperatives underscores that consumer cooperatives were neither inherently reformist nor radical. As long as the working-class movement was militant and strong it sustained a radical definition for those organizations within it.

Two developments clarified the radical potential of socialist cooperation for French socialists: Belgian socialist cooperation and the strike of the glassworkers of Carmaux in 1895. The socialist cooperatives in Belgium were, for French militants, a powerful example of the mutually sustaining strength of socialism, cooperation, and trade unionism through the politicization of the daily material and social concerns of working-class men and women.[18] As *Maisons du Peuple*, cooperatives housed the socialist party, the labor unions, and socialist and labor presses; provided funds during strikes, and sustained the socialist party and party presses financially. A major innovation of the Belgian socialist cooperatives was to inscribe workers automatically on party rolls when they became members of the cooperative. Cooperatives also maintained pharmacies, offered medical consultations, dispersed free legal advice, provided food during strikes, aided with maternity expenses, and provided group insurance. Sociability and education were other concerns, and the cooperatives sponsored libraries, choruses, and gymnastic groups, all of which were designed to involve the entire family in the cooperative's activities.

From the 1880s French workers inspired by the Belgium model transformed existing cooperatives, founded socialist cooperatives, and worked to implement versions of Belgian socialist cooperation. For example, socialist (Allemanist) printers ran a slate of candidates for the administrative council of an existing Parisian cooperative, L'Avenir de Plaisance, in 1893 after attending an international congress of printers in Belgium. Likewise, members of the dyers and finishers union in Amiens founded a new consumer cooperative, L'Union d'Amiens, in 1892 after one of them visited the large socialist cooperatives founded by Belgian migrants in Roubaix. These cooperatives then became dynamic and important local centers for socialist and trade union militancy, mutual aid, sociability and leisure, and education. The symbolic referents of socialist cooperation also placed the movement squarely within the working-class movement. For example, member cooperatives of the Socialist Cooperative Exchange closed on the first of May, flew the red flag of international socialism over the cooperative, and organized expeditions to monuments such as the mur des fedéres in Paris where Communards had been shot. Many socialist cooperators in France also adopted the Belgian strategy of casting cooperatives as Maisons du Peuple.[19] Links with the labor movement intensified as many socialist leaders returned from attending the inauguration of the Brussels cooperative the Maison du Peuple in 1899 with enthusiastic appraisals of cooperation's socialist possibilities. Jaurès for example, argued that cooperation was "socialism in daily life," a "fragment of the new society," and that "with each socialist cooperative created there is a partial expropriation of the capitalist class."[20]

The second event that clarified the radical potential of consumer cooperation for socialists was the extensive financial assistance provided by cooperatives to the striking glassworkers of Carmaux in 1895. The same socialist cooperators who served on the coordinating committee for aid to the strikers then founded the national organization of socialist cooperatives, and cooperatives of the Socialist Cooperative Exchange continued to support and buy glass from the new glassmaking cooperative at Albi.[21] The statutes of the new Socialist Cooperative Exchange stipulated that to become a member, a local cooperative had to agree to the three fundamental principles of socialism (class struggle, socialization of the means of production and exchange, and international entente of workers), and to allocate 2 percent of its profits to socialist propaganda.[22] In short, socialists viewed cooperation as an important means for workers to use the force of their consumption to sustain labor militancy and to achieve socialism in the form of a social republic.

As the wealthiest working-class institution in prewar France, socialist cooperatives contributed large amounts of money to socialist and labor politics. They directly subventioned socialist parties, strike funds, salaries for working class activists, and funds for other radical organizations and activities. Socialist parties, trade unions, and labor presses were often literally housed in local cooperatives. During strikes cooperatives provided free bread and soup kitchens, served as strike headquarters, and coordinated temporary transfers of children of strikers to distant cooperators.

Socialist cooperatives also played an important role in creating and diffusing socialist themes in settings that were not directly connected either to the party or the workplace. Historians of socialism have noted the use by socialists of various social and educational activities. The connection that has been missed, however, is the degree to which these activities extended beyond direct party sponsorship to an institutional web with a shared political culture. Following the Belgian example, French cooperatives sponsored musical events and theaters, festivals, libraries that might house thousands of volumes and that subscribed to worker presses, and children's activities. Children's events were especially popular as a means of indoctrination into socialist political culture.

French cooperators also viewed consumer cooperation as an avenue for women's politicization, the "spenders" in the family economy. Cooperators stressed that women's legal and social inequality was "unjust, ridiculous, and wrong," and insisted that the future socialist society would guarantee equality between men and women.[23] Therefore, as "fragments of the future society" some socialist cooperatives sponsored women's study groups, encouraged meetings and speeches of various feminist organizations at the cooperative, and provided day-care facilities. Some women clearly found some space within consumer cooperation for their political and economic agendas (including feminist ones), and they founded cooperatives, served on administrative councils, and participated in general assemblies. Several women served in high administrative positions in the Socialist Cooperative Exchange. In 1910 women's study groups in Paris formed a League of Women Cooperators (*Ligue des Femmes Coopératrices*) to "develop socialist cooperation and the social education of women" and to "defend women's interests within cooperation."[24] While at least 32 study groups were formed under its aegis, the League of Women Cooperators was never as successful as the British Women's Cooperative Guild in building a large activist organization. The French group's relative lack of success was due in part to the gap that existed between egalitarian rhetoric and discriminatory practices against women in many local cooperatives. For example, the general practice in French cooperatives was for one member of a family—usually the husband—to own shares. Since only share-holders could hold administrative positions, male ownership precluded women's administrative participation. Some cooperatives, such as *L'Union* of Limoges, stipulated that a woman could be a member of the cooperative "only with her husband's permission."[25] The organizational difficulties for women within French cooperation mirrored those of French feminism in general, where despite valiant efforts, the movement was beset by periodic repression and internal divisions. Also, women were not allowed to vote in France, and male cooperators increasingly conceptualized the movement in narrowly political terms.[26]

The roles of socialist cooperation in financing labor militancy and creating a socialist political culture did foster enclaves of socialist political power. It was precisely the shared resources, strength, and interdependence of socialist parties, trade unions, and socialist cooperatives that contributed in large part to the conquest by socialists of national and municipal offices by the 1890s. As one contemporary suggested, "the administration of the cooperative seemed to be the stepping stone for the conquest of municipal power."[27] In French cities such as Lille, Denain, Saint-Claude, and Levallois-Perret, socialist cooperators organized cultures of resistance and gained political power. Cooperatives served as transfer points for relations of power and agents of an expanded vision of socialist commerce where the identities of producers, consumers, and citizens could overlap.

Socialists contributed as well to the ideological debates over the meanings and uses of consumption. In these discussions, socialist cooperators elaborated a theory of consumption that offered a new perspective within the French left. As the economy shifted to one where consumer demand seemed increasingly to influence the organization of production, socialist cooperators sought to organize democratic labor practices and to control production processes through the medium of consumer cooperatives. Employee relations were an important indicator of cooperation's commitment to labor democracy. Socialist cooperatives gave first priority in hiring to those workers fired from their jobs because of labor activism, and supported a six-day work week and union wages. Employees of most cooperatives were represented on administrative councils. However, while some cooperatives paid men and women equally, many did not.[28] As for production, cooperators argued that they should take an active role not only in socializing distribution, but also in creating work-shops and factories that would be "the collective property of the entire prole-tariat."[29] In this way, they argued, cooperation served as a fulcrum for fulfill-ing socialism's goal of the socialization of the means of production and ex-change. Socialist cooperators insisted on the theoretical complementarity of production and consumption (a link that was muted by capitalist commerce), although they placed consumption, rather than production, at the center of their strategies.

Socialist cooperators constructed class-based notions of consumption that challenged those of the department stores and chain stores, as well as those of the rival Cooperative Union. First and foremost, they insisted that consumption was as much a part of the web of capitalism as control over production or the bourgeois Republic. They challenged notions of distribution as a politically neutral free exchange among individuals and of consumption as a personal and individual action. Socialist cooperators argued that workers were doubly exploited—as workers at the point of production in the capitalist mode of production and as consumers in the capitalist mode of consumption. The kinds of goods being produced were increasingly aimed at a working class-market at the same time as workers were increasingly able to think about buying these goods. Yet, both the control of the process and its profits went to the capitalists rather than to the workers. The distribution of products was, they argued, related to social class rather than social needs.[30] Exchanges of goods were one more way for the bourgeoisie to exploit the working class, since capitalist commerce commanded workers' wages. Socialist cooperators argued as well that goods were products of labor, and consequently control over the exchange and distribution of goods indirectly and directly controlled labor. They stressed that "capitalist anarchy" in production resulted in overproduction, division of labor, low salaries, and shoddy products. They envisioned instead a system whereby consumer cooperatives, organized into a national wholesale society, would command production (organized democratically in producer cooperatives), and would focus production on meeting the real needs of consumers.[31] They also, as noted above, insisted that the "profits" from consumption be used for political ends, and that the cooperative function as a kind of "free social space" for working-class politics and culture that included all members of the family. Movement theorists argued that socialist cooperation was both an agent of resistance to capitalism and a worker-controlled space within capitalist society from which to construct an alternative economic system.

Limits to Cooperation's Radical Vision

Despite its strength as the third pillar of socialism, there were boundaries to the growth of socialist consumer cooperation and to the elaboration of a cooperative-based socialist theory of consumption. By the mid-1920s the cooperative movement retained certain aspects of a collective perspective, but its radical thrust had declined. The national consumer cooperative organization, the National Federation of Consumer Cooperatives (*Fédération Nationale des Coopératives de Consommation*, FNCC) founded in 1912 from the merger of the two wings of the movement, represented a small cooperative sector that frequently and defensively adopted capitalist techniques. The explanation for how and why this happened is complicated, and only a few reasons will be briefly noted here.

First, cooperatives in general and socialist cooperatives in particular found their economic growth blunted by other economic interest groups and by an increasingly strong and well-capitalized capitalist system of distribution. For example, cooperatives confronted massive antagonism from both small shopkeepers and antisocialist factory owners. By 1905 small shopkeepers had organized locally and nationally to enlist the state's aid to impose commercial taxation on consumer cooperatives.[32] Factory owners founded their own consumer cooperatives to compete with those of the socialists, a tactic that was especially evident in cooperative strongholds such as the Nord department.[33] On the eve of World War I, capitalist chains had numerically overtaken consumer cooperatives. In 1913 there were 47 capitalist chains uniting 6,446 branches. In the same period, there were 3,250 consumer cooperatives with 716 branches, for a total number of 3,966 cooperative stores. By 1928 there were 102 chains with 18,500 branches compared with 3,513 cooperatives (not including branch stores). While cooperatives provisioned over two million members (5.5 percent of the French population), chain stores provisioned approximately eight million people (around 20 percent of the French population). The most pointed indication of the superior economic strength of chain stores was the difference in sales figures—around three and a half billion francs in total sales for consumer cooperatives and seven billion for chain stores in 1928.[34]

The strength and transformative potential of consumer cooperation relative to capitalist commerce was also undermined by nagging internal divisions between the Cooperative Union and the Socialist Cooperative Exchange. The socialist cooperative movement was further undermined by internal divisions among socialists, notably between Guesdist and Independent socialists, even after the creation of a unified French socialist party in 1905. These divisions inhibited economic cooperation in such areas as wholesaling and absorbed the energies of cooperative activists.

Another internal division within the movement concerned women. Given their role as "spenders" in working-class family economies, there was the real possibility that women would gain power within an organization of consumers. The primary vehicle for muting their demands and for building a cooperative movement that was almost totally male dominated in terms of leadership and politics was the construction of gendered identities within the movement.

Discussions within consumer cooperation characterized women's roles as nonproductive consumers and housewives, while men's roles were linked to production and control over the leadership, political mediation, and theoretical management of the cooperative movement itself. By the 1920s, the prominent cooperator Charles Gide noted: "The role of men is predominant in production, whereas in consumption it is women who are the most important . . . the role

of men is to produce wealth and that of women is to spend it."[35] This bifurcation appeared to resolve the ambiguity: the theoretical and institutional realization of consumer cooperation invoked women's "power" as consumers while
denying the vast majority of women cooperators effective roles in leadership
or administration. By incorporating a dynamic analysis of production and
consumption in cooperative theory and yet ensuring masculine control over the
administration of the movement, male cooperators preserved notions of
strength and masculine authority within a sphere potentially associated with
femininity. The gender identification of femininity solely with consumption
and masculinity with *both* production and consumption thus undermined the
transformative potential of socialist cooperation since it imagined consumption
as a separate women's activity without a link to production.

This position ultimately reveals the instability of the socialist cooperative
movement's assertion of the interrelatedness of consumption and production.
It also reveals the ultimate conservatism of the movement and calls into
question the socialist cooperative movement's claim to be an active
counterexample to capitalist consumer culture. This conservatism was most
evident in two areas. The fixing of sexual difference within consumer cooperation narrowed the possibilities for women's political critique within consumer
cooperation. Also the identifications of masculinity with production and of
femininity with consumption were strikingly similar to those being constructed
by capitalist commerce.

A final reason for the decline of cooperation's radical thread was the
extensive involvement of the cooperative movement with the French state
during World War I, as well as related activities that delegitimated radical
interpretations of consumer cooperation. Movement leaders, self-designated
"neo-cooperators," chose to align the movement within ideological and structural definitions constructed by capitalist commerce and the state rather than
to retain a radical interpretation for the movement. They shifted the theoretical
bases of consumer cooperation from its role as an *alternative* to capitalism to
cooperation as a *regulator* of capitalism. Cooperation was to be a rationalized
movement for all consumers that would offset high prices and help implement
market control.

The origins of cooperation's transformation were in the years immediately
prior to World War I. Cooperators began to stress the similarities rather than
the differences between the Socialist Cooperative Exchange and the Cooperative Union, and to argue that union of the two was necessary to combat the
growing economic threat of capitalist commerce. A group of reformist socialist
cooperative leaders, notably Albert Thomas, Ernest Poisson, and Eugene
Fournière, stated that consumer cooperation should group people as consumers
and use other institutions for "political" purposes. After dismissing the radical
head of the Socialist Cooperative Exchange, Xavier Guillemin in 1910, and
overriding strong protests from many local socialist cooperatives, the socialist

leaders of cooperation began negotiating a merger. In 1912, they formed the FNCC, whose Pact of Unity affirmed Rochdalian principles (especially one person, one vote) and the movement's autonomy and political "neutrality." The economic positions of the FNCC, labeled "neo-cooperation," clearly aligned important aspects of the movement within frameworks associated with capitalist commerce.[36] Fearful of the economic competition of capitalist chains and department stores, cooperative leaders argued they must "adopt the forms and methods dictated by our commercial competition."[37] Neocooperation involved fusing local cooperatives into regional ones for improved economies of scale, raising the cost of shares and encouraging multiple share ownership, and employing professional managers in cooperatives. As associations of consumers, cooperation would aid in price regulation and the restoration of "order" in a market economy.

Prior to World War I, neocooperation existed primarily as a set of prescriptions rather than practices. During the war, however, state and local governments empowered and extended neo-cooperation.[38] Cooperatives served as distribution centers for essential commodities, they were used for price control, and the government sponsored the creation of cooperatives at munitions factories and military cooperatives at the front. In 1917 the French government promulgated the first comprehensive law specifically regarding consumer cooperation, a law that regularized the definition and functioning of cooperatives along neo-cooperative lines, and established the framework for cooperation's receipt of state monies. In the postwar period, the national government relied heavily on cooperatives for provisioning areas liberated from the Germans and for economic reconstruction. In 1918 cooperators adopted a resolution at the national congress of the FNCC that the role of cooperation was "to defend the interests of associated consumers, to serve as public agents for price regulation, and to act in the interest of consumers, therefore in the general interest."[39]

Despite vigorous protests from many local cooperatives, by the beginning of the 1920s consumer cooperation had for the most part changed directions. This change did broaden the appeal of the movement and its membership and economic activities expanded rapidly, although it still lagged behind capitalist commerce. The postwar movement implicitly aligned itself within a consumer culture that fostered individual identification with goods and stressed material rather than social concerns.[40] Consumer cooperation by the 1920s constructed a market culture that addressed consumers as individuals. The movement reversed its position on advertising, and movement leaders cast its use as "consumer education." Ernest Poisson, the President of the FNCC, noted that advertising was necessary "to appeal to consumers, to attract them, to solicit their attention and tastes."[41] Notions of "needs" shifted as well, from meaningful labor and access to basic commodities to a broad range of commodities. Cooperative stores expanded their inventories to include items such as furniture and bicycles, and movement literature stressed "elegance" in fashion and "tastefulness" in home decoration.[42] Like capitalist appeals within the charged consumerist climate of the 1920s, cooperators focused on individual pleasure through leisure, and founded vacation colonies, organized excursions, and added movie "palaces" to cooperatives. Leisure was portrayed as necessary for individual healthfulness and physical fitness.[43] Cooperative leaders framed all of these transformations within a discourse stressing the importance of "rationalization." Cooperation, like capitalism, was to be efficient, rationalized, bureaucratic, and encourage individual pleasure and identification with consumer goods. The reorientation of consumer cooperation after World War I signaled the decline of a collective perspective within the movement. It also eroded the possibility of a collective ideology, of socialized structures, and of a culture of consumption that was socially engaged within twentieth century French commerce and distribution.

Conclusion

Despite these limits, socialist consumer cooperatives were crucial for forging a socialist political presence in the 1890s and early 1900s. Consumer cooperation offered the fullest and most organized challenge to emergent capitalist consumerism. As a grassroots movement rooted in working-class culture and politics, cooperators produced a well-developed class-based critique of capitalist consumerism. As an institutionalized movement, its practices and ideology can be read as a cultural text for the struggles, conflicts, and contradictions within an emerging consumer culture, and as a carrier for working-class visions of a different social and political order. Cooperatives offered socialist and collective theories and practices that were meant to challenge notions of individualist, acquisitive, and profit-oriented consumerism. Modes of consumption, socialists realized, were neither inherently nor necessarily capitalist. Consumer cooperation offered the possibility of constructing consumer institutions that used profits for political and class-specific goals and that could ultimately aid in gaining control of production. As the "third pillar" of socialism, socialist cooperatives demonstrated the radical potential of consumption where workers and artisans constructed commercial institutions that complemented their political and economic visions.

The radical interpretation of consumer cooperation was, in part, related to a particular moment in French history when the working-class movement was strong and militantly self-conscious, and when consumer capitalism was emerging but had not yet assumed its final form. The realignment of consumer cooperation was linked both to broader "reformist" politics within the French working-class movement and to the growing economic strength and cultural appeal of capitalist consumerism. By aligning itself within terms established by capitalist commerce, consumer cooperation abdicated its potential as a carrier for an alternative commerce that was socially engaged rather than materialist and acquisitive. Likewise, the failure of the organized working-class movement to define and support a radical vision of consumption and distribution, and instead to favor productivist discourses and policies, left the movement vulnerable to the appeals of "mass" consumption. The history of French consumer cooperation, then points to the possibilities, and limitations, of counterhegemonic movements.

Notes

1. P. Brizon and E. Poisson, *La Coopération* (Paris, 1913), 3. For fuller elaborations and analyses of the themes and events in this, see Ellen Furlough, *Consumer Cooperative Movement in France: The Politics of Consumption, 1834-1930* (Ithaca, 1991).

2. *Le Coopérator d'Amiens*, April 1929.

3. Representatives of 85 French cooperatives attended the first meeting in Paris, as did visitors from the Belgian, Swiss, and English cooperative movements. The congress created an administrative structure to coordinate activities, obtain statutes of all societies, and keep archives. It also created a commercial committee to serve as a clearinghouse on commercial information and to group purchases. On this meeting: *Premier conqrès des sociétés coopératives de consommation de France (1885)*, 1 and "The Co-Operatives Congress of Consumer Societies—Held at Paris, July 1885," *The Co-Operative News* (Manchester, England), October 3, 1885.

4. Charles Gide (1847-1932) was the major theorist for the Cooperative Union. On Gide, see: the special issue on Gide of the *Revue des études coopératives*, no. 209 (1982); Karl Ealter, ed., *Co-Operation and Charles Gide* (London, 1933); T. Miyajima, *Souvenirs sur Charles Gide* (Paris, 1933); A. Lavondes, *Charles Gide: un apôtre de la coopération* (Uzés, 1953); Henri Desroche, *Charles Gide, 1847-1932: trois étapes d'une créativité: coopérative, sociale, universitaire* (Paris, 1982).

5. *Congrès international des sociétés coopératives de consommation* (1889), pp. 6-7

6. On French chain stores during this period, see: Evariste Curtil, *Des maisons français d'alimentation à succursales multiples* (Dijon, 1933); Pierre Moride, *Les maisons à succursales multiples en France et à l'étranger* (Paris, 1913).

7. Not all cooperatives or chain stores sold this range of commodities.

8. Curtil, *Des maisons français*, 58 and France, Direction de Travail, *Annuaire Statistique, 1907* (Paris, 1908), 125. This number does not include the branch stores of individual cooperatives.

9. Curtil, *Des maisons français*, 103-8 and 25. Many managers were themselves former owners of small shops that had been bought out by the chain.

10. Moride, *Les maisons succursales,* 140 and Paul Gemahling, "La concentration commercial sans grands magasins," *Revue d'économie politique* (March-April 1912): 182.

11. Union Coopérative, *Congrès international (1889),* 6.

12. The cost of shares in cooperatives was kept purposefully low in order to make them accessible to workers. Because purchases of shares by workers who were themselves in precarious economic conditions was the major source of capital, French consumer cooperatives were consistently undercapitalized. Some cooperatives also made economically disastrous decisions, such as borrowing large sums of money for building imposing stores, or from poor management. The best example of the latter was the decline of *La Moissonneuse,* a Parisian cooperative founded in 1874. By 1900 this cooperative had around 12,000 members, nine branch stores, and its own press. Yet, at the same time, the administration was accused of embezzlement and falsification of records. In 1904 remaining members liquidated the society. Jean Gaumont, *Les Sociétés de Consommation à Paris* (Paris, 1921), 15-23 and Charles Gide, "Sauvons la Moissonneuse" *L'Association Coopérative,* 5 July 1902.

13. Union coopérative, *Dixième congrès (1900),* 17.

14. Joseph Cernesson, "Les Sociétés coopératives de consommation," *Revue des Deux Mondes* V (15 October 1908): 899-907.

15. Léon Bourgeois, *Solidarité,* 2nd ed. (Paris, 1897), 12.

16. On Solidarism: Judith Stone, *The Search for Social Peace: Reform Legislation in France, 1890-1914* (Albany, 1985), 25-38; Sanford Elwitt, *The Third Republic Defended: Bourqeois Reform in France, 1880-1914* (Baton Rouge, 1986), 170-216; J. E. S. Haywood, "The Official Social Philosophy of the French Third Republic: Léon Bourgeois and Solidarism," *International Review of Social History* 6 (1961): 19-48; and Theodore Zeldin, *France 1848-1945: Politics and Anger* (New York, 1979), 276-318.

17. Socialist Jean Jaurès cast socialism, trade unionism, and cooperation as the "three pillars of socialism" in a speech delivered in Levallois-Perrot. The speech was reprinted in *La Revue socialiste,* April 1904.

18. For Belgian consumer cooperation see, Emile Vandevelde, *La Coopération neutre et la coopération socialiste* (1913); Victor Serwy, "La Coopération en Belgique," *Les Propagateurs de la coopération* (1943); and two works by Carl Strikwerda, *A House Divided: Catholics, Socialists, and Flemish Nationalists in Nineteenth Century Belgium* (Lanham, Maryland, 1997) and "'Alternative visions' and Working-Class Culture" this volume.

19. For L'Avenir de Plaisance, see Xavier Guillemin, *Bourse des coopératives socialistes de France: Sa fondation jusqu'à la naissance de la FNCC* (1927), 5-9 and Guillemin, "L'Avenir de Plaisance," *Le Mouvement socialiste,* 1 September 1898. For Amiens, the main studies of l'Union are Eugene Cozette, *L'Union d'Amiens: Historioue de la Société, 1892-1923* (1923) and A. Choquet, *L'Union coopérative d'Amiens* (1935).

20. Socialists involvement in cooperatives predated the "official" pronouncements by socialist parties that members should join cooperatives and support the movement. Those official motions passed in national congresses were the P.O.S.R. (Allemanists) in 1896, the P.O.F. (Guesdists) in 1897, and the C.G.T. in 1900. For statements by Jean Jaurès: "La leçon des fêtes de Bruxelles," *Le mouvement socialiste,* May 1899;

"Ouestion de Method," *La Petite République*, October 1899; "Socialism et coopération," *La Petite République*, July 1900.

21. Roger Verdier, "La Longue marche de la coopération: De la verrerie ouvrière (1895) au Pacte d'unité (1912)," (Ph.D. thesis, Ecole des Hautes Etudes en Sciences Sociales, 1981), 30 and 75. On the glassworkers, see Joan Wallach Scott, *The Glassworkers of Carmaux: French Craftsmen and Political Action in a Nineteenth-Century City* (Cambridge, Mass., 1981) and Marie-France Brive, "La verrerie ouvrière d'Albi (1895-1931)," (Ph.D. thesis, University of Toulouse, 1980).

22. *Statutes de la Bourse des Coopératives socialistes de France*. Reprinted in the *Almanach de la coopération socialiste*, (1911), 107-111.

23. *Bulletin mensuel . . . Levallois-Perret*, July 1900 and Arthur Henriet, *La Classe ouvrière et la coopération* (Paris, 1911), 31-39.

24. *Bulletin de la bourse*, August 1910 and Alice Jouenne, *La Femme et la Coopération* (Paris 1911), 31-39.

25. J. M. A. Paroutaud, *Une Coopérative de Consommation: L'Union de Limoges* (Limoges, 1944), 62.

26. On French feminism, see Claire Goldberg Moses, *French Feminism in the Nineteenth Century* (Albany, 1983); Charles Sowerwine, *Sisters or Citizens? Women and Socialism in France since 1876* (Cambridge, 1982); and Maité Albistur and Daniel Armogathe, *Histoire du Féminisme français* (Paris, 1977).

27. Jean Gaumont, *Les mouvements de la coopération ouvrière dans les banlieues parisiennes* (Paris, 1932), 242.

28. *Bulletin de la Bourse*, July 1910.

29. *Premier congrès national et international de la coopération socialiste (1900)*, 47. Socialist cooperators not only monetarily supported existing producer cooperatives, but founded their own, notably the shoe factory at Lilliers (Pas-de-Calais).

30. For one example of this argument, see BCS, *Quatrième congrès national* (1903), 49-50.

31. BCS, *Premier congres* (1900), 52; Georges Boudios, *Le coopérator syndicaliste* (Paris, 1911), 13-14; and *Bulletin mensuel . . . du Nord*, 15 January 1901.

32. Nord, *Paris Shopkeepers*, 21-44. Also, G. Durant, *Le petit commerce et ses sociétés de consommation* (Paris 1901).

33. *Bulletin mensuel . . . du Nord*, January 1903 and May 1905, and Auguste Devaux, *Les Sociétés coopératives de consommation dans le Nord et Principalement dans l'arrondissement de Lille* (Lille, 1907), 61-62 and 81-85.

34. Charles Gide, "France: Consumers' Cooperation," in *Encyclopaedia of the Social Sciences*, ed. Edwin R. A. Seilgman (New York, 1931), 377 and Roger Picard *Formes et Méthods Nouvelles des entreprises commerciales* (Paris, 1936), 96.

35. Gide, *Revue de Metaphysique et de morales*, April-June 1921.

36. The two most important statements for neocooperation were Bernard Lavergne, *Les méthods nouvelles et la lutte contra les sociétés à succursales multiples* (Paris, 1913) and Ernest Poisson, *La Coopération Nouvelle* (Paris, 1914).

37. "Grands magasins et coopératives," *Bulletin de la Confédération des Coopératives Socialistes et Ouvrières de Consommation*, January 1912.

38. On cooperation and World War I, see Gilles Normand, *La Guerre, le Commerce Français, et les Consommateurs* (Paris, 1920); Jean Boulanger, *Les Coopératives de consommation en France pendant la Guerre, 1914-1918* (Lille, 1920); and "Les Coopératives militaires pendant la Guerre," FNCC *Annuaire de la Coopération* (1920).

39. FNCC, *5e Congrès National (1918)*, 137.

40. A good summary of these positions, by the person who was President of the FNCC, is Ernest Poisson, *La Politique du Mouvement Coopérative Français* (Paris, 1929).

41. FNCC, *10e Congrès National (1923)*, 184-89 and 94. In 1922 the FNCC established the National Office for Cooperative Advertising (Office Nationale de Publicité coopérative).

42. *L'Action coopérative*, 15 December 1924; *Le Coopérateur . . . d'Amiens*, April 1930; and *Le Coopérateur de France: Organe de la Fédération Nationale des Coopératives de Consommation*, 7 January 1928.

43. A. Guilleuic, "L'Education physique et sportive de la jeunesse" *Le Coopérateur de France*, 18 February 1928.

Chapter 7

From Self-Help to Konzern: Consumer Cooperatives in Austria, 1840-1990

Gabriella Hauch

This chapter will describe the development of consumer cooperatives in Austria—that is the German-speaking lands of the Habsburg monarchy (Cisleithania) before 1918 and the state of Austria since 1918. A specific constellation of political and legal factors, the growing industrial economy, and, in part, a new consciousness among workers led to the emergence in the nineteenth century of what were called "consumer cooperatives."[1] The main attraction of the earliest consumer cooperatives was the opportunity for economically disadvantaged groups to lessen their dependence on private shops and, instead, to develop new forms of purchasing and distribution of goods which could be tailored to their needs through self-help. Alongside this type of self-help organization developed a type of cooperative that was paternalist, grounded in charitable ideals, and organized by members of the social elites to benefit the poor.

Consumer cooperatives were part of a strategy to enable lower-class people to overcome economic dependence. According to this strategy, "liberation from" was supposed to be understood and realized as both a cultural and political task. How the majority of consumer cooperatives came to embrace and define this utopian ideal during the nineteenth century, World War I, the authoritarian corporatist system of the 1930s, national socialism 1938-1945, and in the post-World War II years is a main theme of this chapter. As we will see, this ideal confronted problems of centralization, elitism, and bureaucratization since conquering economic dependency created new dependencies. These new relationships of power cannot be understood as isolated individual dynamic conflicts, but rather as parts of the framework of capitalistic market relations.

The "cooperative principle," to gain protection against those stronger through self-help, combined with a demand for education and the will to use that education to advantage, is still relevant today. It has, however, moved noticeably to the "alternative culture" and "alternative economy" of the industrial states and to the so-called third and fourth world societies. The basis for this—besides ensuring subsistence—is the belief in an ideal of "the utopia of a free and equal society of an all-inclusive" comradeship.[2] This concept can be traced to the European Enlightenment and utopian socialism—a tradition that the Austrian labor movement embraced.[3]

Another main theme here is that the history of consumer cooperatives is closely linked to the different types of organizations of the workers' movement: the Social Democratic Party, the labor unions, as well as workers' other economic organizations. The "three pillars of the labor movement," which the Austrian Socialist leader Karl Renner in 1909 labeled the triad of political party, labor union, and consumer cooperative, was an important theme from the late nineteenth century on. The basis for creating this movement was an "ideology of classlessness," which in turn depended on the concept of "solidarity"—an ideology that supports the differentiation, individualization, and privatization of social interest groups through raising the quality of social interaction and encouraging collective self-help.[4] Social democracy as a cultural movement tried to form an all-inclusive social network by the social democratization of the work-family-leisure—(*Reproduktion*)—cycle of its members and sympathizers. This creation of an "alternative" to bourgeois-capitalistic society claimed—by expansion and intensification—to break bourgeois "hegemony."[5] It is to be noted, however, that the social democratic concept of the democratization of human life cycles also partly adapted itself to the norms, values, and organizational and representative forms of bourgeois culture. One example of this is "Red Vienna" (*das 'rote Wien'*) of the 1920s. The adaption to bourgeois culture, however, does not negate social democracy's contribution to the democratization of society, and the raising of educational and living standards.

The role of women as consumers and cooperators is one of central issues in this history. In the tradition of socialist theory, going back to Charles Fourier, the most sensitive category for social democratization and emancipation in a society, organization, or program has been the position of women. Analyzing consumer cooperative politics from the point of view of gender, it is clear that the bourgeois picture of women as housewives could be painted in both proletarian and petit-bourgeois tones. Despite Marxian criticism, following Friedrich Engels and August Bebel, of the way the family functioned—the maintenance of authoritarian traits, the inheritance of private property, and gendered roles that produced inequality—only a few young and mainly communist intellectual men and women of bourgeois origin experimented with alternative ways of life.[6] The family as an abstract field of dreams for private happiness and calm remained valid in the Austro-Marxian citizenship concept—especially so for males.

When defined as a political sphere, the history of consumer cooperatives enables us to decode the patriarchal character of the labor movement's ideology centered on the gendered valuation of reproduction and production. The analysis of consumption can be seen as the key for decoding the gender-specific division of labor and the resultant contradictory demands on women.[7] Together with external political and economic pressures, and concessions made to guarantee the success of the politically motivated enterprises, the cooperatives' internal structure played a decisive role. It then becomes clear that their claim of an expanded political idea that included production *and* consumption (*Konsumtion*) cannot really be sustained. With increasing centralization and an economy geared toward profitability, the role of the individual cooperators (both male and female) was often reduced to that of a passive consumer. Furthermore, the organizational structures, the administration, and the member assemblies did not testify to the "power of the housewives" as advertised in the brochures of the consumer cooperatives.[8] These themes raise the question of what was the relationship between the various functions that allowed cooperation to survive and what was the fate of cooperation under various political systems. How did cooperation prove itself as an economic enterprise with sociopolitical claims and as a political organization?

"Conservative Modernization" 1840s to 1880s

The concept "conservative modernization"[9] characterizes the founding phase of consumer cooperatives in the Austrian German part of the Habsburg monarchy (Cisleithania),[10] from the 1840s approximately until the stock market crash of 1873, followed by a renewed boom in consumer cooperatives from the mid-1880s.

Two developments shaped this first phase of consumer cooperative founding. One was the charitable initiatives "from above" under the patronage and dominance of social elites like the bourgeoisie and landed estates. The social and economic situation—poverty and social misery—which was one of the consequences of the Industrial Revolution—formed the background for these initiatives. Cooperation was supposed to arrest or at least lessen workers' poverty. At the same time, "private" groups were to aid in keeping the lower-class populace in its "place" and maintaining social peace. The consequences of modernization were reflected negatively not only in the living conditions of the lower classes, but also of the middle classes. In large part, small tradesmen, civil servants in concentrated city centers, and skilled workers considered themselves to be similar victims of early industrial capitalism and turned to consumer cooperatives as a vehicle for self-help. The protagonist of this social reform trend, Eduard Pfeiffer, therefore, pleaded for open access to consumer cooperatives for all social classes. He hoped to advance the goal of class reconciliation by applying the principle of "countervailing power," that is, workers could be reconciled with other classes once they possessed more resources.

While in other European countries, such as Germany or England, this development was shaped by the existence of paternalistic figures such as Robert Owen, Friedrich Wilhelm Raiffeisen, and Hermann Schulze-Delitzsch (the latter, the father and founder of the cooperative idea according to Ferdinand Lassalle), Austria had no such outstanding founding figure.[11] The earliest Austrian cooperative associations of the 1860s adopted the organizational structure existing in Germany and were listed in the association statistics of the "General Federation of German Purchase and Trade Cooperatives Based on Self-Help" (*Allgemeinen Verbands der auf Selbsthilfe beruhenden deutschen Erwerbs- und Wirtschafts-genossenschaften*) founded in 1864.[12] An appeal for Austria to follow the German example and to organize their own association was not responded to at first. Only when the cooperatives were threatened by tax reform and the imposition of a stamp tax and new fee system was a committee established in 1867, followed by the establishment of the General Association of Austrian Purchasing and Trade Cooperatives (*Allgemeinen Federation der Österreichischen Erwerbs- und Wirtschafts-genossenschaften*). The close personal association between cooperatives in Germany and German-speaking Austria was underlined by the presence of Schulze-Delitzsch at the first Congress of the Austrian *Verband*, in 1875 in Vienna.[13] Soon after the founding, the interests of credit unions (*Kreditgenossenschaften*) and consumer cooperatives began to clash within the *Verband*. In 1881, consumer cooperatives began to form their own sub-associations since they recognized a detrimental conflict of interest with the credit unions.[14]

On a social-economic level, the early consumer cooperatives represented institutions that were meant to increase the purchasing power of underprivileged individuals. Collective economic power was not an aim. The legal counsel of the Austrian cooperative *Verband*, Karl Wrabetz, said in 1889 "that the aim was to provide the little man with as many of the advantages of large capital as possible."[15] A similar impetus lay behind the Austrian association law (*Genossenschaftsgesetz*), which recommended the establishment of cooperatives in order to draw the poorer classes away from the erroneous teachings of communism.[16]

Next to the aims of Schulze-Delitzsch who sought to solve social conflicts with the principle of cooperatives, and the social reform direction of Pfeiffer who followed Robert Owen, there existed another founding figure in the person of the German workers leader, Ferdinand Lassalle. Lassalle wanted to organize against the laws of free market—which only resulted in inequality and injustice—through the establishment of cooperatives. On the other hand, Lassalle defined consumer cooperatives as ultimately "totally incapable" of helping people "where the shoe really pinches"—in their position and function as alienated working producers. Consumer cooperatives, he believed, could only make modest improvements in the sphere of consumption because of the "iron law of wages"; the average wage reduces to the minimum necessary for survival, meaning that the purchase of cheaper groceries in the consumer cooperative would reduce wages.[17] Lassalle leads us to the beginning of the consumer cooperative movement in Austria, which was shaped by the beginning of the organized labor movement.

Perspectives on the "Labor Movement"

The position of the leaders of the early labor movement vis-à-vis consumer cooperatives fell into three categories: disapproval, neutrality, or the view that consumer cooperatives were a means to an end. Even Karl Marx had conceded the possibility of the "cooperative movement" becoming a "driving force" (*Tricbkraft*) in overcoming capitalism—along with the party and unions.[18] In his inaugural address to the International Workers' Association in 1864, he confined his comments on the negative aspects of cooperatives to "individual workers" who were not part of the revolutionary movement.[19] There was little real appreciation, however, of the attraction or potential appeal of cooperation on its own. Yet the actual situation demanded a much deeper engagement with cooperation from the mass of those involved in the early Marxist-inspired labor movement who themselves were largely male workers.[20]

The example of the "Reciprocal Assistance/Support Association of the Factory Workers of Teesdorf" (*Wechselseitiger Unterstützungs-Verein der Fabrik-arbeiter zu Teesdorf*), founded in the small village near Vienna by textile workers in August 1856, and recognized as "the beginning of the consumer cooperative movement in Austria," shows on how weak an economic basis these early self-help initiatives rested.[21] Teesdorf became a legend and was described as the "first modern cooperative in Austria." The stated goal of the association was "mainly the low-cost acquisition" of groceries and their distribution of these to the members. On Sundays, two members took a push-cart to Wiener Neustadt, in the vicinity of Vienna, and acquired the merchandise ordered by the members. Soon, they needed a horse-drawn wagon. In 1866, they abandoned the preorder system and started a small warehouse. In 1873, the year of the stock market crash, they purchased a house in which they set up a retail shop.[22] With this, they turned into professional businesspeople and started down the road to bankruptcy, which could only be stopped by the employment of a professional manager.

This instability characterized the consumer cooperatives for a long time to come. The economic upswing of the mid-1860s translated into faster industrialization and the establishment of new consumer cooperatives. However, the 508 consumer cooperatives registered in the year of the stock market crash—1873—had been reduced to only 276 five years later.[23] Despite this, an increasingly positive picture of consumer cooperatives developed on account of their economic advantages. After the economic upswing of 1895, local authorities and factory owners started to see the advantages and promoted new establishments. It was thus that the Austrian Social Democratic Party—when it started to consider consumer cooperatives as a political issue—was confronted with a situation characterized by the delegate Franz Roscher to the party convention of the SDAP in Prague in 1896 as follows: "Concerning the consumer associations, in my opinion, we'll never get rid of them."[24]

One problem that the organized labor movement had in clarifying its position vis-à-vis consumer cooperatives was the political and religious neutrality established in article 4 of the "*Rochdaler Grundsätze*" (Rochdale principles) modeled after those of the most influential British cooperative. In 1898, six consumer cooperatives were expelled from the Austrian *Allgemeinen Verband* due to their insistence on establishing their own association[25] and their efforts to replace the principle of "political neutrality" with a socialist perspective.[26] Following this, a separate association of consumer cooperatives was founded in July 1901, the *Verband der Arbeiter-, Erwerbs- und Wirtschaftsgenossenschaften* (the Federation at Wozker, Trodl, and Economic Associations). By the end of 1903, 184 associations were affiliated with it; one year later, there were over 300. The number of consumer cooperatives remaining in the *Allgemeinen Verband*—200—had thus been surpassed. In May 1904, a unity conference took place in order to overcome the fragmentation within the cooperative movement regarding wholesale buying. The *Zentralverband der österreichischen Konsumvereine* (Central Federation of Austrian Consumer Unions) was then founded.[27]

The previous year, the party convention had conferred the Social Democratic Party's blessing on the consumer cooperatives. They were even described as "a weapon in the hands of the proletariat."[28] The change had been heralded not only by the attitude and conduct of the members—membership in Austrian consumer cooperatives numbered 240,799 that year and included many party members—but also by theoretical considerations. Karl Kautsky, formerly an opponent of consumer cooperatives, began to support them while calling for expanding their function beyond the procurement of inexpensive foodstuffs. In his opinion, membership represented a learning experience for developing a sense of community and democratic administration. Even socialist thinking and feeling could be learned in consumer cooperatives.[29] The words of Eduard Bernstein, "They are and will exist, whether the Social Democratic Party wants it or not," had triumphed in Austria seven years ahead of the German sister organization.[30] At the 1909 German party convention in Leipzig, advocates of socialist cooperatives pointed to the success of the Austrian party in working with consumer cooperatives.[31] One reason for the delay in the Germans recognizing cooperatives was the quarrel over whether the German Social Democratic Party should drop its revolutionary program and adopt a "revisionist" or reformist strategy.[32] Consumer cooperatives were a central example of revisionism or nonrevolutionary action during the quarrel. No similar theoretical discourse took place in the Austrian party, and thus the Austrian Socialists were freer to accept cooperation.

The expected "rush" to the consumer cooperatives after their acceptance by the Austrian Social Democratic Party failed to materialize, however. This demonstrates how overrated the authority of the party was by contemporaries and by historians—in other words, the propaganda pamphlets (*Agitationsbroschüren*) were accepted at face value without the necessary examination of the sources. Working people became members in consumer cooperatives when the need arose—regardless of what "the party" said. During the 1907 party convention, membership was declared an obligation.[33] Obligatory membership was intended to strengthen the Socialists' hegemonical political concept; "from the cradle to the grave," workers were to be attached to Socialist institutions. The 1909 party convention finally brought closure to the question of what to do about consumer cooperatives in the Austrian Social Democratic Party. These discussions had oscillated between pragmatism and program. While up to then consumer cooperatives had been the "children of Social Democracy" (*Kinder der Sozialdemokratie*), now they became an "equal lever (*gleichwertiger Hebel*) in the war of liberation of the class conscious workers" since they could now secure in the price sector (via workers' purchasing power) what the labor unions had achieved in the wage sector.[34] At least on paper, of course.

The theoretical and strategic discussions and the economic development of the consumer cooperatives progressed unevenly at different times. In 1905, a central buying organization, *Großeinkaufsgesellschaft Österreichischer Consumvereine* (*GOC*) (Austrian Consumer Union Wholesale Society), based on the German model (the *GEG*) was founded.[35] An important consideration for the labor movement was the production of bread since it represented the means of subsistence for the lower classes at a time when one year of inflation was followed by another.[36] Consumer cooperatives had owned their own bakeries since the turn of the century. However, the construction of a milling operation and bread factory near Vienna was more economically risky. In June 1909, with the support of the Socialist party, the time had arrived for the grand opening of the *Hammerbrotwerke* (Hammer breadworks) in Schwechat (near Vienna). The Christian-Social mayor of Vienna, Karl Lueger, had prevented the construction within the city limits.[37] The factory, with the largest mill of the kingdom, was decorated with red flags flying from the roofs. Three years later, the economic downward slide began for the *Hammerbrotwerke*, which was countered with modern advertising methods such as outdoor parties

(*Hammerbrotwochen*)—which required the attendance of the social democratic citizens (male and female) of Vienna. The implication of the *Hammerbrot* as a symbol of identity became clear during the election campaign of 1911: the purchase and consumption of bread from the *Hammerbrotwerke* was seen as a form of political agitation and action. As a party newspaper asserted,

> Purchase your bread where the happy answer to your query regarding the status of the 'eight-hour-day' is going to be: "In this factory, 'the threefold three, the holy three' is at work, the spirit of our red People's Party rules. Therefore remember, if your way of thinking's red (*rot*), then you will only like the taste of *Hammerbrot*.

> *Hammerbrot* is fully nutritional, it does not serve the cause of surplus value which capitalism takes away from us. *Hammerbrot* contains the holy spirit embodied in our great strivings. It will not only satisfy your hunger, it plants confidence in your breast, it will make you strong and self-confident. [38]

(The "threefold eight" = the "holy three" pertained to 8 hours work, 8 hours sleep, and 8 hours leisure.)

The changed position of the Social Democratic Party regarding the organizing of the consumer cooperation cannot be explained only by an intellectual appreciation of the advantages of consumer cooperatives or the pressure of the (party) members, as it was often recorded in autobiographies of Austrian socialist leaders.[39] With the reform of the Austrian election law, the competition between the Social Democrats and the newly developing middle-class parties, especially the Christian Social Party who represented the interests of small shopkeepers or tradesmen, became increasingly important and has to be considered when discussing the changed position. When the 1897 Vienna parliamentary elections did not result in a mandate for the SDAP, the party press blamed the small shopkeepers. Cooperatives were both a means for recruitment to the socialist party and a site for propaganda. For example, Christian Social supporters were called "old grocers" (*Greißlers*) and were considered symbolic of the Catholic environment of the small shopkeepers. Shopkeepers, in turn, looked on the "red" consumer cooperatives as the cause of their economic ruin. When the agitation against the consumer cooperatives was at its peak during the 1907 elections for the Parliament, the Christian Social Party held an election rally in Vienna's city hall. (A similar rally had taken place during the 1897 elections.) It was demanded that consumer cooperatives not be permitted to carry specific goods, such as gourmet foods, fashion articles, and other luxury goods.[40] This demand fits into the image of consumer cooperatives as shops for the poor (*Arme-Leute-L äden*).[41] The "little people" were to have access to affordable consumer goods, which, while still modeled on those of the more affluent, were to be clearly disassociated from those for bourgeois tastes. This was in line with the rational-ascetic thinking of Austrian Marxists who held that "a worker who uses his brain neither smokes nor drinks" (*ein denkender Arbeiter raucht und trinkt nicht*).

By 1913, the *Zentralverband* succeeded in organizing 70 percent of all consumer cooperatives in the Austrian half of the monarchy. This percentage was lower than it might have been because the Czech cooperatives seceded in 1908 to found their own autonomous Federation of Czech Associations (*Zech Zentralverband tschechischer Genossenschaften*) in Prague. This was one of the decisive points in the history of the struggle between German and non-German speakers in the Habsburg monarchy that affected the labor unions and the socialist party equally. The consumer cooperatives remaining in the *Allegmeinen Verband* existed in the shadow of the credit unions (*Kreditgenossenschaften*). In 1933 the renamed *Österreichischer Genossenschaftsverband* expelled the last remaining 26 consumer cooperatives. [42]

Besides the economic dimension—the supply of cheaper goods, the independence from bourgeois small shopkeepers and middlemen—an important place in the publications promoting the consumer cooperative concept was devoted to education, both in socialist solidarity and in democratic administration. In view of the lack of economic profitability of the consumer cooperatives before World War I,[43] this educational mission then became a justification for their existence. If it was the lack of sufficient capitalization and management experience—the members of the boards by and large lacked training in commercial practices—which hindered economic success, during the time of "politicization" it was the mixing of party politics and management that proved that politically motivated buyers, both male and female, were no guarantee of an economically successful consumer organization. [44]

Who Were the Customers in a Consumer Cooperative?

This decisive question is missing from the discussion themes of this chapter listed in the introduction. This is deliberate since it is the main theme of most of the primary sources and existing secondary literature. The sociopolitical aspect of "buying" lies in the acquisition of market goods needed for the daily physical needs that must be differentiated by class. From this, the question arises, who carries out this chore, who shopped in the consumer cooperative? The answer: almost exclusively women.

Reproduction of the gender-specific division of labor is generally accepted as the starting point when searching for the causes of discrimination and oppression against women. It is necessary to note here that the social character of gender relationships created power relationships for one half of humankind in a much broader way than the creation of waged labor.[45] According to

Marx, labor became a gender-neutral concept; in actuality, however, it was thought of as "masculine" and treated accordingly by the various arms of the labor movement. This is not the place to enter into a discussion of the ability of female workers—as a potential—and the female worker—as a reality. In addition, even the definition of these terms and the examination of their relationship to one another—starting from subject and/or object of capitalistic/patriarchal relationships—has to be omitted.[46]

It would appear that in a discussion of loosely defined and socially determined labor under capitalism, the subject of gender can be ignored. Nevertheless, based on the topic at hand that excludes productive work as a paradigm for politicalization, it becomes clear that a "veil" is missing from the genderless criticism of the politics of economics that the labor movement engaged in. The member of the cooperative (*Genossenschafter*) who organizes the consumer cooperatives and who becomes a voting member through the possession of a share of the business was almost always the head of the household, a man. Thus, the frequently conjured up definition of self-help is a relatively abstract one, since women were largely subordinated and found it difficult if not impossible to help themselves through the cooperatives.

For the feminist viewpoint at the end of the twentieth century, the founding phase of the consumer cooperatives offers a measure of ambivalence. The politicization of consumption as a sphere of reproduction opens itself up for research into the gender-specific division of labor in families and its consequences. The finger will be directed to the sore point, the missing gender-specific perspectives and practices. A certain feeling of relief is also noticeable. Thank goodness "they" (Opponents of Cooperation) did not automatically pin the label of women's associations on consumer cooperatives. Nevertheless, within the structure of consumer cooperatives, gender specifics already existed. Without female consumers, without female shoppers, there could be no politicization of consumption or consumer cooperatives.

In 1912, this time had arrived: women, not the female worker but the "housewife" (*Hausmütter*)—as she was called before World War I—were enlisted for and by the consumer cooperatives. The housewife had been addressed and appealed to since 1908 in the magazines of the consumer cooperatives, "*Der freie Genossenschafter,*" "*Der Pionier,*" and "*Für unsere Hausmütter.*" At the same time, this indicates a change in social democratic politics regarding women. Karl Renner, a representative of the *Zentralverband* since 1911, enlisted the Social Democratic Party member Emmy Freundlich for the cooperative movement.[47] In 1912, she became the first female member of the board of the *Verband*. Socialist women founded a cooperative women's organization, and women's commissions were set up with responsibility for advertising to and propagandizing among women. However, no impetus for women's emancipation is to be found in this. The bourgeois image of women became the accepted norm in both proletarian and petit-bourgeois terms. Emmy

Freundlich busied herself with concepts. As editor of the family oriented cooperative publication, *"Der Pionier,"* she demonstrated the new direction in renaming it, *"Für unsere Hausmütter."* It included instructions and hints on how to manage a household, the upbringing of children, personal hygiene, and other matters relating to housewifely concerns. In addition, it was intended to achieve recognition and understanding of the importance of women for the cooperative and the latter's importance to family and society.[48]

The establishment of separate women's sections did not occur without friction—similar to what had happened in the labor unions thirty years before. Many consumer associations were not ready and willing to answer the recommended summons for the establishment of women's organizations.[49] In contrast to the English Women's Cooperative Guild, which was founded already in 1883, collected its own membership dues, and acted independently of the cooperative movement, the Austrian women's committees were subordinated to the Central Women's Committee, which, in turn, was subordinated to the board of the *Zentralverband der österreichischen Konsumvereine.*[50]

The establishment of women's sections in the federation of the Austrian consumer cooperatives has to be seen in conjunction with the founding of the middle class women's federation (*Reichsorganisation der Hausfrauen Österreichs [ROHÖ]*) in 1909. The latter represented a self-help response to the economic distress of the inflation years prior to World War I under the auspices of Christian Social patronage. In addition to aspects of rivalry, the intention to turn housewives into political activists emerged from the agenda of the ROHÖ:[51]

> The influencing of all legal and administrative measures which touch on household interests, the inclusion of housewives in all discussions and decision making, official recognition of the value of domestic work.

For the Social Democratic Party, in its early phase, for the politics of socialism, housewives did not appear to be subjects who could be won over or organized politically. However, a change in the overall activity of women in the Austrian Social Democratic Party in the years prior to World War I can be observed. On the first International Women's Day on March 18, 1911, 20,000 people demonstrated on the streets in favor of women's suffrage. It was obvious that women's suffrage was only a question of time especially after the passage of general male suffrage in 1905. The concept of the "Woman Voter" became a potential vote getter—seen either as a source of increased or decreased power. The Social Democratic Party, which feared the Christian-Social coalition of church and women, tended to reproduce conventional definition of gender. In 1912, for example, two pages of the *Arbeiterinnen-Zeitung* were rededicated to advice on dressmaking and similar issues.[52]

However, it was not until the interwar years that the slogan "the power of the housewife" became a fundamental guiding light in the women's politics of the Social Democratic Party and the Central Cooperative Associations (*Zentralverband*).[53] This was the situation in Austria where Emmy Freundlich was the first female member of the consumer cooperative board (*Präsidium*) and presided over the discussions. The image of the *Zentralverband* of the consumer cooperatives as a place where individual leading women were given a voice is not reconcilable with the reality of the situation of the female members: complaints about unclean consumer shops, expensive merchandise, and the inability to shop on credit went unheeded at party conventions.[54]

World War I: The Politics of Shortages

By integrating into the war economy, the consumer cooperatives of the *Zentralverband*—as happened in most of the European countries—achieved a solid economic basis. In addition, they were able to prove the attractiveness and superiority of their centralized organizational web to the government authorities, they were honest distributors of scarce consumer goods. As in other European countries, they became nationalized or partially nationalized distribution agencies and part of the centralized war economy, and their representatives (male and female) participated in the direction of the war effort.[55] In this way, their activities supported the state and, indirectly, the war effort.

Together with the metal workers' union, the *Zentralverband* founded the Federation of Grocery Stores for Workers Involved in the War Effort (*Lebensmittel-verbände der kriegsdienstleitenden Arbeiter*). It was managed in equal parts by employers and representatives of the consumer cooperatives and took over the provisioning of the service industries involved in the war effort. In Vienna alone, 400,000 people had to be provided with meals every two weeks. It was here that the cooperative distribution system proved most useful. In return for this service, members of the consumer cooperatives were allowed to receive meals as well, which meant a relatively secure supply of food. One condition for this was that the number of new admissions to the cooperatives had to be restricted. Despite this limitation, the number of members in Cisleithania increased from 298,605 at the end of 1914 to 367,530 at the end of 1918.[56] Most of the new members were from social classes, which had, up to then, no connection with the consumer cooperative movement. Their motivation to join was grounded in economic reasons: it was an act to fight hunger and deprivation.

The war made possible the continued existence of the Austrian consumer cooperatives, the central buying organization, the *GÖC*, and the *Hammerbrotwerke*. The *Hammerbrotwerke* worked at full capacity for the first time since its founding with the production of *zwieback* (cracker bread) for the army. The operation could now begin to pay off its debts. Attempts to sell the factory, which had still been ongoing at the beginning of the war, were dropped on a note of satisfaction.[57] Cooperation with local authorities resulted in good governmental contacts, unrestricted access to minister presidents and cabinet officers, state loans, and financial advantages. At the same time politicians recognized that cooperative leaders were worthwhile and important men. The mistrust with which the social democratic "comrades without a country" and cooperators had had to contend appeared to be changing after all. The utility of their structure for the government's purposes initiated a discussion on the question of creating secure and legal representation for consumers. The price that the *Zentralverband* paid for this was the violation of its cooperative principles: restrictions on new members, acceptance of government rationing, no distribution of rebates, and the relinquishing of the internationalist principle to which the International Cooperative Alliance had pledged allegiance following the Second International. In any case, the consumer cooperatives presented themselves as strong, viable organizations at the time of the collapse of the Dual Monarchy and the victory of the Allies.

From Postwar Crises to the Time of Consolidation

In addition to a solid economic basis at the end of the war, the demise of hitherto accepted values, hierarchy, and order constituted an advantageous starting position for the consumer cooperatives. Strengthened by the powerful appeal of the Russian Revolution, social-revolutionary movements gripped all of Europe. At Bavaria's and Hungary's borders with Austria, short-term workers' and soldiers' councils governments were established. In the first years after the war, strikes and demonstrations—the power of the streets—finally brought far-reaching social and political reform, which also benefitted the *Zentralverband* as a part of the labor movement. But the end of Habsburg rule also meant the end of a supranational Austro-Hungarian government structure. With this came the breakup of the Austrian Kingdom's consumer cooperatives into national associations and separation of the common cooperative property into national segments. Hitherto, they had been structured according to linguistic boundaries.[58] It was not until November 9, 1919, that the Federation of German Austrian Consumer Unions (*Verband deutschösterreichischer Konsumvereine*) could be founded in the Austrian Republic.[59]

For the consumer cooperatives, it now became a question of how the position gained during World War I could be maintained in the period of economic transition and in peace time. This was related to the question of the future economic system: was it to be free market, mixed, state-directed, or national-

ized? For the time being, the measures tried and tested in the war were maintained and continued to organize consumer rationing. This translated into
continued growth in membership.

One thing soon became obvious. The new members demonstrated little
interest in the cooperative ideal—consumers' solidarity and economizing in
preparation for a different economic system. The only thing of interest to the
new members was the ability to purchase less expensive groceries in their
respective sales outlets. After the war, the number of cooperative shops expanded due to the fact that they were part of the nonprofit food supply network. Already in 1918 during the establishment of the Economic Committee
for Cooperative Consumer Affairs, Socialist leader Karl Renner had set consideration of the needs of consumer cooperatives during the period of demobilization as one of his goals.[60] In addition, due to the influence of Social Democrats who shared government power with the Christian-Social Party in a
coalition government, state subsidies were granted to cooperatives.

Unlike Germany, the idea of the socialization or nationalization of the
economy continued to be a topic of discussion in Austria. Consumer cooperatives were to be given an important role in the realization of the planned
program of socialization. With the new legal recognition of nonprofit institutions through the law of July 29, 1919, which covered cooperatives because
of their association with *GÖC*—they were to play the part, in Karl Renner's
words, of a "nucleus of socialist means of production in the body of a capitalistic economy."[61]

Already by 1923, Siegmund Kaff, an authoritative critic of the Austrian
consumer cooperative movement, described the mixing of cooperative supply
of needs with capitalistic production for the free market—especially in the
production of textiles and the *Hammerbrotwerke*—as a "fragmentation of
forces." It was his opinion that the cooperative ideal, the organizing of consumer cooperatives and the raising of the necessary financial means, was
becoming more and more obscured. Cooperatives were becoming more similar
to private and profit-seeking enterprises.[62] Another reason for the crisis in the
Austrian consumer cooperatives was the dependence of the Federation (*Verband*) of German Austrian Consumer Unions on state subsidies that, in turn,
were tied to the participation of the Social Democratic Party in the government. This lasted until the summer of 1920, after which the real crisis of the
Austrian consumer cooperatives began.[63]

The political change that was expressed in the election results of 1920 and
the loss of majority status for the Social Democrats had negative consequences.
The state lifted the compulsory government measures to prevent black markets
and marketeering as well as food subsidies, and initiated free trade. The
elimination of consumer goods rationing, mainly foodstuffs, caused a mass exit
from the consumer cooperatives, especially of the new "fluctuating" members.
While the consumer cooperatives had to sell their goods to their members at

affordable prices, the small shopowners kept their shops closed at critical times. Similar to the situation in Germany, this type of abstention from the market was not possible for the consumer cooperatives. On the contrary, it became necessary for cooperatives to return to emergency measures and the rationing of foodstuffs again. This led to another exodus of angry or frustrated members.[64] Meanwhile, the *Verband* of consumer cooperatives had invested in real estate and production facilities above and beyond its financial means because it had had confidence in its protection by the government and party politics. These fixed assets or investments, however, were no substitute for missing liquid assets.

Despite this, the negative balance sheet of this crisis period did not spell ruin. The position of the *GÖC* was firmed up, especially in the production of shoes, textiles, and foodstuffs. The involvement in production operations had succeeded and, finally, the intervention of the Labor Bank (*Arbeiterbank* [*ABAG*])—founded in 1922—saved the day. The concept of a financial institution owned by labor unions and cooperatives had been in existence since before World War I. The Labor Bank, founded in 1922, did not allow ownership of shares of stock by individuals. The labor unions and the *Verband* each owned 40 percent and the organs of the Social Democratic Party and the credit unions each 10 percent. The original idea had been to transfer money from the unions via the Labor Bank to the cooperatives. However, they became self-financing by 1926.[65]

One important factor in the cooperatives' consolidation was the trend of individual consumer cooperatives to combine, i.e., the consolidation of the large Vienna Consumer League in Vienna and the smaller nearby cooperatives into one large organization. This happened also in the provinces. The integration of the large railroad workers food store (the *Eisenbahner-Lebensmittel-magazine*) into the *Verband* also helped.[66] The year 1925 saw the reintroduction of the 1 to 5 percent rebate that had been suspended during the war and the expulsion from membership lists of the so-called "paper soldiers"—members who did not even shop in a cooperative store.

The consequences of the world economic crisis of 1929 led to a rapid decline in living standards and immense unemployment, and the reserves in savings held by the Austrian consumer cooperatives declined drastically. However, the deficit could be balanced out thanks to the stable financial situation and with the help of the Labor Bank. This favorable balance happened despite a drop in sales in the *GÖC* that, under the initiative of its president Andreas Korps, engaged in systematic in-house production.[67] It can be concluded that the Austrian consumer cooperatives, similar to the German ones, were able to maintain their market share remarkably well. Just as in Germany, there was a short-term upswing in membership during the post-stock market crash crisis. This strengthens the thesis that consumers (female and male) were trying to prevent further impoverishment by joining consumer cooperatives—which made the consumer cooperatives that much more attractive in times of economic want.

At the same time, the social polarization and a public backlash against everything "red"—and with this against the consumer cooperatives—in 1930 resulted in legal consequences different from those of the turn of the century. Consumer cooperatives were to come under the trade law (*Gewerbegesetz*), which restricted their operations. This went into effect in 1932. In 1933, the trade regulations were also expanded by emergency order to include cooperatives. This occurred despite the fact that consumer cooperatives had again insisted on their political neutrality and maintained only a loose affiliation with the Social Democratic Party.[68]

A "Different" View of the Red Twenties

In the twenty-year period between the wars, a "Red Vienna" arose in Austria. It represented an experiment in social democratic urban administration—which is still visible today in the material culture of the municipal buildings that date from that era. In the meantime, it has advanced from a beloved topic of labor writers of history to a tourist attraction, mainly of Italian visitors to Vienna. This experiment became possible because of the electoral majorities in the municipal elections and the hegemonic position of the Social Democratic Party in the Austrian labor movement. (There was only a tiny communist party in Austria.)[69] The internationalist left, which had gathered around Friedrich Adler (the assassin of Minister President Count Stürgkh in 1916), Gabriele Proft, and Therese Schlesinge, did not abandon the Socialist party during the time when a whole wave of communist parties were founded all over Europe. That was one reason why the number and influence of Austrian communists, unlike Germany, remained marginal until the party was outlawed in 1933.

In this "Red Vienna" there developed alongside the most modern urban social legislation of the 1920s a distinguished social democratic culture. This reinforced the older familiar quotation "from the cradle to the grave" and was to be understood as the social democratic, proletarian alternative to middle-class society. Increasingly, this socialist counterculture incorporated women who had been given the vote in 1918 and who had been citizens with equal political rights since then.[70] The consumer cooperative sphere now saw a pro-feminist agitation set in. Since women were responsible for consumption, they became the ideal contact persons for the consumer cooperatives. The resultant politicization of every day life, however, appropriated the petit-bourgeois world of gender spheres more deeply among workers' families.

The 1920s brought crucial transformations in the pace of work and time efficiency in the era of production as well as reproduction. These were interrelated but also had gender-specific consequences regarding leisure time. Social legislation and the eight-hour workday—legally in effect since 1918—meant a reordering of the daily routine. This was related to the struggle for a male breadwinner's wage that could support a nuclear family. The family wage (*Familienlohn*) became an expression of the small family unit—hitherto economically unattainable—which was becoming the ideal for workers.[71]

The gender-specific disassociation of work and family life, which let women budget a large part of the income and spend it at the market, was countered by these women's lack of power in the organized consumer cooperative structure. Only he or she who owned a share of the business was able to have a say (vote) and that was, in most cases, the man as head of the household, since very few families could afford a second share. Nevertheless, it became the mission of class-conscious women to consider the consumer cooperatives their own, shopping there exclusively and propagandizing among their own gender.

Georg Büchlein, the deputy managing director of the German GEG, was a guest at the 1925 association day of the *Verband deutsch-österreichischer Konsumgenossenschaften.* He elaborated on the GEG's new advertising strategy directed at women: "We have to recognize the woman for what she is and grab her attention with superficialities. One has to take account of the woman's character/psyche and oblige her accordingly."[72] In this campaign, directed specifically at women, his unflattering vision of women emerges: women are shallow and stupid and can only be reached with references to superficialities. They are not suited for theoretical and probing discourse—which would require an education—on economics. Therefore, they have to be "grabbed" (*packen*), which in the German colloquial can also mean rough physical contact that does not permit resistance. Büchlein puts the German model into concrete terms: evenings with entertainment with, of course, coffee and cake, and short lectures, not too wordy and delivered one after the other. The musical entertainment should be provided by a glee club. Since children were the most important part of a woman's life, Andreas Korp, managing director of the *GÖC*, promoted functions for children with consumer cooperative themes during the cooperative association's celebrations. Not only were future shoppers, female and male, to be reached this way, but the children were to convince their mothers to shop at the cooperative store. This approach, which targeted women, appears especially absurd and revealing when, simultaneously, expansion of the woman's organization was mentioned as the most important part of cooperative "education."[73] Coffee and cake in lieu of economic discourse can neither educate nor be a substitute for political conviction—such as accepting a longer walk in order to shop at a consumer cooperative and with this a longer carrying of the shopping basket, higher prices, or the impossibility of shopping on credit. But this campaign fit into "modern" advertising strategies.[74]

When the rebate program was introduced again in 1926 (at year's end, members received a certain percentage of their total purchases), this was advertised and marketed to women as "pocket money" (Austrian: *Körberlgeld*). It was not a subject of discussion that the consumer cooperatives thereby received an interest-free loan. The failure of a consumer policy directed at women shoppers points beyond the sphere of consumption. It is a valid indictment of a policy that neglected the prevailing gender relationship as a basis of analysis and allowed it to enter unhindered into cooperative goals. In the end, the failure of the consumer cooperative vision rested on norms written in stone that considered shopping and working in a cooperative a female sphere and administrative control a male sphere.

While the experiment of a "socialist female consumer" failed in "Red Vienna" during the politicized period of the 1920s, the model of a social democratic housewife and mother succeeded.[75] Even though Emmy Freundlich, an economic expert well versed in economic theories, sat on the board of the *Zentralverband* of the consumer cooperatives, the bureaucratic administration overseeing this women's activity remained the sphere of men. To be sure, increasingly each branch management committee featured a token woman. But this had no effect on the general structure and direction. In 1931, there were 83 female members of the board as against 455 male; the percentage of women represented only 15 percent of the total.[76]

The Authoritarian Corporative State—Austro-fascist and National Socialist: 1933-1945

In 1933, the Christian-Social chancellor, Engelbert Dollfuß, dissolved the Austrian parliament, basing this decision on the State of Emergency law of 1917. This was followed by a suspension of the constitution, civil liberties, and social political achievements. After the outlawing and dissolving of all political parties, organizations, and associations—including the Christian Social Party—there existed only the unitary organ of the Fatherlands Front ("*Vaterländische Front*"), supported mainly by segments of the armed local militias (*Heimwehren*) and organizations under them.[77]

Consumer cooperatives came under new trade regulations in 1933. This led to a limiting and state control of the numbers of new cooperatives that were permitted. The Labor Bank was dissolved, and the bank accounts of the consumer cooperatives blocked. One year later the government decreed a moratorium on new members, and prohibited the opening of new branch stores. This did not signal the liquidation of the consumer cooperatives. Here, the support of the rural cooperatives—who maintained very good contacts to the ruling "*Vaterländische Front*"—and the only recently improved relationship with shopkeepers groups proved most helpful. As during World War I, the question is to be asked whether the definition of "consumer cooperative" is still applicable since nothing remained of the two principles of self-help and self-administration.

Unlike Nazism, the political system of Austro-fascism could not count on the support of the masses. Therefore, the supervision and inspection of the opposition did not function fully. This translated occasionally even to concessions by the regime and cooperation with different movements. In 1935, cooperative self-direction was partially restored through permission to hold a general assembly of the Vienna Cooperative Association. The GÖC and its associated cooperatives followed a year later. Both instances were not publicly announced. From that time on, they began to recover economically and to consolidate again. Ludwig Strobl, at that time Minister of Agriculture, became the new managing president of the Verband. For the GÖC, there began a new phase of in-house manufacturing—a chemical factory, a printshop, and facilities for the production of paper; a factory for cereal; a wine bottling facility; and a chocolate and candy manufacture were established. As late as 1938, the COOP-Industriegesellschaft was founded, which took charge of most of the production facilities and which consolidated the textile department stores in regional department store corporations (Kaufhausgesellschaften). Almost all of the Austrian consumer cooperatives were consolidated in the Federation of Central Austrian Consumer Associations (Zentralverband österreichischer Konsumgenossenschaften). By feeding the population, the unified organization served the authoritarian regime, which was under Christian Social control. Despite this, pamphlets named "Creeping Socialism" (Schleichender Sozialismus) or "The Consumer Cooperative's Urge to Expand" (Der Expansionsdrang der Konsumgenossenschaften)—both published by Eduard Gudenus in 1937—demonstrated that the political aversion to the cooperatives was not a thing of the past.[78] During this period, however, the social function of the consumer cooperatives was not only reactivated but also expanded under the patronage of the government. The GÖC-Club became an organization devoted to leisure and sports activities. In 1936, an education center (Bildungsheim) with study circles was established—based on Swiss and Swedish models.[79]

Even after Austria's Anschluß into the German National Socialist Third Reich in March of 1938, the consumer cooperatives were not immediately dissolved. In Germany, the formerly social democratic sister organization had been acquiring experience in dealing with the regime since 1933 and had demonstrated by example how political and humanistic principles could be waived for the price of preserving the organization. Until 1938, the German Zentralverband was allowed to exist because of the infighting among competing economic interest groups in the Nazi regime. While this did not allow for expansion, with skillful politicing, it permitted a defense against the demands of the private retailers' organization, which was anticooperative. [80] In Austria, too, all conditions of political conformity or "coordination" (*Gleichschaltung*) were accepted and leading members of Jewish origin dismissed immediately. The priority treatment of "business as usual," which translated into job dismissal for even some non-Jewish and not openly political employees who belonged to the opposition, was justified by the hope for an early end to national socialist rule as well as the hopelessness vis-à-vis the power situation. These were and are slogans that fit reality, but they were also used by the consumer cooperatives and the majority of Austrians to justify averting their faces from the national socialist crimes and readily cooperating with the new rulers. The preservation of the consumer cooperative organization—built up over generations—and the hope for further economic advantage appeared more important than upholding the political principles of the organization. [81]

The hitherto independent *Vorarlberger Verband* and the *Schutzverband österreichischer Konsumgenossenschaften* were now incorporated into the Austrian *Zentralverband*. Because the management of the consumer cooperatives, shortly before the Nazi invasion in 1938, had issued an appeal to vote "yes" for Austrian independence in the announced referendum, [82] Nazi political commissioners were placed at all levels of the organization. A Nazi political cell (*Betriebszelle*) was established in every consumer cooperative. The dairy company and the savings bank were liquidated, and in 1939 the *Zentralverband* was incorporated into the German *Reichsverband*. The privatization, which had been announced time and again, or rather the dissolution demanded by the Nazi trade organization (*Handels- und Gewerbeorganisation*), was not carried out because of the increasingly negative effects the war had on the provisioning of the population. [83]

On February 17, 1941, and after intense struggles between different Nazi groups, a decree was enacted that required the consumer cooperatives to adapt themselves to the war economy (*Verordnung zur Anpassung der verbraucher-genossenschaftlichen Einrichtungen an die kriegswirtschaftlichen Verhältnisse*). The consumer cooperatives were to be dissolved, their assets taken over by the German Labor Front (*Deutsche Arbeiterfront*, *DAF*), and the members were to be compensated for their shares in cash and at par value. After the dissolution of the *GÖC* in January 1942 and its incorporation as the subsidiary, *GW Großeinkauf*, into the Nazi-controlled *Gemeinschaftswerk-Konzern*, the take-over of the last consumer cooperative organization, the Austrian *Zentralverband*, followed on August 1, 1943. It became the Communal Regional Authority-Southeast (*Gemeinschaftswerk-Gebietsleitung Südost*). Even though this meant the end of the independent organization of cooperatives, its inventory and the opportunity to shop for less, in competition with private retail stores, remained intact. The dissolution of a standardized Austrian department of the *Gemeinschaftswerk*, which included the previous Austrian territory, was accomplished by the West-East partitioning into South-East I and South-East II.[84] By their incorporation into the German Labor Front-owned *Gemeinschaftswerk*, the cooperatives recovered the right to expand and the chance to expand sales to all consumers instead of only share-holding members.

The historiography on German and Austrian consumer cooperatives emphasizes that thousands of cooperative members (*Genossenschafter*) remained faithful to their cooperative principles.[85] The question remains open, however, how far the consumer cooperatives and their production facilities contributed not only to the functioning of the Nazi regime—especially during times of food scarcity during the war—but also to the maintenance of popular support for Nazism. It is striking and fits the direction of their historical development hinted at earlier that they were privatized despite the usefulness of their distribution structure: "In Hamburg, for example, official duties had to be carried out temporarily in conjunction with the administrators of the *DAF*."[86] In other words, cooperatives became elements of a dictatorial regime. In this context, the inclusion of gender aspects could possibly open up new discussions on the role of women in the mass organizations of the Nazi state.[87]

1945: Zero Hour?

After the assets of the consumer cooperatives had become part of the property of the *DAF*, they were at the disposal of the Allies after the collapse of the Third Reich in May 1945. In Austria, the Allies had agreed to the establishment of a provisional managing committee as early as April 1945. It consisted of board members from the *Zentralverband* and the *GÖC* from the time before 1933, some of whom, like Ludwig Strobl or Andreas Vukovich, had kept their positions during the Christian-authoritarian corporative state and the period of the National Socialism. After only two years, they succeeded in establishing the General Austrian Consumer Cooperative (*Allgemeine Österreichische Konsumgenossenschaft [AÖKG]*) as an Austrian holding company. At the same time, the Allies—after intervention by the International Cooperative Alliance (*Internationale Genossenschaftsbund*)—waived their claim to the "German" consumer cooperative assets among the *DAF* assets.[88] This was a consequence of the categorization of Austria as the "first victim" of the Nazi expansion, which had been part of the Moscow Declaration of 1943. With this, the foundation was laid for the Austrians coming to terms with their past—in which they would rather forget their voluntary participation in National Socialism.[89]

The *AÖKG* kept the organizational structure that cooperatives had had under Nazi control. Twenty-eight large district cooperatives with standardized statutes replaced the small, local, and regional consumer cooperatives of the

First Republic. Ninety-five percent of all Austrian consumer cooperative members were organized in the *AÖKG*. The 38 independent local consumer cooperatives were concentrated mainly in Vorarlberg where a separate *Genossenschafts-Verband* had existed before 1938.[90] In 1948, the Allies permitted a member assembly of *AÖKG* for the first time. One year later, the *AÖKG*, thanks to tax abatements and state subsidies, was able to pay a 1 to 2 percent rebate to its members, despite the difficult postwar times.

This effective centralization of the Austrian consumer cooperatives was not supposed to honor the past by taking up where the movement had stopped, but rather to use the experiences of the past for a reconstruction of the cooperative organization.[91] The character of the consumer cooperatives had changed. Even if some cooperators who had been active before 1933 appeared to have held on to a piece of the cooperative ideal during the years of Austro-facism and National Socialism, self-help during this period of social disorder was a more urgent necessity than the construction of an alternative economic structure.[92] In light of the uncertain supply of goods needed for survival, the cooperative organizational structure—with state subsidies—proved its worth again, as it had in earlier times of crisis.

The consumer cooperatives set out to erase the image of the 1920s—that of building blocks in a new social and economic order—and to remain neutral, politically and socially. For the "movement," as the union of SDAP members and revolutionary socialists who had been active in the underground called the Socialist Party and its members, the cooperatives established clubs, family events, and afternoon activities for housewives. Even the laws on continuing education and ideas on child rearing were reactivated. However, cooperative and tax policies still played important roles. Because of government pressures, other goals—those of reaching all potential customers both female and male and the exclusive sale to members—were relinquished. With this, cooperatives adapted themselves to the free-market economy; they rationalized and competed. Consumers, female and male, noticed the competition in prices, merchandise, and service. Advertising strategies were conjured up which, however, were only advertising products. Ideas were not to be propagated and disseminated via advertising anymore.[93] The modernization inherent in this new beginning could be seen in the opening of the first self-service supermarket in Austria—in Linz in 1950. It was a branch of a cooperative.

Prospects

Despite the attempt to describe stores for "Everyone," it was obvious during my childhood in the 1960s in Salzburg that certain people in the neighborhood shopped at the *Konsum* and others did not. It is to be noted, though, that the

Austrian political culture in the 1950s was characterized more by class consensus than dissonance. Nevertheless, the categorization of the "red" consumer cooperatives as shops for the poor during the interwar years continued to have an effect, and the cooperative fell into the sphere of certain social groups. Even then it could be recognized that the theory and practice of the consumer cooperative were on a collision course. On the one hand, it was to be a political and group-oriented organization, while on the other, it was an economic enterprise. The primacy of the market economy, and the resultant necessary professionalism, centralization, and rationalization, all favored an unreflective separation of theory and practices that had begun early on.

The dream of a society in which people exercise self-determination and in which consumers, female and male, participate in the managing and in the profits of department stores financed by them is remembered today by veterans and those who take an interest in history. Given the high standards of living of the last two decades, the tendency to shop where one is happy with the merchandise or where it is convenient to the workplace or the home, which started in the 1920s, has prevailed. From the late 1970s on, price-conscious consumers (female and male), either out of desire or economic necessity, were able to do their weekly shopping of larger purchases at discount department stores.

In an entirely different direction from the academic works that question the celebratory historiography, gender-specific questions should be the topic of discussion today. Despite its claim to become the organization for the housewives, the female percentage of consumer cooperative members remained behind that of the Social Democratic Party and the labor unions during the marriage of cooperatives with the Social Democrats in the 1920s. This is not to be interpreted as a "refusal" by the women to participate but as a result of the financial situation and prevailing gender norms. When families could afford only one share, or did not consider more than one necessary, it was issued in the name of the man. It can be seen clearly in the consumer cooperative advertising geared towards women that the disassociation of (male) work from (female) home and shopping was firmly established. This applied also to organizations that made people's emancipation and liberation their task. What matters here is the gender-specific problem that house work (domestic chores) make possible the physical reproduction (*Reproduktion*) of work. Today, it also part of the baggage of conservative middle-class parties and their women's organizations.

Reasons for this questioning of roles are to be found—if one includes the socioeconomic and cultural backgrounds—in the favorable boom of the women's emancipation—even in Austria—since the mid-1970s. Even the massive questioning of the apparent political unworthiness of the reproduction and *Konsumer* spheres can be associated with the new women's movement and their slogan: the private sphere is political and public. The ecological-alternative movement was next with partly different contents and goals. Thus, in the 1980s, the purchase of coffee from Nicaragua was to support the self determination efforts of this small Central American country and serve as a protest against the American economic boycott. Political education regarding the South African apartheid regime was linked to slogans like, "Don't buy South African fruit." In this connection, there were efforts under way during the early 1980s to convince the management of the Austrian Cooperatives to remove South African products from the range of merchandise offered. The men and women who undertook this effort tied it to the political demands from the early years of the consumer cooperatives, or rather the First Republic, without success. The political-economic cooperative that labor unions and the Social Democratic party had once advocated as a new direction in economics, had become passé. As could be seen, the original structure of the consumer cooperatives was especially suited for the provisioning of the population with food during state of emergencies and times of need. Today, there exists, indeed, a broad public awareness about the politicization of the *Konsum*. Recently, Shell gas stations were the target of a boycott—mainly a European one—which had been initiated by the environmental organization, Greenpeace, using media-effective—if not always respectable—strategies. Indeed, the planned sinking of an outdated oil platform by Shell was prevented by this activism.

In 1990, an article on the situation of the ailing Austrian consumer cooperative giant (*Genossenschaftsriesen*), titled "*Konsum-Kosmetik*," reported that the decaying of the aging cooperative was to be arrested with cosmetic measures. This decaying was going on despite the fact that the balance sheet of the chain of retail trade stores was positive and the *Konsum* remained a leader among retail stores. The end came five years later. On March 8, 1995, it was announced in the media that the banks, including the *BAWAG*, founded in 1922 as a bank for working people, were no longer willing to extend credit to the *Konsum Österreich*. With a deficit of 15 billion *Schillinge*, the "Red Giant"—as it was called up to the end—declared bankruptcy.

Notes

1. Anton Amann, "Soziologie und Genossenschaft," in *Handbuch des österreichischen Genossenschaftswesens*, ed. Mario Patera (Vienna, 1986), 441.

2. Peter Natorp, *Sozialidealismus, Neue Richtlinien sozialer Erziehung* (Berlin, 1922).

3. Rudold Ardelt, "Sozialdemokratie und bürgerliche Öffentlichkeit - Überlgegungen zum Hainfelder Parteitag," *Vom Kampf um Bürgerrechte zum burgfrieden. Studien zur Geschichte der österreichische Sozialdemokratie 1888-1917*, Studien zur Gesellschafts- und Kulturgeschichte, (Vienna, 1994), 9-36.

4. Helmut Schelsky, *Auf der Suche nach Wirklichkeit,* (Köln-Düsseldorf, 1965), 375. Alexander Butsch, "Die Bedeutung der Konsumgenossenschaften in der Sozialdemokratischen Bewegung. Zum Verhältnis von Konsumgenossenschaften, Partei und Gewerkschaften in Österreich" (master's thesis, University of Vienna, 1994).

5. On the concept of hegemony according to Antonio Gramsci and Pery Anderson, "The Antnomies of Antonio Gramsci," *New Left Review* 100, (November 1976-January 1977). Gramsci had the view that before taking power "hegemonic activity . . . is not a claim to hegemony over the whole of society, or the ruling class itself, which is by definition is impossible to stage." In contrast to the bourgeoisie, the working class—in a Marxist sense—cannot take a dominant role under capitalism because its social position means that it lacks the intellectual resources to produce cultural achievements. On the other hand, for other classical Marxists, of whom Leon Trotsky was the best known, after the coming to power of the proletariat, the level of consciousness could be reformed from the different facets of bourgeois culture, as the "new" Soviet society was formed out of the "czarist-feudal" mentality. Leon Trotksy, *Fragen des Alltagslebens* [1923] (Dortmund, 1977).

6. Karl Fallend, *Wilhelm Reich in Wein, Psychoanlyse und Politik* (Vienna-Salzburg, 1988).

7. Helga Grubitzsch, "Konsumarbeiterinnen und Lockvögel: Frauen in der kapitalistischen Konsumtion," *Beiträge zur feministischen theorie und praxis 15/16,* (Cologne, 1985), 35 and following.

8. Emmy Freundlich, *Die Macht der Hausfrauen* (Vienna, n.d.).

9. Ernst Bruckmüller, *Landwirtschaftliche Organisationen und gesellschaftliche Modernisierung* (Salzburg, 1977), 176.

10. Robert Blaich, "The Consumer Co-operatives in Austria," and Johann Brazda, "The Consumer Co-operatives in Germany," in *Consumer Co-operatives in a Changing World I,* eds. Johann Brazda and Robert Schediwy (Geneva, 1989).

11. Ferdinand Lassalle, "Offenes Antwortschreiben" [1863], *Gesammelte Reden und Schriften,* ed. Eduard Bernstein (Berlin, 1919), 52.

12. Erwin Hasselman, *Geschichte der Deutschen Konsumgenossenschaften,* (Frankfurt, a.M., 1971), 90ff.

13. Franz Baltzarek, "Die geschichtliche Entwicklung der österreichischen Genossenschaften," in *Handbuch des österreichischen Genossenschaftswesens,* ed. Mario Patera (Vienna, 1986), 28ff.

14. Anreas Vukowitsch, *Geschichte des konsumgenossenschaftlichen Großeinkaufs in Osterreich* (Vienna, 1931), 15.

15. Karl Wrabetz, *Die Erwerbs- und Wirtschaftsgenosschenschaften in Österreich und ihre Bedeutung für die Gewerbetreibenden. Sonderdruck aus der Wochenschrift des Niederösterreichischen Gewerbevereins* (Vienna, 1884).

16. Johann Kaserer, *Das Gesetz vom 9.April 1873 über Erwerbs- und Wirtschaftsgenossenschaften* (Vienna, 1873), 63.

17. Lassalle, "Antwortschreiben," 25.

18. Karl Marx, "Instruktionen für die Delegierten des Provisorischen Zentralrates zu den einzelnen Fragen," in his *Marx-Engels-Werke* [*MEW*], (East Berlin, 1962), vol. 16, 195.

19. Karl Marx, "Inauguraladresse der Internationalen Arbeiter-Assoziation," *MEW*, 11.

20. Franz Seibert, *Die Konsumgenossenschaften in Österreich, Materialien zur Arbeiterbewegung* 11 (Vienna, 1978), 18.

21. Andreas Korp, *Der Konsumverein Teesdorf. Ein Beitrag zur Frühgeschichte der österreichischen Genossenschaften* (Vienna, 1978), 33.

22. Andreas Vukowitsch, *100 Jahre Konsumgenossenschaften in Österreich*, (Vienna, 1956), 3.

23. *Statistische Monatsschrift*, XXI (1895), 375; Neue Folge VII (1898), 660, cited in Baltzarek, *Geschichtliche Entwicklung*, 52.

24. *Verhandlungen des 5. österreichischen Sozialdemokratischen Parteitages Prag 5.-11.5.1896*, (Vienna, 1896), 119.

25. Helmut Huber, "Geschichte der österreichischen Konsumgenossenschaftsbewegung bis 1950" (master's thesis, University of Vienna, 1974), 77.

26. Andreas Vukowitsch, *30 Jahre Zentralverband Österreischischer Konsumvereine* (Vienna, 1935), 8.

27. Vukowitsch, *30 Jahre*, 17.

28. *Verhandlungen des Gesamtparteitages der Sozialdemokratischen Arbeiterpartei in Österreiche, Wein 9.-13.11.1903* (Vienna, 1903), 108.

29. Karl Kautsky, *Consumvereine und Arbeiterbewegung* (Vienna, 1897), 13.

30. Eduard Bernstein, *Die Voraussetzungen de Sozialismus und die Aufgaben der Sozialdemokratie*, new and expanded edition (Stuttgart and Berlin, 1921), 220.

31. *Verhandlungen des Parteitages der deutschen sozialdemokratischen Arbeiterpartei in Oesterreich, Reichenberg, 19.-24. September 1909*, 502.

32. Ernst Klohs, "Die Bedeutung der Konsumgenossenschaften in der deutschen und Österreichischen Sozialdemokratie" (Ph.D. diss., University of Vienna, 1951), 59 et. seq.

33. Gabriella Hauch, "'Revolutionäre im Schlafrock' und Instrumente des Klasenkampfes'. Konsumgenossenschaften in der österreichischen Artbeiterbewegung vor 1914," in *Arbeiterbewegung in Österreich und Ungarn bis 1914*, ed. Wolfgang Maderthaner, Materialien zur Arbeiterbewegung 45, 222 et. seq.

34. Hauch, "Revolutionäre," 222.

35. Baltzarek, "Geschichtliche Entwicklung," 55.

36. Helge Zoitl, "Gegen den Brotwucher! Die Gründung der Wiener Hammerbrotwerke," *Zeitgeschichte* 3 (1988), 79. On the importance of bread, see Roman Sandgruber, *Die Anfänge der Konsumgesellschaft. Konsumgüterverbrauch, Lebensstandard und Alltagskultur in Österreich im 18. und 19. Jahrhundert* (Vienna, 1982), 262.

37. Zoitl, *Brotwucher*, 94.

38. "Nochmals die 'heilige Drei'" *Arbeiter-Zeitung*, April 30, 1911.

39. For Germany, Karl Wissmann, *Wesen und Werden der Konsumgenossenschaften*, (Meisenheim/Glan, 1948).

40. Franz Baltzarek, "Die geschichtliche Entwicklung der Konsumgenossenschaften in Österreich," in *Verbraucherpolitik und Wirtschaftsentwicklung*, ed. Anton E. Rauter, (Vienna, 1976), 205; John Boyer, *Political Radicalism in Late Imperial Vienna: The Origins of the Christian Social Movement, 1848-1897* (Chicago, 1981); and Boyer,

Culture and Political Crisis in Vienna: Christian Socialism in Power, 1897-1918 (Chicago, 1995), 1-110.

41. Erwin Hasselmann, *Konsumgenossenschaften - Aspekte ihrer Enwicklung*, (Hamburg, 1975), 10.

42. Baltzarek, "Geschichtliche Entwicklung," 35.

43. Hasselmann, *Geschichte*, 294.

44. Johann Brazda and Robert Schediwy, "Konsumgenossenschaften im Strukturwandel," *Wirtschaft und Gesellschaft. Wirtschaftspolitische Zeitschrift der Kammer für Arbeiter und Angetelle für Wien*, 1 (1989), 65.

45. Regina Becker-Schmidt, "Frauen und Deklassierung, Geschlecht und Klasse," in *Klasse Geschlecht. Feministische Gesellschaftsanalyse und Wissenschaftskritik*, ed. Ursula Beer (Bielefeld, 1989), 215.

46. Grudrun-Axeli Knapp, "Arbeitsteilung und Sozialisation: Konstellationen von Arbeitsvermö gen und Arbeitsverm ögen im Lebenszusammerhang von Frauen," in *Klasse Geschlecht*, ed. Ursula Beer, 269.

47. Gabriella Hauch, *Vom Frauenstandpunkt aus. Frauen im Parlament 1919 bis 1933*, (Vienna, 1995). Emmy Freundlich, a member of parliament, always presented herself in male circles as an economic expert and distinguished herself as a hardhitting public speaker who engaged in lively exchanges.

48. *Der Konsumverein*, 24, (1913). On Emmy Freundlich, Beatrix Bechtel, "Emmy Freundlich," in *"Die Partei hat mich nie enttäuscht . . .". Österreichische SozialdemokratInnen*, ed. Edith Prost (Vienna, 1989), 89-135.

49. Andrea Ellmeier, "Konsumentinnen. Einkaufen in Wien 1918-1938 (II). Eine Analyse konsumgenossenschatlicher Frauen(presse)politik und bürgerlicher Frauen- und Kundenzeitschriften" (master's thesis, University of Vienna, 1990), 95-112.

50. Emmy Freundlich, *Die Stellung der Frau in der Genossenschaftsbewegung* (Vienna, 1924), 9.

51. Gisela Urban, "Die Entwickung der Österreichischen Frauenbewegung," in *Frauenbewegung, Frauenbildung und Frauenarbeit in Österreich*, eds. Martha Braun et al., (Vienna, 1930), 50.

52. Gabriella Hauch, "Der diskrete Charme des Nebenwiderspruchs. Zur sozialdemokratischen Frauenbewegung vor 1918," *Sozialdemokratie und Habsburgerstaat*, ed. Wolfgang Maderthaner (Vienna 1989), 115.

53. Andrea Ellmeier, "Handel mit der Zunkunft. Zur Geschlechterpolitik der Konsum-genossenschaften," *L'Homme. Zeitschrift für feministische Geschichtswissenschaften* 6 (1995) 1, 62-77; Monika Bernold, "Konsum, Politil und Geschlecht. Zur Feminisierung von Öffentlichkeit als Strategie und Paradoxon," in *Konsumgeschichte als Gesellschaftsgeschichte*, eds. Helmut Kälble, Jürgen Kocka, and Hannes Siegrist, (Frankfurt a.M., 1996).

54. Hauch, "Revolution äre," 224 et. seq.

55. Hasselmann, *Geschichte*, 363 et. seq.

56. Vukowitsch, *Zentralverband*, 24.

57. *Protokoll de* [österreichischen: G.H.] *Deutscher Parteivorstand 24.9.1914* and Heft 7 der handschriftlichen Parteivorstansprotokolle der SdAPÖ protokollierten "Hammerbrotwerke"-Berichte", in Verein für Geschichte der Arbeiterbewegung, Rechte Wienzeile, A-1050 Vienna/Austria.

58. Robert A. Kann, *A History of the Hapsburg Empire, 1526-1918* (Berkeley, 1974), 530-63.

59. Baltzarek, "Geschichtliche Entwicklung," 36.

60. *Ibid.*, 61, n51.

61. *Ibid.*, 63, n52.

62. Siegmund Kaff, "Die Konsumvereine in Deutschösterreich," *Schriften des Vereins für Sozialpolitik - Untersuchungen über Konsumvereine*, (Munich-Leipzig, 1923), 42.

63. Blaich, "Austria," 913.

64. *Ibid.*, 916.

65. Ewald Stöllner, "Die Entwicklung der Genossenschaften in der Ersten Republik", (master's thesis, University of Vienna), 76 cited in Baltzarek, "Geschichtliche Entwicklung," 58, n39.

66. Seibert, *Konsumgenossenschaften*, 94.

67. Blaich, "Austria," 919.

68. Baltzarek, "Geschichtliche Entwicklung," 200; Blaich "Austria," 917.

69. Anson Rabinbach, *The Crises of Austrian Socialism. From Red Vienna to Civil War, 1927-1934* (Chicago, 1983); Helmut Gruber *Red Vienna: Experiment in Working-class Culture, 1919-1934* (New York, 1991). On the question of gender, Gabriella Hauch, "Frauenbewegung - Frauen in der Politik," in *Handbuch des politischen Systems Österreichs*, eds. von Emmerich Talos et al., (Vienna, 1995).

70. An expression of this was that the Austrian labor union congress in 1928 for the first time made "women's work" a separate item on its agenda, Gabriella Hauch, "Arbeite Frau! Die Gleichberechtigung kommt von selbst!?" Anmerkungen zu Frauen und Gewerkschaften," in *"Daß unsere Greise night mehr betteln gehn!" Sozialdemokratie und Sozialpolitik im Deutschen Reich und in Österreich-Ungarn*, ed. Helmut Konrad, (Vienna-Zürich, 1990), 79.

71. Monika Bernold, "Kino(t)raum, Über den Zusammenhang von Familie, Freizeit und Konsum," in *Familie: Arbeitsplatz oder Ort de Glücks? Historische Schnitte ins Private*, eds. Monika Bernold, et al., (Vienna, 1990), 135.

72. *Jahrbuch deutsch-österreichischer Konsumvereine 1923-24*, (Vienna, 1925), 90.

73. Seibert, *Konsumgenossenschaften*, 90.

74. Hauch, "Frauenbewegung," XX.

75. Andrea Ellmeier, "Eva Singer-Meczes, Modellierung der sozialistischen Konsumentin. Konsumgenossenschaftliche (Frauen) Politik in den Zwanziger Jahren," *Zeitgeschichte*, 11/12 (1989), 411, 424.

76. *Jahrbuch des Verbandes deutsch-österreichischer Konsumvereine*, (Vienna, 1932), appendix.

77. Emmerich Tal'os, *Austrofaschismus*. 4. ed. (Vienna, 1988); Charles A. Gulick, *Austria from Hapsburg to Hitler*, 2 vols. (Berkeley, 1948).

78. Both pamphlets were published in Vienna in 1937, Baltzarek, "Geschichtliche Entwicklung," 69.

79. Vukowitsch, *30 Jahre*, p. 16; Seibert, *Konsumgenossenschaften*, 123.

80. Hasselmann, *Geschichte*, 484 et. seq.

81. Hasselmann, *Konsumgenossenschaften*, 87.

82. Baltzarek, "Geschichtliche Entwicklung," 73.

83. Franz Scmidt, *Triumph einer Idee. 100 Jahre Konsumgenossenschaften*, (Vienna, 1956), 40; Andreas Korp, *Stein auf Stein. 50 Jahre Großeinkaufsgesellschaft österreichischer Consumvereine 1905-1945* (Vienna, 1955), 83.

84. Hasselmann, *Geschichte*, 499.; Seibert, *Konsumgenossenschaft*, 132.

85. Vukowitsch, *30 Jahre*, 19; Hasselmann, *Gesichthe*, 508.

86. Hasselmann, *Konsumgenossenschaften*, 108.

87. Johanna Gemacher and Gariella Hauch, "Eine 'deutsch fühlende Frau.' Die Großdeutsche Politikerin Marie Schneider und der Nationalsozialismus in Österreich," in *Fraulenleben 1945. Kriegsende in Wien* (Vienna, 1995), 115-132.

88. Seibert, *Konsumgenossesschaften*, 135 et. seq.

89. The events surrounding the presidential candidacy and election of Kurt Waldheim, as well as the current antiforeigner sentiment, anti-Semitism, and authoritarianism show that a serious collective recognition of this historical period in "comfortable" Austria has not taken place. Gerhard Botz and Gerhard Sprengnagel, eds., *Probleme österreichischer Zeitgeschichtsforschung*, XX.

90. Baltzarek, "Geschichtliche Entwicklung," 75.

91. Franz Schmidt, "Triumph einer Idee," *Konsumgenossenschaften*, Seibert, ed., 139.

92. It is beyond the scope of this chapter to go into the full social-political situation at the end of the Second World War, including the fall of the Nazi regime.

93. Blaich, "Austria," 925.

Chapter 8

Between Farmers and Workers: Consumer Cooperation in Denmark, 1850-1940

Niels Finn Christiansen

In the mid-1990s, the Danish consumer cooperatives represented a market share of roughly 33 percent of the national foodstuffs and beverage consumption. In every town, suburb, and rural community, one could find a cooperative supermarket or smaller shop. In many rural areas, the only retail shop at all was a cooperative. The total membership figure of the National Association of Consumer Cooperatives (the *FDB*) is more than one million, which means that about every second household in Denmark has joined the cooperative movement. The cooperatives pioneered the introduction of sound foodstuffs and initiated campaigns for healthier eating habits. They issued a monthly magazine *Samvirke* (Co-operation), which had the highest circulation of any periodical in Denmark and contained consumer information and articles of a very high quality about history and cultural matters in general. In short, for a very large part of the Danish population of only five million, consumer cooperation is an integral part of their everyday life.

How and why did consumer cooperation become such a formidable institution in Denmark? In this chapter, I shall outline the origins and consolidation of the cooperative movement, and explain its specific Danish social, cultural, and politico-ideological background. The chapter will concentrate on the cooperation's very complex position between the two major national movements of the farmers and the working class.[1]

Origins: Self-help or Self-organization?

In the middle of the nineteenth century, Denmark was still an overwhelmingly agrarian country. Almost 80 percent of the population lived in the countryside and about one half were directly dependent on agriculture. From the late eighteenth century, the capitalist market economy had gradually displaced the seigneurial mode of production. This was accompanied by the creation of a large rural proletariat, which until the First World War formed the major part of the Danish working class.

Most of the towns were very small (between 5,000 and 10,000 inhabitants). Only the city of Copenhagen had more than 100,000 inhabitants. But due to migration in the decades after 1860 both Copenhagen and the provincial towns experienced a massive increase of the population as well as all the social problems that accompany rapid urbanization. Capitalism penetrated the urban economy and market relations much later and more slowly than it did the countryside. Not until the 1840s did capitalists begin to establish factories of some importance. Industry developed gradually until the First World War, with especially intensive phases in the early 1870s and the 1890s. In this period the Danish industry produced almost exclusively for the home market, and it rested heavily on a skilled labor force, except for some branches like the textile and clothing industries in which women formed a major part of the labor force. Most of the urban productive force consisted of artisans who were both protected and restrained by compulsory membership of the guilds. Unskilled labor formed a small but rapidly growing part of the working class. Following the abolition of absolutism and the introduction of a constitutional monarchy in 1848-1849, the guilds were abolished in 1857-1862, and thereafter free labor market relations reigned in the towns as well.[2]

Until 1848-1849, all independent workers' associations were forbidden. Although the press was subjected to severe restrictions under the absolutist regime, a few papers were able to bring rather copious information about the activities of the Left in countries elsewhere in Europe. Some of the ideas of the utopian socialists were introduced and the fate of the Chartists was followed closely. Thus, when the liberal constitution in 1849 allowed a free press and independent associations, a number of workers' societies were established. Few of them, however, were founded by the workers or artisans themselves. Members of the middle class organized most of them with the explicit purpose of bringing workers under the tutelage of liberal leadership and ideology. Education (the German concept *Bildung*, or cultural self-development, is more adequate) became the code word for those societies.

After an abortive attempt at creating a consumer cooperative by the printers of the biggest Danish newspaper, the question was taken up for discussion in the only association led by the workers themselves. The initiative was taken by the first Danish socialist Frederik Dreier who was inspired by French utopian socialism, especially Proudhon. Although Dreier's main interest seems to have been the establishment of producers' cooperatives, he advocated the creation of "The Association for Cheap Necessities of Living." Established in 1853, it managed to survive for two years under very difficult conditions. The model for Dreier's proposal was the association *"l'Humanité"* in Lille, which he had learned about from Andre Cochut's book, *Les associations ouvrières*.[3] In the 1850s, several other attempts were made, but very little is known about them, and it is very doubtful if any of them succeeded in coming into practical function.[4]

Whereas the few initiatives in the 1850s were inspired by continental socialist ideas—no one seems to have had any knowledge of the British/Rochdale system—we can observe a clear change of inspirational sources and motives when the idea of consumer cooperatives was relaunched in the mid-1860s. Now the projects were taken over by liberal philantropists from the middle class under the ideological banner of "self-help." There is no connection to the vague socialism of the 1850s. On the contrary, cooperatives were reintroduced as a prophylactic means to prevent the invasion of socialism in Denmark.

A small, but very effective group of middle-class liberals acquainted themselves with the ideas and experience of the Rochdale pioneers and especially the activities of Schulze-Delitzsch in Germany. A number of doctors, clergymen, and politicians became convinced that cooperatives might serve to alleviate the poverty among the rapidly growing class of working people in Copenhagen and other towns. This was to be done without interference with the forces of the free market. The proposals were not directed toward those poor people who were permanently supported by the poor-law administration. These were considered to be doomed to eternal poverty. The self-help institutions should assist those working-class families who were only hit by temporary poverty caused by illness, accidents, or unemployment, i.e., the "respectable" workers.

Beginning in the early 1860s, a number of sick-benefit and old age provision associations, savings banks, and building societies were established within the framework of artisans' organizations and nonsocialist worker associations. All of them were initiated and led by people from the middle class. They were guided by the motive of securing the workers' acceptance of liberal capitalism and bourgeois politics. They got full ideological, but no practical or financial, support from the state, which was held firmly in the hands of the conservatives until the turn of the century.[5]

Among the middle-class philantropists we can, however, observe a clear divergence between two groups. The first put their highest priority on the raising of the moral and educational standards of the workers. This group saw all practical initiatives as a means to these ends. The second group found it impossible to demand higher ethical standards as long as the workers were forced to engage themselves in a daily struggle to make both ends meet.[6] Within this last group we find the initiators of the first consumer cooperatives that managed to survive.

The Danish consumer cooperative movement dates its start from 1866 when the Rev. H. C. Sonne in the small town of Thisted in Northern Jutland helped the local workers to establish a consumer cooperative. Sonne was well informed about the various cooperatives on the continent and in a series of

lectures given to the Thisted workers he referred in greater detail to the
Rochdale example. He had probably for some years subscribed to *The
Co-operator* and in 1868 he wrote a letter to this journal relating the events
that led to the opening of a cooperative shop in Thisted. It is characteristic that
he chose to call it Thisted Worker Association (*Thisted Arbejderforening*). It
was designed to help the relatively well-off workers in the town, not the poor,
and from other classes. This he stressed explicitly when, shortly afterwards, he
became engaged in a polemic with the local retailers who accused him of
destroying their trade.

The Thisted Worker Association became a success. Soon after its establishment, Sonne distributed the statutes to anyone who showed interest in the
experiment, and they served as a model for most of the urban cooperatives that
were created during the following decade. Equally important, however, was a
small pamphlet *On Worker Associations* (*Om Arbejderforeninger*), which
Sonne published in 1867. He drew massively on material from *The
Co-operator* and combined practical information with an outline of cooperative
ideology as it was understood within the liberalistic, self-help framework.

In accordance with his occupation as a clergyman, Sonne put a high
priority on the moral effects of cooperative associations. The ultimate goal was
to "raise . . . the lower, dependent and oppressed part of the population to a
higher moral, intellectual and social level, thereby securing them a more
respectable position in society."[7] This, however, could be achieved only if the
workers' material welfare reached a certain level. The task of those who shared
his views was to help the workers help themselves through education, information, and practical assistance. By compelling workers to save in order to buy
cheap commodities of good quality, cooperation would serve as a moral and
material lever for their welfare in general.

In the following years, Sonne became a central figure in the rapid development of cooperation in Denmark. But the geographical center was moved to
the east, to the city of Copenhagen and the towns on the island of Zeeland.
More importantly, however, was the spread of cooperatives in the rural areas
all over Denmark. Already in 1869 there were more consumer cooperatives in
the countryside than in the towns. I shall return to this remarkable development in the following section. Although the rural and urban cooperation cannot
be totally separated, there were many differences, and here I will concentrate
on the relationship among urban workers, cooperation, and the early socialist
movement.

Sonne, in his pamphlet, had drawn the outline of a comprehensive nonsocialist welfare program designed to help both the rural and urban proletariat.
Cooperation was meant to form an essential part of this program. It was
adopted immediately by many middle-class people in the towns. As early as
1871 we know of about thirty urban consumer cooperatives. The initiatives
came from master artisans, teachers, clergymen, and civil servants. In no case

did the workers themselves take the lead. But in some cases they seem to have been educated to take over the leadership of their cooperative. The number of urban cooperatives stagnated in the mid-1870s and declined in the second half of the decade whereas the number of rural consumer cooperatives continued to grow (in 1879 there were only nine urban cooperatives against 185 in the country).

The center for the diffusion of the cooperative ideas and information became *The Worker. A Monthly Journal for Self-Help and Co-operation* issued between 1868-1876 by an organization called the "Association." The indefatigable editor and leader of the organization was the state controller of the Danish saving banks Viggo Faber. He published extensive information about cooperation abroad and in Denmark. He tried to build up a central association for the consumer cooperatives, and he gave basic and elementary advice about all practical problems involved in running a cooperative store. Like Sonne, he argued for consumer cooperation in the context of a wider social policy program based on self-help. He drew up plans for mutual insurance funds, credit associations, saving banks, and building societies. But according to his fundamental liberalism, he warned against any state-intervention that went beyond the poor-law.

From the early 1870s on, however, the cooperative movement in Denmark was enmeshed within Danish political struggles—in the country between the farmers and the landed aristocracy, in the towns, and especially in Copenhagen, between socialist and nonsocialist strategies for solving the social problems of the working class. In 1871, in the wake of the Paris Commune, a vital socialist movement was founded in Denmark. As a proclaimed section of the First International, it managed within a year to lay the foundations for a very strong labor movement. In terms of organization, it was based on the extraordinary unity of trade unions and party functions, and thus the movement engaged in both economic struggles and political mass demonstrations. It was, of course, met with massive opposition and repression from the ruling classes and the state. But it also met opposition from the already existing worker associations no matter what their ideological and practical standpoints were.

The consumer cooperative movement opposed the socialists vehemently. *The Worker* served as one of the most outspoken and constant advocates for self-help as the alternative to socialism. Its editor Faber rejected the assumption of a contradiction between capital and labor. Capital is "if not the worker's only friend then his first and best and the indispensable condition for his well-being," he argued already before the advent of socialism.[8] The problem of the workers was not insufficient wages, he insisted, but their lack of ability and will to spend their wages in the most appropriate way. The task of the consumer cooperative movement was exactly to teach the workers how to do so.

In principle, the consumer cooperatives were politically neutral. But there could be no doubt that the most important spokesmen rejected any attempts at changing the foundations of capitalism. Thus, they also tried to dissuade the workers from engaging in strikes. Strikes were, if not harmful, then useless because increasing wages would necessarily be followed by higher prices. Moreover, strikes would break the fundamental harmony between capital and labor.

No wonder then, that the socialists regarded the consumer cooperative movement with the utmost scepticism and, at times, with open hostility. This was not only because of its antisocialism but also for more fundamental reasons. To some extent, the socialists of the 1870s were influenced by Ferdinand Lassalle's ideas, especially "the iron law of wages" when every lowering of the costs of living would immediately result in a corresponding lowering of the wages. Paradoxically, this theory came very close to the liberalistic arguments against trade unions and strikes. But in that respect the socialists rather illogically did not adopt the Lassallean theories. The socialists gradually dismissed Lassalleanism and after 1880 his theories were left behind and replaced by a Marxism influenced by Karl Kautsky.

The labor movement's second argument against the consumers cooperatives was of more lasting impact. Cooperatives would destroy the trade of the small retailers, a class that in terms of living conditions was very close to the working class and a potential ally in the struggle for socialism.

Nevertheless, the socialists left a door open for a more positive attitude toward consumer cooperatives. If the workers could oust the bourgeois leadership of the cooperatives and take them over themselves, cooperation might, in the end, help to ease their social misery. In practice, however, it was to be several decades before the labor movement adopted this tactic. It is doubtful whether the decline of the urban consumer cooperatives in the second half of the 1870s was in any way caused by the negative attitude of the socialists. Rather, it was a result of the general economic crisis.[9]

In one area the early labor movement militants adopted the idea of cooperation. They were strong adhererents of producer cooperatives. At first, influenced by Lassalle, they appealed for state-aided producer cooperatives as an important element in the strategy for socialism. This, of course, was rather illusory since state power remained firmly in the hands of the landed aristocracy and the upper middle class. Gradually therefore, the idea of state aid was left behind. But the idea of producer cooperatives was taken up by the trade unions for several purposes. In the absence of strike funds, artisans established cooperatives in connection with strikes in order to keep their trade going. Producer cooperatives were also taken up by workers who were blacklisted by the employers for political reasons. The labor movement wanted to prove to itself and the employers that it was possible to organize production without capitalists, to introduce better working conditions, and eventually, to pay higher wages. None of these producer cooperatives succeeded in surviving for any longer period of time. Thus, by the end of the 1870s, both urban consumer cooperation and producer cooperation lay in ruins.[10]

Cooperation as an Instrument
in the Farmers' Democracy

In this section, I shall deal with a paradox: cooperation, which was originally designed to solve the social problems of the urban proletariat, within a few years after its introduction, became a vital element in an impressive movement for self-organization by the Danish farmers.

During the development of capitalism in the Danish agrarian sector, the peasants were able to buy most of their land. Thus, a class of farmers possessing small or middle-sized farms grew up alongside the agrarian capitalists. About 1870, this class of farmers owned some 75 percent of the land, cultivating it with the help of a few farmhands and maids, and the occasional use of wage labor. From the 1830s, they were gradually integrated in the world market, selling surplus grain and livestock primarily to England and Germany.

Unlike the peasants and farmers in many other countries, the Danish farmer class developed a high degree of independent class identity based on economic, political, and cultural self-organization. In the 1840s, the farmers participated actively in an alliance with a small—mainly intellectual—urban middle class and constituted the necessary basis for the establishment of the constitutional monarchy, as it was laid down in the liberal constitution of 1849. Also from the 1840s, the farmers gradually gained a dominant position in local politics. Gaining a majority in almost every parish council, they were able to put a heavy imprint on the administration of the poor-law, the local schools, and eventually the church.

The farmers' struggle for an independent class culture originated in a widespread religious revival movement beginning in the first decades of the nineteenth century. It was directed against the rationalism of the state church and its clergy-dominated structures. This lay movement, which crossed class barriers between farmers, cottagers, and landless laborers, served a dual purpose. First, it provided schooling in capitalist norms. Second, it built up a grassroots organization, fostering a combination of individual responsibility and collective solidarity, which, in a different context, could become the mainspring of political struggle. Unlike Sweden, for example, the religious revival movement stayed within the framework of the "people's church," which had been established in accordance with the constitution in 1849 as a replacement for the absolutist state church. The increasing cultural and ideological class consciousness had its biggest effect on the educational structure. The farmer class built up an alternative to the state system, introducing free schools and "folk" high schools for young men and women. Between 1860 and the First World War, a very large percentage of the rural young people attended these schools, which helped to build up an outstanding sociocultural identity in the farmer class by reviving the teaching of religion and Danish history combined with practical subjects.[11]

In the local communities, the farmers from the early 1870s on began to establish village halls (forsamlingshuse) as centers for local cultural activities. By the First World War, one could find such a village hall in almost every parish, in many regions with the addition of a "mission house." These were built by people who represented the "inner Mission," a pietistic branch of the revival movement.

This extensive complex of cultural institutions was only one aspect of the farmers' achievements. As a parallel movement, they created a network of socioeconomic associations and societies, many of which were established on the basis of cooperative principles. Beginning in the 1840s, the farmers organized insurance institutions, real-estate credit associations, savings banks, and sick-benefit associations. All of these institutions were established on the principle of self-help. They were also democratically organized with a high degree of membership-influence.

Thus, when the idea of consumer cooperatives was put forward in the second half of the 1860s there were in many local communities people who had acquired some experience in managing their own affairs. Also, information about cooperation was spread not only through Viggo Faber's The Worker, but by a rapidly expanding network of local newspapers founded by leading members of the farmers' political party Venstre (the Left).

From 1869 to the early 1880s, when the consumer cooperatives gained a foothold in the country, it appears that the founders followed two goals. First, like the urban cooperators, they wanted to improve the living conditions of the poor, the rural proletariat, and the small cottagers with the principle of self-help. In this way, they imagined that the expenditure for poor relief could be diminished. Second, they aimed to break the trade monopoly of the towns. Even after the law of free trade in 1857, the towns were surrounded by a protection belt of 7-11 kilometers within which no retail shop was allowed. Consumer cooperatives might be established as long as they distributed goods only to their members.

The consumer cooperatives became one element in an on-going antagonism between town and country, which raged not only in the economic field but also, as dealt with below, in the area of politics. Whereas the consumer cooperatives succeeded in breaking the monopoly of the towns it is more uncertain if they fulfilled their first goal, alleviating rural poverty. Though very little is known about the actual functioning of the rural cooperatives, it appears as if they came to serve the economic interests of the agrarian middle class to a much greater extent than they helped to alleviate the situation of the proletariat. Even if the latter formed the majority of the members, the leadership lay firmly in the hands of the farmers, local schoolteachers, or ministers.[12]

The consumer cooperatives in the country spread from the island of Zealand toward Jutland at a solid and uniform rate in the decades from 1880 to 1920. The numbers of cooperatives are as follows; 1880: 201; 1890: 598; 1900: 1043; 1910: 1406; 1920: 1739. In the towns, the development was much slower, as I shall deal with below. As a whole, around the First World War one might be certain to find a consumer cooperative in the vast majority of the parishes.[13] Brugsen (the Danish shortened name for co-ops) had become a permanent and central part of everyday life and trade in the local communities. Like almost every other Danish social or economic network of organizations, the consumer cooperatives established a central organization in the 1890s. In 1896, the National Association of Consumer Cooperatives (FDB) came into effect. It was immediately joined by one-third of the local co-ops, and by 1915 roughly 90 percent had joined the FDB.

Despite the obvious success of the consumer cooperatives, the picture of Denmark as a pioneer land of cooperation is much closer associated with another sector, cooperative diaries and bacon producing factories. Beginning in 1882, they expanded with dramatic speed. In terms of economic importance, they gained a crucial role in relation to both the agricultural producers and the national economy. They played a decisive role in the transformation of agricultural productions from grain and livestock to animal products, processed in the dairies and bacon factories.

While the consumer cooperatives had been inspired mainly by British models and partly by German experiences, the dairy cooperatives grew out of domestic traditions, or rather created a completely new model for organizing production. During the 1860s and 1870s, several hundred privately owned dairies had attempted to cope with the rapidly increasing output of milk from the farms and estates. For many reasons, the independent farmers were discontent with the inefficiencies of private dairies. Thus, when a few technical improvements, such as the cream separator, and the market conditions allowed for large-scale dairy production to emerge, the farmers needed only one example in order to set the whole country in motion. In 1882, in a small village situated in Western Jutland, a handful of farmers drew up what was eventually to become the very simple basic principles of a dairy's constitution: joint liability of the members for the debts incurred by the dairy, distribution of profits according to the amount of milk each had delivered to the dairy, and finally, one vote at the annual general assembly for each member regardless of his herd's size and the amount of milk delivered.

After a couple of years with only a handful of dairy foundations, the farmers speeded up their development. In 1887 and 1888 the number of dairy cooperatives virtually exploded with the establishment of 158 and 248, respectively. By 1890, 699 had been established, covering about 30 percent of the holdings, and by the outbreak of the First World War, the number reached 1,168. Roughly 90 percent of the holdings had joined the dairy cooperatives, thus securing them a nearly monopolistic status.

What gave them this unique position was the ability to absorb all holdings irrespective of size. The medium-sized farms dominated in the early phase, but the smallholders, including those with only one cow, very soon joined the movement. Finally, even most of the proprietors of the big estates gave up their private dairies and joined the cooperatives.

Although the dairy cooperatives within twenty-five years managed to cover almost all milk production in Denmark and all sizes of holdings, the initiative and leadership in all these years were almost exclusively in the hands of the farmers from middle-sized holdings. From this class came about 80 percent of the chairmen of the local dairies. The second largest group represented in the boards was the school teachers who often served as accountants or auditors.

The introduction and spread of the farmers' cooperatives, especially the dairies, caused a radical shift in the gender division of labor. Traditionally, the milking of cows and the processing of the milk into cream, butter, and cheese had been performed by the (young) women in the household. The milking for a long period of time remained a women's job whereas all the others function were moved into the dairies and performed exclusively by male labor force. Consequently, in the decades before World War I, the number of female employees on the farms was drastically reduced, and many of the young women migrated to the big cities or to overseas countries, primarily to the United States.

In 1887, the cooperative movement spread to bacon manufacturing. The development in this area came somewhat slower and was more problematic than was the case for the dairy cooperatives. The cooperative bacon factories in the early 1890s had to go through a tough struggle with some very large factories owned by the biggest capitalists in the country. By 1913, however, forty-one cooperative bacon factories had been established, accounting for about 85 percent of the total value of products manufactured from pigs. To these two basic areas of cooperative production were soon added products like eggs and poultry. In the mid-1890s, regional and national centralized organizations were established to take care of wholesale and especially export for the world market. After the turn of the century other areas were included. Cooperative insurance companies, a bank, and a cement factory were built up.

Thus, by the outbreak of the First World War the agricultural cooperative movement formed a network that covered virtually all aspects of the rural population's production and consumption. Together with the above mentioned cultural institutions and the churches, it tended to structure the whole existence of the farmers and smallholders, excluding only the landless proletariat.

Many attempts have been made to explain this formidable achievement. The traditional myth linked cooperation and inspiration from the folk high-schools directly, seeing the economic organizations as a result of the education that the young people received at those schools. Recent research, however, has pointed to the fact that the explicit motives given by the initiators themselves and those who joined the cooperatives were exclusively based on economic rationality: cooperation was the solution for Danish agriculture when it was struck by a severe crisis in the 1870s and threatened by exclusion from the world market. Cooperation combined economic advantages for the individual with means of survival and expansion for the trade as a whole.[14]

It is true, indeed, that the strength of agricultural cooperation lay in the fact that it secured the survival of individual ownership of the main bulk of medium-sized farms and small holdings. Cooperation in a very flexible manner mediated the integration of the individual farm into the world market. It combined traditional independence and individualism with solidarity in purely economic matters. In this way, cooperation became the most important means of the farmers preserving for another century an agrarian structure of ownership, which contradicted most of the laws of capitalist development.

We must not, however, overlook the fact that cooperation was not envisaged as an anticapitalist instrument. It was conceived of as an instrument of survival and expansion within capitalism. Also, cooperation in terms of wage labor functioned in a purely capitalist way. In no case at all did the employees in the dairy cooperatives or bacon factories have any kind of co-ownership. Nor was industrial democracy ever introduced. On the contrary, in the labor movement the agricultural cooperatives very soon got the reputation of being harsh employers.

Even if it is obvious that economic motives were the dominating force behind the creation of the cooperative movement it cannot denied that the effects went far beyond the influence on the national economy. Officially, all branches of the agricultural cooperation declared themselves neutral in political matters. No doubt, many different attitudes were represented among the membership. Nor did the local or central organizations ever declare open support for any single political party.

Nevertheless, agricultural cooperation served as an extremely important powerbase for the farmers. Most of them were staunch supporters of the Left party (*Venstre*). The overwhelming number of leaders in local as well as central cooperative institutions were associated with this party. For many of the party's representatives in Parliament (*Rigsdagen*), experience in the cooperative institutions had served as an elementary education in democracy and organization. Cooperation was a vital element in the Danish farmers' massive effort to disprove Marx's view that farmers were incapable of establishing themselves as an independent, self-conscious and politically dynamic class.

When, finally in 1901, the farmers conquered natural political power after a thirty-year-long struggle with the Right (*Højre*), it was no doubt due also to the impressive economic power they had built up through cooperation. Even today, when the number of those occupied in agriculture represents less than 5 percent of the population, *Venstre* remains a dominating force in local and national politics. The historical traditions of farmer politics and cooperation still saturate Danish society.

Cooperation and the Labor Movement

By 1900, the agricultural cooperative movement had proved to be a dynamic instrument in ensuring farmers' economic independence and political power. In contrast, the labor movement was still very reluctant to give cooperation a central position in the overall socialist strategy. In fact, until the 1890s, the cooperative idea and practice played only a secondary role in the total economic and political activities of the labor movement. But between 1880 and 1920 some important changes took place in the attitudes of socialists, especially toward the consumer cooperatives.

The early socialist movement went through a severe crisis at the end of the 1870s. Economic hardship and the emigration of the leaders to America almost crushed the movement. In 1878, the unitary organization of party and trade unions was dissolved into a Social Democratic party and a formally independent trade union movement. The Danish/Scandinavian labor movement in terms of organization and ideology followed the Continental "model."

Within two decades, the reorganized trade unions proved able to organize the majority of the skilled male workers and a significant proportion of the unskilled male and female workers. By 1910, it is estimated that 90 percent of the skilled workers and about 50 percent of the unskilled had been organized. While the proportion of organized women was considerably smaller, compared with international standards, it was very high. During the 1880s and 1890s, a national union network took shape in all trades. In 1898, union leaders established the National Trade Union Association, which became the central organization for negotiations and conclusion of collective agreements with the corresponding Employers Association. The organizing effort was closely linked to an intensive class struggle that reached its climax in the great 1899 lock-out—one of the longest and most comprehensive labor disputes in the history of the Second International. This wave of disputes played an important role in the development of the cooperative movement.

Parallel to the trade unions, the Social Democratic party experienced a breakthrough in terms of membership and voters. By 1914, it had become the biggest party in Denmark in terms of voters, but, due to electoral procedures, not in the number of parliamentary representatives. From 1883 to 1901 the Social Democrats formed an alliance with the farmers' party *Venstre* with the aim of ousting the government of the Right.

While the Social Democrats in this period adopted the basics of Marxist analysis of capitalism, the party, in its struggle for socialism, followed an unambiguously reformist strategy, placing itself in a center-right position within the Second International.

Consequently, one might expect that both the alliance with *Venstre* and the party's reformism would have led to a full-scale engagement by Socialists in cooperative activities. That was not the case. For almost three decades, their attitude toward cooperation remained ambiguous. The Social Democrats and the trade unions continued to distinguish sharply between consumer and producer cooperatives.

Although all traces of Lassalleanism were eliminated during the 1880s, the Social Democrats did not change their attitude toward consumer cooperation. While they were well informed about the success of consumer cooperatives in other European countries such as Belgium and Switzerland, the Danish Social Democrats still denied that cooperatives would be of any importance in improving the workers' material welfare. On the contrary, they believed, the expansion of consumer cooperatives would only create new proletarians by robbing the small retailers of their means of existence. In this connection, it seems as if the aim of winning over the urban petty bourgeoisie for the social democratic cause was much stronger than the requests of many workers that the party should drop its opposition to consumer cooperatives. The leadership retained the old scepticism toward any initiatives that might have the smell of liberalistic self-help. Although the pressure from below had become stronger, the party congress as late as 1898 flatly refused to have anything to do with the consumer cooperatives. The activities of the labor movement ought to concentrate solely on political and trade union activities.

The liberal self-help cooperators were unable to break the staunch social democratic opposition. Consequently, in the 1880s and 1890s, the establishment of consumer cooperatives in the towns stagnated totally. In 1900, there were only twenty-one urban consumer cooperatives (compared to the more than 1,000 in the rural districts). Those very few established in the towns seem to have been initiated by workers who disagreed with the party-line and especially by specific groups of workers such as the railway employees. [15]

In spite of the opposition to consumer cooperatives, the labor movement engaged itself very actively in other forms of cooperative projects. Producer cooperatives were still considered to be an important supplementary instrument, especially in connection with the large number of labor disputes. A number of short-lived producer cooperatives were established by the workers and trade unions in the 1880s and 1890s. The movement culminated in 1899 during the above mentioned, very comprehensive lock-out when the first permanent producer cooperatives were set up in the building trades. Several of those have managed to survive until today. But their economic potential and market share have been very modest.

Bread, milk, and beer became the true success stories of the workers' cooperative movement. All three of them may be considered as parts of both consumer and producer cooperatives, in the sense that they combined the efforts for cheap commodities of high quality with cooperative ownership. Also, in the initial phase at least, they were meant to serve as an alternative to private capital and its dominance on the market.

Founded by the workers themselves or by local federations of trade unions, cooperative bakeries from the mid-1880s spread all over the country. The initiative came from the provincial towns and the reasons given for the creation of the bakeries were primarily the gap between falling prices on grain and stable if not rising prices on bread. Consideration for the workers in their capacity of consumers seems to have been the overriding motive and not any general acceptance of cooperatives as a strategic tool. The cooperative bakeries were directed against the small private bakeries and immediately became great successes. At the turn of the century, about twenty cooperative bakeries had been established, all of them with a considerable market share.

Hesitations about consumers cooperation, however, had not been abandoned. In 1886, in connection with the founding of what was to become a very large bakery in Copenhagen, the *Social-Demokraten* wrote explicitly that the bakery was meant to break a monopoly and would not become a base for a war against "the numerous group of small retailers."[16]

The bakeries were organized as limited liability companies. The trade union federations and party organizations were in full control of the management which allowed no influence for the bakers employed. Any thought of the cooperative bakeries as some kind of laboratories for industrial democracy was far from the minds of the social democratic leadership at that time.

The establishment of the first labor-controlled dairy cooperative combined several aims of the labor movement. While the farmers' dairy cooperatives aimed at earning a reasonable profit for the producers, the labor dairy cooperatives aimed at supplying the urban population with good quality dairy products at the lowest possible price. Second, they aimed at breaking milk supply monopolies in the towns, especially in Copenhagen. Third, the idea of a dairy cooperative sprang out of the struggle for the right to organize. In 1896-1897, during a strike of the drivers against the Copenhagen Milk Supply Company, the leadership of the unskilled workers' union fostered the idea of replacing the privately owned company with a cooperative dairy. Within a few months, they organized a big dairy plant owned by the union. After initial difficulties, the dairy had to enter into an agreement with a private competitor. Coexisting with the private dairies, the cooperative dairy soon obtained a considerable market share. In spite of this relative success, the initiative never spread to the provincial towns, mainly because of the hard competition from the farmers' dairy cooperatives.[17]

The unskilled Working Men's Trade Union also tried to move into another field of the urban population's daily consumption, margarine. In 1897, the union bought a private margarine factory in the provincial town Svendborg. It was reorganized as a cooperative factory with the aim of benefitting the workers in their capacity as both consumers and producers. The attempt ended in a spectacular failure. After severe losses, the factory was closed in 1908.

Thus, at the turn of the century, the experience of the labor movement with combined consumer and producer cooperatives was rather mixed. This fact, however, did not prevent the movement as a whole engaging in the rapidly expanding market of beer consumption. A shift in taxation in the 1890s changed the drinking habits of the workers from distilled spirits to beer. In 1902, the labor movement established a brewery in Copenhagen based on capital from the cooperative bakeries and the trade unions. Once again, the beginning was very troublesome. The brewery not only faced severe competition from the giants in the market, Carlsberg and Tuborg, but also the quality of the beer did not satisfy the taste of the workers. Further, the trade union of the brewery workers opposed the initiative, fearing unemployment. Finally, the fairly strong temperance movement criticized the labor movement for instigating the workers to continue to drink, thus adding to the social miseries caused by drinking. The Danish labor movement never officially adopted temperance in its program and, in the following years, made a great effort to consolidate the brewery. Although the brewery never managed to make a serious inroad on the near-monopoly of the big breweries it obtained a market share sufficient to secure the survival of the brewery for almost sixty years. However, in spite of great efforts and a lot of money, the workers' cooperatives never succeeded in cutting more than very marginal slices of the capitalist economy in the field of production.

Changing Attitudes toward the Consumer Cooperation

Immediately after the turn of the century the question of consumer cooperatives became a very urgent one for the labor movement. Several factors helped to provoke a change of the hitherto negative attitude: a pressure from below, several requests from the much more positive labor movements in the other Scandinavian countries, and a new generation of party leaders who were not influenced by the negative experience of the self-help movement.

As late as 1898, the Social Democratic party congress flatly refused to have anything to do with the consumer cooperative movement. The elimination of poverty could only be achieved by the socialization of the means of production and the only means to that end were the organization of the workers in the trade unions and the Social Democratic party.[18]

The rank and file of the labor movement, however, totally disregarded the warnings against cooperation. In the years from 1901 to 1914 almost seventy consumer cooperatives were founded in Copenhagen and the provincial towns. Many of these seem to have been created by members of the Social Democratic party or the local trade unions. Although very little research has been made into the gender question in this connection it seems as if this pressure can be ascribed partly to a growing influence of women in the labor movement. Both in the trade unions and in the party their voices were heard more clearly after the turn of the century, and the concerns of the women as responsible for the daily consumption and shopping sharpened their awareness about the possibilities connected with the consumer cooperatives. It is, however, characteristic of the extremely male-dominated Danish labor movement that in the debates about attitudes toward cooperatives and especially in the leadership of the individual shops and the cooperative movement as a whole the women were totally absent for a very long period of time. The party faced an immediate danger of becoming isolated from a rapidly growing grassroots movement if it did not engage itself actively in the movement, or even take the initiative.

Furthermore, the international pressure for consumer cooperatives became constantly stronger. Several parties of the Second International actively supported the movement. Especially the sister parties in Norway and Sweden put pressure on the Danish labor movement, which until then had been the leading party in Scandinavia in questions of theory as well as tactics. In 1907, at a Scandinavian congress, the Danes were urged to vote for a resolution the contents of which totally reversed the attitude toward the consumer cooperatives. The cooperative movement was regarded as an important instrument in the struggle for the liberation of the working class. When, in 1910, the Copenhagen congress of the Second International passed a resolution to the same effect, the Danish delegates voted for it without hesitation.

Between those two congresses the Danish party had set the course for a revision of its attitude toward the consumer cooperatives. In 1908, at the Danish party congress, the most prominent parliamentary spokesman and indefatigable supporter of the cooperative movement, F. J. Borgbjerg, urged the delegates to pass a resolution in favor of cooperation. After a partial success he went on the next year in a speech to the national conference of the trade unions where he elaborated the perspectives of cooperation. To the two pillars of the labor movement, the party and the trade unions, the cooperative movement ought to be added as a coordinate support for liberation. The workers were exploited as producers and as consumers. Quoting Jean Jaurès, he characterized the consumption of the workers as a "revolutionary force." Furthermore, cooperation represented the seeds of socialism, teaching the workers the administration of production and their own life situation. Through cooperation, the labor movement might create a steadily growing sector of socialist economy and thus roll back capitalism. On the very touchy question of the small shopkeepers, he flatly envisaged their future demise. Capitalism would make them superfluous and, consequently, they might as well join the socialists immediately.[19]

Borgbjerg's energetic campaign for the consumer cooperatives resulted in the formation of a joint party and trade union committee, which, finally, in 1913, for all practical purposes, brought about the long overdue revision of the attitude toward the consumer cooperation. In the following years party members in great numbers joined the consumer cooperatives and leadership in almost all urban shops was taken over by the Social Democrats. In 1916, all consumer cooperatives in Copenhagen became associated in *Hovedstadens Brugsforening* (The Consumer Cooperative of the Capital). Though it was officially politically neutral there was no doubt that the leadership was firmly in the hand of the Social Democrats. The urban cooperatives associated themselves with the agrarians in the *FDB*, but for the next half-century there was a clear distinction between urban and rural consumer cooperatives in terms of party affiliation and ideology, representing the major political opponents in twentieth-century Danish politics, *Venstre*, and the Social Democrats.

The consumer cooperatives as a whole consolidated their position in the interwar period. The membership grew about 33 percent, and the turnover almost doubled. The urban, worker-based cooperatives expanded somewhat, but they never conquered a position in the local communities which corresponded to the dominance of the rural cooperatives. The division between town and country in 1922 was formalized by the formation of the Central Union of the Urban Cooperative Societies (*Det kooperative Fallesforbund-DKF*). This union organized all cooperatives associated with the labor movement and may be considered as a parallel to the central organization for the agricultural cooperatives, the Central Co-operative Committee (*Andelsudvalget*) founded in 1898.

In fact, the backbone of the expansion of workers' cooperatives during the interwar years was not the consumer cooperatives but a rapidly growing number of cooperative building societies. After a modest start before the First World War, the Workers' Cooperative Housing Association (*Arbejdernes Andelsboligforening*) and the Workers' Cooperative Building Society (*Arbejdernes kooperative Byggeforening*) pioneered a very strong housing cooperative movement with local sections in almost every town. The expansion in the housing sector was due partly to financial support from the state and partly to a close collaboration with the local authorities. In one town after another, the Social Democrats obtained a majority in this period. They initiated grand building programs, frequently with the cooperative building associations in the role of entrepreneurs.[20]

Conclusion

Probably, the cooperative movement has had a greater impact in Denmark than in any other country in Europe. In the general opinion, cooperation is closely associated with the Danish farmers' exceptional development into an economically very strong and politically dominant force. In almost every textbook, the agricultural cooperative movement is described as the characteristic feature of the Danish historical and national heritage whereas the workers' urban-based cooperation is hardly mentioned. This fact cannot only be ascribed to the dominance of what has been termed as the "Farmer Interpretation" of Danish history.[21] To a very large extent, this view corresponds with reality.

As demonstrated above, the agricultural cooperative movement constituted the backbone of the farmers' economic form of organization. In contrast, the urban workers' cooperative achievements remained less significant in several respects. First, it did not succeed in fulfilling F. J. Borgbjerg's optimistic visions of cooperation as a tool in the struggle for socialism. The idea of cooperation undermining capitalism proved to be illusory. Second, within the labor movement as a whole, cooperative ideals and practices always came in the third place in relation to party politics and trade union engagement. Both the leadership and the majority of the members always considered it to be a subsidiary to parliamentary reform politics and trade union activities.

There are many explanations of this situation. The role of cooperatives, in the initial stage, as a tool in the hands of bourgeois liberals against the socialists caused deep-rooted suspicions among the workers in the formative years of the labor movement. Also, the constant attention to the role of the urban petty bourgeoisie as a potential ally for the Social Democrats strengthened the reluctance to engage actively in especially the consumer cooperative movement. When the Social Democrats finally adopted the idea, they did not throw in the whole economic power of the labor movement as they did in, for instance, the very successful building cooperation. Moreover, the takeover of the urban consumer cooperatives took place in a situation where the rural consumer cooperatives had consolidated and totally dominated the movement as a whole. In the half-century after the First World War, the urban consumer cooperatives had very little influence within the central organizations of the cooperatives (the *FDB*). It was not until the second wave of urbanization, beginning in the mid-1950s that the urban consumer cooperatives came to play a major role in the *FDB*. But that is a whole new story.

Notes

1. A brief, general outline of Danish Cooperation in English is given by Clemens Pedersen, ed., *The Danish Co-operative Movement* (Copenhagen, 1977).

2. Lennart Jörberg, "The Industrial Revolution in Scandinavia," in *The Fontana Economic History of Europe*, vol. IV, (London, 1970); and Sevend Aage Hansen, *Early Industrialisation in Denmark* (Copenhagen, 1970).

3. André Cochut, *Les associations ouvrières: Histoire et théorie des tentatives de réorganisation industrielle operees depuis la révolution de 1848* (Paris, 1851).

4. Preben Dollerup, *Brugsforeningerne 1866-1896* (Albertslund, 1966), 29-30; and Poul Thestrup, *Narbutik og neringslovsomgaaelse. En undersoegelse af brugsforeningerne og deres placering i innovationsprocessen i Danmark mellem 1850 og 1919* (with an English summary), (Odense, 1986), 112-21.

5. Thestrup, *Naerbutik*, 128-33.

6. Claus Bryld and Niels Finn Christiansen, *Det sociale spoergsmaal i den offentlige debat i 1860'erne og 1870'erne* (Copenhagen, 1965), 17-29.

7. H. C. Sonne, *Om Arbeiderforeninger* (Copenhagen, 1867), 5.

8. *Arbejderen*, January 1871, 1; and Jens Christensen: *Rural Denmark 1750-1980* (Copenhagen, 1983).

9. Dollerup, 122-33 and Thestrup, 158-63.

10. K. D. Larsen, "Arbejderkooperationens historie 1871-1923," *Arbejderhistorie* 22 (1984): 25-29; and Henry Bruun, *Den faglige Arbejderbevoaegelse i Danmark indtil Aar 1900*, vol. 1, (Copenhagen, 1938), 546-72.

11. For this development, see the brief survey by Niels Finn Christiansen, "Denmark, End of the Idyll," *New Left Review* 144 (1984): 5-32; and Christiansen, *Rural Denmark*.

12. Claus Bjørn, "The Co-operative Movement in Denmark—a Historical Sketch," in ed., Pedersen, 110.

13. Thestrup, *Naerbutik*, 235.

14. This survey is based on Claus Bjørn, "Co-operative Movement," and Claus Bjørn, *Det danske landbrugs historie*, vol. 3 *1810-1914* (Odense, 1988).

15. Thestrup, *Naerbutik*, 444.

16. Kaj Lykke, *Arbejderbevaegelse og Arbejderkooperation i Danmark 1871-1898* (Copenhagen, 1974), 87.

17. Lykke, *Arbejderbevaegelse*, 111-13.

18. P. Christensen and Fr. Dalgaard, *Kooperation* (Copenhagen, 1931), 89.

19. F. J. Borgbjerg, *Kooperative Foretagender* (Copenhagen, 1909).

20. The rapid development of the building cooperatives that continued after World War II was until now very underresearched.

21. Thorkild Kjaergaard, "The Farmer Interpretation of Danish History," *Scandinavian Journal of History* 10 (1985): 97-118.

Chapter 9

Swedish Consumer Cooperation as an Educational Endeavor

Peder Aléx

Consumer cooperation has often been seen as a successful and influential part of Swedish social democracy, but much about the history of consumer cooperation in Sweden is not widely understood. Despite the importance of the Socialist tradition in Sweden, cooperation began as a liberal movement and played a large role in popularizing liberal economic ideas. Although Sweden has been a model social democracy for the rest of the world, foreign influences—from Britain, Belgium, France, Austria, Denmark, and Germany—helped shape the rise of Swedish consumer cooperation. Consumer cooperation was not only an economic and social movement, but an intellectual one as well. Through workers' education, the cooperative movement transformed liberal economic ideas and foreign models. The movement advocated, especially to women, the values of savings and socially conscious consumerism and ultimately helped create the modern consumer movement in Sweden.

In examining how liberal economic ideas could be combined with the working-class movement to form Swedish cooperation, it is important to begin with the social and economic history of mid-nineteenth-century Sweden. Seen from an international perspective, liberal economic ideas and the industrial revolution came to Sweden relatively late. The economy was long characterized by mercantilism. In 1846, freedom of trade was extended, the guild system disappeared, and it became easier to conduct business. Merchants in the cities could leave the guild-system, but were still forced to establish commercial associations. In the countryside, free trade was also proclaimed, but under two conditions. First, the proprietor of a village store had to apply for an operating permit at the county administrative board. And, second, he was not allowed to open his store within thirty kilometers of a city. Trade did not become totally free in the countryside until the legal dissolution of separate orders—aristocracy, townspeople, farmers—in 1864. From that point on, commercial activity increased with enormous rapidity.[1]

Sweden was then an extremely poor country on the periphery of Europe. The rise of industrialization, beginning in the 1850s and expanding in the late nineteenth century, however, was a clear sign that society was in the process of changing drastically. Despite Sweden's geographical isolation, many people carefully followed European intellectual and political debates. In the spirit of liberalism, reformers were in favor of changes in the constitution, while also wanting to avoid the social strife they observed in the rest of Europe. The continental revolutions of 1830, and especially 1848, frightened many Swedes, as did the misery and class conflicts caused by industrialization in England. Class struggle and even revolution seemed to be sweeping over Europe with gale force. This wind had to be combated before it blew in over Sweden.

Liberal Workers' Societies

The liberal educational tradition was important in the Swedish debate over the "social question" throughout the nineteenth century. The idea was that social conflicts in society could be avoided through general adult education, intended to raise the "spiritual" level of the populace to a higher, more middle-class one. Middle-class reformers saw education as the cornerstone in achieving self-sufficiency and a responsible and enlightened civic spirit, even among the lowest strata of society. In time, the cooperative idea came to be inextricably associated with this educational ideal. The two ideological traditions were two sides of the same coin, both aiming at educating and cultivating the lower strata until its members grew into responsible citizens. An educated populace would solve the problems confronting society by using its reason instead of relying on emotions that fueled class hatred. Physician Johan Ellmin pioneered the organized education movement in Sweden from the 1840s on. According to Ellmin, general education was the only way to solve society's social conflicts. He was the leading figure of a group in Stockholm that took the initiative to start an educational circle in 1845. The idea was that education would offer an alternative to a night at the local pub, while at the same time act as an intermediary in meetings between different social classes. Politics was not considered to be a part of education, and consequently was forbidden. Until the rise of the peasant party in 1867, politics was confined to a small elite divided between librals and conservatives. The circle gained a large membership from among Stockholm's artisans, and the idea soon spread to several other cities.[2]

It was these educational activities, as well as rural cooperatives, which brought consumer cooperation to Sweden. In 1850, a group of workers who had been members of one of Ellmin's reading clubs created a new society. The reading club itself had been taken over by more conservative forces, and Ellmin had been outmaneuvred. The new workers' society issued an appeal to the nation's workers, encouraging them to found societies of their own. A number of them were indeed established in several other cities throughout Sweden. It was out of these new workers' societies that cooperatives would eventually grow. The time was not yet ripe for a more comprehensive workers' educational movement, however, due perhaps to the fact that commerce and economics had not yet succeeded in liberating the populace from the structures of agrarian society. Although Swedish peasants were legally free and most owned their own land, few produced much beyond subsistence, and markets were small-scale. Yet the idea of "cooperation" was not foreign to agrarian society; in fact, it was a natural component of rural life, as manifested in local householder associations and village meetings.

Thus the first cooperative organizations in Sweden were established among the rural population. The first was the Lagunda and Hagunda District Commodity Supply Company, founded in Öresundsbro by County Governor Robert von Kraemer in 1850. Von Kraemer was a close friend of author and history professor Erik Gustav Geijer, who had visited England and been pleasantly surprised by the workings of the cooperative movement there. Von Kraemer probably got the idea for a cooperative society from Geijer. The society consisted primarily of farmers and dealt in herring, salt, lime, and tar, which were traded for commodities produced by farmers themselves.[3] The second society was founded in 1858 in the province of Dalecarlia, at Kloster's Mill.[4] During the 1850s, several accounts appeared in the newspapers describing both the French and English cooperative movements. For example, *Aftonbladet* published an article by the authoress Fredrika Bremer, in which she described the English cooperatives in positive terms. The flow of information concerning the cooperative movement culminated in 1852 when the liberal S. A. Hedlund lectured at the Stockholm Working Men's Society, giving an account of the French and English cooperative movements.[5] Despite this, the development of both workers' societies and the cooperative movement did not really take off until the 1860s.

Worker Societies and Cooperative Ideas

In 1860, a number of artisans and middle-class reformers founded the Workers' Society of Norrköping, immediately providing a model for future workers' societies. In its wake, similar organizations were established in numerous localities. All of these societies emphasized information and educational activities, though often in an extremely diluted form, as in the following policy statement: "The object of the society is to promote the education of its members and devote itself to goodness, refinement and beauty."[6] The subjects to be dealt with had to be all-round educational and politically harmless.

The workers' society in Gothenburg, Sweden's second largest city, provides one successful example. Created in 1866, it boasted over 3,000 members only two years later. Again, educational activities and cooperation went hand-in-hand. The society organized lectures and language classes, ran a library and arranged health insurances for its members, along with a cooperative-influenced trade enterprise, which after some years went bankrupt. Furthermore, the society planned programs featuring various kinds of diversions and outings. Axel Krook, the society's most prominent figure, wanted it to raise the intellectual and moral standards of the workers. According to Krook, the health insurance plan, along with the business enterprise, were meant to teach the workers the values of self-sufficiency.[7]

Around the same time as workers' societies were being founded in more and more towns, the cooperative idea gained its first advocates among the intellectual elite. G. K. Hamilton, Professor of Political Economy at the University of Lund, held a series of lectures in Stockholm in 1864, which were later published as a book entitled *On the Working Class and Workers Societies*.[8] Hamilton was mainly interested in promoting producer cooperatives, following the exmaple of those created by Schultze-Delitzsch in Germany. The purpose of these societies was to build character and promote personal development; cooperative manufacturing societies would instill in their members a sense of personal responsibility and independent progress. The soul was to be cultivated through cooperative labor: "A more extensive association for common manufacture presupposes the development of spiritual self-control and intelligence amongst the participants, as it appears nearly unthinkable to expect such to occur on a wider basis."[9] According to Hamilton, the central government, municipalities, and private charities were incapable of achieving any significant solution to social problems. Whenever they attempted to do so, there was always the risk of idleness, neglect, and "debauchery" setting in among the aided population. Instead, one must prevail upon the people to help themselves. That is why the cooperative manufacturing society was such an excellent alternative for Hamilton, because it demanded a high degree of personal commitment from individual workers. But Hamilton also drew attention to the consumer cooperative in England, notably those influenced by the Rochdale model. According to Hamilton, participation in these stores taught the workers the essential virtue of exercising their own judgement. By being a member of an active consumer cooperative, the family had access to inexpensive provisions, developed itself, and achieved a state of comfort and well-being in the home. Moral qualities such as thrift, tidiness, and considerateness followed. Hamilton wanted his educational project to promote the personal development of each individual working man. The soul would be cultivated, and using the cooperative manufacturing society as a means, the working class would ascend to become the newest members of the middle class. This would also indirectly strengthen the existing middle class, something that may have been deemed necessary since the recent abolition of the four-estate parliament in 1864.[10]

C. E. Ljungberg, a statistician and federal politician, was equally influential. Both his Stockholm lecture, and subsequent book *On the Association System in Foreign Lands, With Particular Regard to the Advance-Payment Associations of Schultze-Delitzsche* (1865),[11] had an immediate impact. Several consumer and credit cooperatives were established in Stockholm following Ljungberg's lecture (businesses that soon declared bankruptcy, however). Ljungberg also advocated producer cooperatives and viewed consumer cooperatives as a way for workers to learn to economize prior to the formation of producer cooperatives. Ljungberg further hoped that the workers' manners would improve through associational activities. This would occur not only by working together for the common aspirations of the society, but also through the adult education program the society would offer and the example set by the best and brightest individuals for the other members.[12]

One individual who wanted to unite the ideals of the consumer association with the fundamental motivations behind the workers' society was Abraham Rundbäck, lecturer in mathematics in the small Swedish town of Växjö. Rundbäck strongly advocated the English style consumer cooperative and established a cooperative society in Växjö himself in 1867. In his book, *Treatise on Consumer Societies* (1869), Rundbäck develops his ideas in greater detail.[13] Cooperatives would be started up in order to help working people learn "self-sufficiency." Through "self-sufficiency," the workers could gain their share of the improvements and heightening of the level of civilization currently underway in all nations. According to Rundbäck, the economic progress of cooperation was a prerequiste for "increasing development in other ways as well," by which he meant the development of both the national economy and the morals of mankind. Rundbäck felt that the network of workers' societies existing throughout the country had started out at the wrong end by being educational first and engaging in cooperation second. By beginning with a cooperative society, not only would the financial situation of the membership be improved, but that development would also have an effect on the individual members' "ethical, social and political development." The cooperative society ought therefore to function as an educational institution for its members.

As we can see, by the end of the 1860s there existed a tradition of liberal workers associations advocating education as a means to solving social conflicts. These ideas were partly absorbed by the growing cooperative movement, which often had as its initiators or propagandists members of the same middle-class circles who started up the workers societies. A large portion of this movement disappeared during the 1870s only to resurface the following decade in another form.

The Late Nineteenth Century

Despite marked failures in the 1880s and the initial opposition of the growing Social Democratic party, consumer cooperation grew during the last decades of the nineteenth century into a genuine working-class phenomenon. The individual who most avidly pursued the cooperative ideal during the 1880s was L. O. Smith, who had been inspired by the French cooperative movement, the association *Humanité* in Lille in particular. Smith borrowed the idea of a special organization, which he called the "ring movement" from *Humanité*. A society, or (in Smith's terminology) a "ring" of individuals, would conclude agreements with various suppliers. Each member of the ring would purchase products from these suppliers, who in turn would offer them sizable rebates. The rebates obtained by the ring would be paid out to the members afterwards. The ring movement spread quickly, above all throughout Stockholm, but also in many other towns around the country; figures show that between 1883 and 1885 some 20,000 to 22,000 members had joined.[14] Two factors, however, soon caused the rings to collapse. In the first place, few businesses were really in a position to offer rebates, for the marginal costs in retail trade were so small. Second, the burgeoning Social Democratic movement, led by ideologue August Palm, was strongly opposed to any form of cooperation.[15] The Social Democrats had long considered cooperation as a way of diverting the workers from the path of class struggle. They opposed cooperation just as they opposed the adult educational activities and lecture series that had embarked upon a strong comeback in the 1880s and that the Social Democrats also saw as essentially liberal movements.

The growth of the Social Democratic movement was a product of increasing industrialization. Industrialization gained momentum in Sweden during the 1890s as the country experienced a boom beginning in the year 1894. Sweden was at last able to industrialize as the country earned capital via the sale of oron ore from newly opened mines. Hand in hand with the industrial boom, the number of workers increased, as did membership in trade unions and in the still-fledgling Social Democratic party. The number of new cooperative businesses increased enormously, not the least because legislation from 1895 now permitted the ownership of stores by members of an organization. Not including the ring movement, 1,150 consumer cooperative were founded in Sweden between 1865 and 1900; 490 of them, or almost half, were created during the 1890s alone. However, despite the fact that the birth of cooperatives was commonplace, one cannot say the same thing about their rate of survival. Only eighty-five survived beyond the year 1908.

Cooperatives founded during the 1890s differed significantly from their predessesors. Rank and file members established most of the later cooperatives without sponsorship by middle- and upper-class individuals. For all these "lower class" members, cooperatives were one part of a pragmatic, down-to-earth strategy: the trade union raised wages, and the temperance movement contributed to healthy development in family life. The most appealing aspect of cooperation for working-class members was its financial aspect. Almost none of the new cooperatives pursued the ideal of enlightenment and education. Nor did they view the cooperation as a means of solving the "social question." These new members wanted access to good, inexpensive merchandise; this was often the sole motivation for creating a society. Few and far between were those societies that continued to speak about cooperation as a means of uplifting, informing, and educating the working class.[16]

The Founding of the Swedish Cooperative Union and Wholesale Society

When the Swedish consumer cooperative movement formally organized itself as the Cooperative Union and Wholesale Society (KF)[17] at its 1899 conference, two nineteenth-century traditions were at work. The first was the liberal tradition inherited from the workers' societies and early nineteenth-century cooperative movements. That tradition was introduced to KF by one of the initiators of the conference, an aristocratic firebrand named G. H. von Koch. During a trip to England in 1898 he had become enamoured of the cooperative idea. Not only was he interested in the economic aspects, that individuals in fellowship should answer for their own finances and provisioning in order to share the profits among themselves, but the educational program of English cooperation also fascinated him. Von Koch became the first secretary of KF, and from the beginning was its sole full-time steward. As such he pursued his particular version of consumer cooperation with great enthusiasm, primarily in the form of a comprehensive lecture series arranged during the first years. Some of the leading Swedish political economists—Gustav Cassel, Eli Heckscher, and Gustaf Steffen—gave von Koch ideological support. They had all read Beatrice Potter's *The Co-operative Movement in Great Britain*, and had been convinced that the cooperative movement really could mean something for the poor in terms of higher living standard.

A Social Democratic cooperative tradition, however, also existed. Many of the consumer cooperative societies established from 1895 onwards had been created by workers influenced by the Social Democrats' critical attitude toward liberalism. The Social Democrats had long been vocal opponents of the cooperative idea; they did not begin revising their position until positive appraisals of cooperatives had been expressed by Eduard Bernstein, writing in exile from London for *Die Neue Zeit* in 1895, and Karl Kautsky, in his book *Consumer Societies and the Workers' Movement* (*Consumvereine und Arbeiterbewegung*) of 1897.[18] Social Democratic newspaperman Axel Danielsson had by 1898 become so convinced of the future possibilities of cooperatives that he proposed creating a cooperative society in Malmö, Sweden's third-largest city. In Stockholm, Axel Rylander had long been gravitating in the direction of a positive position toward cooperatives. He belonged to the leading group of Social Democrats in Stockholm, and was the initiator of the first trade union for commercial employees. Although he, in common with the more radical wing of the party, had first been highly critical of the cooperative idea, he became increasingly fascinated by it. His conversion began as he became interested in the Belgian cooperative movement, which saw cooperation as an essential element in the work of the Socialist Party and in its financial growth since financial profits reaped by the cooperative societies would be turned over to the party. By 1895, however, Rylander had abandoned that thought and become a partisan of the English cooperative movement's method of turning all the profits of the cooperative back to the members.

Rylander and von Koch were two of the driving forces behind KF's first conference in 1899. Forty-four cooperative associations attended the conference, representing 8,900 members.[19] It was not until 1905, however, that the consumer cooperative movement began its forceful development, which by 1939 had led to a formidable organization of 5,171 KF stores for 669,429 members—and with stores also open for nonmembers—and the starting up of a number of industries.[20]

Cooperation and the Idea of Progress

The early twentieth century saw cooperation finally brought into Social Democratic thought along with other reformist notions. Axel Rylander was one of the first leading Social Democrats to advocate the cooperative model. He acted from the same motives as those workers who would rather be engaged in practical work for reform than thinking in terms of restructuring the whole of society. Practical restructuring of society could take the form of working for trade unions, franchise reform, the temperance movement, or cooperation.

Consumer cooperation was seen as a way to begin the reformation of society in the here and now. As members of the cooperative, people were provided with a steady supply of quality provisions, something that was far from insignificant especially when industrialization was incapable of providing them with acceptable products. The cooperative was a nonprofit organization, with all profits being shared among members in the form of rebates proportional to the size of their purchases. Membership was voluntary and every member of the society had a vote. Thus the cooperative, in contrast to society at large, was democratic, although voting members were usually male heads of families. Cooperatives can be seen as the manifestation of a very down-to-earth and practical reformism, which directly and immediately made life easier for its members.

From the outset of the 1890s, social and intellectual changes had developed at a dizzying rate and encouraged a marriage of cooperation and socialist thought. To many observers, the idea broached by the new natural and social sciences concerning the evolution of life on earth from a lower to a higher stage was proven to be true in day-to-day life. The theory of progress was given strong support by actual economic development. The radical wing of the Swedish Social Democratic party experienced increasing difficulty in attempting to defend the economic theories of both Marx and Lassalle from the frontal attacks of social liberal political economist Gustav Cassel and the expert on political science Ponthus Fahlbeck. Both used statistical material to demonstrate that economic development in Sweden had gone forward, something that many a working man had also noted.[21] By the turn of the century, the idea of progress and reformism had defeated the revolutionary currents within social democracy. Thus the cooperative movement could now be offered unreserved support, since it could be understood as the idea of progress being implemented in concrete terms. The cooperative movement, despite the fact that it has always remained politically unaffiliated in Sweden, fit in perfectly with the reformistic system of the Social Democrats, where practical reformism and the idea of progress go hand in hand. In the true spirit of reformism and the belief in progress, Swedish consumer cooperation, despite its more radical elements (profit being shared out in the form of dividends) aimed at contributing to society's material progress. It became increasingly common to state that the goal of the cooperative movement was to attain higher levels of consumption as a worthwhile means to other goals.

Credit and Ethics

In the tradition of Swedish reformism, the consumer cooperative movement emphasized cooperation, profit sharing, and education. KF stated its educational focus in its charter, composed at its first conference (1899). Paragraph 11 of the KF charter states that the association's secretariat was to "always keep watch to see that the movement developed into an important factor in the dissemination of general civic training and elevation of the stature of the populace as regards both moral and economic matters." Two and half percent of the financial profits were earmarked for educational activities.[22] Social Democrat Axel Rylander lent his support to this educational idea, originating in the liberal tradition, and restructured it to suit his tastes. Rylander, like the liberal workers' societies before him, believed that the workers were in need of a certain amount of education in order to be able to function as sound citizens. But the project Rylander had in mind did not intend to "elevate" the workers to the middle class: cooperation should not just be means to a middle-class career. Instead, the workers must transform themselves so that they inspired confidence, i.e., they must become informed and responsible. When they began to behave in this proper manner, then they could take power and administer a society deeply in need of reform.

This was the context in which Rylander's battle against consumer credit took place, a struggle maintained by Swedish consumer cooperation long after his death. Rylander developed his argument against credit in the pamphlet *Consumer Credit: A New Century Better Habits* (1900).[23] Rylander believed that the use of credit quickly led the worker into insolvency. Dependence upon credit meant workers did not live on what they earned, but on what they were going to earn in the future. The customer learned to live rashly; offering credit made it easier for the retailer to fob his merchandise off on the customer than when dealing strictly on a cash basis. In the long run, this led to depravity. Buying on credit, the customer became indifferent toward household econo-mies, which spawned an indifference toward paying bills and taxes. Credit "led to demoralization, financial ruin, poverty, deceit, and crime in numerous cases. It helped no one, while bringing thousands and thousands more to ruin." The customer, that is, the male citizen, who had become accustomed to being punctual and correct, became accustomed to negligence, and "thereby lowers people's confidence in his endeavours." The workers' movement had no use for such a careless and irresponsible sort, who would be unable to contribute to the creation and administration of the new society. On the contrary, says Rylander, it is always "the most thoughtful, well-behaved, and correct workers (who as a result of such qualities are also the best situated ones) who can do something and win something for their class." Thus it was not enough to speak out against social injustice; one was to instill the general public with confi-dence in the ability of the working class to take over and administer society. As long as the workers shoped on credit they proved their financial indepen-dence, and thus their ability to administer the finances of an entire society. The most pressing task of the cooperative movement, according to Rylander, was to relieve the material and spiritual misery created by credit. People must get used to making cash purchases, "to know the value of money, in other words, the value of a sound economy." The ultimate result of such a policy would be citizens who have "happier dispositions, are nobler of mind, feel themselves stronger and more independent, have greater confidence in themselves and others who act as they do." The worker who makes purchases with cash in hand "will become the workers' movement's most reliable support, and conse-quently, society's finest individual."

The idea of citizenship also manifested itself in Rylander's thought. Coop-eration was to aid in developing lower-class people (or the more diffuse category of "the consumers") as citizens with a sense of responsibility, whether they performed their services to society within the confines of the workers' movement or elsewhere in society. One is tempted to say that, according to Rylander, cooperation would aid in disciplining the lower strata of society in order to adapt them to that which Norbert Elias calls "the civilizing process." Those who are poised to take control of society in the future must be taught etiquette and civilization, which also means controlling one's inner emotional life. With the advent of democracy at the beginning of the twentieth century, the lower classes were forced to travel the same road that the aristocracy and middle class had already traversed at an earlier stage of the historical process. Participation in the ever more complicated systems of government and bureaucracy demanded a greater check on internal emotions: behavior must be disciplined. The modern, responsible worker/citizen must not be guided by his sense of pathos, but rather must heed only his (hopefully) mature sense of reason.[24] The cooperative movement distributed Rylander's pamphlet in several large editions. Up to the 1930s, the fight against credit was one of the leading themes pursued by the cooperative movement. In an editorial of *Kooperatören* from 1925, one can read the same opinions on the credit system as expressed by Rylander a quarter of a century earlier. Credit does not raise the standard of living. On the contrary, states the paper, it only tempts people to overconsumption. Moreover, "credit inflicts not only economic damage, but moral damage as well . . . The order lacking in the household's finances engenders a constant state of unrest, which can prove extremely depressing. Peace of mind, a feeling of freedom and of taking pleasure on one's work, all disappear."[25]

From the beginning of the 1930s there was no need of keeping on with the anticredit campaign. But still it seemed to be important to save money; KF, together with some of the bigger banks, launched a campaign to exhort a spirit of saving, especially among younger citizens. (Saving was possible in the 1930s, despite the Depression, because Sweden weathered the worldwide crisis almost better than any other countries.) From the credit-and-save campaign, the idea of cooperation as a democratic liberation movement was developed. Democracy consisted in the fact that all members had a vote, and by freedom one meant freedom from economic dependency, i.e., from credit.

The battle against credit, like other important ideological questions, was engaged mainly in the pages of the cooperative press. The newspaper *Kooperatören* began publishing in 1904, and by 1914 had established itself as a theoretical organ for the cooperative movement. At the same time, the weekly *Konsumentbladet* was started up, and its subscription list grew steadily. In 1927, it had a circulation of 259,000 copies per week and by 1939, under the new name *VI* (WE), it had become Sweden's most widely read weekly, printing 570,000 copies every week. This was extremely large, considering that Sweden at that time only had six million people.

Cooperative Studies are Organized

The propaganda activities stipulated by KF's charter were carried out right from the beginning, in an intense and extensive fashion. Publishing operations began immediately (for example, with the pamphlet by Axel Rylander mentioned above), along with lecture and agitation tours on behalf of the cooperative movement, and the establishment of a cooperative press. As far as female membership was concerned, special women's guilds were established beginning in 1907 (an activity without any tangible propaganda effect until the great upswing of the 1930s).[26] Study circle operations flourished around the years 1917-1918. The first priority of teaching in the form of the study circle was to master the difficult art of bookkeeping, but study groups concurred with the still undeveloped cooperative theory were also organized. Part of this activity was transformed shortly thereafter into correspondence courses, wherein the participants, whether working in groups or as individuals, studied forms and textbooks and sent their completed assignments to KF's Correspondence Institute in Stockholm to be corrected. These activities also grew substantially through the years. In 1939, 2,803 groups throughout Sweden signed up for correspondence courses, with a total number of 48,127 participants.

The new type of study circle, which went under the designation of "group activities," was to become even more widespread than the correspondence courses. Axel Gjöres, who became KF's organizational leader in 1920 started group activities, received the impulse for this idea from England. In 1929 KF's central study department began to publish discussion booklets listing subjects that could be discussed at meetings. The intention was that the discussions would be open and without a moderator. Answers could be sent in to the study department, which in return commented on every answer received. In this manner, a dialogue between the grass roots and KF's central leadership was established. While discussions centered on cooperative themes, they also attached great importance to domestic economy, i.e., discussions that dealt with how to run a household rationally and economically. A few examples of the subjects discussed include "Infants, Tykes and School Children," "What We Eat," and "Rational Cleaning." The group activities of the cooperative movement grew to such an extent by 1939 that there were 3,853 groups meeting, hosting over 52,000 participants.[27] In the process, a subtle but important shift occurred from the late nineteenth century focus on the male citizen to an emphasis on the woman in the home caring for her children and family in the twentieth century.

The Swedish People as Political Economists

The growth of workers' education through the cooperative movement reveals the debate going on within the working-class movement over how to defend the liberal economic system from Marxist, statist intervention, and capitalism's own illiberal defects. Diligent publishing activity, which gained real momentum during the 1920s, was an important part of KF's extensive educational program. Like the rest of its educational operations, book publishing was dominated by economic topics. Cooperation taught its members fundamental business economics so that they could take part in the administration of the cooperative stores. Leaders of the cooperative movement were also, and somewhat surprisingly, interested in classic liberal political economy. When the ninth edition of political economist Gunnar Westin-Silverstolpe's book *Political Economy for Everyone* was published in 1939, sales had reached some 60,000 copies.[28] This can be seen as a reflection of the interest the cooperative movement showed for political economy, an interest that also spread to all forms of cooperative educational activities. A cascade of books and articles originating from the cooperative movement defended the classic theories of political economy against Marxist-influenced attacks, while also going on the offensive against "deviant" variations of the free enterprise system including trusts, cartels, and monopolies.[29] The cooperative movement and the trade union movement were portrayed in these books as supporters of free enterprise, something that could not always be said about private business. Free price formation was considered crucial, especially in the mind of Anders Örne, Swedish cooperation's major ideologue. Örne held strategic positions within KF between 1910, when he became editor-in-chief of *Kooperatoren*, and 1954, when he finally left its administrative board (one of the key central governing bodies).

During the 1910s and 1920s, Örne was influenced by the theory of "the cooperative republic." He was at that time in favor of a cooperatively controlled economy embracing everything from production to consumption,[30] but with one very important restriction: prices. The only obstacle to a cooperative economy for him was the danger of price fixing. How could the consumer know whether a particular price was the correct one in such a model? According to Örne, the only economic system providing the opportunity for the correct price to develop was free enterprise. A correct price demands that one not see Sweden as the sole market; the cooperative movement must consider the whole world its marketplace. That is why Swedish cooperation rejected all forms of customs as well as other variants of government subsidy—quite simply because such measures inhibited market-determined prices, which in turn did not favor the consumer. Örne and the cooperative movement opposed the customs system, protectionism, and government support as vehemently as they opposed private trusts and cartels. A planned economy was the most deformed type of economic system according to Örne; it was reminiscent of the medieval guild system. Just like the guild system, a planned economy ultimately demanded restrictions on democracy and freedom. On the other hand, in Örne's view, there was nothing inherently wrong with the theory of liberal political economy; the only problem in its application was that it could lead to the creation of deviations such as trusts, cartels, and monopolies. In this specific context the cooperative movement could play an especially key role.[31] The cooperative could fight these problems, which is just what it did during the 1920s and 1930s when it began operating mills and manufacturing oil, rubber, and lightbulbs. Trusts or cartels already existed in one form or another in all of these fields, and prices sank when KF engaged in competition.[32] Thus KF's theoreticians believed that cooperation was a better and more secure basis for sound competition than liberal private enterprise; it could regulate capitalism better. That the cooperative was also democratically constructed and had eliminated profit through the rebate system did not harm its case either. Anders Örne articulated the cooperative movement's opposition to state intervention in the economy in a 1936 article, where he castigated government subsidies to business: "Just as soon as it supports such an undertaking, the public treasury could instead offer good wages to all the anglers of the nation, even if each one of them provided the national economy with nothing more than the odd measly little perch or roach per day or week."[33] The policy advocated by the cooperative movement helps explain why Sweden, despite the Social Democrats' participation in government from 1930s, did not resort to the nationalization of industry, which Socialists brought about in countries such as Britain and France.

The leadership of KF believed in the movement's mission in spreading a healthy sense of economic responsibility among the population at large. The struggle against credit and classes in political economy would be two aspects of a good popular educational program. Many outsiders also agreed that the cooperative fulfilled this role. Thus in his opening address to the 1939 KF conference, the chairman of the Swedish trade union movement, August Lindberg, said "The importance which the cooperative movement has had and continues to have for the working class has often been stressed. I wish to emphasize that strongly. And the greatest significance lies, in my view, in the fact that cooperation teaches the workers to think economically. And the trade union movement too reaps the benefits of this economic know-how."[34]

That KF should exert such strenuous efforts on economic education on behalf of its own members is perfectly normal. It is also obvious that the educational program had meaning for society as a whole, insofar as many members of the cooperative movement were or later became engaged in politics; they brought to the society an understanding of economics and organizational skills. What may seem a little more peculiar is the fact that such intense interest was shown in the theories of political economy. This can partly be explained by the interest in the French thinker and activist Charles Gide (early translated into Swedish). In his theory of political economy, Gide strongly supported cosumer cooperation. Gide can be seen as the link uniting KF and liberally minded political economists in Sweden. Gide emphasized the educational value of cooperation, while at the same time admitting that cooperation did not intend to abolish capitalism but rather to topple it from its dominant position. The cooperative movement contributed to this by setting the needs of the masses at the center of its activities and giving priority to consumption over production.[35] There is also evidence of the influence of Austrian political economist Carl Menger's theories in the emphasis placed on the role of the consumer by Anders Örne, when he submits that it is not labor that determines the value of an object, but rather marginal utility. In the theory of marginal utility, the consumer plays a much larger role in controlling society's production than in the theory of the labor value as formulated by David Ricardo and Karl Marx.

Thus we see that a liberal element continued to exist in consumer cooperation during the early twentieth century. The criticism directed at liberalism as an economic theory by the cooperative movement was that it was naive and lacked self-knowledge; liberals failed to see that it eventually led to cartels and monopolies. Cooperators believed, however, that there was nothing wrong with competition in and of itself. This meant that the cooperative movement ended up swimming against that current within the Swedish Social Democratic movement, which had a positive view of nationalization and a certain degree of planned economy. Such a policy (according to Örne, for example) was nothing but an expression of a "guild mentality." When KF's leadership wrote on topics of political economy, they also rejected Marx' surplus value theory, wherein the exploited workers created a surplus, which ended up in the pockets of the capitalists. In many ways, cooperation became a very powerful non-Marxist (as opposed to "anti-Marxist") wedge in the workers' movement, on the basis of its ideology combined with its successful business side, which continued to expand even during the first years of the Depression.

Women in the Cooperative Movement

According to the cooperative movement, consumption mostly dealt with buying and economizing the most important daily products. While KF never was and never became a part of the articulated women's liberation movement, the cooperative movement knew that women had primary responsibility for consumption. In the Swedish cooperative movement, "the woman with the basket" became a symbol for power of the consumer and women. The idea

was that "the woman with the basket" with her purchases could control production. In the first discussion about women's consumer power in
Kooperatören in 1908, the paper cites an article from the German magazine
Genossenschaftliches Volkblatt saying that women, if they want, can have
extensive economic power. They can dominate consumption because through
their purchases they can decide whether or not "rubbish" will be produced.[36]

The Swedish cooperative movement drew on other foreign influences as
well to create its model of the woman consumer who had the potential to
control production. In one article, the German cooperator Franz Staudinger
argued that the consumer, i.e., the woman, in the context of society as a whole,
employs those who produce. All wives are in this perspective nothing else than
"the employer of their husbands."[37] But above all, it was the Danish cooperator Julius Eskildsen who developed a theory for women, who in the home
could be "the domestic minister of finance." His thoughts were in 1919 published in a booklet edited by the Danish Women's Guild Cooperative. Here
Eskildsen developed his view on cooperation as being foremost a women's
organization:

> The consumer is the natural ruler of the society, and women are the biggest
> consumers. From this we can conclude that, if there is a demand for a product,
> machines will be working and workers occupied, but in a factory, whose prod-
> ucts nobody wants to purchase, the wheels stop turning and the workers get
> fired and are unemployed. Women, house-wives and daughters of all classes
> in society no matter what religious and political views you ever have, you are
> in truth the utmost commanders of trade and production.[38]

The organizational leader of KF, Axel Gores, invoked the image of "the
woman with the basket" in an article in 1926, saying that the housewife of
today is not as big a producer as the woman in nineteenth century. The present
housewife is more of a consumer, but in this role she is very important: "The
housewife of today has the power of consumption in her hand, and this can
steer the economy of a society, something only dreamt of in previous generations. Consumption is the base of production, and decides the direction and
formation of the whole of economic life."[39]

Women in the 1920s and 1930s were often seen as the "woman with the
basket" or "the domestic ministers of finance." Consumption, if it were organized correctly, could make women to be "their men's employer." Through
this, women could develop their power in society, although inside the cooperative movement men still had the majority of membership and power. Some
critical voices, however, were raised against the idea that women were only
consumers, albeit important consumers. The Finnish political economist Laura
Harmaja argued in her 1928 book, *The Economical Deed of the Housewife*,
that women in the home were more than consumers, that they were both

productive and capable of also creating new national economic values.[40] Her theory was cited with approval in *Konsumentbladet* and in study circle activities.[41] Cooperation's view of women seemed to encourage them as housewives in the home sphere, as the people ultimately responsible for consumption, but it also had the potential to see women as both affecting production in society and as important producers in the home sphere.

Good Taste and the Consumer Movement

By teaching its members the importance of political economy and consumption, the Swedish cooperative movement eventually made perhaps its greatest contribution to twentieth-century Sweden, the creation of a consumer movement. Consumers, according to the movement, should eventually be taught to buy high-quality, tasteful products without wasting resources. When KF was first established in 1899, a pattern of market-controlled consumption already existed in Swedish society. Numerous stores offering goods of reasonable quality provided Sweden's population of five million with what it needed, often sold on credit. KF wanted to change all that. The battle against credit, which bound the people not only to their local storekeeper but also to debt and over consumption, led to the fact that KF primarily stressed the functional needs of consumption. Anders Örne spoke about the "demand" of man, but never explained what he really meant. For him cooperatives were a broadened household system. In this system, as opposed to the profit-economy, merchandise should be seen first of all "as a means of satisfying human needs."[42] Instead, in a profit-driven economy, the psychological and sociopsychological needs of mankind were often seen as superfluous, something with which the storekeeper manipulated citizens. Thus all through the twentieth century, KF grew extremely skeptical toward commercialism and mass consumption. A tradition of consumer information soon grew forth, wanting to limit consumption to these basic "needs." In the beginning of the 1930s the discussion to define these "needs" began, and it became important to have the "right taste."[43]

The liberal educational movement of the nineteenth century continued to develop during the first decades of the twentieth century. A number of organizations were active in arranging various public lectures and distributing books and pamphlets. The information that these societies wished to disseminate among the people was the common denominator uniting them. The people would learn about the new triumphs of science, including everything from how children ought to be brought up in accordance with nutritional and psychological theories to the importance of light, air, and cleanliness in the home, in order to destroy filth and poor hygiene. Clean apartments or houses were linked to the aesthetic ideal—beautiful furniture and bright wallpaper—which ought to be taught by educators. By holding correct views in questions of taste and beauty, we would grow to be educated individuals; via that process, we would learn how to differentiate ourselves from the uncivilized or the ignorant.[44]

In other words, an educational program existed at the turn of the century that intended to have a normative effect on the pattern of people's lives and, ultimately, on their patterns of consumption. We can certainly view the liberal workers' societies as one such movement, but the temperance movement in Sweden too aimed at urging citizens toward proper patterns of consumption. The Swedish cooperative movement joined that discourse, attempting (in its own way) to make a contribution to the broad Swedish tradition of education. KF, however, primarily stressed what was to be considered good and healthy consumption, the products that modern and rational individuals should consume in order to fulfill their functional needs. As we shall see, the movement was to emphasize (under the banner of "Beautiful Household Articles") the aesthetic value of the product, which in turn was often a reflection of its functionality.

The newspaper *Kooperatören* stressed the right sort of food to be eaten and how the individual and the home should be cared for, but it did not begin engaging in a systematic program of consumer information until 1911 with a series of articles entitled *Our Food*.[45] In this series, author Harald Huss addressed all imaginable foodstuffs, and sought proper labelling of contents.[46] Soon after, Gertrud Bergström, one of the country's leading experts on household matters, began contributing a regular column. Bergstrom followed modern ideas concerning how the home ought to look and how it should be organized, often in conflict with her readers who mostly came from the working class. Neatness and rationality were key points of reference in her articles. The housewife should make sure she is nicely dressed while cleaning and preparing meals. This may have to do with the determined conviction that cleanliness and health were all part of a whole. The house, in order to contribute to everyone's well-being, ought to look nice, that is, be bright, warm, and dry. A good home accords its inhabitants calm, rest, and comfort, and helps them maintain even temperament. The housewife had to fortify her professional role, keeping abreast of all the latest discoveries from the world of science where they concern the home, including new research results in the fields of chemistry, bacteriology, child care, health care, hygiene, and cooking. All professionals are required to constantly increase their intake of information, and the housewife is no exception to this rule. Thus, she ought to read and attend lectures regularly. Rationality and the ability to keep to a schedule are just as essential for the housewife as for society in general.[47]

During the 1920s, KF broadened the discussion concerning product information and taste. At the conference retreat Vår Gård, opened in 1924, KF personnel and elected representatives received practical education in good taste and the knowledge of merchandise. In these classes, the participants might be asked to choose between various household articles, thereafter discussing why one thought a particular utensil was aesthetically pleasing. During these discussions the teachers would explain the prerequisites that must exist in order for a household article to be declared beautiful. Pure, clean lines were stressed. Worst of all, naturally, were cheap, mass-produced items that imitated richly ornamented aristocratic tastes, that is, the democratization of luxury, which the majority of consumers might think was the most beautiful.[48]

In 1925, KF opened its own architectural offices to design modern, hygienic stores. The office soon expanded, and in 1936 over 60 architects were working there. Most of the inspiration came from new German architects such as Walter Gropius and the Bauhaus-group, but this new architecture was adapted to the local environment. KF became a vanguard for a new rational store culture; architects drew plans for over 2,000 stores and pieces of store equipment during the first ten years.[49]

In 1923, KF began to publish the yearbook *Home and Housekeeping* together with the Association for Rational Housekeeping, wherein commodity knowledge and questions of taste were discussed and analyzed.[50] In the era leading up to the Second World War, the yearbook's ideal home was portrayed as modern and rational, tidy and hygienic, a home where the latest educational principles were applied, and where each meal was part of a light, vitamin-rich and nutritional diet, in contrast to the traditional heavy Swedish fare featuring copious amounts of flour and fat. The yearbook's readership was offered everything from the proper way of furnishing a room to the latest nutritional news.[51] The information and ideals that the consumer cooperation played its part in promoting were often the same ones that more enlightened, middle-class liberal women represented and disseminated within their own social circles.[52]

Consumer education became an enormously important issue in women's guilds and study circles beginning in the early 1930s. The connection between food and health dominated, but discussions soon expanded to include questions concerning modern housing problems and population and family matters. Gunnar and Alva Myrdal's *The Population Crisis*,[53] published in 1935, had above all turned these into burning issues, and the cooperative "groups" were discussing them.[54]

The study circles also discussed the actual meaning of "aesthetic household articles," the same topic being engaged at Vår Gård. The debate really took off in 1935 when the newspaper *Konsumentbladet* published an essay in which art critic Gustav Näsström declared that "the public does not have taste, but it can acquire it." Leaders of KF, such as business manager Albin Johansson and organization head Axel Gjöres agreed: the cooperative movement had been negligent in questions of taste.[55] Art critic Gregor Paulsson and furniture designer Carl Malmsten both found themselves involved in this discussion, Paulsson by giving lectures at Vår Gård and Malmsten by helping KF with its furniture manufacturing, which began in 1939.[56] The most interesting aspect here is the fact that KF now fully admitted that style and taste were important social phenomena, something to be discussed and taught.

The Cooperative Woman Guild succeded during the late 1930s in making KF more interested in women's household labor and bettering the conditions of the housewife. In 1938, KF initiated the "Easier Household Work" campaign. In practice, the campaign did not result in much, but it had at least zeroed in on the problem.[57] During the Second World War, KF started a "housewife department" with its own experimental kitchen. Along with others, such as the Institute for Household Research,[58] KF conducted extensive research concerning nutrition and commodities. Consumer information was considered more important than ever. The government, in which Social Democrats had been the major party since 1932, was positive toward these activities, and in 1957 the Institute for Household Research was converted into the National Institute for Consumer Questions. This in turn became the National Board for Consumer Policies in 1973, a government civil service department.[59] The former voluntary consumer information campaign in which the cooperative movement had been one of the leading actors had now been almost entirely taken over by the widen society. Now it was the government who would teach citizens to consume the correct product with impeccable taste.

Conclusion

The Swedish consumer cooperative movement grew to see itself as a "Third Way," an alternative to both liberal capitalism and state-planned socialist economics. In contrast to capitalism, profit did not exist in the consumer cooperative movement, since economic surplus after consolidation was returned to the customers in the form of dividends. The abolition of profit can be seen as an inheritance from the traditions of the nineteenth-century utopians. The fact that the cooperative, as opposed to private enterprise, was a nonprofit business was long employed in cooperative propaganda as a sales pitch. Each member of the cooperative movement had one vote, another feature differentiating it from capitalist businesses. Furthermore, in contrast to both capitalism run rampant and state-sponsored socialism, the cooperative movement stressed free price formation without any government involvement.

A worldwide cooperative system was seen as a guarantee for a non-monopolized economy and a peaceful society, where all citizens would have access to products, which were as sound and as inexpensive as possible. An extensive information campaign, running until the beginning of World War II, stressed these economic issues. When the Swedish Social Democrats came to power in 1932 and began building the Welfare State (or as future Social Democratic Prime Minister Per Albin Hansson called it in a 1928 speech, "the Good Home for Man"), thousands of Social Democratic functionaries were already well acquainted, thanks to KF, with the idea that a road travelling the middle ground between capitalism and state socialism existed, a development based on sound market principles. There was a connection between the liberals, Social Democrats, and KF in the analysis of this "third-way" in the economy.

KF waged a diligent campaign against credit, which interlocked with the educational civilizing project conducted at the turn of the century by various enthusiasts in a number of different ways. But while the majority of them only spoke of the importance of order, cleanliness, and education, KF's struggle against the lack of financial responsibility among the citizenry contributed in a practical manner to creating the "orderly consumer" (who as far as the consumer cooperative was concerned was usually also a worker or a farmer). Axel Rylander was a prime exponent of this consciousness within KF. In the general economic education program, horizons are significantly broadened; there we meet the ideal consumer, the creation of liberal economic theory, according to which it is the consumer who determines production. However, this only occurs after consumers have joined together and associated their strength. Only when the consumer becomes aware of belonging to a group can he induce the producer to manufacture inexpensive, aesthetically pleasing quality goods. Thus in this theory, the consumer ascends to the position of strategic power in society. By providing them with power (for example, through educational programs), the power of the producers would be diminished. In the existing conflict between producer and consumer, KF always stressed the role of the consumer as the motivating subject.

The conscious consumer must be in control of his or her personal economy, but that alone was not enough. An understanding of products, which ought to be beautiful and functional, was just as essential. The individual consumer was assumed to have no sense of taste from the outset; however, through extensive educational activities concerning taste and goods, the consumer would be led to reflect and discuss issues of taste. Thus Swedish consumer cooperation also functioned as a modernizing movement standing on two pillars. First, KF created clean, rational and profit-making stores and distribution system for all its members, and as a result of this, the price was lowered in the economy as a whole. Second, a steadily expanding study and educational movement contributed to the creation of the modern, educated consumer-citizen. This new modernity consists of always being extremely conscious of manipulations and new fashions when we consume—through active reflection, we are able to choose useful and functional products. The "new" was generally considered good: new ideas about diet, new functional housing, the redesigning of everything from dishes to furniture, new methods of house cleaning (the vacuum cleaner, the dishwasher, washing machines), new spotless kitchens and shops. At that point in time, most of the KF membership could not afford to consume these things. Still, learning the art of consuming conscientiously was considered essential, in order not to be distracted by the siren call of commercialism, which cynically appealed to people's possessive instincts.

Ever since the 1970s, Swedish consumer cooperatives (and other chain-store organizations) have been in a state of crisis. Fewer and fewer people feel attracted to the fundamentals of the cooperative. KF is experiencing particularly serious problems in the big cities, with Stockholm at the head of the list. When product choice literally exploded in the 1950s, KF met the new patterns of consumption by building first self-service stores and then department stores in all the larger towns throughout the country. Once again, KF felt it was thereby taking the lead in a modernization movement.

New specialty stores, however, soon appeared to compete against the department stores, which by the 1980s had lost a large portion of their appeal. The explosive increase in choices on the market also served to undermine the idea that the purpose of consumption was first and foremost to satisfy the consumer's functional needs. KF found itself in a market aiming at the seemingly ever expanding dreams and wishes of the citizen. The idea of a more "puritanical" utilitarian consumption was no longer transmitted by KF; this role had now been taken over by the government, through the National Board for Consumer Policies. Many could therefore no longer see what role the consumer cooperative had to play in modern society, especially when economic setbacks forced the cooperative to eliminate dividends in most parts of Sweden.

In the 1990s, however, Swedish consumer cooperation has regrouped somewhat. Once again, KF wants to be in the avant-garde of a new consumer movement, and to spearhead a movement of social modernization. It becomes increasingly apparent that the new, socially aware consumer must think in terms of global environment—and it is just that trend the cooperation wants to lead. Private chain stores have also discovered this new market, and cooperation is confronting hard competition. Perhaps the long heritage of cooperative ideas will give KF an advantage, with its emphasis on active membership, democracy, and the dissemination of information via a broad-based educational program, along with the distribution of profits among its membership in the form of dividends. It remains to be seen if KF can emerge successful.

Notes

1. Walter Sjölin, *Detaljhandeln och krediten* (Stockholm, 1968), 20; *Svensk kooperation under 180-talet* (Stockholm, 1960), 13ff.

2. Axel Påhlman and Walter Sjölin, *Arbetarföreningarna i Sverige 1850-1900* (Stockholm, 1944), 35f, 88ff.

3. Axel Gjöres, *Svensk kooperation före attiotalet* (Stockholm, 1919), 34ff.

4. Påhlman and Sjölin, 201ff.

5. *Ibid.*, 198.

6. *Ibid.*, 137ff.

7. Gjöres, *Svensk*, 122-26.

8. G. K. Hamilton, *Om arbetarklassen och arbetarföreningar* (Lund, 1865).

9. *Ibid.*, 34.

10. *Ibid.*, 77-114.

11. C. E. Ljungberg, *Om associationsväsendet i främmande länder med särskilt hänseende till de Schultze-Delitzschska förskottsföreningarne* (Stockholm, 1865).

12. Gjöres, *Svensk*, 54-73.

13. Abraham Rundbäck, *Afhandling om konsumtionsföreningar* (Stockholm, 1869).

14. Axel Gjöres, *Stormar: En folkrörelse växer fram* (Stockholm, 1963), 14-22.

15. Sjölin, *Detaljhandeln och krediten*, 127f.

16. Påhlman and Sjölin, 35ff., 66, 107f.

17. Henceforth the Swedish name "Kooperativa Forbundet" will appear in its short form, "KF."

18. Gjöres, *Stormår* (1963), op cit., 41-45.

19. *Ibid.*, 91f.

20. From KF's annual report, 1939. It is difficult to establish the market share of the consumer cooperation. According to *Kooperationens ställning inom svensk näringsliv* (Stockholm, 1934), 52, KF had approximately 10 percent of the retail trade and 12 percent of the food trade by 1934. According to Etti Widhe, *Kooperationen - Hemmens folkrörelse* (Stockholm, 1950), 37, KF had by 1949 12-13 percent of the retail trade and 20-25 percent of the food trade. *An Overview of the Swedish Cooperative Movement 1976 to 1984* (Stockholm, 1986), 6, says that the co-op societies' share of the total retail trade went up continuously until the beginning of the 1970s (18 percent), but then decreased (16 percent by 1984). The number of societies differed a lot from time to time, from 941 (1920) and 681 (1950) to 137 (1987). But the total membership increased the whole time, from 235,000 (1920), 962,059 (1950) and 2,013,254 (1987). Sven-Åke Böök/Tore Johansson, *The Co-operative Movement in Sweden* (Stockholm, 1988), 99.

21. Walter Sjölin, *Svensk kooperation under 1800-talet* (Stockholm, 1960), 33.

22. From KF's annual reports, 1899-1905, *Berättelser över Kooperativa förbundets Krongresser ären 1899-1906*, eds. Martin Sundell and Axel Påhlman (Stockholm, 1912).

23. Axel Rylander, *Konsumtionskredit. Nytt sekel - bättre varor* (Stockholm, 1900).

24. Norbert Elias, *Über den prozess der zivilisation: soziogenetische und psychogenetische untersuchungen* (Basel, 1939). Ronny Ambjörnsson writes about civilization and self-discipline in Swedish popular movement in *Den skötsamme arbetare* (Stockholm, 1988); *idem*, "The Conscientious Worker: Ideas and Ideals in a Swedish Working Class Culture," *History of European Ideas* 1 (1989): 59-67.

25. H. S. "Kredit och konsumenten": in *Konsumentbladet* (1925): 3.

26. In 1910 there were 97 women's guilds with 3,882 members. In 1939, 342 guilds with 11,800 members. From KF's annual reports, 1910 and 1939.

27. From the annual reports of the cooperative movement's conferences.

28. Gunnar Westin-Silverstolpe, *Nationalekonomi för alla* (Stockholm, 1922).

29. For example Gösta Bagge, *Det moderna näringslivets uppkomst* (Stockholm, 1925); Bertil Nyström, *Hur arbetet betalas* (Stockholm, 1929); Karin Kock, *Svenskt bankväsende i vara dagar* (Stockholm, 1930); Gustav Cassel, *Grunddragen i penningväsendets utveckling* (Stockholm 1931); Bertil Ohlin, *Den världsekonomiska depressionen* (Stockhoom, 1931); Gunnar Westin-Silverstolpe, *Depressionen och guldmyntfotens kris* (Stockholm, 1931); Gunnar Myrdal, *Konjunktur och offentlig hushållning* (Stockholm, 1933); Eli Heckscher, *Tvångshushållning och "planhushållning"* (Stockholm, 1934). On the debate between statism and liberalism, Sven E. Olsson, *Social Policy and Welfare State in Sweden*, 2 ed. (Lund, 1993), 43-89.

30. Anders Örne, *Kooperatismen* (Stockholm, 1921); *idem*, *Det kooperative programmet* (Stockholm, 1921).

31. See e.g., Anders Örne, "Konkurrens och kooperation" in *Kooperatören* (1923): 5-6; *idem*, "Kooperatören och staten" in *Kooperatören* 1929 Anniversary Edition; *idem*, "Kooperationens ideologiska grundvalarw" in *Kooperatören* (1939): 23-24.

32. KF's factories was founded only with capital accumulated inside the movement. In turn the following factories were bought or founded: factory for margarin (1921), three biggest flour mills (1922-24), shoe factory (1925), rubber factory (1927 and 1933), superphosphate factory (1929), bulb factory (1931), vegetarian oil factory (1932), factory for cashboxes (1932), rayon factory (1936), porcelain factory Gustavsberg (1937), and several local bigger bakaries and butcheries. *Kooperationens ställning inom svenskt näringsliv* (Stockholm, 1934); Etti Widhe, *Kooperationenhemmens folkrörelse* (Stockholm, 1950).

33. Anders Örne, "Mellanfolkligt samarbete och konsumentkooperativa grundsatser" in *Kooperatören* (1936): 3-4.

34. Conference proceedings, 1939.

35. Charles Gide, *Nationalekonomins grunddrag II* (1899), 4th ed. (Stockholm, 1916), 181-87.

36. "Kvinnans ekonomiska makt" *Kooperatören* (1908): 14.

37. Franz Staudinger, "Hustrurna som sina mäns arbetsgivare" in *Kooperatören*, (1912): 24.

38. Julius Eskildsen, *Hemmets finansminister* (Hälsingborg, 1919), 15.

39. Axel Gjöres "Kvinnan med korgen" in *Konsumentbladet* (1926): 20.

40. Laura Harmaja, *Husmoderns ekonomiska gärning* (1928), 3d ed. (Stockholm, 1937).

41. "Böckernas värld" in *Konsumentbladet* (1928): 35; the study circles *Hemekonomiska fragor* (Stockholm, 1933 and 1934), and *Hemenkonomi* (Stockholm, 1938).

42. Örne, *Det kooperativa programmet*, 15.

43. In his book *The Romantic Ethic and the Spirit of Modern Consumerism* (Oxford, 1987), Colin Campbell describes how a new consumer mentality grew out of the focus on the desires and imagination of both Puritanism and Romanticism. In *Dream Worlds: Mass Consumption in Late Nineteenth-Century France* (Berkeley, 1982), Rosalind H. Williams partly addresses the same process, wherein human dreams fuel the urge to consume. Socialists most often opposed these dreams, which created "unnecessary needs" and "irrational wishes."

44. Jonas Frykman, Orvar Löfgren, and Alan Crozier, *Culture-Builders: A Historical Anthropology of Middle-Class Life* (New Brunswick, 1987), 125-53.

45. *Vår Mat.*

46. Harold Hass, "Vår Mat," *Kooperatören* (1911): 32, 34, 35; 1912: 3, 5, 8, 13A, 20, 21.

47. *Konsumentbladet* (1914): 14, 15, 16 "Om utbildning i huslig ekonomi"; (1915): 15 "Några ord om hemmakläder"; (1915): 38 "Våra bostäder"; (1916): 4 "Renlighet och hälsa"; (1916): 25 "Tid är pengar".

48. Orvar Löfgren, "Swedish Modern: Nationalizing Consumption and Aesthetics in the Welfare State," Rutgers Center for Historical Analysis, 1993.

49. Lisa Brunnström, *Den rationella fabriken* (Umea, 1990), 185-89.

50. *Hem och Hushåll.*

51. *Hem och Hushall* (Stockholm, 1923-1943).

52. Jan-Erik Hagberg, *Tekniken i kvinnornas händer* (Vimmerby, 1986).

53. *Kris i befolkningsfrågan* (Stockholm, 1935).

54. Oh the study circles, Herman Stolpe, ed. *Bostadsfragor* (Stockholm, 1935), and Herman Stolpe, ed. *Familjefrdgor* (Stockholm, 1936).

55. Gustav Näsström, "K.F. smakodlare för svenska folket" in *Konsumentbladet* (1935): 12; "Smakdebatten i gang" in *Konsumentbladet* (1935): 13; "Smak och bohag" in: *Konsumentbladet* (1935): 15-16; "Hem och bohag" in *Konsumentbladet* (1935): 19.

56. Harald Elldin, *Kris och bakgrunder till kooperativt fostringsarbete under ett halvsekel* (Stockholm, 1950), 352-60. Carl Malmsten was a furniture designer, craft instructor, and professor who was strongly critical of cheap mass-production. He wanted instead to achieve a renewal of handicrafts on a traditional Swedish foundation. Greger Paulsson was a professor of art history who became a powerful advocate for functionalism in Sweden. As early as 1919 he published the book *Vackrare vardagsvara*, whose title (Aesthetic household articles) inspired discussions in taste up to the time of Second World War. In his theoretical project Paulsson wished to discern the connection between art and the development of society.

57. Widhe, *Kooperationenhemmens*, 52f.

58. Hagberg, *Teknihen*, 229-33.

59. "Varje dag stöter man pa saker som man skulle vilja veta mer om", in *Vi kan Vi behövs*, ed. Brita Åkerman (Stockholm, 1983), 99-105.

Chapter 10

The Rise and Fall of Consumer Cooperation in Germany

Brett Fairbairn

The history of German consumer cooperatives is largely a story of how the working classes discovered cooperatives as tools to assert collective economic power, to strengthen working-class families and communities, and to exert influence on the shape of urban environments. It is also a story of how that tool was destroyed by political enemies, repression, and ultimately by the new social and economic realities of the post-1945 era.

Consumer cooperatives arose in Germany, as in most countries, as a social response to modernization and industrialization. First intellectuals and benevolent citizens, then broad groupings in the population, seized on cooperatives as tools to articulate communitarian values and relationships in what they saw as an increasingly unstable, individualistic world. Cooperatives appealed to these social movements precisely because they combined two divergent aspects. Cooperatives were business enterprises operating and able to compete in the liberal market economy. At the same time, they were democratic associations of people embodying the nineteenth-century impulse of voluntary associationism. While both of these basic ideas—the market economy and associationism—were distinctive institutions of liberalism, those who combined the two in cooperatives were by no means all liberals. Mid-nineteenth-century German liberals were for the most part classic advocates of laissez-faire, stressing the freedom of the economy and nonintervention of the state, alongside their characteristic political program of constitutional civil rights and liberties. Liberals looked to free competition of individuals in the economy as the agency of progress. Those liberals who supported cooperatives generally understood them as mechanisms to help individuals compete. By the 1860s, when liberal economic ideas dominated, this point of view suggested that cooperatives were a means to shore up what had become the prevailing economic order. Yet increasingly, those who joined and led cooperatives saw them not as stepping-stones to individualism, but as permanent collective entities; not as institutions by which individuals could adapt to the market economy, but as a means by which the market economy could be adapted to the needs of people.

In Germany as in other countries, a cooperative movement born in part of
liberal ideas increasingly became a tool for those who struggled against what
they saw as the failings of liberalism. Most German cooperatives after the
1870s were inspired by social Catholicism, rural conservatism, social democracy, minority ethnic nationalism, even sometimes by anti-Semitism. All of these
tendencies protested the loss of community values and institutions under the
corrosive action of markets. These diverse social and ideological impulses—all
part of a groundswell of popular reaction against the effects of economic
individualism—made the cooperative movement the largest mass movement
in German history.[1]

Despite these similarities to other countries, the German consumer cooperative movement differed in important ways from many others. Two general
features of German modernization heavily influenced the development of consumer cooperatives. First was the timing and intensity of industrialization.
Germany industrialized late in the nineteenth century, later than other, western
European countries. When it came, industrialization was rapid, turning Germany from a largely agrarian economy to an urbanized, industrialized world
power in two generations after 1860. Due to the relative lateness of industrialization, German intellectuals heard about cooperatives from France and Britain
considerably before any large, organized working class had emerged in Germany. Cooperative models were therefore defined first and fundamentally for
artisans, peasants, and small business. Working-class leaders were slow to
adopt the cooperative vision, seeing it as a vision more suited to these traditional social groups. When workers did turn in large numbers to consumer
cooperatives in the 1890s and early 1900s, however, the rapidity of German
industrialization made itself felt. Consumer cooperation blossomed in connection with the polarization of German society between workers and employers.
The German consumer cooperative movement quickly grew to become the
second-strongest consumer cooperative movement in the world; by 1914 only
the world-leading British movement was both larger in membership as well as
economically stronger in volume of business.

A second structural parameter affecting the development of German
consumer cooperatives was the late and incomplete resolution of the question
of national integration. A German nation-state was formed only in 1871—the
Prussian-dominated German Empire—and it contained deep religious, ethnic,
and regional differences. Tensions between Protestants and Catholics, between
Prussians and Bavarians, between ethnic Germans and ethnic Poles, between
advocates of democracy and its enemies, between increasingly radical German
nationalists and those they saw as traitors, were basic features of the new state.
One effect on cooperatives was that such polarizations undermined the unity
of the movement. Eventually the largest consumer cooperative federation was
associated with the Social Democratic labor movement and was mainly urban,
Protestant, and ethnic German in its support. While this was a large constituen-

cy, it was nevertheless perceived by others as sectional, closed, and politically marginal. Consumer cooperatives increasingly became objects of attack by nationalists and antisocialists, and were subjected to punitive municipal, state, and federal taxes and regulation. Later the National Socialists, when they took power in 1933, built up this preexisting current of opposition to consumer cooperatives and hounded them into dissolution. Following 1945, the difficult task of rebuilding consumer cooperatives from the ground up was hampered in West Germany by rapid changes in retailing, by increasing competition, and by a not entirely sympathetic conservative regime, while in East Germany cooperatives were restored for the most part in name only and allowed little genuine autonomy. In the end (with a few notable exceptions), the movement that had once been a world leader and one of the "three pillars" of socialist labor, that had survived Nazism and been rebuilt, died with a whimper, amidst scandal and confusion, in the Federal Republic of Germany.

The Origins of Cooperatives

For historical, political, and perhaps cultural reasons, German cooperatives came to be associated with the good works of first one and later a few "great men." The historical record, however, does not support the idea that cooperatives were invented by individual genius. Cooperatives emerged in Germany as a fusion or preexisting models—the business enterprise and the voluntary association. With similar fusions developing in many other countries at about the same time, this might be regarded as an almost inevitable development: an idea that was simply "in the air." There is evidence to support this view. By the late 1840s and early 1850s, many kinds of cooperative-like institutions had been created in cities, towns, and rural communities across Germany, generally characterized by benevolent impulses (that is, charity: the well-off helping the poor) more than by cooperative ideas of mutual, democratic self-help. The Spar und Konsum-Verein Ermunterung, founded in May 1845 for working people in Chemnitz, may not have been Germany's first consumer cooperative, but it was a step toward being a cooperative.[2] Others of the early associations likely should be accepted as cooperatives. In rural Westphalia, for example, there were credit associations, governed on the basis of one member, one vote, which mutually guaranteed loans contracted by their members. These organizations were formally constituted, economic in function, voluntary, democratic in governance, with an identity between members and users: in a word, cooperatives.[3] All of these creations took place before any of the legendary founders of German cooperatives could have exerted any influence.

The distress of the 1840s and the revolutions of 1848 reinforced the associationist impulses in German society. Among workers, building on the foundation laid by workers' educational associations in the 1840s, the *Allgemeine Deutsche Arbeiterverbrüderung* (General German Workers' Fraternity) was created in 1850. The *Arbeiterverbrüderung* pursued economic progress through education and mutual self-help among working people. It rejected the old guild system as well as state intervention, and experimented with forms of cooperative group activity among workers. A number of cooperative-like associations were created in the late 1840s and early 1850s, many of them dissolved by the police. One writer has identified twenty-six production cooperatives; sixteen consumer, raw-material, and warehouse cooperatives; three cooperative banks; and four other cooperatives founded in 1848-1850 under the influence of the *Arbeiterverbrüderung*.[4]

While the cooperative idea was "in the air," it was a handful of intellectuals and political leaders who formalized and articulated specific concepts of cooperation. It was significant for the German consumer cooperative movement that none of these early system-builders was of working-class origin, nor was any primarily interested in the cooperative retailing of the necessities of life. The birth of the German cooperative movement—unlike, for example, the English or the French—was guided by men who were thinking mainly about relatively traditional producers and communities, not so much about the situation of wage labor in a market economy. The first intellectual to promote the cooperative idea as a solution to the social question was a conservative writer, Victor Aimé Huber.[5] But the first actually to create, test, and replicate cooperative models in the 1850s, and to draft legislation for them in the 1860s—the man recognized as the definer and founder of the German cooperative movement—was a Progressive (left-liberal) jurist and deputy, Hermann Schulze-Delitzsch.

Schulze-Delitzsch and German Liberalism

Hermann Schulze-Delitzsch was a notable from the Prussian province of Saxony, a region known for small industry and artisanal production.[6] In the 1840s, after decades of decline, there were more masters than apprentices, with many of these "masters" struggling with chronic underemployment and poverty. Schulze-Delitzsch became acquainted with these problems first as a local judge, then as a deputy in the Berlin National Assembly in 1848 where he was chair of a committee to investigate the artisanal economy. The failure of the liberal revolutions in 1849 and the onset of a new period of reaction seemed to end the possibility of political action in a liberal sense. With the door closed to any overt political action, Schulze-Delitzsch turned instead to cooperatives as a means to organize artisans and address their social-economic problems.

The distress of artisans posed a fundamental threat to the kind of world desired by German liberals. Liberals saw a healthy society as one that was based on broad middle classes, a group they referred to as the *Mittelstand*, best rendered in English as the lower middle class. "Remember that the German *Mittelstand*," Schulze-Delitzsch said in 1862, "whose economic independence we have undertaken to strengthen, has the great task of being one of the chief bearers of the culture and political development of our fatherland."[7] Liberals conceived of themselves—in an age of poorly developed party and interest-group organization—as the representatives of "the people," a vague concept that acquired substance to the extent that the *Mittelstand* provided liberalism with broad popular support. The threat that the *Mittelstand* would be torn apart—poorer artisans becoming impoverished or proletarianized—was a threat to both the strength of the liberal movement and, as they saw it, to German society and civilization. Ironically, of course, the distress of artisans was caused in substantial measure by the elimination of guilds and the effects on artisans of a spreading market economy: by liberal economic policies, in other words. Liberals were aware of the possibility that social distress could lead to renewed intervention in a conservative sense by the absolutist state—for example, through legislative reintroduction of compulsory guilds. What German liberals needed was a solution to the social question that was consistent with liberalism—in other words, a solution that did not involve state intervention or interfere with market forces.[8]

Schulze-Delitzsch's thinking about the reasons for and roles of cooperatives is illuminating. In a speech to the Reichstag he called cooperatives "the guilds of the future," and tied them directly to the transformation then being experienced by Germany's economy: "in the instant in which the guilds in their old sense cease to exist, free cooperatives begin . . . which are destined to play as powerful a role in the social development of the near future as the old guilds did in their own time."[9] His classic book on credit cooperatives, written in the early 1860s when German industrialization was taking off, opened with his observation that the need for cooperatives "for our artisans and small businessmen" was "pressing and . . . generally recognized."[10] Cooperatives were an answer to the fact that "the development of industry in our time tends more and more toward big enterprises." "The monstrous development of big industry," he wrote, "threatens the independence of our lower-middle-class tradespeople (*gewerblichen Mittelstand*)." But "instead of complaining about the inroads made by the factory and by commerce, about the excessive power of capital, one should instead empower oneself with the advantages of factory-like, businesslike enterprise, and put capital at one's own service."[11] The threatened classes could make themselves stronger, could achieve economies of scale and become more competitive, by banding together in cooperatives. Schulze-Delitzsch saw this as a "rejection of all socialist fancies," a practical way to resist the tendency toward big industry. It is true that Schulze-Delitzsch also wanted to help wage laborers, and promoted the concept of consumer cooperatives partly for their benefit. The first indisputable consumer cooperative in Germany was the 1850 association in Eilenburg in the Province of Saxony, established with Schulze-Delitzsch's inspiration.[12] At root, however, his vision of cooperatives was less one of helping the proletarian working class, than one of preventing the formation of a large proletarian working class. While he was aware early in his work of the famous cooperative established by British workers at Rochdale in 1844, his vision differed in notable respects from theirs.

Schulze-Delitzsch advocated, and developed practical models for, various kinds of cooperatives including credit, input-purchase, warehousing, production, marketing, and consumer cooperatives. In 1858, Schulze-Delitzsch claimed twenty-five well-developed credit associations. Cooperatives multiplied in the 1860s—especially the credit cooperatives, followed by the consumer associations, the two kinds that were not exclusively for artisans. At the end of August, 1867, Schulze-Delitzsch counted 1,571 cooperatives in Germany, of which 1,122 were credit cooperatives, 250 were consumer cooperatives, and 199 were raw materials cooperatives and other trade-related cooperatives. Not all of these were members of his federation, the *Allgemeiner Verband* (the General League). The known consumer associations were located mainly in the more industrialized parts of Germany, notably the Kingdom of Saxony (39), the Rhine province (33), and Brandenburg (27).[13] They were also attracting a broad and diverse membership, not only artisans but other people of modest means who had an interest in obtaining low-cost goods or credit. It was estimated at the time of Schulze-Delitzsch's death in 1882 that perhaps two-thirds of the members of his most successful kinds of cooperatives—the credit and consumer associations—were made up not of artisans but of groups such as farmers, industrial workers, and civil servants.[14]

The evolution of German cooperatives after the 1860s shows that Schulze-Delitzsch's vision of cooperation—the *Mittelstand*, independent of state help, shoring up a liberal society—encountered limits. The declining attractive power of his cooperative vision paralleled the decline of the Progressive or left-liberal world view, as liberalism became increasingly splintered and marginalized in German politics. Social and political tensions were rising, reflecting sharper polarizations of class and ideology. The *Mittelstand* was increasingly reactionary, less liberal, and made less use of cooperatives than Schulze-Delitzsch had hoped. Two groups that did begin to turn in large numbers to cooperatives after the 1870s and 1880s, farmers and workers, were not particularly liberal. Those who founded many of the new cooperatives after Schulze-Delitzsch generally shared his concept of cooperatives as a tool by which marginalized groups could defend and assert themselves in industrial society. But they invested that concept with different ideological content.

Raiffeisen and Consumer Cooperatives for Farmers

Not long after Schulze-Delitzsch had popularized the cooperative idea, a social-reformist Prussian provincial official named F.W. Raiffeisen came up with his own version of cooperatives.[15] These differed from Schulze-Delitzsch's in a number of structural and legal ways that today seem rather less important than they did in the 1870s, when a full-blown *Systemstreit* (conflict of systems) raged between the two cooperative leaders and their respective camps. For present purposes, two features of Raiffeisen's system are relevant. First, Raiffeisen brought the concept of cooperatives to the service of rural communities and of farming. As it turns out, this is the environment in which cooperatives the world over have been most successful—leading to the result that Raiffeisen's name is better-known internationally than Schulze-Delitzsch's; Raiffeisen may in fact be one of the half-dozen most widely known nineteenth-century Germans. Second, in regard to consumer cooperation, Raiffeisen taught that each village should have only a single cooperative, which would conduct all necessary economic functions including credit (the main business) along with marketing agricultural products, selling farm inputs like feeds and fertilizers, and selling food and articles needed by village people. The Raiffeisen legacy includes multipurpose village cooperative stores and facilities that still exist in Germany today and have been replicated in dozens of countries abroad.

The social and political implications of the Raiffeisen cooperatives were far different from those of the urban Schulze-Delitzsch and other cooperatives. The urban cooperatives were mostly liberal or later Social Democratic and secular. Raiffeisen himself was nonpartisan but clearly a social conservative, comfortable in his career as a mayor appointed by and responsible to the conservative Prussian state. His followers tended to be patriotic defenders of traditional rural society, with not a few clergymen among them. Given these differences, there were few contacts between the urban cooperative movements and the Raiffeisen movement.[16]

In the 1870s and 1880s, a new rural cooperative movement was built as an alternative to the Raiffeisen system, this time focused initially around special-purpose rural consumer cooperatives. The patron of this new movement was Wilhelm Haas, a National Liberal politician, deputy, and government official from the state of Hesse in west-central Germany. Haas did not himself take issue with Raiffeisen, but Haas's followers explained that they found Raiffeisen's movement too clerical, too idealistic, and too monolithic. They preferred to form cooperative institutions that were more businesslike and pragmatic. They also preferred to organize separately within each state, rather than to join the nationwide Raiffeisen organization known as the *Generalverband*, founded in 1877. Haas's consumer cooperatives initially provided the backbone of this movement. They sold seed, feed, fertilizer, and machinery, epitomizing the underlying practical and improvement-oriented philosophy. As it grew, however, the movement branched out into special-purpose cooperatives of all kinds, from dairy cooperatives to cooperatives for generation of electrical power. Haas's movement soon surpassed Raiffeisen's in size and extent.[17]

As with the Raiffeisen cooperatives, the Haas rural consumer cooperatives had little or nothing to do with their urban counterparts. They did not normally handle groceries and general consumer goods, but only farm supplies, so there was no compatibility of economic function with the urban consumer associations. And once again, the politics were very different. The National Liberal Party, of which Haas was a prominent member, was a more patriotic and right-wing breakaway from the left-liberal Progressive party of which Schulze--Delitzsch was a longtime leader. The National Liberals favored cooperation with the conservative German and Prussian states, while the left liberals did not. The National Liberals were receptive to protectionist tariffs and certain forms of state interventionism and social policy, while the left liberals were dedicated to free trade and free enterprise. Finally, the National Liberals were more determinedly nationalistic and antisocialist than were the left liberals. Among other things, these differences illustrate how broad the cooperative idea is and how adaptable it is to a wide variety of political ideologies. In the historical example of Germany, however, the different kinds of cooperation did not all succeed to the same degree, and they experienced much different treatment at the hands of the state.

The rural cooperatives on the Raiffeisen and Haas models came to the attention of other government officials. At first in the 1840s and 1850s, officials had been suspicious that cooperatives might be subversive. But officials concerned with agriculture, first in the Rhineland and eventually in Berlin, came to believe that rural cooperatives offered a way to educate farmers, help them modernize, strengthen rural communities, and thereby to strengthen the social and political order of Germany. It was also relevant that agrarian protest movements grew after 1890 and became influential within conservative circles allied to the government. Helping agriculture made for political stability in quite a direct way. By 1892 the Prussian government gave official, systematic encouragement to rural cooperatives. Officials helped form and sponsor new rural and artisanal cooperatives, gave them donations and low-interest loans (in 1895 the Prussian Central Cooperative Bank was created as a state bank for this purpose), and generally encouraged them in every way possible without interfering overly in their internal affairs. Other state governments outside Prussia followed suit. But this encouragement was limited to cooperatives for farmers and those for artisans and shopkeepers. By the late nineteenth century, urban consumer cooperatives had developed a close association with the urban working classes. As it turned out, working-class cooperatives were *not* encouraged by the state. Instead, they evolved on their own fitful and erratic path from tentative beginnings in the 1860s, to real strength in the early twentieth century the face of growing hostility from opposing interests.

Consumer Cooperatives and Workers

The first substantial consumer cooperative movement in Germany that was ideologically focused on workers arose in the state of Württemberg in the 1860s. Despite the regional success of this movement, however, it was premature and geographically isolated. The German workers' movement as a whole turned its back on the cooperative idea for decades.

The southwestern German state of Württemberg was noted more for its wines and (at least in the nineteenth century) for its peasantry and small towns—not for industry and large populations of urban wage laborers. This was not the first place one would expect worker-oriented consumer cooperatives to have developed on a significant scale. The social-structural limitations of the Württemberg environment may well explain why cooperatives did not grow further or sink deeper roots. That they developed at all was largely due to the work of a provincial intellectual, Dr. Eduard Pfeiffer.

Pfeiffer was a young, educated son of a Jewish banker. Interested in social reform to help the working class, he heard about the Rochdale cooperative in England and the movement that had grown up around it. In 1862 he visited Rochdale, and it impressed him. The English cooperatives appealed to Pfeiffer because they were self-consciously working-class institutions, imbued with a doctrine of participation, democracy, and transformation of society. Pfeiffer decided to promote consumer cooperatives on the Rochdale model for workers in Stuttgart and nearby towns.[18] In 1863 Pfeiffer published a book, *Über Genossenschaftswesen* (*On the Nature of Cooperation*), which established the idea that working-class consumer cooperation had a social program. Pfeiffer envisaged a gradual advance of working-class organization and consumer cooperation until cooperatives controlled the bulk of the economy. The working-class cooperative movement beginning with consumer goods could move on to a more advanced stage of production cooperatives. This non-Marxist vision of gradual social transformation through working-class action of course closely resembled the English movement's philosophy, as epitomized, for example, by the Fabian socialists. Pfeiffer was the first to promote such ideas in Germany, but he seems to have had little influence outside Württemberg.

The Württemberg consumer cooperatives achieved some success on a regional scale. Pfeiffer called together interested individuals, advised them on rules and bylaws, and succeeded in bringing a number of cooperatives to life. The first was the 1864 consumer association in Stuttgart, founded by fifty-two members of a workers' educational association. Pfeiffer's social and political connections were of some help to the small groups of working people who formed the early cooperatives. Pfeiffer was a leading figure in the Württemberg German Party, the governmental party in that state (equivalent to the northern German National Liberals). He represented the interests of the cooperatives to local and state governments and helped them obtain official legal recognition. One estimate is that, by 1875, 12 percent of all households in Stuttgart were connected to the Stuttgart cooperative.[19] Other cooperatives were started in other centers, and Pfeiffer considered attempting to create a national association and a national wholesale on the English model. He did not like the Schulze-Delitzsch federation because of its commercial emphasis and its concentration on more well-off social classes and on other kinds of cooperatives than consumer cooperation. But the consumer cooperatives were not strong enough to form national institutions in the 1860s, and, with the failure of Pfeiffer's efforts, the cooperatives decided to join the Schulze-Delitzsch movement.

Pfeiffer and the Württemberg cooperatives did not merely copy English models; they also developed some organizational variations that remained features of German consumer cooperatives for half a century. Chief among these was the use of tokens or *Marken*. The cooperative association sold these tokens to its members, and paid out its annual refunds in the form of tokens. The tokens were redeemable at the premises of local merchants who had entered into contracts with the cooperative association. In this way, the cooperative expanded its business without having to open new stores or handle new products. One can argue that the use of tokens in the Württemberg cooperatives was a unique contribution to cooperative history: cooperatives operated in partnership with private merchants, instead of against them.[20] But merchants' associations later complained that the *Marken* made merchants too dependent on the worker-run cooperatives, which had the bargaining power to dictate favorable prices for their members.

Despite Pfeiffer's efforts, the German workers' movement and working-class cooperatives remained separate. When lasting German working-class organizations were built in the third quarter of the nineteenth century, they gradually came under the influence of ideas hostile to cooperatives. This was unlike France in the same period, where cooperatives continued to be a dominant theme of the French labor movement in its "associationist" phase.[21] A major difference seems to be the greater politicization of, and earlier dominance of Marxist ideas within, the German labor movement. After some tentative beginnings of workers' organization in 1848-1850, a lasting national-level workers' movement first emerged in the 1860s under Ferdinand Lassalle. Lassalle founded the General German Workers' Association in 1863. He was a colorful personality who advocated, among other things, nationalization of industry to set up worker-run productive facilities—an idea reminiscent of

Louis Blanc's writings in France in the 1840s. In Germany, however, neither the labor movement nor the state actually created many such societies; they remained mostly an abstract concept, unlike France where hundreds were created in the early 1850s and again in the 1860s-1870s. Even Lassalle and his followers limited their advocacy to production cooperatives, and did not broaden their cooperative proposals to distribution, services, and consumption. Meanwhile Lassalle's critics and opponents, led by Marx, generally rejected the cooperative idea. Cooperatives, according to the Marxists, were a waste of effort, a distraction from the necessary political and economic class struggle, and stood no chance of helping workers within a capitalist society. When in 1875 the Lassallean group united with the Marxists at a meeting in Gotha to found the *Sozialdemokratische Partei Deutschlands* (Social Democratic Party of Germany or SPD), many of the Marxist ideas predominated, including the basic antipathy to cooperatives.

The outlawing and repression of Social Democratic organizations after 1878 hardened the party's class-conscious Marxist orientation, even as the Social Democratic movement became large and well-organized. When the ban on Social Democratic activities was lifted in 1890, the SPD adopted its Erfurt program, which began with an ideological preamble that rang with Marxist ideas. Non-cooperation with the government and other parties, and language of class warfare, remained features of the national party's propaganda and campaigns. The SPD became the largest party in popular vote in 1890, surpassed even the combined liberal parties in 1898, and elected the largest delegation to the Reichstag in 1912. Parallel to this political development, the Social Democratic movement developed a diverse array of organizations ranging from labor unions to social and recreational clubs. These increasingly well-organized working-class institutions complemented and supported the centralized and bureaucratically organized mass party. Through all of these organizations, the working class, particularly the working class in Protestant areas, was integrated into a Social Democratic milieu. This milieu satisfied many working-class aspirations without, as it turned out, provoking a cataclysmic revolution. Among the organizations that were developed within the Social Democratic milieu were a number of consumer cooperatives—despite the party's official opposition to cooperatives, which was reiterated, for example, in a party resolution in 1892. The local activists who built these cooperatives contributed to the creation of a mass movement. Ultimately, the fact of a large, working-class movement of consumer cooperatives forced the SPD to alter its Marxist ideological stance as it applied to cooperatives.

The New Movement of the 1890s

The rate of formation of new consumer cooperatives increased sharply in the late 1880s and early 1890s, and took another jump after the turn of the century. Of 653 consumer cooperatives known to have been founded in Germany before 1905, over one-third (232) were founded in the 1890s, and another third (222) were founded in the five years from 1900-1904.[22] Three general trends lay behind this development. First was the industrialization and urbanization of Germany, which was creating larger populations of urban wage laborers. Having organized themselves into trade unions, in many cases, to improve their wages, more and more of these workers also decided to form or join consumer cooperatives in order to make their wages go further. Second, the period after about 1895 was generally one of an expanding economy, rising prices and wages, and rising real income. This may well have sped the development of consumer-oriented values and ideas. Finally, after 1890 came the massive development of the Social Democratic movement and its many mass-membership organizations and auxiliaries. The networks of trade unions and Social Democratic clubs were used by cooperative organizers to get their associations started. The new cooperative law of 1889 also aided the spread of cooperatives by permitting cooperatives with limited liability. Both Schulze-Delitzsch and Raiffeisen had opposed the introduction of limited liability, seeing it as deleterious to self-reliance; the liberal Schulze-Delitzsch saw it as undermining the concept of self-responsibility in the marketplace, while the conservative Raiffeisen saw it as undermining moral solidarity among members. Limited liability was of crucial importance to working-class consumers, however. To achieve economies of scale, urban consumer cooperatives wanted to be large; but this was risky if every individual member was exposed to unlimited liability in the event of financial failure. After 1889 working-class people risked only their shares, not everything they owned, to join cooperatives. Cooperatives spread more widely and grew much bigger in the urban areas.

The consumer cooperatives concentrated, at least initially, on easily handled, staple foodstuffs, but, where successful, soon branched out with their own bakeries, specialty shops for meat, and so on. While real wages were beginning to rise for workers, there was not yet a perception of prosperity. With memories of boom-and-bust cycles (and there was yet another short, sharp recession in 1901), working-class families cannot have felt economically secure. Consumer cooperatives offered a means to stretch family food budgets a little further, to accumulate small savings in cooperative accounts, all of which promised security. Later, as increases in real wages became noticeable, consumer cooperatives offered outlets for expanding purchasing power and rising material aspirations. The beginnings in the 1890s, however, were modest.

The expansion of the movement corresponded to an increasingly clear and deliberate working-class orientation. Many of the members of the consumer cooperatives in the Schulze-Delitzsch movement were artisans, public servants, peasants, and officers. The social composition of consumer cooperatives changed in the 1880s, as more and more workers were organized. Some of these new cooperatives were closely associated with the Social Democratic labor movement. The 1884 cooperative in Leipzig-Plagwitz, for example, took shape because organized workers were incensed that many local shopkeepers had signed a proclamation against the election of a Social Democratic candidate.[23] The foundation of the *Vorwärts* consumer association in Dresden in 1887 was a key step. Despite its name ("Forwards," which was also the name of the Social Democratic party newspaper) and the fact that it was an authentic worker-organized cooperative, the majority of the SPD's delegates and decision makers disapproved of the association and criticized it. Nevertheless, it made substantial inroads, demonstrating the potential for working-class consumer cooperatives to expand in big industrial centers.[24] More and more predominantly working-class cooperatives were created, which fit less and less comfortably within the liberal Schulze-Delitzsch federation. When, as described below, in 1903, the Schulze-Delitzsch movement expelled a number of consumer cooperatives, these cooperatives were estimated to have a membership that was 78 percent working class.[25]

A new group of consumer-cooperative publicists and leaders also emerged, overlapping with the functionaries in the Social Democratic movement. One of the key leaders was Heinrich Friedrich Kaufmann, son of a village pub-owner in Schleswig, who became an adult educator in Hamburg and a co-founder of the Hamburg People's Theatre. Kaufmann gave up teaching to manage and edit a local SPD newspaper in 1894, and from there entered the consumer cooperative movement and became a publicist and federation secretary. Like Pfeiffer before him, Kaufmann argued that the progressive advance of consumer cooperation would achieve a socialization of the economy, and that among all different kinds of cooperatives only consumer associations could achieve this. His prominence as a leader and spokesperson was so great that after his death some spoke of the "Kaufmann Era."[26] Even more closely tied into the SPD was Adolph von Elm, who led a career as party politician, labor unionist, and agitator in favor of cooperatives. From 1883-1891 Elm was manager of a "Friendship Club for Cigar Sorters," which acted as a labor union during the period of the antisocialist law. Elm was one of the cofounders of the General Commission of German Trade Unions, the powerful central body of Germany's largest labor union movement, and as a member of the Reichstag was one of the SPD's prominent national leaders. Apart from defending cooperatives within the party, he took part in founding several key cooperatives.[27]

As a result, significant departures in the organization of the consumer movement came in the 1890s. In 1894 the *Großeinkaufsgesellschaft deutscher Konsumvereine* or GEG (Wholesale Society of German Consumer Associations) was created by 47 consumer cooperatives. As a wholesale society owned by consumer cooperatives, its primary function was to order collectively on behalf of its members, achieving better wholesale prices than the individual consumer cooperatives could obtain on their own, and to operate a nationwide distribution system for these wholesale goods. Soon, instead of merely purchasing directly from factories, the GEG began buying and building its own factories and production facilities—all of this in conscious imitation of the English and Scottish Cooperative Wholesale Societies, which were visited by delegations of German consumer cooperators. The growth and vertical integration of cooperatives through the GEG reflected the aspirations of many of the urban cooperatives to grow into an expansive, interconnected, British-style movement with powerful central agencies. Members saw no practical limit to the areas of production into which the GEG might enter, raising the prospect of an entire consumer-dominated economic sector integrated from the retail level back to primary production. The progress of the GEG, however, depended on the multiplication of strong local cooperative societies, for without sufficient volume and sufficient density of cooperatives, there would be little a national wholesale could do.

Parallel to the growth of the GEG, new cooperatives were created in major urban centers across the country, either by neighborhood groups of working-class activists operating independently, or by the coordinated effort of local labor unions. In Berlin there were a number of false starts. One of these was interesting for its ideological overtones. In 1894-1895 a group of anarchists who were incarcerated at Plötzensee prison came across Schulze-Delitzsch's writings in the prison library. They conceived of a consumer cooperative for Berlin workers as a mechanism toward the creation of production cooperatives. This idea took shape in 1895 as the short-lived workers' consumer cooperative *Befreiung* (Liberation). "The greatest power that the worker has today lies in his consumption," wrote the organizers in their proclamation.[28] Though the *Befreiung* cooperative was short-lived, the idea that had been raised by the anarchists—the idea of mobilizing the power of workers as consumers in order to change society—was in the air. In 1899, new cooperatives in north and south Berlin got off to a better start. The new cooperatives amalgamated in 1902 to create a united "Consumer Cooperative Berlin and Area" that became, through growth and through further amalgamations with other Berlin cooperatives, one of the largest and strongest associations in the German movement.[29]

The *Produktion* cooperative founded in Hamburg, also in 1899, inaugurated a new model for consumer cooperative development across large urban regions. *Produktion* began during a large strike of port workers in which food relief had to be organized for the strikers; these efforts led to consideration of creating a consumer cooperative.[30] Local executive members and delegates of the SPD-oriented Free Trade Unions spent many months studying the idea, and, after deciding to proceed, used the Hamburg-area network of trade union organizations to publicize the idea and to sign up members. *Produktion* quickly branched out into construction of worker housing complexes and many other fields, and expanded to a massive network of productive and distributive facilities around the Hamburg area. Within a decade the cooperative operated 42 shops and 612 units of housing in complexes in neighborhoods across Hamburg.[31] *Produktion* provided an example for big, centralized, consumer-owned cooperatives in urban areas that would be active in many or all aspects of the economy. The Hamburg-based GEG, together with the model *Produktion* cooperative, and Hamburg-area leaders like Kaufmann and Elm, made up what was called the "Hamburg Tendency" (*Hamburger Richtung*) in consumer cooperation.

The example of the *Darmstädter Consum-, Spar-, und Produktions-Genossenschaft,* founded in the provincial Hessian city of Darmstadt at the turn of the century, shows the direction in which many of the new cooperatives were headed. Already the name of the cooperative ("Consumption, Savings, and Production Cooperative") shows the vision of a large, multipurpose business serving varied member needs. By just its ninth year of operation (1908-1909), this cooperative reported 2,229 members, who were overwhelmingly working class. The largest groups among them were identified as metal workers (333), factory workers (266), followed by "widows and private individuals" (231), joiners (226), masons (215), and officials and city employees (210). These members were served by a cooperative that decried price increases in foodstuffs as "taxes" upon the common people, and proudly advertised its own prices in its annual report. The goods advertised included beer, bread, butter, chocolate, eggs, salami, oatmeal, cheese, oil, and tea. The cooperative also sold clothing and had its own shoe division. These products were handled through 11 branches in the city and outlying centers, most of which had 100-200 local members. Further, the Darmstadt coop announced that it had agreements with nine bakers, eight butchers, four milk handlers, three hat and glove sellers, one glass and porcelain merchant, eight clothing handlers, one jeweller and watchmaker, and two hairdressers—from whom the co-op members could purchase while receiving credit toward their accounts with the cooperative. While the co-op shops as such were limited mainly to basic groceries and dry goods, members could in principle satisfy most requirements through some shop affiliated to the co-op. As the average purchases per member were only 150 Marks, however, it seems members were not buying exclusively from their cooperative. The directors exhorted members to buy more through the co-op, stating that they knew of co-ops where sales averaged 300-600 Marks per member.[32] It should be noted that average annual earnings in this period were only about one thousand Marks annually for waged workers; even 150 Marks might represent a significant percentage of total income.

The Darmstadt example shows that the goal was to develop cooperatives that reflected and served every need of the working-class household—initially through contracts with other merchants for specialized items, but increasingly over time through the cooperative's own production and distribution. The key advantages that the cooperative promised, aside from variety of goods, were lower prices. (In the case of the Darmstadt co-op, there were no patronage refunds being paid: the annual surplus was mostly put into reserves to finance further growth, after small deductions for education and charitable purposes.) The cooperative, then, was to provide a range of services that mirrored the needs of the working-class household, and provide low prices that would enable the household budget to be stretched further, all within a worker-controlled economic sector or system. While achievements of course fell short of the ideal, cooperatives were mobilizing growing numbers of members and volumes of business. The multiplication and expansion of these kinds of cooperatives exacerbated the conflicts with the older cooperatives built on the Schulze-Delitzsch model.

The Split with Liberalism:
The Rapprochement with Social Democracy

The development of the Hamburg-style cooperatives came into increasingly open conflict with the principles of the Schulze-Delitzsch movement for two main reasons. First, the new working-class cooperatives were associated with local Social Democratic and labor union functionaries. This class and political association was seen by liberal cooperators to be dividing society instead of uniting it and was thought by them to be a violation of the principles of neutrality and good business practice. Second, the Rochdale-style idea of large, centralized consumer cooperatives with many branches, owning production and processing enterprises as well as houses and savings banks, contradicted the Schulze-Delitzsch structure in which cooperatives were to be more specialized, more limited in scope, and reliant on the pledges of members' solidarity with each other. The consumer cooperatives' use of limited liability to create bigger and bigger enterprises violated Schulze-Delitzsch's teachings. In a wider theoretical sense, the claims of consumer cooperatives that they could expand indefinitely, until the whole economy would be socialized, left little room for the Schulze-Delitzsch artisanal cooperatives (or their artisan members) to continue to exist. The growth of such consumer cooperatives was increasingly perceived to take gainful employment away from the kind of people Schulze-Delitzsch had set out to help.

The conflict between the two models grew heated. Increasingly, *Allgemeiner Verband* leader Hans Crüger accused the consumer cooperatives of pursuing an illegitimate form of cooperation that amounted to socialism, a form that violated principles of political neutrality. The consumer cooperatives responded that the federation was being unsympathetic to the needs of their kind of cooperative. In the 1890s, they showed a distinct tendency to look to England for inspiration rather than to the *Allgemeiner Verband*. They organized a major study trip to visit the Cooperative Wholesale Society, the Cooperative Union, and Rochdale for just this purpose.

Matters came to a head beginning in 1900, when Crüger, still thinking of the *Mittelstand*, raised the idea of a cooperative organization of retailers. While credit and artisanal cooperatives could easily cooperate with such an organization, to consumer cooperatives it would be an organization of their competitors and, in the case of working-class cooperatives, of those considered their class enemies. As tensions increased, Crüger brought a motion to the September 1902 congress of the *Allgemeiner Verband* meeting in Kreuznach calling for the expulsion of ninety-eight consumer cooperatives identified with the Social Democratic and Hamburg movements. After the motion was passed, the expelled consumer cooperatives formed their own federation in 1903, the *Zentralverband deutscher Konsumvereine* or ZdK (Central League of German Consumer Associations). The ZdK became the umbrella organization for a consumer movement that swiftly surpassed the entire *Allgemeiner Verband* in the number of people and the volume of business it represented. Comparable to the partnership of the Cooperative Union CWS in England, the *Zentralverband* joined the GEG as the key central institutions of an increasingly strong and self-confident system of consumer cooperatives.[33]

The independent organization of the consumer cooperatives, and their growth among the working classes, led to a rapprochement with the Social Democratic movement. In 1892, consumer cooperatives had not even been discussed when the party passed a resolution condemning cooperatives in general; the debate at that time still revolved around the Marx-Lassalle argument concerning production cooperatives.[34] In 1897, SPD party ideologue Karl Kautsky published a pamphlet denouncing the idea that consumer cooperatives offered any answer to the social question.[35] But at the 1899 party conference in Hanover, consumer cooperatives were widely debated. Kaufmann and Elm spoke in their defense, against critics like Rosa Luxemburg from the left of the party. This debate paralleled the debates at about the same time over revisionism and reformism. In general, cooperatives were considered a reformist cause and hence opposed by the party's revolutionary wing. The Hanover conference finally passed a resolution recognizing the contributions of consumer cooperatives to the well-being of the working class, and approving of them as a means of educating the working class toward control of its own institutions, but adding that they were of no decisive importance in the proletariat's struggle for liberation. On balance, the resolution stated that "the party is neutral toward the creation of cooperatives."[36]

Finally at the Magdeburg party conference in 1910, the SPD actively encouraged its members to join and be involved in consumer cooperatives. Cooperatives were to provide jobs for the movement's members and activists, support striking workers with emergency funds, provide model working conditions, and train the working class to manage its own enterprises.[37] The strongest position, expressed by Elm, was that social democracy was a movement resting on three completely independent but equally important pillars: the party, the trade unions, and the consumer cooperatives. The "three-pillars" theory achieved wide currency in the German Social Democratic movement in the era around the First World War as it did in many European socialist movements. And, indeed, one 1913 study concluded that as many as 80 percent of the members of consumer cooperatives were also members of the SPD.[38] The difficult evolution from 1892 to 1910 shows that the SPD opposed consumer cooperatives for ideological reasons, until consumer cooperatives had developed numbers and an ideological perspective of their own that could no longer be ignored.

Political Catholicism and Consumer Cooperation

The massive expansion of consumer cooperative membership in the 1890s and early twentieth century was driven by that part of the movement that was associated with Social Democratic labor. Not all workers and not all cooperatives, however, were Social Democratic in their sympathies. Most of the Catholic parts of Germany remained politically supportive of the Catholic *Zentrum* (Center) Party, which around the turn of the century was increasingly antisocialist. In industrialized Catholic areas such as, notably, parts of the Rhineland and Westphalia, this raised the question of whether Catholic workers ought to join trade unions or consumer cooperatives that were associated with social democracy.

In the first decade of the twentieth century the Catholic movement decided, following the lead of an aggressive social Catholic intellectual leadership, to go out and win back the workers for Catholic institutions. Just as a Catholic labor union movement emerged from this impulse, so, too, did Catholic consumer cooperatives. These cooperatives could be justified on the basis of religious doctrine and traditions of social thought. Authorities interested in the "Christian restructuring of economy and society" saw consumer cooperatives as a modern mechanism to achieve "the economic ideal of the ancient church":

the just price that rewards everyone in proportion to their labor without exploitation.[39] One prelate active in the Catholic workers' movement noted, "we see in consumer associations a moralization of today's capitalist order."[40]

The Catholic cooperatives seem, like the trade unions, to have rested on a kind of middle ground between conservative and progressive social Catholicism, though perhaps somewhat closer to the latter. On the one hand, by emphasizing that Catholic workers ought not to be members of cooperatives associated with social democracy, the Catholic movement was accepting that religion transcended class: workers of different religious and political ideologies should not cooperate on common economic interests. This differed from the view of some radicals within the Catholic community, who believed non-Catholic and Catholic workers should strike and work for higher wages and better standards of living together. But while the idea of separate Catholic cooperatives was in this sense not radical, it nevertheless embodied the notion of organizing Catholic workers (as consumers) separately from other classes of Catholics. This assertion of working-class autonomy and self-organization within the Catholic community implied, to some degree, a repudiation of the corporatist doctrines that dominated conservative Catholic thought.

The motivation for the new cooperatives arose from Catholic labor union circles. In 1901 a new Social Democratic consumer cooperative, *Hoffnung* (Hope), was organized in the Cologne area. Christian workers declined or were discouraged from joining it by Catholic leaders. A young Catholic labor unionist named Peter Schlack helped lead a campaign to form a separate consumer cooperative, which took shape in 1902 as *Eintracht* (Harmony). For ten years, Schlack served as its chief publicist and the chairperson of its board of directors *(Aufsichtsrat)*.[41] Other cooperatives quickly followed, usually organized by Catholic labor unions for Catholic workers. In Werden, for example, the local council of Catholic trade unions decided in 1903 to form a consumer co-op; membership grew in one year from 63 to 1,080, of whom 73 percent were miners.[42] Schlack's *Eintracht* cooperative remained the flagship of the Christian cooperative movement, and the focal point for developing a Rhenish-Westphalian regional federation in 1908. Finally, in 1913, organization was extended to the national level in a *Reichsverband deutscher Konsumvereine* (Imperial League of German Consumer Associations) with Schlack as director. Soon a central cooperative wholesale organization was set up to parallel the GEG. Within little over a decade, then, the Catholic trade unions had created a movement whose form paralleled the consumer movement of the Social Democratic unions: worker-oriented urban consumer cooperatives growing as large as possible and joined in strong central organizations. The movement's size, however, was limited by the fact that Catholics were a minority, and by the fact that most Catholic areas were little industrialized. There was little strong basis for the Catholic urban consumer movement outside of western Germany.

Geography and demographics were not the only limits. Catholic labor unionists found that clerics and Catholic politicians were happy to resist Social Democratic consumer cooperatives, but less happy to support separate Catholic ones. The advocates of Catholic consumer cooperation had to argue against other interests that were influential within political Catholicism. Schlack and leaders like him fought to establish the legitimacy of their project against arguments raised by the Catholic *Mittelstand*.[43] This argument within political Catholicism reflected a similar, even more vociferous confrontation within the mainstream, Protestant society.

Mittelstand Activism and the Opposition to Consumer Cooperatives

As workers were won over in larger numbers to consumer cooperatives, activists speaking on behalf of the *Mittelstand* became increasingly opposed to them. Schulze-Delitzsch's vision of a *Mittelstand* embracing cooperatives of all types, including consumer cooperatives, was undermined by the polarizations of industrial society. German liberalism's ideals of social harmony, and the strength of German liberalism itself, were in decline.

By the turn of the century, protecting the *Mittelstand* had become a conservative cause, an antisocialist, antiliberal, and, in some respects, even an antidemocratic cause. The *Mittelstand* had not been won over to Schulze's "guilds of the future." Activists still hoped, through state intervention, to reestablish the guilds of the past. They also demanded restrictions on modern forms of retailing that competed with traditional shopkeepers. This included department stores, traveling salesmen, and not least of all consumer cooperatives. So-called chain stores became an issue later, in the 1920s. Until that time German consumer cooperatives were the pioneers in multiple-outlet retailing. *Mittelstand* demands were received with some sympathy by conservative governments.

In Germany generally, the *Mittelstand* lobby became increasingly well-organized and influential during the 1890s and especially after 1900. Associations of small retailers defended shopkeepers' interests and influenced politicians and public opinion. Some of these associations were purely political, like the *Schutzverbände* (Protection Leagues). Others combined economic and political action, like the *Rabattsparvereine* (Discount Savings Associations). In 1902-1903, a *Verband der Rabattsparvereine Deutschlands* (League of Germany's Discount Savings Associations) was created under Heinrich Beythien, with the express purpose of fighting consumer cooperatives and department stores. Beythien was also, after 1905, the secretary of the *Deutsche Mittelstandsvereinigung* (German *Mittelstand* Union) and was an advocate of open participation in party politics. He was later a functionary of the ultranationalist, antisocialist German Fatherland Party of 1917-1918.[44]

These associations were not isolated. The campaigns of such *Mittelstand* groups were given publicity, ideas, and legitimacy by middle-class writers, among whom the most prolific was likely Professor E. Suchsland, a senior teacher of Latin from Halle.[45] At certain stages the lobby also received assistance from authoritarian antisocialist interests like the Imperial League against social democracy, which in 1908 issued a publication entitled *Die Sozialdemokratie als Arbeitgeberin und Unternehmerin* (Social Democracy as Employer and Entrepreneur) that criticized consumer cooperatives as examples of social democracy in action.[46] Similarly the *Deutsche Arbeitgeber-Zeitung* (German Employers' Magazine) published a story in 1909 that claimed an "intimate connection between the Wholesale Society of German Consumer Cooperatives and Social Democracy," alleging that the social support funds of the wholesale organization were used to help socialist activists, and referring to the enterprises owned by the wholesale organization as socialist.[47] The head of the *Allgemeiner Verband,* Crüger, also joined in this campaign, publishing a chapter in a 1909 book in which he claimed that consumer cooperatives had been taken over by people who saw them as instruments to establish a socialist state, that this had led to labor unions and the working class supporting them, and therefore to the loss of their former middle-class character.[48] These attempts to link socialism and consumer cooperatives were an effective tactic for convincing Germany's antisocialist governments to take action against consumer cooperatives.

Increasingly after the turn of the century, governments at all levels responded to the *Mittelstand* lobby by taking incremental steps to restrict consumer cooperatives. In fairness to German public servants and legislators, they demonstrated some restraint and some inclination to uphold the rule of law, avoiding measures that would have banned or shut down consumer cooperatives outright. But under pressure from conservatives and nationalists, laws and regulations were bent in restrictive and oppressive ways.

A clear example was the way in which urban consumer cooperatives were harassed under the Reich cooperative law. The law had been amended in 1889 to forbid trade by cooperatives with nonmembers. As a general principle, this was certainly acceptable to most cooperators, who believed that it was bad cooperative practice to do much trade with nonmembers. The law was amended in the 1890s, however, to make this more than a general principle, and created stiff fines to punish any transgressions. Three features of the changes were particularly noxious. First, by making it a criminal offence *ever* to sell *any* goods to nonmembers (rather than, for example, establishing a percentage limit on nonmember business), the law opened consumer cooperatives to harassment. *Mittelstand* and antisocialist activists could frequent stores to try to catch examples of any sale to a nonmember, or perhaps even to try to entrap the cooperative into such a sale. Cooperatives were forced to put elaborate control procedures in place to try to ensure that every customer was a member. Given the scale of cooperative enterprise in the cities, total control was impossible. Second, the fines under the law were not fines *to the cooperative*, but *to the salesperson* who transacted the business. In other words, working-class employees were subject personally to a fine if they accidentally or deliberately sold to a nonmember. The provision was calculated to intimidate. Finally, the law specifically exempted agricultural consumer cooperatives from the restriction on nonmember business. In other words, only the cooperatives of the working class were to be restricted and regulated by criminal provisions; cooperatives of similar structure, but serving farmers, were exempt. This was ideologically based favoritism by the state.[49] The government's attitude was also clearly expressed where, as in Prussia and Saxony, state officials were forbidden to serve on cooperative boards of directors, or even were forbidden to join cooperatives.

It is more difficult to write about the question of taxation of cooperatives, because the relevant business and other taxes were imposed at the local or state level, resulting in variations across the country. Lobbyists proposed all manner of special taxes from taxes on volume, to taxes on the number of branches, and taxes on cooperatives greater than a certain size. In 1896, the Kingdom of Saxony imposed a special tax on the sales volume of large businesses, which had particular impact on consumer cooperatives because they operated branch systems and were larger, generally speaking, than the retailers with whom they competed. In 1900, Prussia introduced a warehouse tax (again, it was usually consumer cooperatives and other large businesses, not independent shopkeepers, who operated warehouses), and it permitted municipalities to create their own special taxes on consumer cooperatives. Consumer cooperatives were, in addition, made subject to income taxes, despite the objections of cooperators that a consumer cooperative has no income of its own and is only an agent for its members.[50]

Despite some successes by the cooperatives in fending off the more extreme taxation proposals, it appears that taxes on consumer cooperatives climbed sharply after 1900. The Stuttgart consumer cooperative paid taxes equivalent to 0.26 percent of its sales volume, or 3.4 percent of its member refunds, in 1880; after a new tax law of 1905, taxes were proportionately eight or ten times as high: 2.2 percent of sales or 25 percent of the value of the refunds to members.[51] A weavers' consumer cooperative in the Eulengebirge, according to cooperators an especially poverty-stricken group, faced a 94 percent increase in taxes from 1906 to 1909, while its volume increased only 32 percent. The RM 19,543 in taxes was equivalent to 22 percent of the net surplus. As the context makes clear, *Mittelstand* activists wanted to use such taxes to drive consumer cooperatives out of business altogether. "When the business tax was brought in, the store could not make it and was closed again," one cooperation told the Saxon legislature, referring to a town he knew. "Then one could remove the business tax, since its purpose had been achieved."[52] It was not lost on consumer cooperative leaders that they were paying hundreds of thousands, even millions of Marks in taxes, while the same governments that taxed them punitively were subsidizing rural and agricultural cooperatives.

The argument for restricting consumer cooperatives, apart from political considerations, rested on the claim that they were a form of unfair competition. This argument is an interesting one because it appealed to a nonliberal, nonmarket standard of fairness: that small business people were essential to German society, no matter whether they could match their competitors' prices or not. The reason for the wildfire spread of consumer cooperatives appears to be, apart from working-class organization, that the German system of small retailing was inefficient by modern standards. Cooperators estimated that small retailers operated with margins of 20 percent, which allowed the cooperative to sell more cheaply and still regularly pay 10 percent patronage refunds, as most of them did in the 1890s and early 1900s. The large patronage refunds were undoubtedly an important factor in the cooperatives' success, even though the ideologues in the movement criticized the cooperatives for overemphasis on large refunds to the detriment of other uses for their surpluses. Whatever the reasons, the *Zentralverband* and its consumer cooperatives became by 1914 Germany's largest cooperative federation in members and business volume, despite the increasingly shrill opposition and harassment from right-wing groups and governments. Among the countries of the world, Germany had the third greatest number of consumer cooperatives (2,311) after Russia and France; the second most consumer cooperative members (1.6 million), amounting to two-thirds of Britain's total; and the world's third largest cooperative wholesale organization, the GEG, after the English CWS and the Scottish CWS.[53]

Visions and Limits: Consumer Cooperatives
in the Weimar Republic

The First World War gave a noticeable boost to consumer cooperation in Germany, ushering in a period of expansion and maturity for the consumer cooperative movement in the 1920s. In many respects the Weimar period proved to be the golden age for German consumer cooperation. The prewar trends of development were continued to their logical conclusions, and German consumer cooperation reached its highest historical level of support.

The First World War and the immediate postwar period brought improvements in the relationship of consumer cooperatives with the German central and state governments. The need to organize the wartime economy, regulate supply, and control prices made consumer cooperatives useful allies of the state. It was easier for state officials to work with the centralized, integrated, and nonprofit system of consumer cooperatives than with thousands of independent shopkeepers. The most useful allies of the government were in fact the ZdK/GEG cooperatives. Even though these were the cooperatives associated with social democracy, they were the largest and most centralized—hence, the best able to help the government to control price increases and regulate distribution.[54] In any case, the isolation of the Social Democratic movement was decreasing. The revolution of 1918 eventually put the Social Democrats into power nationally. Both the Social Democratic party and the other two "pillars" of the movement, the trade unions and the cooperatives, enjoyed considerable prominence in the interwar years. In part this reflected a considerable degree of recognition and influence—these were social, political, and economic institutions to be reckoned with. But the radical right was never reconciled to their strength or perhaps even their existence.

On balance, the 1920s favored the growth and further centralization of the consumer cooperative system. Of course the economic instability of the early Weimar years took its toll on a number of consumer cooperatives, as it did of many businesses; but economic instability and hardship also gave more Germans a reason to support consumer cooperatives. The wartime experience of profiteering, followed by the postwar chaos of recession, inflation, and demobilization, made thousands of Germans turn to consumer cooperatives for help for the first time. Cooperatives offered a degree of stability and planning, a possibility of reduced prices and increased refunds, and trustworthiness as community-run, nonprofit enterprises. The restructuring of the economy also favored the cooperatives. Small independent shopkeepers faced serious challenges and rapid decline; chain stores, department stores, and other more integrated and large-scale forms of retailing multiplied. Cooperatives had the economic scale advantages of regional chain stores, and were furthermore inclined toward innovation in marketing and advertising. Large-scale buying, large-scale advertising and marketing, integration on regional and national levels: consumer cooperatives had advantages over most of their direct competitors in operating efficient, modern retailing systems. It is difficult to argue that consumer cooperatives became more pragmatic or more like their capitalist competitors, since there had always been a strong practical emphasis on price, and since consumer cooperatives had generally been leading rather than following in the development of "capitalist" practices like integration and multiple retailing. It may be, however, that the initial ideological gloss on these activities began to wear thin in the 1920s; or perhaps that the economic ups and downs made the practical benefits and the dreams of long-term growth less compelling. Instead of triumph, the peak of the German consumer cooperative movement seems to have been a reaching of limits—as is perhaps inevitable in social movements that justify their activities with far-reaching goals of social transformation.

Consumer cooperatives faced not only economic changes, but also social ones. In one respect, social and demographic trends favored the cooperatives. Urbanization increased the potential membership base; urban consumer culture potentially meant continuing, keen interest in low-cost goods and services, provided consumer aspirations could be channeled through cooperative institutions. Other social trends, however, posed clear challenges for consumer cooperation. Greatest among these were the changing roles of women and of youth.

Women had always been the main customers of consumer cooperatives (as of other retail stores), but the movement's structure had been thoroughly male-dominated, in the image of the trade unions that in fact sponsored the creation of many co-ops. The role of women was inversely proportional to the power exercised at each level of involvement. Shoppers were women. Members included women, especially widows, but married women often used memberships in their husbands' names, so most members were men. Front-line service staff included women, but the majority of employees overall in most cooperatives were men. The senior managers and elected leaders of the movement were almost exclusively men. Prior to the First World War there was only gradual change. Among the cooperatives of the ZdK, for example—still by far the largest federation—the proportion of shares owned by women increased after 1910, amounting by 1919 to more than one-fifth of all shares.[55] The real debate over involvement of women began in the Weimar Republic, driven in part by women activists in the movement, but also by a sense among some of the established cooperative leaders that the movement was stagnating, and that better support from women might be the way out of the impasse. Changing gender roles in the wider society were undoubtedly the key: it was not in cooperatives alone that the issue of women's roles was raised. However, the broad membership base of the co-ops, their democratic structures, and their progressive ideals compelled them to deal with such questions. The record, in the 1920s, was mixed at best.

The creation of more and more women's groups was an important step, and provided a platform for advancing the issue of women's participation. Within the ZdK, such groups multiplied at the local and regional levels, growing from seven in 1923 to forty-four in 1931.[56] Separate, usually regional women's groups existed in affiliation with the various kinds of cooperative umbrella federations; no centralized national women's cooperative movement emerged. Possibly due to the educational and organizing work done by the women's groups women did become more visible in leadership positions of local cooperatives. Between 1923 and 1926 there was a quadrupling of the number of women directors on local cooperative boards from 25 to 101, of women on cooperative councils (*Genossenschaftsräte*) from 144 to 641, and of women in delegates' assemblies (*Vertreterversammlungen*) from 258 to 1,130. In percentage terms this was still a small portion of the leadership of the movement, but it was clear that the issue had been raised. Many male and female cooperators both began to realize how long women's representation was, and conclude that women had to be involved in cooperatives not only passively, as customers, but also actively as committed members, if their loyal support was to be retained. There remained philosophical resistance among the male cooperative establishment, however, to the ideas of special organizations or measures for women's involvement. In 1928, the federation of eastern German consumer cooperatives made a statement to a conference of women cooperators held in their region, assuring the women activists that "the cooperative movement serves women: it strengthens their purchasing power"—therefore women had a moral obligation to support cooperatives. In return, the movement would sponsor educational programs for women, and activities for mothers with children.[57] These were positive steps forward in the context of the times. They did not, however, begin to address the structural and hierarchical questions of *power* within the cooperatives.

Within the Catholic consumer cooperatives, there was also increased discussion of the role of women in the 1920s, though this resulted in few changes in organization or leadership. Nevertheless, in the 1920s a number of women were important leaders in the Catholic cooperative movement, including Reichstag deputy Christine Teuch, and the secretary of the Catholic German Women's League, Christine Hölzgens.[58] The latter wrote that "the cooperative idea is a most fundamental property of women," because cooperatives embody community (*Gemeinschaft*). "Women, as nurturers . . . of the smallest community, the family, have by their nature, by their deepest sensibility, a much stronger drive for community than men." It may be, as Hölzgens argued, that women were inherently more supportive of cooperatives than men. In the 1920s this did not yet translate into large numbers of leadership positions for women in Catholic cooperatives.

The question of youth was perhaps even more problematic. Like the wider Social Democratic and trade union movements, the cooperative movement was aging. Its leadership and officials were mostly of the prewar generation. Cooperatives were beginning to be seen as old-fashioned and overly bureaucratized, with little to offer in terms of inspiration or idealism for the young. The economic turmoil of the early and late Weimar years probably did not help, since it implicitly questioned the old cooperative assumption of gradual, steady progress toward a cooperativized economy.

These vulnerabilities of the Social Democratic consumer cooperative movement were fully exploited by the Social Democrats' bitter enemies, the Communists. After the German Communists split from the majority Social

Democrats in 1919, Communist activists contested the control of local working-class institutions in order to wrest from the Social Democrats the legitimacy of speaking on behalf of workers. These contests for control were conducted within the consumer cooperatives as well. The constant attacks by the hard Left helped weaken and delegitimize the consumer cooperatives. While Communist followers did not gain control of the cooperative movement as a whole, they did score successes in electing "opposition" delegates within many of the cooperatives, and in taking control of a few of them, particularly in eastern Germany and notably in Saxony.

Communists seized on every scandal and every questionable managerial decision in order to demonstrate that the cooperatives and their Social Democratic leadership were betraying the working class. These attacks became especially vociferous after the onset of the Depression, when many cooperatives were forced to cut back and lay off staff. The Communists argued that the cooperatives should stand up for the working people, keep workers employed, spend their surpluses, and run deficits. In making this argument, the Communists realized that these actions would have driven many cooperatives into bankruptcy. The point was rather that they did not care a great deal about the consumer cooperatives as such, instead seeing them only as tools in the battle for the hearts and minds of the working class—all this in agreement with the rather ruthless tactical view of the Communist International.[59] The Communists' organizing efforts may, however, have helped mobilize excluded and marginalized groups such as youth and women.

Where the early 1920s had seemed so promising for consumer cooperatives, a decade later they seemed crippled by age and institutionalization, besieged from outside by economic forces, and undermined from below in some of their key regions of the strength by Communist organizing. Possibly it seemed that matters could hardly get worse, but the National Socialist seizure of power in 1933 put the state in the hands of activists and an ideology that were systematically and ruthlessly opposed to consumer cooperatives.

Nazism and the First Destruction of Consumer Cooperatives

As the National Socialist movement developed in the 1920s, it dealt opportunistically with cooperatives: sometimes as an issue around which polarizations could be exploited; sometimes as tools for influence and for the penetration of the movement into society—much, indeed, as the Communists used them to organize support. The variety of different signals given by the Nazis represented the tendency of different arms of the movement to cater to different constituencies. Some Nazi propagandists, speaking to audiences of cooperators, argued that Nazism and cooperatives were akin to each other, in that both strove for the common good, to transcend individualism and arouse a spiritual dedication to higher causes. Even these propagandists tended to be critical of the practical and economic concerns of cooperatives, arguing that cooperatives within a liberal society were tainted by materialistic and class concerns. Only under National Socialist leadership would cooperatives achieve their true destiny.[60] The so-called "left" of the National Socialist party, led by men like Otto Strasser who believed the party should be worker-oriented, made rhetorical statements about a Nazi future in which factories would be organized as cooperatives of managers, workers, and representatives of the state as owner. On the other hand, the party's *Mittelstand* activists, united in the *Kampfbund des gewerblichen Mittelständes* (Combat League of Middle Class Tradespeople) shamelessly exploited the preexisting agitation against consumer cooperatives as an alleged threat to the *Mittelstand*. Consumer cooperatives were denounced as "Marxist-capitalist" enterprises, in league with big business and financed by Jewish capital with the express purpose of wiping out German small business. The radical *Mittelstand* activists were important to the party. They were influential enough to organize Nazi-supported boycotts of consumer cooperatives in the early 1930s, and to voice the opinion in 1932 that shopping in a consumer cooperative was grounds to be expelled from the Nazi party. Prior to the Nazi seizure of power in 1933, it was possibly not clear which of these various strains would win out.

Once in power, National Socialism could not avoid conflict with cooperatives for two reasons. First, a large part of the working class, of farmers, and of the *Mittelstand* were organized in cooperatives, and these cooperatives valued their autonomy. The Nazi organizational principles of *Gleichschaltung* ("co-ordination" or organization of society under Nazism) and the *Führerprinzip* (appointment of leaders from above) meant that cooperative systems had to be subjugated and assimilated into a National Socialist state. Second, a number of groups of cooperatives were associated with ideologies like liberalism and social democracy, which the Nazis were dedicated to destroying. This was not true of all cooperatives: the conservative rural cooperative systems were relatively little-touched by the Nazis. Consumer cooperatives, which were usually urban and Socialist, however, were another matter.[61]

In power, Nazism moved slowly but inexorably from subjugating consumer cooperatives to destroying them utterly. Soon after Nazi paramilitary forces smashed and occupied the offices of German trade unions in May 1933, they began to move against consumer cooperatives as well. The administrative buildings of the ZdK and the GEG were occupied by the SA, the Nazi paramilitary units, the so-called brown-shirts. Deputy Nazi party leader Rudolf Hess issued a circular on Hitler's behalf, forbidding further attacks on consumer cooperatives by the party's street fighters. Instead, the regime proceeded more slowly and systematically after that point. Gradually the consumer cooperatives were drawn into and finally amalgamated with the German Labor Front, a mixed party-state administrative entity headed by senior Nazi Leader Robert Ley. For a time, the consumer cooperatives remained as centers of quiet resistance to the regime by the underground SPD However, a law of May 21, 1935, began the winding up of consumer cooperatives. In the following months 72 cooperatives, including many of Germany's biggest, were dissolved, their shareholders paid off with state funds where necessary, and the co-ops converted into state-run or private distribution centers. Political supervision and Gestapo action cleaned non-Nazi functionaries out of the remaining consumer cooperatives. Finally, a decree of February 18, 1941, systematically liquidated consumer cooperatives and made their assets and facilities part of Ley's empire.[62] More than three generations of enterprise and organization-building by, particularly, working-class people had been wiped out. When—after the horrific destruction brought by Nazism on all of Germany in 1944-1945—consumer cooperators began to rebuild, in the midst of bombed-out cities and a shattered economy, they began with nothing.

The Challenge of the Mid-Twentieth Century

In western Germany—from 1949 onward the Federal Republic—consumer cooperatives faced the twin challenges of rebuilding a distribution, retailing, and production system starting with no assets, and of adapting to rapidly changing and increasingly Americanized retailing practices such as the spread of self-service shops. They were successful in the first challenge, somewhat so in the second, but were hamstrung among other things by unfavorable state policies. The dedicated work of the labor and cooperative movements to rebuild consumer cooperatives in the 1950s ended decades later in widespread failure.

In some respects, the Federal Republic provided an environment less favorable to consumer cooperatives than what they had enjoyed before 1933. There were, to be sure, some benefits of the open and competitive society of postwar western Germany. In terms of the legal environment, a 1954 law allowed consumer cooperatives to sell to nonmembers—a practice that could bring helpful volume and profits, but of which cooperative theorists had usually disapproved.[63] Other changes were clearly negative; for example, the size of refunds was legally limited to 3 percent. Cooperatives were thus no longer permitted to pay substantial dividends on patronage refunds. Even if they were successful enough to pay dividends, it became more difficult to demonstrate their advantages over other retailers.[64] Legal and regulatory decisions concerning business practices and taxation likely hindered the healthy membership development and capitalization of the consumer movement. On balance, however, it may be that social and cultural changes were greater threats to the movement. These included a newer and more individualistic kind of consumerism, which undermined member loyalty to cooperatives, and a gradual decline in the size, strength, and unity of the kind of working-class movements that had created large numbers of consumer cooperatives in the first place.

These adverse factors were perhaps implicit from the beginning, nevertheless, western German consumer cooperatives made considerable strides from the mid-1950s to the mid-1960s. A new emphasis on competitiveness and modern marketing helped them. The movement grew again in numbers and sizes of cooperatives, as before in partnership with the trade unions. In terms of membership development, 1958 was the peak year of the women's cooperative movement: in that year the reconstituted ZdK had 114 associated women's groups representing some twenty thousand women activists.[65] The subsequent decline in separate cooperative organizations for women in the 1960s appears to have been a trend in various countries. It may reflect, in part, generational change among women and in their concerns and priorities. It seems probable that it reflects growing opportunities for women in other areas—not only work, but also other political, educational, social, and recreational organizations and activities—that reduced the importance of cooperative women's groups in their lives. It may also reflect a conclusion by women activists (in retrospect, perhaps mistaken) that separate women's organizations were no longer needed. The economic success, satisfaction, and complacency of cooperatives in the postwar world may have contributed to their downfall; they succeeded in making themselves commonplace and uncontroversial.

Starting in the late 1960s, the consumer movement encountered growing difficulties, related to the need for increased capital and increased centralization and efficiency. At stake was the ability of consumer cooperatives to match the modernization of competing, capitalist chain stores. While it is beyond the scope of this chapter to analyze the ultimate collapse, a brief sketch is in order. The last of a series of restructurings came in the 1970s when most of Germany's consumer cooperatives were converted into share companies. These companies amalgamated regionally to form a tightly integrated system, dominated by a centralized national company, "Co op AG" (that is, "Coop, Inc."), effectively controlled by a number of labor union leaders. This conversion and centralization was to provide the kind of large-scale organization, integrated marketing, and economic strength needed to compete in modern retailing. The joint-stock company form was chosen to facilitate raising additional capital, which the consumer cooperatives felt they needed in order to match their competitors.[66] As of 1984 the Co op AG group had drawn in about two-thirds of the consumer cooperative movement, and it had roughly ten billion DM in sales volume through a couple of thousand local outlets.[67] But Co op AG encountered financial difficulties and collapsed in the 1980s—scandal was involved; a number of functionaries were convicted of embezzlement. Because the system had been centralized, it all went down together. Today, a few strong consumer associations that never joined Co op AG remain in existence, notably the consumer cooperative in Dortmund, which is one of the largest in the world. But 1986 figures for fourteen European Community countries plus Japan and Israel found that Germany ranked *last* of the countries studied in the percentage of its population who were members of consumer cooperatives—in Germany's case, only 1 percent.[68]

In Communist-controlled East Germany after 1945, true cooperatives never had a chance. Consumer cooperatives and housing cooperatives were re-established by the German Democratic Republic in the 1950s (and new agricultural production cooperatives were created, among other forms), but in practice these did not function independently of Communist party and state control. Centralized planning and the dictatorship of the Socialist Unity Party (SED) meant that autonomous cooperatives were hardly possible. Ironically, though, eastern Germany preserved vestiges of institutions, including retail cooperatives, longer than they survived in the increasingly Americanized west. Much of the east German retail sector remained organized in "Konsum" stores that were ostensibly cooperative in structure. The reunification of eastern Germany into the Federal Republic in 1990 released the Konsum system from state control, permitting reorganization into genuine cooperatives, but at the same time these cooperatives were exposed quickly to full competition from modern western chains. Not surprisingly, with so little time to adapt, burdened by debt and capital shortage, most of the rather unmodern stores were quickly closed. If enough consumer co-ops manage to survive in the east, however, they may strengthen the faltering German consumer cooperative movement.

Conclusion

Consumer cooperatives were conceived in Germany as a means by which all classes and people could improve their family economies. Schulze-Delitzsch believed they would help artisans; later on, diverse groups including civil servants and white-collar employees found considerable utility in them. In a separate line of development, rural consumer cooperatives became a fixture of German agriculture, supplying agricultural inputs and other commodities to rural households. But urban consumer cooperatives thrived only in the period from the 1890s to 1933 when trade unionists and working-class leaders promoted them as class-conscious, collective tools for the self-advancement of working people. Consumer cooperatives changed the face of urban Germany by building stores, housing projects, and production facilities that were statements of working people's strength and enterprise. They contributed to the creation of a communal and, to a degree, participatory culture. They opened a debate concerning the involvement of women in the economy and in the leadership of community businesses. At their height, they expressed a variation of consumerist ideas according to which consumers should act jointly to shape an economy in their own interests.

The story of German consumer cooperatives also illustrates the importance of politics and political culture to popular institutions. Consumer cooperatives faced determined and at times well-connected ideological and economic interest enemies. It was the ideas articulated by these enemies that triumphed through Nazism and brought about the first death of German consumer cooperatives. Nevertheless, while the dramatic political events that destroyed consumer cooperatives in 1933-1945, and that hampered their development in the two Germanies in different ways after that time, should not be underestimated, the political drama obscures the fact that there were also underlying social and economic causes for the ebbing of the movement compared to its height in the Weimar Republic. Chief among these underlying causes is surely the decline by the late twentieth century in the size and strength of the working class, and of the kind of ideology and activism that had once made consumer cooperatives the "third pillar" of the socialist labor movement. Also, the post-Second World War consumer culture in the west was increasingly individualist, contributing to a sense that consumers should act by opportunistic individual choices rather than by collective commitments. And finally, notions of participation and control have evolved since the democratic centralism of the early twentieth-century labor movement. The "new social movements" of the 1980s in Germany stressed decentralized, flexible, and grassroots organization, not the cumbersome and bureaucratized institutions typical of the earlier era. These movements created many new cooperatives, but mostly small and alternative ones not connected to the older movement. Apart from all the other problems that were not under their control, German consumer cooperatives failed to adapt to these social-cultural changes. The result was a second death, under capitalism this time rather than under Nazism, of most consumer cooperatives. The few strong ones that remain are last bastions of a movement that was once among the strongest in the world.

Notes

This article is part of an on-going research project into the history of German cooperatives. The author is grateful for the financial support of the Social Sciences and Humanities Research Council of Canada and the Alexander von Humboldt-Stiftung.

1. (Excepting churches, if one wishes to consider churches as mass movements.) On the German cooperative movement generally, see Helmut Faust, *Geschichte der Genossenschaftsbewegung: Ursprung und Aufbruch der Genossenschaftsbewegung in England, Frankreich und Deutschland sowie ihre weitere Entwicklung im deutschen Sprachraum*, 3rd ed. (Frankfurt a.M., 1977). On German consumer cooperatives, see Erwin Hasselmann, *Geschichte der deutschen Konsumgenossenschaften*, (Frankfurt a.M., 1971); Arnulf Weuster, *Theorie der Konsumgenossenschaftsentwicklung: die deutschen Konsumgenossenschaften bis zum Ende der Weimarer Zeit*, (Berlin, 1980); and Theodor Cassau, *Die Konsumvereinsbewegung in Deutschland*, (Munich, 1924). In English there is Erwin Hasselmann, *Consumers' Cooperation in Germany*, 3rd ed. (Hamburg, 1961). Too late to be used in preparing this chapter was the important new study by Michael Prinz, *Brot und Divbidende: Konsumvereine in Deutschland und England vor 1914* (Göttingen, 1996).

2. Hasselmann refutes Paul Göhre's claim that "Ermunterung" was the first consumer co-op. Hasselmann, *Geschichte der deutschen Konsumgenossenschaften* 47-48; Paul Göhre, *Die deutschen Arbeiter-Konsumvereine*, (Berlin, 1910), 32.

3. The International Cooperative Alliance defines a primary or local cooperative society as "an autonomous association of persons united voluntarily to meet their common economic and social needs and aspirations through a jointly owned and democratically managed enterprise." (Statement of Cooperative Identity adopted by the I.C.A. in congress at Manchester, England in October 1995.)

4. Christiane Eisenberg, *Frühe Arbeiterbewegung und Genossenschaften: Theorie und Praxis der Produktivgenossenschaften in der deutschen Sozialdemohratie und den Gewerkschaften der 1860er/1870er Jahre* (Bonn, 1985), Anhang A. See also Hasselmann, *Geschichte der deutschen Konsumgenossenschaften*, 43ff.

5. On Huber, see Faust, *Geschichte der Genossenschaftsbewegung*, 167-92; Hasselmann, *Geschichte der deutschen Konsumgenossenschaften*, 100-108.

6. On Schulze-Delitzsch, see Rita Aldenhoff, *Schulze-Delitzsch: Ein Beitrag zur Geschichte des Liberalismus zwischen Revolution und Reichsgründung* (Baden-Baden, 1984); "Schulze, Franz Hermann S.," *Allgemeine Deutsche Biographie* (Leipzig, 1891). Deutscher Genossenschaftsverband (Schulze-Delitzsch), *Schulze-Delitzsch: ein Lebenswerk für Generationen* (Wiesbaden, 1987), has some quite good pieces in it, especially Volker Beuthien's.

7. Speech to Allgemeiner Verband meeting in Potsdam, 1862, quoted in Eberhard Dülfer, "Des Organisationskonzept 'Genossenschaft'—eine Pionierleistung Schulze-Delitzschs", *Schulze-Delitzsch: ein Lebenswerk für Generationen*, 59-126.

8. James J. Sheehan, *German Liberalism in the Nineteenth Century* (London, 1982), 92-94.

9. "Die privatrechtliche Stellung der Erwerbs- und Wirthschafts-Genossenschaften 1868-76." Bundesarchiv Berlin, Reichstag, Film 30735, Nr. 406. The phrase *Innung der Zukunft*, "guild of the future," goes back at least to his *Assoziationsbuch für deutsche Handwerker und Arbeiter* (Leipzig, 1853), 56, and was also in the title of a newsletter he published in the 1850s.

10. Schulze-Delitzsch, *Vorschuß- und Creditvereine als Volksbanken. Praktische Anweisung zu deren Gründung und Hinrichtung*, 3rd ed. (Leipzig, 1862), 1 (and the same for the following quotations).

11. Schulze-Delitzsch, *Assoziationsbuch für deutsche Handwerker und Arbeiter* (Leipzig, 1853), 56.

12. Hasselmann, *Geschichte der deutschen Konsumgenossenschaften*, 68-69.

13. "Statistische Uebersicht über Zahl und Geschäftsresultate der Deutschen Genossenschaften in den letzten Jahren," Reichstag des Norddeutschen Bundes, 1. Legislatur-Periode, Sitzungs-Periode 1868, No. 60, attachment, Bundesarchiv Potsdam, Reichstag, Film 30735, Nr. 406.

14. "Schulze-Delitzsch," *Allgemeine Deutsche Biographie*.

15. For reasons of length and internal unity, this chapter gives disproportionately short shrift to rural consumer cooperatives in Germany. While such cooperatives were numerous and important to rural communities they were so totally unconnected to the larger urban associations economically, socially, and politically that it is difficult to deal with both at once or in parallel.

16. On Raiffeisen and the Raiffeisen movement, see Faust, *Geschichte der Genossenschaftsbewegung*, 323-86.

17. Faust, *Geschichte der Genossenschaftsbewegung*, 387-416.

18. On Pfeiffer, see Karl Bittel, *Eduard Pfeiffer und die deutsche Konsumgenossenschaftsbewegung*, Schriften des Vereins für Sozialpolitik: Untersuchungen über Konsumvereine, Band 151 (Munich/Leipzig, 1915).

19. Hasselmann, *Geschichte der deutschen Konsumgenossenschaften*, 141.

20. Hasselmann, *Geschichte der deutschen Konsumgenossenschaften*, 133-34.

21. Bernard H. Moss, *The Origins of the French Labor Movement, 1830-1914: The Socialism of Skilled Workers* (Berkeley, 1976), 3.

22. Heinrich Kaufmann, *Kurzer Abriß der Geschichte des Zentralverbandes deutscher Konsumvereine*, (Hamburg, 1928), Table II., 332.

23. Göhre, *Die deutschen Arbeiter-Konsumvereine*, 122ff.

24. Adolph von Elm, *Die Genossenschaftsbewegung* (Berlin, 1901), 10.

25. Kaufmann, *Kurzer Abriß*, table, p. 341. The precise definition was people employed for wages in industrial enterprises; agricultural laborers and civil servants were in addition to this number.

26. Weuster, *Theorie der Konsumgenossenschaftsentwicklung*, 157-58.

27. Weuster, *Theorie der Konsumgenossenschaftsentwicklung*, 234-35.

28. Gert-Joachim Glaeßner, *Arbeiterbewegung und Genossenschaft: Entstehung und Entwicklung der Konsumgenossenschaften in Deutschland am Beispiel Berlins*, Marburger Schriften zum Genossenschaftswesen 68, (Göttingen, 1989), 63; Göhre, *Die deutschen Arbeiter-Konsumvereine*, 72ff.

29. Glaeßner, *Arbeiterbewegung und Genossenschaft*, 67 ff.

30. Göhre, *Die deutschen Arbeiter-Konsumvereine*, 424.

31. *Produktion*, (Hamburg, 1910), last (unnumbered) page. This is a trilingual English-French-German publication issued by the Produktion cooperative.

32. *Bericht der Darmstädter Consum-, Spar-, und Produktions-Genossenschaft über das Neunte Geschäftsjahr 1908/09* (Darmstadt, c. 1909).

33. F. Staudinger, *Von Schue-Delitzsch bis Kreuznach: Eine Festgabe zur Errichtung des Gesamtverbandes der deutschen Konsumvereine am 17. und 18. Mai 1903*, (Hamburg, 1903).

34. Hermann Fleißner, *Genossenschaften und Arbeiterbewegung*, 2nd ed. (Jena, 1924), 19.

35. Karl Kautsky, *Consumvereine und Arbeiterbewegung* (Vienna, 1897).

36. Fleißner, *Genossenschaften und Arbeiterbewegung*, 21.

37. Heinrich Kaufmann, *Die Stellungnahme der Sozialdemohratie zur Konsumgenossenschaftsbewegung* (Hamburg, 1911), 40-49; Weuster, *Theorie du Konsumgenossenschaftsentwicklung*, 164 and 235; Elm, *Die Genossenschefts bewegung*, 16-18.

38. Oskar Dorth, *Geschichte der Konsumvereinsentwicklung in Rheinland und Westfalen*, Diss., Münster, 1913, 48, cited by Klaus Kluthe, *Genossenschaften und Staat in Deutschland: Systematische und historische Analysen deutscher Genossenschaftspolitik bezogen auf den Zeitraum 1914 bis zur Gegenwart* (Berlin, 1985), 48.

39. Reinhold Henzler, "Genossenschaft und christliche Gesellschaftspolitik," *Christliche Neuordnung von Wirtschaft und Gesellschaft*, ed., Heinrich Krehle (Munich, 1950) 51.

40. Quoted by Fritz Klein, "Die Konsumgenossenschaften," in Krehle, 157.

41. On the Catholic consumer cooperatives generally, see Fritz Klein, *Selbsthilfe aus christlicher Verantwortung: Die Geschichte der christlichen Konsumverein* (Recklinghausen, c. 1967.) On Schlack, see also Weuster, *Theorie der Konsumgenossenschaftsentwicklung*, 255-57.

42. *Festschrift zum 25 jährigen Bestehen des Konsumvereins Wohlfahrt e. G.m.b.H. Essen-Altenessen*, (n.p., 1928), 26.

43. Klein, *Selbsthilfe aus christlicher Verantwortung*, 18.

44. Robert Gellately, *The Politics of Economic Despair: Shopkeepers and German Politics 1890-1914*, (London, 1974), 70-71.

45. E. Suchsland, *Notwahrheiten über Konsumvereine: Eine Diskussionsrede vom Kampfplatz mit der Sozialdemokratie*, (Halle, 1904, and *Los von den Konsumvereinen und Warenhäusern. Eine Mahnung und eine Bitte an alle Vaterlandsfreunde zur Erhaltung des gewerblichen Mittelstandes in Stadt und Land, als des Fundamentes unseres Staatswesens und unserer Kultur* (Halle, 1904).

46. On the Imperial League against social democracy and its campaign against consumer co-ops, see Max Radestock and Heinrich Kaufmann, *Der Zentralverband deutscher Konsumvereine im Jahre 1909: Berichte des Vorstandes und des Generalsekretärs über die Entwicklung des Zentralverbandes deutscher Konsumvereine im Verbandsjahr 1909* (Hamburg, 1910), 215.

47. *Ibid.*, 221.

48. *Ibid.*, 223.

49. The parliamentary debates became earnest with the government's bill of December 1895 (*Stenographische Berichte über die Verhandlungen des Reichstages 9. Legislaturperiode, IV. Session 1895/96*, No. 34). See the minutes, motions, petitions, and so forth collected in Bundesarchiv Berlin, Reichstag, Film 30737, Nr. 412 (Der Gewerbebetrieb der Konsumvereine 1891-1903).

50. See Kluthe, *Genossenschaften und Staat in Deutschland*, 84; Hermann Fleissner, *Zur Geschichte der Umsatzsteuer in Sachsen: Nebst Urteilen und Gutachten über die Umsatzsteuer* (Hamburg, 1904). In 1904, the ZdK's newspaper, the

Konsumgenossenschaftliche Rundschau, carried 98 articles in one year concerning the taxation question.

51. Erwin Hasselmann, *und trug hundertfaltige Frucht: Ein Jahrhundert konsumgenossenschaftlicher Selbsthilfe in Stuttgart* (Stuttgart, 1964), 85.

52. Fleissner, *Zur Geschichte der Umsatzsteuer in Sachsen,* 18.

53. J. F. Schill, "Internationale Statistik des Konsumgenossenschaftswesens," 1913 (printed 2-page chart found in Bundesarchiv Berlin, Materialsammlung "Geschichte der Konsumgenossenschafte", Nr. 24).

54. On consumer cooperation during and after the First World War, see the appropriate sections of Hasselmann, *Geschichte der deutschen konsumgenossenschaften.*

55. Arnd Kluge, *Frauen und Genossenschaften in Deutschland: Von der Mitte des 19. Jahrhunderts bis zur Gegenwart* (Marburger Beiträge zum Genossenschaftswesen 24), (Marburg, 1992), Graphik 1, 32. In the other federations, women held only between 5 and 15 percent of the shares.

56. Kluge, *Frauen und Genossenschaften,* Tabelle 2, 77; also 38ff.

57. Vorstand des Verbandes ostdeutscher Konsumvereine, "Was Habe ich beim Einkauf zu beachten? Die Frau in der Genossenschaftsbewegung" (Hamburg, c. 1928), 25.

58. Klein, *Selbsthilfe aus christlicher Verantwortung,* 20 (and the same for the following quotation).

59. See, for example, the clippings from the Communist press in 1931 concerning consumer cooperatives in Bundesarchiv Berlin, Materialsammlung "Geschichte der Konsumgenossenschaften," Nr 13; and the articles from the SPD press in Nr. 14.

60. For example, Anton Kiesewetter, *Genossenschaft, Stand und Volkstum: Vortrag, gehalten am 13. November 1927 . . .*; and later and more definitively Eugen Schach, *Nationalsozialismus und Genossenschaftswesen* (Nationalsozialistische Bibliothek, Heft 32), (München, 1931).

61. See, generally, Kuno Bludau, *Nationalsozialismus und Genossenschaften,* (Hanover, 1968).

62. Bludau, *Nationalsozialismus und Genossenschaften,* 94ff and esp. 120-26.

63. The argument is that business with nonmembers is essentially speculative and profit-seeking in nature; it encourages the cooperative to expand without a solid foundation of committed members and their share capital on which to base the expanded volume of business in the long term.

64. Gunther Aschoff and Eckart Henningsen, *The German Cooperative System. Its History, Structure and Strength* (Frankfurt a.M., 1985), 96.

65. Kluge, *Frauen und Genossenschaften,* Tabelle 4, 78.

66. Erwin Hasselmann, *Von der Lebensmittel-Association zur Coop. Die unternehmerische Verbraucherselbsthilfe im Wandel der Zeit* (Hamburg, 1984), 89ff.

67. Aschoff and Henningsen, *The German Cooperative System,* 99.

68. Oswald Hahn, "Konsumgenossenschaften im internationalen Vergleich," in *Forschungsinstitut für Genossenschaftswesen an der Universität Erlangen-Nürnberg, Veranstaltungen,* Band 10: *Konsumgenossenschaften,* 16 November 1987, Tabelle 2, 28.

Chapter 11

The Consumer Co-op in Japan: Building Democratic Alternatives to State-Led Capitalism

Ruth Grubel

While in many other industrialized countries consumer cooperatives are struggling to survive and find a meaningful role, these organizations are thriving in Japan. Not only are there 19 million members nationwide, consumer co-ops represent 20 percent of the households in Japan. In fact, the Japanese Consumers' Cooperative Union (JCCU) has become the largest consumer organization in the country. Therefore, it is not an unexpected revelation that the largest consumer cooperative in the world is in Japan; Coop Kobe with over 1.2 million members.[1] As we consider why consumer cooperatives appear to be so successful in Japan, we must ask whether that success is based on uniquely Japanese characteristics, or whether their experience provides lessons that can be replicated around the world. For example, are there unique aspects of Japanese society which make it especially fertile for consumer cooperation? Has the cooperative movement there been the beneficiary of particularly skillful management? Are government policies in Japan unusually supportive of co-ops? Has competition from the private sector been weak enough to allow energetic growth in the cooperatives? Perhaps most important of all is the question that will be the focus of this chapter: Have consumer cooperatives in Japan achieved financial stability by "selling their souls" and trading their core value of democracy (member participation) for business acumen?

The case of cooperatives in Japan has been particularly compelling because, in spite of rapid economic growth and a nominal democratic system, the pervasiveness of government influence in Japanese economy and society has made many observers skeptical about the presence of any genuine bottom-up initiatives in organizations such as consumer co-ops. Can participatory democracy flourish when civil society is moving according to state directives? In *Civil Society and Political Theory*, Jean Cohen and Andrew Arato state that a democratized civil society is a vital factor in making political parties and government bodies more open.[2] Furthermore, Robert Putnam extols the virtues of "civic engagement" and mourns its decline in the United States because he argues that community groups can supplement government efforts to address social problems.[3] However, in Sheldon Garon's analysis of various Japanese groups, he cautions that Putnam's understanding of "civic tradition" precludes the traditional participation of organizations in Japan where there are close ties between community groups and the government.[4] In fact, even without coercion, many of these groups concur with state directives, often because they themselves have been involved in formulating the policies. Furthermore, a number of cooperatives, including some consumer co-ops, have political affiliations, making them less than neutral players in the system.

However, in contrast to many of its fellow consumer cooperatives, Coop Kobe is not aligned with any political party and does not receive any government funds, but with its large membership, it has the potential to influence community life and public policy in the Kobe area. In the search for factors leading to the success of Japan's cooperatives, I believe that Coop Kobe offers a valuable case study for two reasons. First, in a country of strong businesses and strong government, the Coop developed into a successful alternative for shopping and participatory decision making. Second, Coop Kobe addresses some of the most vexing problems that persist in established democracies around the world: how to sustain economic vitality without achieving pathological income gaps, how to encourage environmental responsibility without government regulation, and how to encourage grassroots participation, particularly by women, in making and implementing community-building decisions.

After briefly describing the features of civil society and democracy in the Japanese setting, this chapter will introduce an abbreviated history of the consumer cooperative movement in that country, and follow with a case study of Coop Kobe, the largest and most financially successful of its type. A second case study will focus on the Seikatsu Club, a group that concentrates on environmental issues and has been particularly adept at maintaining member participation and activism. Finally, an attempt will be made to assess the factors that have contributed to the success of these cooperatives.

Civil Society in Japan

Positioned between the state (government bureaucracy at all levels) and private business and industry is the third sector known as civil society. Here are all the associations that are independent of the other two sectors, beginning with families, and ranging from religious groups to social movements. Their primary role is to mediate between the individual and the economic and state sectors by filling gaps in services and providing refuge from the alienation common in large, impersonal institutions. Ohta Hiroshi[5] is particularly positive about the function of third sector associations:

Such mediating structures are indispensable in a robust democratic society because they generate and maintain certain values that are constitutional to the society. Often the most innovative and enduring citizens' efforts . . . come from the independent, third sector.[6]

As independent bodies, associations within civil society are established and maintained by their own members, but Cohen and Arato emphasize the necessity of institutionalizing their existence through laws. Without both self-creation ("independent action") and institutionalization, the survival and progress of civil society are threatened.[7] It is this point of institutionalization that creates problems in Japan. Within the Japanese context, can any organization that meets the institutional requirements of national laws actually maintain its independent action?

Karel van Wolferen, one of the foremost analysts of the Japanese "system," doubts that any true civil society exists outside the control of government and the power system.[8] Chalmers Johnson also focuses on the ubiquitous role of the state in directing economic and social policy. Johnson argues that most American observers of the Japanese political system attempt to find examples there of pluralist dynamics more familiar to their own experience in the United States, but they do not recognize the power wielded by the national government bureaucrats working either through their ministries or through the influential positions they attain in private firms after retirement from government service.[9] However, the control exercised by the state in Japan is not usually overt, but what John Owen Haley calls "administrative guidance" or "authority without power" because there are few legal means of coercing compliance. Yet because of the close relationship between the bureaucrats and powerful economic and social groups, a consensus is sought early in the discussion process, even if it requires compromise, so that once a directive is issued, compliance will follow without pressure.[10]

In spite of the perception that private associations in Japan are constantly under the influence of the state, the dynamics of administrative guidance demonstrate that this oversight is more complex than heavy-handed regulation. In fact, Sheldon Garon's case studies of selected Japanese groups both before and after World War II indicate not only that many middle-class group members collaborated with government directives but also that a significant number of the public policies were actually initiated by the groups themselves. As Garon argues, Japanese "moral suasion" programs were relatively successful in addressing a myriad of social problems because of the active involvement of citizen groups in formulating and implementing them. Therefore, it is too simplistic to see such groups as either antigovernment victims of repression or as fanatical jingoists, ready mindlessly to do the state's bidding.[11]

Although there are significant examples of Japanese civic groups organizing volunteers to accomplish important social goals, Ohta claims that Japan has an "underdeveloped" third sector or civil society, primarily because of political and legal barriers to private, nonprofit public interest groups. However, let us examine the case of the consumer cooperatives that were created by public-minded citizens, often in defiance of government resistance, and have attempted to institutionalize a range of social programs as well as a democratic alternative to traditional retail stores.

Background on the Cooperative Movement in Japan

Cooperative societies developed in a variety of forms before the nineteenth century, but the beginning of the modern cooperative movement is generally recognized as 1844 when the Rochdale Equitable Pioneer Society, or the Rochdale cooperative, was established in Great Britain. By 1854, the basic rules for operating their cooperative had been refined into eight principles:

1. Democracy—one member, one vote
2. Open membership—low down-payment, unlimited membership
3. Fixed and limited interest on capital—guaranteed interest on down-payment
4. Distribution of the surplus as dividend on purchases
5. Cash trading—no credit purchases
6. Pure and unadulterated goods
7. Education—intellectual improvement of members and their families
8. Political and religious neutrality[12]

These principles developed by the Rochdale founders served as the basis for the world cooperative movement and the International Cooperative Alliance, which in turn helped to establish cooperative societies around the world, including many in Japan.[13]

In Japan, mutual assistance groups were organized during the Edo period (1603-1867) to alleviate the hunger and poverty that affected large segments of the population. At about the time that the Rochdale cooperative was being established, rural credit unions came into existence in Japan, and when the Meiji period began in 1868, cooperatives were created in a variety of industries. Most noteworthy among these new cooperatives were those for the silk and tea industries, which utilized their new associations to achieve quality control and increase exports. In order to encourage the development of guild-like organizations as seen in contemporary Germany, the Japanese parliament passed the Industry Cooperative Law in 1900. Although little progress occurred in the first decade, sustained government assistance, the improvement of the Industry Cooperative Law in 1921, and the establishment of the Central Industry Cooperative Bank (Norinchukin) in 1923 demonstrated that the government was serious about organizing cooperatives. Independent, public-spirited individuals, such as Kagawa Toyohiko, founder of Coop Kobe, breathed life into the cooperative movement at this time. However, as Japan became more involved in wartime activities in the 1930s, government control of the cooperatives increased apace. In fact, in the final years of World War II, Japanese agricultural cooperatives were being used as a means of organizing the rural populace, and for ensuring food supplies for the war effort.[14]

After the war, significant policy changes were carried out during the Occupation by Allied Forces. For the rural population, the dramatic land reform program, which eliminated absentee landlords and redistributed farm land to tenant workers, and the 1947 Agricultural Cooperative Law which created smaller local cooperatives, made cooperative organizations more democratic.[15] However, because of management problems, government assistance had to be sought again for the agricultural cooperatives. Furthermore, because a large percentage of farmers belonged to cooperatives, those organizations became potent allies for the conservative political parties they supported. In turn, the long postwar reign of the conservative Liberal Democratic Party made the cooperatives more closely linked to government agencies in their administration.

Of course agricultural cooperatives were not the only variety that evolved in postwar Japan. In 1945, the Cooperative League of Japan (CLJ) was begun as a national organization for Consumer Co-ops, and in 1951 it was superseded by the Japanese Consumers' Cooperative Union (JCCU). The Kobe activist, Kagawa Toyohiko, was instrumental in organizing the CLJ, and served as the first president of the JCCU. The latter organization continues to represent Japan's consumer cooperatives through its membership in the International Cooperative Alliance, and through a variety of other functions. For example, a broad spectrum of co-op brand products are manufactured and marketed through the coordinating efforts of the JCCU. Even today, the cooperative philosophy of Kagawa is the foundation for JCCU's activities, and this attitude has influenced policy in many of the member co-ops. His principles, obviously inspired by the Rochdale founders, are as follows:

1.   Profit sharing
2.   Human economics
3.   Sharing of capital
4.   Non-exploitation
5.   Delegation of authority
6.   Political neutrality
7.   Focus on Education[16]

Unlike the legal perspectives established in many other countries in relation to their cooperatives, Japan's laws treat these associations differently according to their type. As a result, agricultural co-ops, for example, have a very different legal position compared to credit unions or consumer cooperatives, each of which has a separate document to establish its parameters. Although restrictive elements were added to the 1948 Consumer Cooperative Law, which was created specifically for such associations, it was forged during the Allied Occupation when Japanese authorities were strongly encouraged to incorporate democratic ideals, so Article 1 of the Law describes its purpose as: "To provide for the spontaneous development of consumers association organizations, with the hope of enhancing the stability of the people's livelihood and improving the culture of daily life."[17] However, the Consumer Cooperative Law made consumer co-ops newly liable for income taxes, both to the national and prefectural governments, and prohibited them from expanding beyond a single prefecture.[18] Nevertheless, consumer cooperatives sprang up around the country, and were joined by similar associations based on separate legal foundations providing insurance, health care, housing, university stores, and financial services, among others. Although government regulations may have helped or hindered the establishment of cooperatives at various points in Japanese history, the reality is that the ideological orientation of the founders and the subsequent political affiliation of the association affected the nature of government relations with each cooperative group. For example, many cooperatives, including consumer cooperatives, were formed as an outgrowth of the labor movement, and a significant number had communist or socialist origins. As a result, ties were often established with sympathetic political parties, and in response, government policies were formulated to support or restrict them, depending upon the ideological preferences of those in power.

In addition to experiences with government interference, co-ops in Japan also have had a history of resistance from business and industry competitors who felt threatened by the success of the consumer cooperatives.[19] By charter, they are required to return profits to members. However, in order to stay alive, consumer cooperatives must compete with a variety of for-profit retailers, so must be sensitive to quality and price factors that dominate the capitalist enterprise. Because they are to be member-directed and oriented organizations, anticooperative actions have often focused on preventing nonmembers from shopping at co-op stores. The 1948 Consumers Cooperative Law clearly prohibits non-members from utilizing co-op services. However, the strictness with which this rule is enforced has varied according to the political pressure from competitors. Although the provision was included in the 1948 law to protect the cooperatives from exploitation by nonmembers, anti-co-op movements have attempted to force stronger government monitoring of the co-op stores and refusal of sales to nonmembers.[20] The cooperatives argue that potential members cannot make educated decisions about whether to join without first using the services.

In contrast to consumer cooperatives in Europe and North America, which developed in the nineteenth century as a means of addressing poverty, the cooperative movement in Japan began to grow most dramatically in the 1960s when concerns for food safety and consumer rights came to the forefront. Consequently, the dividends based on purchases and membership investments are not regarded with the same importance in Japanese co-ops that they are in their Western counterparts, although they continue to be an integral part of member benefits. In fact, the difference between worker-orientation in the European and North American cooperative movement compared to the consumer-orientation in Japan has led to differences in membership makeup. For example, as household managers, women constitute the overwhelming majority of members in Japanese co-ops, while there is a comparatively larger proportion of men in the Western associations.[21]

In spite of problems resulting from government involvement, competitor resistance, internal management, and even economic conditions, the current total membership in Japanese cooperatives is around thirty million people.[22] Due to the significant variation in member participation and government support for different cooperatives in Japan, I have selected two case studies; associations that have little direct government subsidy, but that attempt to involve members as much as possible in the organizational decision making. The first case concerns of one of the oldest consumer cooperatives in Japan. In fact, without including the predecessors of Coop Kobe, the history of cooperation in Japan is a great deal shorter. Much of the pioneering effort to establish such associations occurred within the Kansai cooperatives, which became Coop Kobe, so that history is summarized below. In contrast, the second case describing the Seikatsu Club is representative of the numerous cooperatives that had their origins in the 1960s.

Consumers Cooperative Kobe (Coop Kobe)

The current entity known as Coop Kobe is the result of a merger between two consumer cooperatives in Japan's Hyogo prefecture. In 1962, the Nada Coop and the Kobe Coop were the two largest in Japan, so when they merged to form the Nadakobe Coop, they formed one of the biggest consumer cooperatives in the world. Twenty-nine years later, when the total membership exceeded the one million mark, the Nadakobe Coop was renamed "Consumers Cooperative Kobe" or Coop Kobe. Although these milestones may appear to reflect an organization growing steadily in a supportive environment, considering the many crises along the way, its survival, much less growth, has been miraculous.

History of the Co-op

Both the Kobe and Nada Coops were established within two months of each other in the spring of 1921, and they both shared the common involvement of Kagawa Toyohiko, a social activist, Christian leader, and prolific author. In the years following World War I, the Japanese economy began to decline, and laborers who had not benefited from the boom years of the war faced even worse conditions such as unemployment and food shortages. Despite government disapproval, labor union activities attracted increasing numbers of supporters and mass protests such as the Kobe "rice riots" took place to bring attention to high prices and shortages of food. Kagawa was living in the slums of Shinkawa near Kobe, trying to alleviate the stark poverty and hopelessness there with a variety of social programs and religious activities. He believed that Christianity demanded social involvement and personal sacrifice to improve the lives of the powerless.[23] Because he was unusually well-read and familiar with community development efforts around the world, Kagawa was seen as a valuable resource for reformers and activists across Japan. Although he believed that the capitalist system exploited workers to benefit the few, as a pacifist, he did not agree with the violent revolutionary tactics favored by communists trying to create a worker-centered society. Kagawa argued that labor unions needed to have legally established rights, and that they should work through the system to transform it into a just society for all.

In addition to his efforts on behalf of labor groups, Kagawa began to organize cooperative associations to establish member-owned enterprises. His first cooperatives, a restaurant and a toothbrush factory, were failures, but he learned from his mistakes, and continued to believe in the British guild socialist model to empower the poverty-stricken Japanese, both in the cities and in the countryside. Of particular merit, in Kagawa's estimation, was the democratic organization of the cooperatives in which each member, regardless of the amount of investment made, had just one vote.[24] His work with laborers naturally led to the support of worker cooperatives to provide goods and services to employees of various companies. Farm laborers were in particularly difficult circumstances, so cooperatives to provide credit and other forms of assistance made a significant impact. Of course Kagawa did not single-handedly build these many cooperatives. Although he invested all of the income from his books in the co-ops and charity programs in the slums of Shinkawa, the consumer co-ops, in particular, needed significant financial backing and management expertise.

Together with a number of labor activists, Kagawa established the Kobe Purchasers' Cooperative on April 12, 1921. The initial membership included six hundred households and eighteen employees. As the elected president of the new organization, Fukui Suteichi brought many years of experience in business, which was especially valuable for the venture.[25] Nearby in Sumiyoshi, a wealthy businessman, Nasu Zenji, was concerned about the poverty and degradation he saw in many of the urban communities around him, so he organized a group to discuss means of improving society. Kagawa Toyohiko was one of the "experts" consulted by the group to recommend specific strategies, and he suggested that they organize a cooperative. This idea was supported by Hirao Hachisaburo, a future Minister of Education, who had spent some time in the West and had first-hand knowledge of cooperatives there. So the Nada Producers' Cooperative was founded on May 26, 1921, with three hundred members and six employees. Because Nasu was selected as the first president, the new Coop benefited from his successful business experience and his social conscience.[26]

Unfortunately, the young cooperatives had to struggle immediately, not only with the expected trials of establishment, but also with strong resistance from businesses that viewed them as competitors, and from government officials who regarded the co-ops as communist, or at least akin to the labor unions. However, the capable leadership and efforts of the members allowed both organizations to overcome financial crises and expand their operations. One of the factors that contributed to the growth in membership was the establishment of women's guilds or *kateikai*, which organized educational opportunities and activities for the co-op women. In fact, the focus on educational and cultural activities has been an on-going strategy for these cooperatives because the founders (Kagawa in particular) saw them not just as retail operations but as tools for improving members' lifestyles as well. An example of the educational material produced by the early Coop was a series of nine "Consumers' Cooperative Pamphlets" published between 1922 and 1924. Each was focused on a different theme, and written with a different style. One particularly successful Pamphlet included an article entitled "Consumers' Cooperative Story" by Hayashi Hikoichi, and described a Coop campaign in the words of Shizuko, a hypothetical young woman. Because Hayashi was the managing director of the Kobe Consumers' Cooperative at the time, he was well aware of all the trials and joys involved with the cooperative movement.[27]

During World War II the co-ops and several leaders, including Kagawa, were targeted for special scrutiny because they were suspected of inappropriate activities. Kagawa himself became an apologist for Japan and severely criticized the actions of the Allied Powers, but he remained suspicious of Japanese government motives toward his domestic programs. Most of the Coop buildings in the Kobe area were destroyed by air raids, and many employees were called into military service, but as in the past, extraordinary efforts by members revived the associations after the war. In fact, the immediate post-war years demonstrated again the urgent need for cooperative activities. With food scarce and communities in turmoil, the co-ops attempted to secure dependable sources for food, and reinstated the culture and education programs to enrich the lives of members who felt so deprived.

In the early years, co-op members were served by the "roundman" system in which employees visited homes each morning to take orders, and then delivered them later in the day. Some small self-service stores were opened early on as an additional service, but the main focus was on the delivery system. After the war, changing social conditions and competition from other retailers led the co-ops in Kobe to open more self-service stores, and in 1961 the first supermarket opened its doors. By that time, the two co-ops were beginning to overlap geographically, and the decision was made to merge.[28] The new Nadakobe Coop redoubled its efforts to produce healthful items, and established a testing laboratory to evaluate products itself. In many respects the organization was adapting to the changing times, but difficulties began to emerge within the Coop.

As the co-op continued to grow and provide more services, the employees began to demand a bigger voice in decision making, and a period of labor-management disputes ensued. When the 1973 OPEC oil embargo created shortages in Japanese stores, co-op membership actually went up dramatically as consumers sought means of ensuring dependable sources for their necessities. A much larger membership gave the co-op strength but it was far more difficult to maintain the democratic participatory system, which had been part of the "Kagawa Spirit." Many of those in leadership positions did not have the expertise to efficiently direct a huge organization while incorporating opinions from members and employees. Until after the war, it had been difficult to recruit university graduates into co-op management because the stigma of retail operations as the lowest in the social hierarchy made it unattractive to well-educated young people. Most of the top co-op managers had worked their way up through the organization or through other businesses, and had valuable experience, but few tools to deal with the rapidly changing situation. As a result, the rift between labor and management widened further, a strike took place, and the survival of the co-op was threatened. In 1978 the labor dispute reached a climax. The union elected new leadership and the management side replaced all permanent directors who had been in their positions since before the War.[29] Many young leaders with experience in the successful university co-ops were recruited to help define a new direction for the organization. Under their guidance, competition from new retailers was met more aggressively with new store openings, and more emphasis was placed in developing co-op name products, which could be trusted for high quality and competitive prices.[30] Because the new leaders were committed to more collaborative labor-management relations, significant adjustments were made, and employees were given new cooperative management education and training opportunities that would, in turn, give them additional promotion options and make them more valuable members of the co-op team.

During the late 1970s and into the 1980s, a large number of the community cooperatives in the United States struggled with similar problems of adjusting to social changes and competition from other stores. A significant number, including the Berkeley Coop, with which the Nadakobe Coop had a sister relationship, went bankrupt as they focused too much on how the world should be, and not on the challenges of the real world.[31] However, post-mortem evaluations of failed cooperatives in the United States produced recommendations that were far different from the path taken by successful Japanese cooperatives. In one such analysis, Craig Cox notes that:

> Participatory organizations are like that. They mature, they become bureaucratized, they lose track of the larger world. . . . As members age, the organization becomes gradually less interesting, less fulfilling, less revolutionary. In order to survive and flourish, in fact, coops and other alternative groups need to stay small, on the fringe, always on the brink of collapse. Their workers must be underpaid and transient, or the organization loses track of its real purpose: changing society.[32]

In contrast, the co-op response to the crises of the 1970s in Japan was to instill more professionalism into the workforce and to strive for financial stability. Daiei, the largest retailer in Japan, also originated in the Kansai area, and recently moved its headquarters to Kobe, thus intensifying the competition. However, the presence of such able competitors as Daiei and Jusco may have prevented the co-op from becoming complacent. The non-profit status of the organization allowed it to reduce prices and compete on that basis, but the co-op also offered members a biannual rebate based on their purchases, together with interest on their capital investment as specified in the early Rochdale Principles. Additionally, technological innovations such as computerization of many functions were adopted aggressively, and in 1989 Coop Kobe was the top retailer in Hyogo Prefecture with sales of 298 billion yen and 141 stores, while Daiei was a close second, commanding sales of 249 billion yen through their forty-eight stores.[33] In spite of their business successes, co-op decision makers also recognized the need to experiment with methods of keeping the cooperative message alive and meaningful to its members, employees, and to the communities where they were located.

Opportunities for Participation of Coop Members

Ironically, one of the management changes made as a result of the labor disputes had the side effect of improving the participatory nature of the Japanese cooperatives. For the sake of economizing, the roundman system, which was labor intensive and inefficient, was discontinued and it was replaced with a group purchasing system. The core of the new group purchasing method was a concept that originated in Japan—the *han*. Each *han* group is made up of five to ten members who make weekly orders of co-op items on forms that today can be computer scanned. One *han* member is chosen as the leader to coordinate the orders and to accept their delivery on the appointed day each week. In recognition of the effort required to sort group orders, a refund is made to each *han* member every six months based on the value of items ordered during that period. From the co-op perspective, *han* involvement builds loyalty to co-op products and activities among the members, and permits more efficient distribution of the food orders. For example, because orders are received a week before delivery, it is possible for the distribution centers to arrange transport of perishable items just in time without expensive long-term storage in a supermarket or warehouse.[34]

Although the *han* system allows the co-op to stay competitive with other retailers, the groups have also proven to be an effective means for members to participate in the decision making for the organization as a whole. Not only are the *han* groups represented by their own members selected for local steering committees, they are ultimately represented on the *Coop Board of Directors*. Each of Coop Kobe's eight business districts selects a member representative who is approved by the Annual Congress to serve on the thirty six-member Board of Directors. Then within the eight districts are a total of 92 localities, each of which has a thirty- to forty-member steering committee, bringing the total membership of these local steering committees to 2,900. Through the committees, *han* members are asked to test new products, give feedback on Coop policies, and help plan autonomous volunteer, sports, and cultural activities for their own localities.[35] The opportunities available to *han* members give them a voice in Coop affairs and a ready-made community group that can be mobilized for a variety of purposes. For each level of participation, the Coop offers courses for the members to understand the structure of the organization and how they can contribute to the decision making. However, even for Coop members who are not able to participate in a *han* group, there are means of becoming involved in the organization's affairs. In 1982 a Coop channeler system was established to allow 2,000 members to express their viewpoints by completing detailed questionnaires four times during their one-year terms. Additionally, a member forum is held in each local area twice a year to allow all members to meet with Coop executives and discuss a full range of issues, including complaints. Other opportunities for member input include a merchandise committee made up of member representatives who screen the quality, pricing, and labeling of goods, which are being proposed for introduction, as well as a Coop hot line that accepts collect calls from members who discuss a wide variety of opinions. Finally, each Coop store has a suggestion box so that anyone with a comment or suggestion can submit it in anonymity, if so desired.

In order to assist the members in staying abreast of Coop developments, a weekly newsletter is delivered to *han* groups together with the merchandise order forms. News about the range of Coop activities, new products, member interviews, and producer profiles are just some of the items included in the newsletter titled *Kyo-do-*. In addition to recipes and tips for achieving a healthier lifestyle, *Kyo-do-* also publishes notices of upcoming Coop meetings, descriptions of meeting proceedings, the annual budget, and appeals for members to participate in decision making, cultural, and volunteer bodies. It is through the *Kyo-do-* that the Coop philosophy of sharing and caring for the earth is reinforced. Personal testimonies are often featured, not only to inform readers about the merits of a particular Coop product, but also to thank member volunteers for assistance rendered, or to describe the satisfaction of participating in a particular activity as well. The last page of *Kyo-do-* usually highlights a particular Coop item and the individuals who produce it. Often the item is a food product, and a description is made of the location, the methodology, and the people who produce the rice, onions, or peaches. With the generous use of photographs and maps, the effort to bring the producer and consumer closer together is made effectively.

Production of Food Items

Even in the early years of the Nada Coop, the high quality of the products was seen as essential to the organization's survival. To earn the trust of the consumer, particularly in times of unscrupulous business practices, it was critical that the co-ops be able to maintain consistent high quality and stable pricing. When there were shortages, it was necessary for the Coop to maintain long-term relationships with dependable producers or even set up production facilities of their own. For example, as early as 1924, the Nada Coop built its own miso production plant.[36] Later, soy sauce, tofu, and *konnyaku* (devil's tongue jelly) were also produced at Coop facilities. Quality control was easier when the Coop was in charge of production, and today over 400 different items are made in the Coop "factory," but it is not practical to establish their own production facilities for all the items sold in Coop stores. Instead, arrangements have been made with subsidiaries to produce a broad range of food and nonfood items to Coop specifications. The role of the workers and Coop members is essential in determining what new products should be made by the association and its subsidiaries.

In addition to directing food processing operations, the Coop is active in maintaining links with agricultural producers of all kinds. Since the early

years, contracts have been made with rice farmers, and today, the list includes
a large variety of fruit and vegetable growers. The Coop has been working
with farmers to reduce chemical use in agricultural operations, and in 1991, the
"alternative food program" was established to create a category of items that
have been developed with special attention to safety and nutrition.[37] This
program includes eggs from free-range chickens as well as organic crops of
various kinds. Although many of the food items are produced in Japan, the co-
op has begun establishing ties with food producers overseas. For example, it
is importing bananas from a worker-owned plantation in the Philippines, which
is attempting to improve the lives of the laborers and their customers by
growing organic bananas. The story of this plantation and its bananas was
featured in one issue of *Kyo-do-*. For several months in 1996, positioned just
above the fresh produce displays in the Coop stores, were photographs of the
workers and their banana farm in the Philippines.

Outreach Programs

From the beginning, the Kobe and Nada Coops were dedicated to reaching
out to the disadvantaged in the community and the world. Many of the
Kateikai study groups focused, not just on building better lives for the co-op
members but on how these members could reach out to others in need. A
recent development from this outreach mission is the establishment, with
assistance from local governments, of several subsidiaries expressly designed
to offer job training and employment opportunities for the mentally and physically challenged.

Other outreach activities include coordination of volunteer activities,
primarily to serve the elderly and disabled with home assistance or just provide
companionship. Government officials have taken an interest in these volunteer
activities, and have cited them as models for community-based social support
programs. While this sort of government recognition may be completely
benign, it brings to mind the "moral suasion" campaigns recounted in Garon's
case studies wherein community volunteer activities are encouraged by the
government in order to limit the state liability for providing such social services.

In addition to local volunteer activities, Coop Kobe has a long history of
involvement with international peace and development issues. Donations for
victims of the atomic bombs in Nagasaki and Hiroshima amount to more than
ten million yen per year, and UNICEF contributions are usually double that
amount.[38] Through the years, thousands of co-op members have participated
in antinuclear and peace demonstrations in Japan and around the world. During
1997, awareness campaigns have been launched to educate co-op members

about land mines and the international movement to curtail their use. Some local co-op groups have focused their volunteer efforts on welcoming and assistance programs for international students and foreign nationals living in their neighborhoods.

Environmental Programs

As postwar co-op members became more educated and aware of health risks in the environment, their study groups and agenda representatives began to note the dangers of chemicals used in farming, food processing, and daily tasks such as laundry. Campaigns were launched to reduce chemical use among co-op producers, and development began on nonpolluting laundry and cleaning products. An "Environment Protection Fund" was created in 1991 with an initial investment of 50 million yen in a tax-exempt account to finance a range of environmental projects. In addition, June was designated as "Environment Month" to promote special activities, and these were followed-up by projects in October and November, which were selected as "reinforcement months."[39] In 1992, environmental issues were seen as so essential to the organization's philosophy, that the Coop Kobe Environmental Foundation was established.[40] Through the efforts of this Foundation, environmental sensitivity has been increased within the co-op family, as well as throughout the prefecture. For example, the product testing center checks toxicity levels in name-brand products in addition to the co-op brands to supplement government testing, which is irregular at best. The Environmental Foundation goes so far as to monitor acid rain and nitrogen dioxide levels in Hyogo prefecture to inform citizens of developing conditions. Unlike most retail operations, the co-op regularly encourages its shoppers to reduce waste and consumption of polluting substances such as detergents.

Recycling has become a big enterprise as well, with each co-op store placing bins near the doorway to encourage deposits of used milk cartons, styrofoam trays, and metal cans. Because many municipalities do not require, or even provide opportunities for recycling, the co-op has become famous for its promotion of package reuse. Thanks to the cooperation of thousands of members, the co-op reprocesses the milk cartons into paper products (toilet paper, tissues, paper towels, etc.), and the styrofoam into plastic benches and shopping baskets used in the stores. Other earth-friendly efforts include children's programs to increase environmental awareness, nonfreon refrigeration systems in the stores and warehouses, solar heating systems in some of the buildings, delivery trucks fueled by natural gas, vegetables grown with compost from waste created by fresh produce processing, and sturdy, affordable, and reusable shopping bags promoted as a better alternative to regular, disposable plastic shopping bags. In fact, shoppers at co-op stores, as at most Japanese supermarkets, bag their own groceries, but as an incentive to reuse bags, cashiers stopped handing out bags at check-outs beginning in June 1995.[41] Instead, if their own bags have not been brought along, co-op consumers are asked to donate five yen for each new regular plastic shopping bag taken to carry their purchases.

Perhaps in order to appear environmentally responsible, several of the co-op's major competitors have initiated recycling programs for items such as shopping bags and plastic bottles, and have been marketing various recycled products. Daiei also sells a line of sturdy canvas shopping bags to reduce the need for disposable plastic bags. Although there may be some question about the incentive for these actions and the philosophical commitment to protecting the environment, the recognition by regular retailers that consumers are attracted to responsible actions is an important first step. Of course the co-op goes far beyond the superficial efforts of its competitors, but it may have been instrumental in pressuring the other retailers to join in earth-friendly activities.

One of the most effective aspects of the Coop Kobe environmental programs is the educational effort. Through the special activities, recycling opportunities, shopping bag policy, earth-friendly food and household products, and weekly articles in the *Kyo-do-* newsletter, it is difficult to ignore the need for action and the role that each member can take in ameliorating the current situation.

Other Activities and Services

Because each local steering committee has the authority to organize unique activities on behalf of its members, there is a broad range of activities being pursued by Coop Kobe. Some of the primary ones have already been mentioned, but two more should be noted. The first is the sports program begun in 1985 and that by 1991 had 16,000 members involved with thirty-five different sports in 250 locations such as the twelve tennis courts around the Kobe area.[42] Evidently there was a great need for organized sports, which catered to co-op families. The second type of activity is specifically for children. Many of the co-op localities organize youth activities under the program known as Coop Rainbow Kids. Some of the activities include camping, gardening, excursions to farms (usually co-op producers) in Hokkaido and Kyushu, puppet shows, and special camps at one of the co-op resort villages.

In response to member suggestions, there are also many services that the co-op has established, either directly through its organization, or through subsidiaries. Some examples of these services include a special package delivery service for the elderly and disabled (*Fureai-bin*), full-service divisions for both wedding (*Annipa*) and funeral (*Cleri*) needs, mutual insurance, a travel agency, and three resort villages.[43] Like many of the large Japanese corporations, the co-op provides a full range of benefits to support members in almost every aspect of their lives.

The Earthquake Experience

When the Great Hanshin Earthquake hit on January 17, 1995, the Coop Kobe headquarters were completely destroyed and many of the stores were demolished or seriously damaged. Even more tragically, many Coop employees, their family members, as well as thousands of Coop members were killed or injured. Ironically, after the 1923 Great Kanto Earthquake in the Tokyo area, Kagawa Toyohiko had been one of the first to deliver food and and assistance. Now his home territory faced similar devastation, and coops around the country mobilized to help. Coop associations as far away as Okinawa sent personnel and relief goods as soon as possible. However, the city of Kobe had a standing commitment from Coop Kobe to supply food and other items in the case of an emergency, so the director of product planning called on the frantic city office on the day of the disaster to see what was needed. In spite of damage to their own stores and difficulties with logistics, Coop Kobe trucks were able to deliver 5,000 *inarizushi* meals, 3,000 boxed lunches, 792 liters of drinking water, 25,520 bread buns, and 2,700 flashlights to the nine ward offices on the initial day of the earthquake. By the second day, other co-ops joined the effort and delivered seven times the goods that had been sent the day before.[44]

Although thirteen of the Coop's 363 facilities, including the head office, were completely destroyed and 33 were partially damaged, operations were resumed as quickly as possible, not only to provide needed goods and keep the business going, but also to reassure the public. Kobe's mayor, Sasayama Kazutoshi, asked that as many Coop stores as possible be opened, because with nearly 70 percent of the households in the area holding membership, panic could be averted by having their familiar neighborhood landmark functioning as usual. On the first day, 97 out of the 155 total stores were able to open.[45] All of the central computers in the headquarters building were out of commission, but because there were still managers who remembered how records were kept twenty years earlier (before computerization) the contingency plan of accounting by hand required relatively little adjustment.

Perhaps even more noteworthy than the Coop's efforts to organize relief and resume operations, was the extraordinary performance of many individual Coop employees. After the earthquake, news reports were filled with stories of personal heroism, but many government officials and large company employees were reluctant to make decisions without approval from their superiors, and bureaucratic paralysis was the result.

"Street-level" Coop employees had been making requests for more discretion since the reorganization of the late 1970s. Innovations and quick responses to customer inquiries could not be realized without adequate authority in the hands of all the employees. Coop managers had struggled with the demands for more dispersal of power, while they worried about how decentralization would affect personnel matters such as promotion, salary, and educational development. Through their regular input opportunities and education on Coop philosophy, the workers were receiving some training in decision making, but the extent of their autonomy was not known until the earthquake crisis. A postearthquake survey found that under those extreme circumstances, even part-time workers were able to make decisions on the spot.

In his study of women and cooperatives, Sato Yoshiyuki discusses the superior performance of Coop Kobe members during the earthquake crisis.[46] Although they too were victims, that experience helped them understand instinctively what was needed. They worked at whatever remained of the Coop stores, not because they wanted to be paid, but because they were human. Because they happened to be Coop employees they had access to the personnel, goods, and the organization that could assist with the disaster response. According to Sato, administrative rules and procedures are not useful except in peaceful situations. A community must have developed a habit of cooperating if the members are to work effectively together during an emergency. If five Coop employees gathered to respond to the disaster, they would not ask where the supervisor was or what the procedures were. They would determine what they could do with the resources they had on hand, and act accordingly. Sato goes on to say that information and relationships are symbiotic in Japan, and the two are crucial in a crisis.

After the earthquake, an effort was made to rebuild the Coop by using the successes in the emergency performance as lessons for improvements. The *han* groups provide regular relationships for members in their daily life, and model a type of participatory democracy. They were shown to have been helpful relationship builders for earthquake response, so *han* membership has been promoted as a valuable aspect of the Coop system. Perhaps because of their *han* experiences, many Coop members have willingly continued to be involved in volunteer activities since the earthquake. As a result, eight Coop Volunteer Centers have been set up around the region to support those "grassroots" efforts by assisting with coordination of the volunteers and support given by the Coop itself.[47]

Coop Kobe and the Government

As with many social relationships in Japan, the public image of the Coop may hide a different dynamic, which is its true identity. Nevertheless, we can evaluate the extent of overt government involvement in its operations, and determine how the Coop has impacted the efficacy of its employees and greater membership.

One of the six basic principles of a cooperative society delineated by Kagawa Toyohiko is political neutrality. During his lifetime, Kagawa had many conflicts with the state, but he collaborated with government-sponsored activities when they pursued his shared goals of social service. Today too, Coop Kobe works with government bodies to maintain harmonious relations and to achieve mutual objectives such as the the establishment of a workplace for the mentally and physically challenged. However, anti-Coop campaigns have continued to recur, and government scrutiny has periodically caused difficulties for the Coop. Some of the product testing and environment monitoring efforts by the Coop could also be judged as adversarial efforts to embarrass government regulators. In each case when the Coop has been under fire from state restrictions, it has appealed to the public and its own members, and has received much positive support. In fact, the periods of attack on the cooperatives have been followed by increased Coop membership.[48]

The primary legal restrictions on consumer cooperatives appear to protect their competitors. For example, the prohibition against expanding beyond prefectural borders, or against allowing nonmembers to utilize Coop services serve to restrain Coop growth. As a result of competitor pressure on the government, consumer cooperatives have also had to comply with the Large-Scale Retailing Store Law, which necessitates consultation with local retailers before a new store can be built in a particular area.[49] Therefore, taken together with a substantial tax liability—30 percent national tax and 10 percent prefectural tax[50]—the restrictions on cooperatives in Japan are substantial. Of course the presence of state restrictions does not necessarily imply an adversarial role, but we may be able to conclude that the relationship between major traditional retailers and government officials is closer than that between Coop Kobe and representatives of the state.

Seikatsu Club

While Coop Kobe is the largest and most economically viable consumer cooperative in Japan, there are others that have attracted members who actively participate in environmental programs, and who enter politics as a result of their cooperative experience. One of the most noteworthy of these environmentally activist cooperatives is the Seikatsu (Lifestyle or Living) Club in Tokyo. Unlike Coop Kobe, which had its origins between the world wars, the Seikatsu Club began in 1965, but both cooperatives provided economic motivation for their initial members. Coming at the time when Japan was focusing all its energies on economic development, particularly for producers, prices had begun to rise, working hours were longer, education was focused on entrance examinations, and increasing pollution was seen as an inevitable side effect of industrialization. A group of young activists organized about 200 housewives in Tokyo's Setagaya ward to purchase 329 bottles of milk per day. With economies of scale permitted by the large purchase, each family could obtain milk at a significant discount. In just two years, the number of members had increased to 800, and the daily bottles purchased grew to 2,000.[51]

As the Seikatsu Club grew, it began to offer a larger variety of food and household products. Although the lower prices allowed by bulk purchasing were important to members, concern for product safety was at least as critical. The Seikatsu Club strove to select only those foods that were produced with minimal toxic chemicals and that were not full of artificial preservatives so that members could order items with confidence. At most other retail outlets, it was difficult to know how foods had been grown or prepared, and the push to achieve profitability encouraged many farmers and food companies to choose chemical shortcuts.

Like Coop Kobe, the Seikatsu Club was organized into *han* groups, which were the basic unit for ordering products, but they also became the core of activist movements and the setting for homemakers, in particular, to discover their voice by taking initiatives for themselves and their families. Participating in Club purchase decision making also proved to be a significant eye-opening experience for many members. For example, a decision was made to purchase mikan oranges from the former fishing community, which had contracted Minamata Disease (mercury poisoning) from the fish they caught in heavily polluted waters. However, as the relationship between the Minamata community and the Seikatsu Club members developed, the awareness emerged that herbicides and pesticides used in the cultivation of mikan were toxic to the growers as well as to their consumers in the Seikatsu Club. As a result, the Club members worked with the growers to significantly reduce the use of chemicals, and thereby to improve the health of all involved.

The Pure Soap Movement

In the early 1970s, many members of the Seikatsu Club began to notice that the detergents they were using for cleaning and laundry were chapping their hands and causing rashes on their children's skin. They also learned that such detergents were polluting the waterways and affecting the ecosystem. As a result, the Club decided to switch from these synthetic detergents to pure soap products, and began an information campaign in 1974. Three years later, a majority of Seikatsu Club members were using pure soap rather than detergents, so the cooperative stopped carrying detergents altogether.

In Kawasaki, a city near Tokyo where Seikatsu Club activities had spread, the pure soap movement progressed even further. A synthetic detergent council was formed, and in 1983 adopted a pure soap promotion policy so that by 1991, most of the 117 schools in the city were using pure soap in their cafeterias.[52] However, the rejection of detergents did not progress rapidly in all regions. In spite of efforts to pressure local governments to switch to pure soap, none of the municipalities petitioned (with more than twice the required number of signatures) agreed to stop using detergents. Frustrated with the resistance by bureaucrats in these government offices, Seikatsu Club members decided to run for local city council positions. The fact that most Club members were female and homemakers made them unusual candidates, but in 1979 the first Seikatsu Club member was elected in Nerima Ward of Tokyo, and more followed. By 1995, a total of 109 Club members had been elected to public office.

Among the most influential of these Seikatsu Club politicians was Terada Etsuko who began an effort to establish a Kawasaki City soap factory as soon as she was elected to her municipal council. With the backing of the mayor and the financial support of the citizens who made contributions in units of 1000 yen each, the Kawasaki Municipal Soap Plant began operation in November of 1989, and has become a business enterprise for the city.

Another spin-off of the pure soap movement was based on the relationship between the Seikatsu Club and an agricultural cooperative in Yamagata Prefecture. This Shonai Agricultural Coop provided much of the rice sold by the Seikatsu Club, and a strong relationship had developed between the members of the two organizations. A group of Seikatsu Club homemakers visited Yamagata each year to assist with aspects of rice production, and it was natural that they would discuss the issues of concern to them, including the use of synthetic detergents. In response, the Shonai Coop store eventually stopped carrying synthetic detergents, and soon pollution-sensitive whitebait fish, which had disappeared earlier, returned to nearby rivers.

Growth of the Seikatsu Club

Today the Seikatsu Club movement has spread to twelve prefectures and has well over 200,000 members. In 1989 the organization was granted the Right Livelihood Award, and thus achieved international recognition.[53]

Through this cooperative movement, many women, in particular, have gained the motivation and means for choosing a more healthful, more humane lifestyle for themselves and their families. Although the Club has not become the huge retail operation that is Coop Kobe, the activism of its members has affected politics, agriculture, and education in the regions where the Seikatsu Club exists.

Conclusion

Whether or not there is collusion between the state and Coop Kobe or the Seikatsu Club, opportunities for participatory decision making, particularly for women, indicate some autonomy at the local levels, and the embryonic development of an independent third sector. Several articles in issues of *Review of International Cooperation*, which refer to Japanese consumer cooperatives, describe the *han* groups as the key to maintaining participatory democracy in a large, modern organization.[54] Because these groups are voluntary and they require input from all the members, the *han* can be regarded as training grounds for autonomous decision making. In his description of the Seikatsu Club cooperative in the Tokyo area, Sato, too, is enthusiastic about the role of the *han*, which he calls "subgroups":

> The subgroup is not only the basic purchasing unit, it is also an independent core group which makes many decisions concerning the Seikatsu Club itself. Subgroup activities help foster harmony between the consumer and the producer and the ordering system results in reduced production costs by ensuring stable supply and demand. In addition, the subgroup provides housewives with a forum for information exchange. It also serves as an intermediary in forming human relationships establishing a spirit of mutual Cooperation and providing housewives with an opportunity to look at society as a whole. The subgroup is also a place where each member's ability for self-management, the very basis of democracy could be developed.[55]

As Sato indicates, much of the *han* activity is dependent on the presence of homemakers who are available for group meetings and Coop deliveries. An on-going concern of Coop Kobe, and the Japanese consumer co-ops as a whole, is the increasing number of working women, and the resulting growing proportion of inactive to active members.[56] Efforts are being made to solicit suggestions for accommodating women working outside their homes and attracting the inactive members to integrate them into Coop operations once more.

As important as the *han* groups are to the participatory activities of the co-op, the earthquake crisis demonstrated that a critical role is played by the employees as well. It is often the co-op worker, perhaps one of the nearly 10,000 part-time employees (80 percent of whom are women), who initiate *han* involvement and encourage member participation in the many opportunities available through the co-op. Of course each co-op employee, from the president to the most junior part-time worker is also a single-vote carrying co-op member. Although high-level management positions are still disproportionately held by males, the Japanese Consumers' Cooperative Union established an affirmative action program in 1994 to ensure that women would be recruited into management within its member organizations.[57] Furthermore, the official policy to decentralize the decision-making process is already giving women more discretion in the workplace.

Credit must also be given to the managers of successful cooperatives like Coop Kobe. It is remarkable that those cooperatives have been able to survive in such a competitive environment. While utilizing the most sophisticated management strategies, the decision makers are working diligently to maintain the flow of information and guidance coming from the membership. It is a difficult balance, but for now, Coop Kobe seems to have achieved such a balance between its democratic values and its business success.

No matter how free the voluntary involvement of co-op members may appear, we must continue to return to Sheldon Garon's conclusion that state-directed social management permeates even citizen groups. Because they accept the notion that as Japanese they need protection from a chaotic world, and are willing to join efforts to maintain order and stability, Garon asserts that civic groups in Japan ultimately acquiesce to state management. In other words, popular associations are not truly autonomous, but depend upon direction from the state.

> Few Japanese in the twentieth century have embraced the sort of American-style free-market liberalism that conceives of the world as borderless and the individual as the basic unit of economic well-being. The belief persists that the Japanese people must regulate themselves, make sacrifices, or at least "rationalize" their behavior for the greater good.[58]

The fear of "degenerating" into a society pursuing individual rights at the expense of community values[59] is understandable, and, in fact, the thorough enculturation of group participation in Japan is a real advantage for cooperation. One Japanese sociologist interviewed for this project suggested that it is in individualistic Western cultures that cooperatives are bound to flounder because members do not wish to commit their support to such an organization for the long term. Whether Japanese society promotes group activity or not, the consumer cooperatives there are attempting to provide more opportunities for individual initiative and decision-making power. Sato Yoshiyuki is one such co-op proponent who addresses Garon's points directly:

The individual does not exist for the cooperative; rather the cooperative exists for each individual. It is no longer acceptable for individuals to be sacrificed for the sake of the organization. Neither is it appropriate for individuals to be sacrificed for the sake of the home or the country. It is an age in which each individual is called upon to live to their full capacity. . . . The cooperative movement is far ahead of politics and administration. By setting a precedent in its treatment of problems that the government cannot or will not solve, it illustrates that government authority and power is relative, not absolute. . . . No matter how local or personal the problem, whether it be food safety, garbage reduction, recycling, the local environment, nuclear weapons, peace, poverty, overpopulation, the economy, or women, we must view all issues from a global perspective. Now more than ever, we need this kind of approach in which Cooperation exceeds national boundaries.[60]

Broad-based cooperative programs are reaching many participants who would have few other options for activism or services. Their outreach to weaker members of society and opportunities for equal participation make the co-ops particularly sensitive to justice issues. Although groups in other countries may not be able to duplicate all the conditions found in Japan, it is encouraging to know that with perseverance, skill, and good fortune, consumer cooperatives do have the possibility of thriving economically while pursuing their human values.

Notes

1. Japanese Consumers' Cooperative Union, *Coop: Facts & Figures 1995* (Tokyo, 1996).

2. Jean L. Cohen and Andrew Arato, *Civil Society and Political Theory*. (Cambridge, Mass, 1992), 19.

3. Robert Putnam, "Bowling Alone: America's Declining Social Capital," *Journal of Democracy* 6 no. 1 (January 1995): 65-78.

4. Sheldon Garon, *Molding Japanese Minds: The State in Everyday Life*. (Princeton, N.J., 1997), 234.

5. Japanese names are written with the surname first as is customary in Japan.

6. Ohta Hiroshi, "The State and Civil Society in Japan," *Japanese Public Policy Perspectives & Resources* (Washington, D.C., 1995), 212.

7. Cohen and Arato, ix.

8. Karel van Wolferen, *The Enigma of Japanese Power: People and Politics in a Stateless Nation* (London, 1989).

9. Chalmers Johnson, *Japan: Who Governs?* (New York, 1995), 14.

10. John Owen Haley, *Authority without Power: Law and the Japanese Paradox*, (New York, 1991), 158.

11. Garon, 17.

12. Jonathan Birchall, *Coop: The People's Business* (Manchester, 1994), 54-62.

13. Takamura Isao, *Principles of Cooperative Management* (Kobe, Japan, 1995), 14.

14. Mark Klinedinst and Sato Hitomi, "The Japanese cooperative Sector," *Journal of Economic Issues* 38, no. 2 (1994): 511.

15. Klinedinst and Sato, 511.

16. Takamura, *Principles*, 13.

17. Nomura Hidekazu, ed., *Seikyo: A Comprehensive Analysis of Consumer Cooperatives in Japan* (Tokyo, 1993), 30, 31.

18. Takamura, Isao, "All About Coop Kobe," unpublished report prepared for the ICA INCOTEC Workshop, Berlin (1991), 35.

19. Takamura, "All About," 35.

20. *Ibid.*, 78.

21. Nomura, *Seikyo*, 49.

22. Klinedinst and Sato, 509.

23. Robert Schildgen, *Toyohiko Kagawa: Apostle of Love and Social Justice* (Berkeley, CA, 1988).

24. Schildgen, *Toyohiko Kagawa*, 168-69.

25. Takamura, "All About," 4.

26. *Ibid.*, 3-4.

27. Takamura, *Principles*, 261.

28. Takamura, "All About," 11.

29. Takamura, *Principles*, 268.

30. Birchall, *Co-op*, 193.

31. Takamura, *Principles*, 18.

32. Craig Cox, *Storefront Revolution: Food Coops and the Counterculture* (New Brunswick, N.J., 1994), 141.

33. Takamura, "All About," 7.

34. Birchall, *Co-op*, 194.

35. Takamura, "All About," 39

36. *Ibid.*, 5.

37. *Ibid.*, 5

38. *Ibid.*, 19.

39. Consumers Cooperative Kobe, *Annual Report: from April 1991 to March 1992* (Kobe, 1992), 7.

40. Consumers Cooperative Kobe, *Coop Guide Book* (Kobe, 1995), 3.

41. Consumers Cooperative Kobe, *Coop Guide Book.*

42. Takamura, "All About," 41.

43. Consumers Cooperative Kobe, *Coop Guide.*

44. Yomiuri Shimbun, ed., *Chronicle: The Great Hanshin Earthquake* (Osaka, 1996), 143.

45. Yomiuri, *Chronicle*, 142.

46. Sato, Yoshiyuki, *Josei to Kyo-do- Kumiai no Shakai Gaku (The Sociology of Women and Cooperatives)* (Tokyo, 1996), 190-92.

47. Consumers Cooperative Kobe, *Coop Guide.*

48. Takamura, "All About," 36.

49. *Ibid.*, 82.

50. *Ibid.*, 35.

51. Sato, *Josei*, 256.

52. *Ibid.*, 263.

53. *Ibid.*, 265.

54. MariaElena Chavez, "The Role of the ICA in the Advancement of Women in Cooperatives," *Review of International Cooperation* 89, no. 1 (1996): 42-51; Kurimoto Akira, "The Cooperative Response to the Aging Society in Japan," *Review of International Cooperation* 90, no. 1 (1997): 18-24; Kurimoto Akira, "Restructuring Consumer Coops and Coop Principles," *Review of International Cooperation* 86, no. 2 (1996): 6-74; Yamagishi Masayuki, Lou Hammond Ketilson, Per-Olof Jonsson, Iain Macdonald, and Loris Ferini, "Joint Project on Participatory Democracy," *Review of International Cooperation* 88, no. 4 (1995): 27-43.

55. Sato, *Josei*, 257.

56. Takamura, "All About," 83.

57. Chavez, 49.

58. Garon, 236-37.

59. Onuma, Yasuaki, "Norm Setting: A Challenging Role for Japan in International Society," in Sakio Takayanagi and Katsuya Kodama, eds., *Japan and Peace* (1994, 45-54.

60. Sato, *Josei*, 268-69.

APPENDIX A
Coop Kobe Statistical Data
Fiscal Years Beginning April 1[*]

	1991	1996
Membership	1,043,105	1,286,828
Employees	12,348	15,461
full time	5,972	5,501
associate	186	239
part time	6,190	9,721
Retail Stores	148	174
department store (Seer)	1	1
general merchandise store (Coop Days)	1	6
regular supermarkets	76	84
satellite stores	8	6
mini shops (Coop Mini)	58	70
home improvement centers	4	4
(Coop Echo)		2
specialized equipment outlet for		
elderly and disabled (Heart Land)		1
Other Facilities and Services (Partial Listing)		
cooperative college (Kyodo Gakuen)	1	1
group purchase depots	19	19
member activity centers	7	8
mausoleum vaults	2,002	2,002
resort villages	1 3	
wedding service (Annipa)		1
food plant	1	1

[*] Consumers Cooperative Kobe. *Annual Report 1991* (and) *1996*, pages 10 and 34, respectively.

APPENDIX B
Coop Kobe Balance Sheet

Fiscal Years Beginning April 1[**]

(in millions of yen)

	1991	1996
Current Assets (cash, accounts receivable, etc.)	57,730	47,802
Fixed Assets	116,557	154,273
tangible fixed assets (buildings, land, etc.)	89,414	111,470
intangible fixed assets (utility rights, etc.)	410	776
investments	26,733	42,027
Total Assets	174,287	202,07
Current Liabilities (accounts, bills, taxes payable)	65,198	74,980
Fixed Liabilities (Coop bonds, reserves, etc.)	36,760	46,849
Total Liabilities	101,958	121,829
Share Capital (from members)	25,679	38,824
Surplus	46,650	41,422
statutory reserves	15,200	20,410
optional reserves (education, welfare, etc.)	25,265	17,504
unappropriated surplus	6,185	3,508
Total Members Equity	72,329	80,248
Total Liability + Member Equity		
Sales Income[3]	174,287	202,075
Sale of Merchandise Minus Sales Refund	352,763	379,528
Cost of goods sold	268,474	288,389
Expenses	75,128	88,459
Net Surplus from Sales	7,560	2,680

[**] Consumers Cooperative Kobe. *Annual Report 1991* (and) *1996*, pages 11 and 25, respectively.

[3] Consumers Cooperative Kobe. *Annual Report 1991* (and) *1996*, pages 12 and 26, respectively.

Chapter 12

Of Spheres, Perspectives, Cultures, and Stages: The Consumer Co-operative Movement in English-Speaking Canada 1830-1980

Ian MacPherson

The consumer cooperative movement has played a pivotal role in the history of the general English-Canadian cooperative movement, a role far greater than its size might suggest. It has been the most consistent guardian of cooperative orthodoxy; it has been the sector that has most faithfully espoused the cooperative philosophical position associated with the Rochdale tradition. It has also been one of the more effective forms of cooperative enterprise in helping span the deep divisions within Canadian society, most particularly in its capacity at various times to serve both the working-class and rural populations.

The consumer cooperative movement had a powerful impact within general cooperative circles throughout the 1920s and 1930s when it profoundly shaped English-Canadian understandings of cooperativism. During the 1940s and 1950s it seemed to offer rich potential and the range of people interested in it—somewhat contradictorily as both a way to meet their growing consumer needs and as a way to limit "conspicuous consumption"—was remarkable. During the 1960s, it seemed on the verge of becoming a major force in the Canadian economy, but significant economic swings in the 1970s undercut the capacity of the movement to realize its earlier promise.

In exploring the history of the English-Canadian consumer cooperative movement, this chapter uses a framework for understanding the dynamics that typically characterize the history of cooperative organizations. The framework is the result of historical inquiry; it is also the result of the author's long involvement as a volunteer within several cooperative organizations on a local, provincial, regional, national, and international level.

The framework proposes that most cooperatives, regardless of type, essentially have functioned and continue to function within five spheres of activities: membership relationships, community activities, state relationships, associations with other cooperatives, and the managerial practices they create to help themselves. Cooperatives can and should decide clearly and aggressively how they work within all these spheres, each of which is substantially open to being controlled: none can be ignored if a given cooperative is to achieve its full potential. The framework further suggests that cooperators reflect at least one of three broad perspectives, articulated and assumed: one flows from the movement's deep and diverse ideological heritage; another emanates from the economic and social situations within which they function; the third reflects the merely utilitarian needs a given cooperatives meets.

This framework also accepts that cooperatives typically are and have been dominated by one of three kinds of institutional cultures which here are called "populist," "managerial," and "structural." In other words, they are shaped at different times by the insights of economic democracy, a concept open to innumerable interpretations; the needs of managerial cadres, including in the ways distinctive to cooperatives, some of the needs of elected leaders; and the priorities and visions associated with the institutional structures cooperative leaders develop to meet the needs of their societies. While any of these cultures may be dominant at any given point in time, they can coexist in the same organizations and can create tensions, even acrimony. Their differing priorities often created the keen debates that have usually preoccupied cooperative people throughout the history of the movement.

Most cooperative movements and their organizations typically go through four stages of development characterized by preoccupations with local, regional, national, and international issues. Each stage has its own imperatives that profoundly affect how cooperatives "manage" the five spheres over which they must exercise control. Each stage can draw into question the broad perspectives that shape their outlook and govern their activities. Unlike the stages of a butterfly's life, the stages are not distinct. Indeed, they often co-exist in a given organization or movement, a circumstance full of remarkable potential for what might be done, but also replete with opportunities for fragmenting debate.

This framework is a useful, though hardly fully satisfactory, guide to the patterns, debates and issues that shaped the history of the English-Canadian consumer movement. It can help in trying to understand a rather diverse movement typified more by centrifical than centripetal forces.

The Formative Period 1864 to 1928

The English-Canadian consumer cooperative movement has a long history. Its beginnings, as in so many other countries, were associated with the rise of

Dynamics of Cooperative Organizations

SPHERES				
Members	Community	State	Structure	Management

PERSPECTIVES		
Movement	Situational	Adaptable

CULTURES		
Populist	Managerial	Structural

STAGES			
Formative	Regional	National	International

an industrial economy. There is some evidence of discussion about consumer cooperatives as early as the 1830s, when industrial unrest first became a feature of Canadian society. The first known continuing consumer cooperatives, however, were organized in Nova Scotia in the 1860s in Stellarton and Sydney Mines.[1]

These early cooperatives displayed three characteristics common in one of the main streams of consumer cooperatives organized during the movement's formative period, or until 1926 when the first independent consumer wholesaling services were organized. First, they were much influenced by the European, and especially the British, experience with consumer cooperatives. Indeed, it can be argued that the consumer movement first emerged essentially from the cultural baggage many European immigrants, but especially those familiar with the Rochdale tradition of consumer cooperatives, brought to North America. Second, they were developed by members of the working class, for the most part people from the skilled trades, the so-called "labor aristocracy." Third, they were organized in mining communities where bonds of work, class, and place created strong feelings of solidarity and a pervasive sense of being exploited.

For the next sixty years, several societies were started in the mining districts of eastern Nova Scotia. Between 1900 and 1926 they also became common in the mining communities of northern or New Ontario and the mountains that spanned the Alberta/British Columbia border. Some of the stores started in this period displayed remarkable staying power and lasted for decades. One of them, the British Canadian in Sydney Mines, Nova Scotia, became the largest consumer cooperative in North America for several decades.[2]

The British Canadian store, in fact, became something of an institution frozen in time: a grocery, furnishing, and clothing store that still functioned in the early 1970s much like a large English cooperative department store of the 1920s, replete with a pneumatic communications system, a strongly hierarchical and formal management structure, a commitment to the educational priorities of another time, and a staff still referring in hushed tones to the cooperative experience of the "mother country." For its leadership, at least, Holyoake, Mitchell, and Gide were still potent names decades after most Canadian cooperators had forgotten them; the triumphs of English cooperativism during the late nineteenth and early twentieth centuries were still models for contemporary life. Its history demonstrates the depth of feeling and commitment one could find within the forces that led to the creation of the first wave of consumer cooperatives.

The working class also spawned consumer cooperatives in other economic contexts during the formative period. During the 1880s, the same circles as produced temples for the Knights of Labour created consumer societies, generally organized in the Rochdale tradition, most of them tied directly to local lodges. In communities like Toronto, London, Hamilton, Brantford, and Victoria, about forty consumer cooperatives appeared, all of them lasting for only short periods. Working-class support for cooperation was broad but it was not deep.[3]

Another band of consumer cooperatives developed in enclaves of industrialism throughout Canada, particularly Ontario, during the early years of the twentieth century. Their primary networks were drawn from trade unionists and social democrats (in the case of northern Ontario, Marxists). They flourished—or did not—depending upon the nature and strength of working-class culture. Most of them lasted for between three and five years, the main exception being in northern Ontario where some lasted into the 1970s. The demise of most of them was explained by the depression of the early 1920s, mistakes made by poorly trained leadership, the emergence of chain stores, and by the changing middle-class aspirations of their memberships. The most serious set of failures occurred in southern Ontario where the movement, building upon a base of about a dozen stores in industrial communities, expanded rapidly during World War I, in large part as a way for people to withstand the ravages of inflation. One by one, they disappeared in the five years following the war, a particularly serious setback, not only for the movement in Ontario but also for the national movement as well: without a strong presence in the heartland of English-speaking Canada, consumer cooperation would not have automatic access to government or easy recognition by the media.[4]

Their failures can also be seen as part of the cooperative fallout from the ideological wars that beset much of the Canadian working class as the twentieth century progressed. As in so many other parts of the industrializing world, the rather gentle, inclusive and inadequately developed ideology of cooperativism lost out to the more militant appeals of Marxism, various forms of social democratic thought, the blandishments of liberalism, and the emergence of "bread-and-butter" unionism. All these other ideological positions occasionally supported cooperative enterprises, but their flirtations were brief and usually for ulterior purposes: they used cooperatives as a medium for communicating other messages or for meeting obvious immediate needs until (hopefully) other levers of power could be grasped; few among their adherents had any real understanding of cooperative ideology or practice.

The most important network responsible for the development of consumer cooperatives lay within the ranks of the agrarian movements of the late nineteenth and early twentieth centuries. The Patrons of Husbandry or Grange developed consumer cooperative enterprises to supply essential commodities to farm families during the 1870s and 1880s. The Patrons of Industry in the 1890s fostered a farmer-owned binder twine company that demonstrated, until its demise in 1912, the possibilities of collective, "class"-based ownership. While these activities did not lead directly to the creation of cooperative stores, they helped create a receptive climate for such endeavors among two, arguably three, generations of farm families.

Similarly, the widespread support for local cheese factories in Ontario and Québec (some 4,000 at their greatest extent) and the tradition of supporting mutual insurance companies demonstrated the possibilities inherent in pooling resources and sharing risks. There were few dairy areas in central Canada that did not have cooperative creameries at one point or another. Stories of their successes were taken westward by Canadian settlers and became part of the context within which prairie cooperative enterprises would thrive.

These nineteenth-century precedents, coupled with a gathering crisis emanating from rural depopulation, inadequate rural services, and apparent government disinterest, fueled an agrarian revolt in many parts of central Canada in the early twentieth century. In Ontario, the revolt ultimately became focused within the United Farmers of Ontario. This briefly powerful organization created the United Farmers Cooperative in 1914, a system of local cooperatives engaged to some extent in marketing farm products but, even more, in the provision of the kinds of supplies increasingly needed by commercial agriculture. Its stores, numbering some forty outlets by the early 1920s, became a common feature of the rural regions of the province.

Throughout its history (until its amalgamation with GROWMART, a U.S.-based cooperative, in 1990), United Farmers Cooperative experimented unsuccessfully with the sale of consumer goods, even venturing into the outskirts of several regional towns and cities in Ontario. It never developed this side of the business effectively, however, at least partly because the primacy of producer interests always overpowered the interests and needs of consumers, a reflection of the common enough producer-consumer tension in the history of the international movement. Its failure to do so, however, had a profound impact upon the history of the general cooperative movement in English Canada: it was another important reason why consumer cooperatives never became an important force in Ontario society.

To a somewhat lesser extent, the awakening of the countryside also assisted in the formation of a consumer movement in the Maritimes.[5] That awakening, roughly coincidental with that of Ontario, was primarily concerned with the organizing of the numerous small farms that dotted the region, relying for part of their income on the production and sale of sheep, poultry, cattle, vegetables, and small fruits. The organization of the rural people was undertaken by federal, and particularly, provincial departments of agriculture;[6] it was assisted by teachers from the Truro Agricultural College and by socially engaged priests from St. Francis Xavier University. Their efforts ultimately culminated in the formation of Canadian Livestock Cooperative (Maritimes) (CLC) in 1927. In time, it would become one of the pillars upon which a stable cooperative movement would be built.

Agrarianism's most lasting contribution to the cooperative movement was on the Prairies where, to some extent, consumer cooperatives were a natural consequence of the settlement process. Without casting a romantic glow of mutual aid over the entire settlement process, it is reasonable to claim that the challenges of creating permanent households and communities inevitably led many settlers to work together: building bees, harvesting bees, buying clubs, jointly owned machinery, "bull rings," quilting bees—they were common strategies for overcoming shortfalls in family labor pools.

In addition to these essentially spontaneous examples of cooperation, prairie farm people developed a wave of cooperative institutions in the early years of the century. The most prominent were in the grain industry. The first of these institutions was the Grain Growers Grain Company established in 1906,[7] although from the beginning its cooperative *bona fides* were questioned. Shortly thereafter, with varying degrees of government support, provincial marketing organizations were developed for and by grain producers in Saskatchewan and Alberta. Early in the 1920s the pooling movement swept much of the region, championed by Aaron Sapiro the great "apostle" of pooling who had organized many commodity organizations among fruit growers and wheat producers in the United States.

Consumer cooperatives flourished in the wake of the agricultural marketing campaigns, albeit not without serious threats of being overwhelmed. Primarily, they prospered because of the great impetus the grain marketing campaigns gave generally to the cooperative movement. Farm families marketing other commodities, such as eggs, poultry, livestock, and dairy products, also organized cooperatives. Local groups and governments explored the possibilities of cooperative credit institutions and cooperative implement businesses. Buying clubs developed into full-fledged stores. In Saskatchewan by the mid-1920s there were an estimated 600 stores or significant buying clubs at any given time,[8] with about ninety of them being relatively permanent cooperative stores. Some of the prairie stores, like those in Moline, Minto, Davidson, Melfort, Lloydminster, Young, Edgerton, Killam, and Wetaskiwin, were particularly successful adaptations of the consumer model to the Canadian experience.

Arguably the most important figure during the formative period was George Keen, the general secretary of the Co-operative Union of Canada, from its formation in 1909 until his retirement in 1944. Keen was a formidable figure. In appearance and mind-set he was "Victorian" (in the traditional meaning of the word). He was a deeply committed advocate of the cooperative movement as a "social religion." An English immigrant who took up residence in Brantford, Ontario, he was a devout disciple of George Holyoake and a devoted admirer of the consumer cooperative tradition built on Rochdale and by the English Cooperative Wholesale Society. He believed in the consumer theory of cooperation, envisioning a society in which local consumer cooperatives through their wholesale and its associated businesses—from banking through insurance to labor copartnerships and cooperative housing—would democratically control the entire economy.[9]

While Keen showed tolerance, even sympathy, for other kinds of cooperatives, his heart was always with the consumer movement. The Union, therefore, essentially brought together consumer societies and the services it provided, particularly managerial advice, was directed almost entirely to consumer cooperatives. Consequently, Keen developed a range of like-minded contacts across much of English Canada. Invariably, they were strong proponents of the correctness of the "Rochdale rules"[10] and of the British view of cooperative development. While few of his associates subscribed to the full consumer theory of cooperation as he did, most accepted the centrality of the consumer movement, and this significantly affected how cooperative legislation was developed in most provinces.

The consumer cooperatives created during the formative period generally evinced a deep commitment to democratic practice and volunteer leadership and participation: they were, in their culture, essentially "populist" in their deep faith in the capacity of "ordinary" people to manage economic enterprises through democratic practices—and direct democratic practices at that.

The early stores placed great emphasis on the role of volunteers and expected them to become missionaries for the cause and, often, willing unpaid workers in the stores. They relied to some extent upon employees but the underlying assumption was that the heart of the stores was the wishes of the membership transferred into good business practice by the elected leadership: in the formative years that meant the directors typically did much of the work.

Many of the stores evinced a general and sincere devotion to training and education. They purchased or produced pamphlets, held information meetings, and distributed propaganda about their stores and the nature of the movement. They emphasized that members had duties—to patronize and to participate—in the operation of their stores. They paid considerable attention to the training of directors and managers in sound business practice, most particularly how to monitor inventories, set prices, select dividend levels, and build reserves. In fact, it was generally true that the cooperative stores that survived were the ones that stressed this kind of training.

For many of the leaders, however, and most especially George Keen, "cooperative education" was ultimately far more important than training. Keen helped a significant group of Canadians to understand that the movement had a deep history, could provide a critique of contemporary society, and possessed an ideology worthy of being considered as a force at least equal to liberalism, social democracy, and communism. Of all the Canadian leaders of the time, in the consumer as well as other sectors, his cooperative knowledge was the most profound. No other person played a more decisive role in helping to shape the consumer movement's distinctive ideology in its formative years.

Keen's perspective was deeply imbedded in a movement culture that sought to apply the principles and philosophy of the movement to a wide variety of circumstances. For him the ultimate battle was one of ideas not economics or politics. While not alone, he was in a minority among the many cooperative leaders and enthusiasts whose perspective were more typically shaped by local circumstances—the needs of a mining or agrarian community or the desirability of combatting the exploitive practices of local merchants. The resultant differences created an abiding tension between those whose perspectives ranged back in time and over a significant body of thought and those who sought immediate benefit and for whom the movement was either a tool or a convenient organizational form to develop business opportunities. Debates among those who held these contrarian views were at the heart of the institutional culture evident in the cooperatives of the period.

Keen was also committed to developing appropriate legislation for the movement, a necessary basis upon which to build strong cooperative organizations. In 1906 he had tried—from a very small base of support—to join Alphonse Desjardins[11] and several farm leaders in lobbying the federal government for national cooperative legislation. When those efforts failed, he turned to securing good cooperative legislation at the provincial level. His intent was to create a framework in which governments would assist in the development of cooperatives but would promote, even organize, them in such a way that they would soon be operating independently.

Keen found his greatest support in Saskatchewan where an English immigrant, W. Waldron, was responsible for government cooperative activities during the 1920s. The two men collaborated in the writing of a new cooperative act for the province in 1924, an act that became a model for all provincial legislation for twenty years. Keen also gradually built up his contacts with other governments and by the time of his retirement in 1944 there was a reasonably good body of cooperative law across the country. The result was a relationship with the state that protected the cooperative requirements for democratic control structures and education. Perhaps most important, the emerging legislation tried to balance the need for independence with the need for government sympathy and support analogous to that which governments and their officials extended to farm organizations or, indeed, traditional private enterprise.

From a business perspective, the cooperatives established during the formative years were operated in a necessarily conservative manner, the common maxim being that they should "cut the suit to fit the cloth": in other words, that they should offer services and products to meet known demand and within an established, secure budget. They were "no-frill" stores, completely controlled by local memberships. They vigorously resisted any idea of "chain-stores," even though one of the first significant Canadian advocates of that approach, Thomas Loblaw, learned his trade and developed his ideas about how chain stores might be organized when he worked with the United Farmers Cooperative in Ontario. In fact, Loblaw tried unsuccessfully to turn that organization into a chain store.[12]

From a social perspective, the stores of the formative period typically demonstrated class backgrounds, interests, and needs, although it is also true that most of them sought to attract people from outside of their working class or agrarian bases. They were clearly community organizations, drawing upon community involvement through their democratic procedures and committee systems. Many of them made significant efforts to reach out to women, through appeals to the "power of the breadbasket" and to the provision of special services (such as rooms to feed children). In a few instances, consumer cooperatives organized women's guilds and attempted to recruit women for boards and committees, but with limited success.

In the mining towns the consumer cooperatives were centers of resistance to the domination of mining companies, especially their explorative use of "company stores." In some instances, though, notably in Nova Scotia, they found themselves in particularly awkward situations when prolonged strikes affected their memberships. In those circumstances, where did their ultimate loyalty lie? Was it to support the memberships until they were forced into bankruptcy? Was it to stop support when providing food and supplies on credit threatened the store's existence? It was a Hobson's choice that most stores made in favor of their own survival, never an easy alternative because of the inevitable animosities that decision created from within the memberships.

Nevertheless, the overall impact of the consumer cooperative movement in its formative stages was remarkable, especially when one remembers that cumulatively it was not a large movement. Although there were always debates and differences within the ranks, the movement had developed, largely in imitation of English experience, a strong adherence to traditional cooperative practice. It projected a relatively clear vision of the nature of the movement as an independent force, seeking appropriate legislative frameworks and capable of reaching out to a relatively large segment of the population. Thanks largely to the network that George Keen had forged, it had developed a respected national voice. A strong base had been built, though its size was small and its impact restricted to a relatively few places in a vast country; it was a tender and slender plant, beset with problems common to the international movement and limited by Canadian realities, but nevertheless, even in its early years, of some significance.

Creating Regional Strength, 1926-1958

By the late 1920s, strong concentrations of consumer cooperatives were to be found in eastern Nova Scotia and in each of the Prairie provinces; there was a frustratingly small but still promising movement in Ontario and some small beginnings amid the diversities of British Columbia. Following the pattern established by the English movement and imitated by the Scots, Scandinavians, Germans, and others, most of these groupings began to consider establishing wholesale societies.[13] Indeed, in some ways, wholesales were seen as the most effective way to ensure that new cooperatives could survive and old ones thrive.

The importance of creating wholesales, the most obvious manifestation of a growing regional consciousness, therefore, can scarcely be overestimated. The wholesales were expected not only to benefit the entire movement through economies of scale in the purchase and distribution of goods but also to enter gradually into the manufacture of consumer goods. They were expected to provide enhanced educational and training opportunities for members, directors, staff, and managers. They were to be the conduit through which consumer cooperatives would work with other sectors in the movement and they would represent the consumer cooperative viewpoint before government.

Formally structured wholesales first appeared in Prairie Canada (the provinces of Manatoba, Saskatchewan, and Alberta). In 1926, a grouping of stores and buying clubs, scattered around the rural areas of Manitoba, organized a wholesale.[14] Although the movement was arguably less well developed than in Saskatchewan and Alberta, it relied to a great extent upon gaining volume discounts, primarily from Winnipeg wholesalers.

In Saskatchewan the drive toward creating a wholesale actually began in 1925 with the organization of the Saskatchewan Cooperative League. For the next three years many of the consumer cooperatives and buying clubs in the province sought volume discounts for consumer and farm products. They found themselves enmeshed in a difficult relationship with producer cooperatives who were also trying to develop the farm supply business, and in fact had relied on income from it for a number of years. Nevertheless, by 1928, the League was able to enter into the formation of a wholesale owned jointly by the consumer cooperatives, the Saskatchewan Grain Growers Association, and the United Farmers of Canada (Saskatchewan Section). It was an uncomfortable beginning, however, including many participants who possessed a limited and, for some, even a misguided, understanding of the cooperative movement.

In Alberta, the consumer cooperatives undertook joint purchasing in the early 1920s through the Alberta Cooperative League formed in 1923. Arguably even more than in Saskatchewan, though, the tender plant of consumer cooperation had tremendous difficulty maturing beneath the woods of the producer cooperatives. Indeed, Alberta, through the energetic leadership of Henry Wise Wood and William Irvine, developed the most exclusive agrarian movement in Canada, perhaps North America: it envisioned creating farm organizations, economic, social and political, that were tied entirely to rural interests. That kind of narrow agrarianism contrasted strikingly with the more inclusive approach typical of consumer cooperation and reduced collaboration to occasional possibilities not systematic partnership. Nevertheless, the leaders of the provincial movement did make progress, partly because of the potential business offered by the existing cooperatives, partly because of the interest of the Alberta government formed by a farmers organization, the United Farmers of Alberta. In fact, the wholesale started on a too grandiose scale, in part because of government pressure, a beginning that would long cripple its effectiveness.

In the ten years that started with the collapse of the stock market in 1929, interest in cooperatives expanded steadily on the Prairies. The consumer movement, although it encountered serious difficulties,[15] ultimately took on new life as rural communities reeled amid the economic catastrophe and as people on declining income sought to limit the amounts they had to spend on food. The Dirty Thirties, as the Great Depression became called on the Prairies, triggered a deepening of ideological commitments to the cooperative movement. Those already evident tendencies toward seeing the cooperative movement as a significant force in improving and reshaping society took on new meaning. The result was the rapid expansion of interest in all kinds of cooperatives, including credit unions, insurance, petroleum, heating fuels, farm supplies, medical services, arenas, and stores. The existing cooperative stores ultimately benefitted from this growing interest and it would help produce economic strengths when the Depression ended.

During the 1930s, too, as Brett Fairbairn wrote, "the most important episode in the history of the consumer cooperative movement in western Canada"[16] occurred: the creation of Consumers' Cooperative Refineries Limited. It was the result of more than a decade of farmer efforts to secure reliable, inexpensive petroleum products for the machines then starting to revolutionize agricultural production. The refinery was started in 1934 when a group of frustrated farmers representing eight consumer cooperatives near Regina organized a refinery association. Led by Harry Fowler, an intrepid cooperative warhorse,[17] they fostered support for the refinery idea through their cooperatives and through public meetings. They navigated their way through difficult issues connected with what kind of business they should undertake, how they should raise money, and how they should relate to government. After a difficult birth, the refinery began operations near Regina in 1935. Almost from the beginning, it was a success, a success that would become the cornerstone for the prosperity of the western cooperative movement.

In British Columbia, the Depression also provided considerable stimulus for the development of the movement. Unfortunately, the movement was deeply fragmented for many years, partly because of the geography of the province. It had some strength in the mining districts of the Kootenays and occasional bursts of interest in the mining districts of Vancouver Island, but these did not form a sufficient base upon which to build a strong provincial movement. Nor was there much potential for collaboration with the agricultural marketing movement that took off in the 1920s and the 1930s, primarily among fruit producers and orchardists but also among small tender fruit producers as well. Unfortunately, the consumer and the agricultural producers did not mix easily together: not only were they separated by geography and ethnicity but also by ideology—the liberal and conservative farmers distrusted the social democratic and Marxist working-class leaders. Some local farmer organizations, however, such as in Surrey were supportive.

The fishing cooperatives along the Pacific coast were a different matter, however, and they became an important factor in the development of a provincial wholesale. They had started in the late 1920s with a membership that included many Scandinavians with a strong knowledge of cooperative forms of organization. As the fishing movement developed, particularly in Prince Rupert, they became interested in consumer issues, firstly in finding inexpensive supplies for their fishing activities, then in consumer goods generally. They became a crucially important support for the always tenuous wholesaling activities in British Columbia.[18]

In May 1938, on the initiative of Robert Wood of the Armstrong Cooperative, a meeting was called in Vancouver to discuss the formation of a wholesale. Perhaps prematurely, those in attendance, drawn from a small but diverse groups of cooperatives, decided to form a wholesale. It went into business shortly afterward, destined to struggle for its existence for a number of years.

In Atlantic Canada, the Depression also encouraged many people to explore the possibilities of cooperative action. The Antigonish movement of St. Francis University sparked the formation of many kinds of cooperatives among fishing and farming people, initially in eastern Nova Scotia and then throughout Atlantic Canada.[19] While its primary emphasis was upon the development of credit unions, because of the comparatively easy way in which they could be formed, it also contributed significantly to the development of consumer cooperatives. Perhaps even more importantly, the Antigonish movement preached the inter-connectedness of cooperative forms and manifested an inclusive view of cooperativism that profoundly affected the Canadian movement, helping to distinguish it from other national movements, particularly that of the United States.[20]

As a result of the work of the Antigonish leadership (notably Moses Coady, J. J. Tompkins and A. B. MacDonald) and a band of men and women organizers associated with the Extension Department, literally hundreds of cooperatives appeared throughout Atlantic country, organized at any crossroad or, as Stefan Haley put it, "wherever anybody wanted to."[21] They were too often best intentions unconnected to practical realities, and they needed the discipline and expertise a wholesale could provide. The first discussions of the possible benefits of wholesaling in the region took place in 1934.[22] Two years later, W. H. McEwen, then working for Canadian Livestock Cooperatives, and A. B. MacDonald brought leaders of many of the cooperative stores together to discuss the possibilities further. Developing a wholesale, as in other regions, was not an easy task. The enthusiasms of the Antigonish movement had created too many small, uneconomic stores. The divisions between Cape Breton and the rest of Atlantic Canada ran deep, and the divisions between the British Canadian and the rest of the Cape Breton cooperatives were significant. The relationship between the urban and rural cooperatives was also often strained if not antagonistic.[23]

A central wholesale, however, did struggle to life in 1938 as a branch of Canadian Livestock Cooperative. It was, from the beginning, a doubtful venture. It was particularly difficult for cooperators in Maritime Canada to develop a regional perspective; the calls of home and community usually overwhelmed appeals from wider loyalties. By 1940 cooperatives in the eastern portion of the Nova Scotian mainland were organizing their own wholesale and the stores of Cape Breton, disdainful of the agrarian roots of CLC and led by a dynamic individual, Ted MacDonald, were doing the same. Similarly, on Prince Edward Island and in the Acadian areas of New Brunswick, the consumer leaderships were following the same route.[24] Soon CLC would be just a supply service for a group of small regional wholesales, none of them large enough to have an easy economic future. Nevertheless, it was a beginning.

The emergence of the wholesaling activities in Atlantic and western Canada can be explained largely by the development of a managerial perspective within the consumer movement. That perspective, however, was not just the preserve of those who technically were employed in managerial positions. As with most cooperative movements in their formative stages, the lines between boards and management verged on being indistinguishable: volunteers often did much of the work, from stock-taking to shelf-filling to accounting, usually thought of as managerial responsibilities; most managers came to their positions from an elected director's chair. That situation applied at a local level and it would apply for some years at the wholesale level as well. Moreover, partly because of the example of the producer cooperatives, individuals elected as presidents typically took aggressive positions in relations with members, in negotiations with other cooperative organizations and governments, and in the everyday affairs of the organization.

The new "managerial" influence was evident in two main ways. First, many local societies, led by such managers as W. C. Stewart in Sydney Mines, E. D. Magwood in Deloraine, W. F. Popple from Minto, A. P. Moan of Wetaskiwin, T. Swindlehurst of Edgerton, W. Halsall of Killam, H. W. Ketcheson of Davidson, C. G. Davidson of Lloydminster, and Robert Wood in Armstrong, were at the heart of the drive to create regional structures that could support the activities of their local organizations. Second, although progress was slow, the wholesales ultimately developed their own managerial cadres with their own specific aspirations and needs; that cadre would become increasingly important as the years went by.

During World War II, the consumer movement made significant progress in all parts of English Canada except for Ontario, although even in that province the leaders of the United Farmers Cooperative once again entered into one of their periodic discussions of the need to develop consumer co-ops in the urban centers. The important point, though, was that co-ops prospered in relative terms while government restrictions on new buildings meant that they and their wholesales accumulated savings rather than spending them; nor did the leadership make the mistake of distributing all of them to members in the form of patronage dividends. Significant accumulated savings were thus available for the expansion of the wholesaling, retailing, and production capacity of the consumer movement when wartime restrictions on expansion were ended.

The times were propitious in other ways. The late 1940s ushered in a quarter century of generally continuous economic prosperity and an imperfect but nevertheless significant search for an extensive welfare state. It was also a time of growing Canadian nationalism, manifested in a desire to build up Canadian institutions and to create a society, as it was often put, "worthy of the sacrifices made in the Great Wars." Within cooperative circles, that viewpoint, plus the growing needs of the various sectors, stimulated a powerful national cooperative vision, a vision that consumer cooperatives helped significantly to design. It was the consumer movement's first foray into helping to develop a national cooperative superstructure.

In part, the possibilities had been perceived even before the war had started. In the last years of the Depression, the consumer leadership had played a significant role in the development of Canadian Cooperative Implements Limited, a Winnipeg-based selling and then manufacturing plant concerned with reducing implement costs for prairie farming people.[25] Of more direct concern for the consumer cooperatives, the leaders of the three Prairie wholesales formed Interprovincial Cooperatives in 1940 to undertake joint purchasing for the three wholesales. While developing slowly because of war-time restrictions, it ultimately undertook some production in the 1940s and gradually expanded to include consumer and producer organizations from the other Canadian regions.[26]

In 1943 and 1944 the consumer movement played a significant role in the restructuring of the Co-operative Union of Canada (CUC). That restructuring was an attempt to make the CUC an important focus for the national movement. It was only a partial success because the strengths of the English-Canadian movement were really at the local and provincial level and to some extent the regional level. This weakness was further reaffirmed by the fact that, unlike consumer cooperative movements in other, smaller countries, there was no national wholesale organization, only a national joint purchasing organization, IPCO.

The most important element of the postwar vision, was the creation of a strong national financial system. That initiative led to the formation of two insurance companies, a national trust company and a national organization (the Canadian Co-operative Credit Society) for the national credit union movement.[27] All of these organizations in their formation were envisioned as being closely allied to the consumer cooperative movement, providing financial services and funding the development of the movement. The consumer movement in both the Prairie and Maritime regions, therefore, played central roles in developing this vision and in helping create the four organizations. It also played a central role in the development of the Co-operative Institute in 1955 (Western Co-operative College in 1959, Co-operative College of Canada in 1972), an attempt, arguably not as well conceptualized as it might have been, to create a strong educational resource for the Canadian movement.[28] All of these initiatives were indicative of a growing national perspective within the consumer movement.

The consumer cooperative movement, too, changed significantly. Some of the cooperative societies, thriving in particular communities, most of them at that time small, were becoming more complicated institutions: they were expanding to serve the limits of their own, natural regions. As they grew, they faced the inevitable problem of how to relate to more diverse memberships.

The bonds of "populist" cultures were being stretched. Larger stores, the advent of branches and increasing competition from chain stores stimulated the emergence of increasingly more effective management cadres. Several important managers—or board members with strong "managerial" casts of mind—emerged in the wholesales serving eastern, central and western Canada. They included such individuals as Robert McKay, W. H. McEwan, H. H. Hannam, Leonard Harman, Harry Fowler,[29] George Urwin and "Ted" Mowbrey.

They were a remarkably capable group of individuals who were largely responsible for putting organizational strength onto the cooperative vision that was then blossoming. As a group, they were increasingly, "organization" men, strong protectors of balance sheets and able to create effective managerial structures. For those reasons, they were praised for their results but often viewed suspiciously by the leaders of local organizations for their centralizing tendencies.

The emerging managerial culture within consumer cooperatives significantly altered the movement. On both local and wholesale levels, it created obvious needs for better accounting, marketing, and personnel systems; it articulated a growing need for better trained people, both within management and among directors. On a local level, it tended to de-emphasize the role of members in the daily activities of the cooperative; it saw member relations in less broad terms, as a kind of advertizing and informational activity.

On the wholesale level, there were also important manifestations of an increasing management culture. From one perspective, the main aim of the wholesale was to harness the strengths of local organizations in the common interest. The board and management of the wholesale must constantly strive to create efficiencies through the appropriate pooling of financial and human resources, the careful investment of accumulated funds, the prudent employment of technology, and the careful development of employees. The wholesale must also be continually interested in questions of structure, and the leaders of all the provincial/regional institutions devoted considerable time to structural issues, particularly in the 1950s.

Overall, therefore, the consumer cooperative movement had developed considerable complexity by the later 1950s. While there was a range of kinds of relationships with members across the diversity of cooperatives, there was a definite trend away from the informal and deep ties of the formative period. There was also a migration to market relationships based more on conventional retailing practice. At the same time, there was a decline in the ways in which members could affect the nature of their store. As the bonds of membership changed so too did the relations with communities. Originally, stores were outgrowths of communal feeling, often derived from work, ethnic, or class associations. They lost some of those specific orientations as they reached out to all segments of the community.

The relationship with the state also changed. In the early days of cooperative development, the environment for cooperative development created by the
state was vitally important. The more supportive state in Saskatchewan and the
quiet roles of public servants in the other two Prairie provinces and in Atlantic
Canada,[30] significantly helped and shaped the movement. The reverse in
Ontario was yet another reason why cooperatives did not flourish. But the
relationship did change after World War II. State paternalism, in the form of
information sessions, regular inspections, and unofficial advisory services gave
way to aloofness as cooperatives gained maturity and as government policies
and personnel changed. It was not a quick or easy separation but it proceeded
steadily throughout the postwar period, reflected in legislative changes reducing the scope of government in cooperative affairs.

The debates over structure, both for the consumer movement and the wider
cooperative movement, became a significant factor in the period. Within the
western wholesales, the need to maximize purchasing power, to contain costs,
and to increase capacity led to the amalgamation of the Manitoba and Saskatchewan wholesales in 1955 to form Federated Cooperatives; six years later
Federated united with the Alberta wholesale to provide a single wholesale for
prairie Canada.[31]

In the Maritimes there was a similar rethinking of appropriate structures
that, however, took much longer to be resolved. In 1944, in the wake of
wartime prosperity, Canadian Livestock Co-operatives (Maritimes) was reorganized and renamed Maritime Co-operative services. While it remained in the
farm supply business and even expanded aspects of that business, it persevered
in its efforts to become the regional wholesale for consumer societies. It had
difficult and often volatile relations with smaller wholesales, notably Eastern
Co-operative Services and Cape Breton Co-operative Services, an unfortunate
set of divisions that, at least from one perspective, would long limit cooperative development in the region.[32] The move to a regional stage in eastern
Canada, reflecting the underlying regionalisms and the economic patterns of
the region, would be a slower and more difficult process.

Nevertheless, the movement in the Maritimes, partly because of the effectiveness of those—A. B. MacDonald, W. H. McEwen, Lloyd Matheson,
Alexander Laidlaw—who represented it, was from the 1940s onward a significant presence on the national level. Like leaders from the consumer movement
in western Canada, they played a major role in reshaping the national movement between 1944 and 1955. They were central to the reorganization of the
Cooperative Union of Canada in 1944 and in the development of the provincial
cooperative unions associated with that restructuring. They were significant
forces in the development of the insurance companies and the trust company.

All of the changes within the spheres within which the consumer cooperatives functioned were not accomplished without extensive debate and sometimes vigorous disagreement. The consumer cooperatives of this period were

rapidly changing and innovative organizations caught up in extensive change. Rather remarkably, they sustained a relatively high "movement" commitment. While each cooperative functioned in a specific environment, which markedly affected its culture and priorities, cumulatively the consumer societies were well steeped in the conventional cooperative philosophy associated with Rochdale. Most of them sought to retain that association as their cultures were transformed from populist to managerial paradigms, not an easy task. And, as they moved into regional and national frameworks they still saw themselves as creating an alternative to, not just an imitation of, the private business against which they competed.

In short, while there were problems the future was bright, at no time more obviously than in June, 1958, when Red River Cooperative in Winnipeg opened its new supermarket. It seemed to be a particularly propitious entry into the main stream of a major city. It seemed to signal that the movement could work through the dynamics typical of its activities to reach out to the young and the urban; if not quite a brave new world than at least a promising vision of what might be.

Gathering Challenges, 1958-1980

While wealth was far from shared equitably across Canada between 1958 and 1980, it was in general a prosperous period. As a result, the biting edge of social criticism engendered by the Great Depression and transformed by the idealism emanating from World War II gradually lost its edge. The development of the welfare state, particularly the creation of health care systems and increased access to postsecondary education, reflected a vaguely liberal, communitarian value system empathetic to some kinds of cooperative ethos. The steady expansion of suburbs heralded a new kind of affluence in the growing cities, an opportunity for the cooperatives more typically found in rural areas. The mass migration of the young from the countryside camouflaged a monumental change in agriculture and rural life, an often difficult process, which cooperatives, as in the past, could help soften. It was also preeminently an age of consumerism, reflected in the power of advertising, the pervasive quest for the gadgets of the middle class, and the growth of consumer credit. It was a trend that could be potentially supportive of a movement dedicated to "wise" consumerism.

And, in fact, the consumer cooperative movement did make substantial advances in the period. It became a significant retailing force in western Canada[33] and it developed pockets of strength in Atlantic Canada. Generally, it seemed to find a competitive niche within the small towns and villages inadequately served by the chain stores. It appealed best to the generation that matured in the Depression but it also had resonance with those wishing to create a more equitable Canadian society after the war through an assertive role for the government and economic institutions with a strong social commitment.

In the West the refinery made substantial progress and surpassed any of the predictions made for its development. Year after year, it produced substantial funds for the movement and helped many stores survive that were in very difficult competitive situations in the food business.

The main problem was the cities where the overwhelming majority of the population lived and the dominant consumer trends were set. Ultimately, only the Calgary consumer cooperative solved the puzzle of how to compete in the Canadian suburbs. Because of sound management and a careful plan for expansion made possible by the securing of inexpensive land early in its history, the Calgary Coop became a multibranch operation able to compete with the largest chain store operations in western Canada. It found ways to retain a comparatively high level of member commitment and sense of ownership; it sustained a sense of difference in the market place. Unfortunately, Calgary was the exception and the other urban cooperatives in the West failed to keep pace with the market and with the perceived needs of their members.[34]

In retrospect, the consumer movement seemed to reach the limits of its potential; its "niche" was somewhat less than the vision that had ennobled the work of the pioneers. In large part, that limitation was explained by the nature of the business in which the stores largely competed, primarily groceries but also clothing and hardware. The retail trades became large volume, low margin businesses; competition could be fierce and consumer demand was fickle. Significantly, the dominant players in the business, such as Safeways and Sobeys, made much of their profits from their wholesaling and trucking businesses not through their stores. While the cooperative "systems," as they increasingly were called, could match parts of the wholesaling economies, they were ultimately unable to keep pace with them.

In some ways, too, the dynamics of the cooperative system made the desired expansion of the movement difficult. The growth of managerial cultures within large cooperatives and the wholesales, manifested in the drive to create stores similar to those built by the chains, inevitably created a reaction; there was a debate over what the culture of the organizations should be.

One set of reactions came from Ottawa, ironically enough from the Cooperative Union of Canada (CUC), the national organization for all kinds of cooperatives that was in part funded by Federated Cooperatives. One of the most powerful leaders of the CUC in the period was Ralph Staples, a deeply committed and idealistic cooperator who served as President from 1953 to 1967. Writing under the pseudonym Ernest Page, he became one of the voices of conscience for the movement, a role not always appreciated by everyone in the movement he led.[35]

A rather severe, deeply religious teetotaler in one of the then powerful traditions of Old Ontario, Staples did not approve of the conspicuous consumption of the period, nor did he accept that everyone was benefiting from the expansion of the middle class. Influenced by social critics like Ralph Nadar, aware of the "War on Poverty" in the United States, he championed a different kind of cooperative, the service fee or direct charge cooperative to serve those who were not being well served (in his mind at least) by the chain store system—or by the conventional consumer cooperative stores.

The service fee cooperative was based on the simple idea that members should pay a fee cumulatively equal to at least the overhead costs of operating a store and then purchase their goods at close to cost. He wished to see a high degree of member involvement retained and so he also advocated that members help in the store, at the very least by pricing the articles they purchased. In keeping with the broad approach to education, he advocated that members be "educated" to understand the nature of the retailing system: to comprehend the unnecessary costs created by advertizing, to understand the costs of having frivolous choices among essentially the same products, to realize the value of purchasing products produced by cooperatives, and to appreciate the advantages of member loyalty.

After having only limited success in starting such stores in Ontario, Staples took his idea westward. He found a kindred spirit in Rod Glen, a credit union manager in Nanaimo, British Columbia. One of the truly visionary leaders of the Canadian cooperative movement between 1960 and 1980, Glen was a powerful figure in the provincial, national, and international credit union movement. He was a prominent figure within a decreasing band of cooperators who believed that credit unions should be a catalyst for all kinds of economic activities on behalf of their members. In 1964 he started a service fee cooperative, Mid-Island Consumer Services Cooperative. It became an almost instant success, and the idea spread to other British Columbian communities, primarily through credit union circles.

Amid his idealism, Glen was something of an iconoclast who throve on controversy. The leadership at Federated Cooperatives was not convinced that the service fee idea was ultimately viable, most particularly in more affluent areas where there was significant consumer choice; they saw more future in the careful adaptation of conventional retailing practices. Disagreeing and tending to divide the world between those who supported him and those who did not, Glen was often vigorously critical of the wholesale. His crusading zeal, however, did lead to the creation of ten service fee cooperatives on the Pacific Coast, and several of them flourished for a number of years before converting to more orthodox kinds of consumer cooperatives.

The service fee experiments may be considered as an imaginative way to repackage old cooperative approaches[36] or as a needed new way to create a consumer society based on education and fair costs (the version preferred by the participants). They might even be seen as the consequence of the force of a powerful personality. Perhaps most important, though, they should be seen as an attempt to continue the expansion of the movement, to find ways to reach out to new populations, different kinds of people, and emerging communities. In large part, they were the outgrowth of Glen's deep concern that the movement had started to lose its grander vision as it settled into the convenience of a small established store system.[37] It is unfortunate that the service fee concept never achieved the momentum it might have; a more supportive reaction from the conventional cooperatives and a more conciliatory approach by Glen might have given it a longer and more potent life.

At the same time, other groups of critics of the conventional consumer cooperative emerged on the west coast. They were largely to be found among disaffected young people in Vancouver and Victoria. Reflecting similar trends in the United States, they were concerned with selling food uncontaminated by pesticides and with developing stores in which the management culture was democratic rather than conventional, participatory rather than directive. In their disgust with the existing cooperative system they formed their own wholesale, Fed-Up Coop, a not-so-subtle reflection of their views of Federated Cooperatives.

The emergence of these bands of critics did not mean that the advocates for the expansion of conventional cooperatives in western Canada were without dreams or ambitions. All the major urban cooperatives on the prairies struggled with the challenge of penetrating the urban market, with only Calgary making significant gains. On the west coast, responsibility for cooperative promotion and development passed in 1971 to British Columbia Central Credit Union, after the provincial wholesale had been amalgamated with Federated Cooperatives and when the provincial cooperative union ran into financial and managerial problems.

Shortly afterward, the leadership of Central, in collaboration with consumer leaders and extensive financial assistance from Federated Cooperatives, started an extensive development of consumer cooperatives in the Okanagan and Fraser River valleys in British Columbia. Undercapitalized, soon caught in a rapid rise of interest rates and inadequately based on local memberships, the initiatives soon failed. It was a bitter lesson that would daunt future development in arguably the most logical region for growth for decades that followed.

The failure also spoke to a fundamental problem that had emerged in the consumer cooperative movement, arguably in much of the Canadian movement: it was the problem of regeneration. The movement had been built upon the effective use of sympathetic networks, ideological commitments, educational activities, and a supportive state. The networks of the 1970s were not the networks of an earlier age. Members of farm movements, trade unions, political parties, women's movements, even associated cooperative movements such as credit unions, were not as easily engaged, in some cases they had become disinterested. As the ideological simplifications associated with the Cold War overwhelmed more subtle ideological quests such as cooperativism, the intellectual excitement typically found among earlier generations was rarely encountered. Cooperative education, "the life blood of the movement" in Holyoake's phrase, became increasingly member information and marketing allurements despite the best efforts of some dedicated cooperators. The state, even in Saskatchewan, became increasingly only a registration and supervisory agency, losing nearly all commitment to the expansion of cooperative endeavor. To some extent, all these trends were evident in the failures of the British Columbia experiments.

The weakness of the regenerational impulse emanated from the dynamics of cooperative endeavor in another way. Generally, the consumer cooperative were reacting to changes, not only in how they worked in the five spheres of member relations, community ties, state relations, structural bonds, and management systems, but also in their governing perspectives, institutional cultures, and stages of development. Preoccupations with the markets in which they operated lessened their commitment to a broader movement; the development of management cultures often meant a devaluation of member involvement; the ending of the formative period marked the decline of the kinds of commitment upon which much early member support had been based.

Moreover, the experience of the previous fifty years created a comfortable acceptance of the status quo that made consolidation and change in the face of new technologies, management practice, and communications systems difficult. Cooperative systems have had an inevitable and sometimes commendable bias in favor of sustaining what has been built rather than envisioning what might be possible. It can also be a liability. Thus efforts to create larger, more competitive units were resisted when the economic—and potentially the social—benefits were reasonably transparent. [38]

More seriously, cooperatives had difficulty in accumulating the kind of capital and other resources needed to sustain growth. It was the rare board and management that could effectively harbor the funds, assemble the land and develop the human capacity to continue expanding the membership base and developing new facilities.

Meanwhile, in Atlantic Canada, the consumer cooperative movement went through a similar and yet quite different history. As in western Canada, there were several local stores in both urban and rural places that were sound economic organizations, able to meet member needs and to fulfil their social obligations as cooperatives. Structurally, though, there was a surplus of organizational enthusiasms, a predilection towards more wholesale than was profitable. In the early 1950s, the Island Cooperative Service on Prince Edward Island had encountered difficulties and nearly took down all the local societies. The movement was saved by a difficult economic restructuring, partly engineered by Maritime Cooperative Services. A few years later Cape Breton Cooperative Services and Eastern Cooperative Services amalgamated under the name of the latter after they both encountered severe economic difficulties. The experiment lasted until 1965 when a financially troubled Eastern Cooperative Services was merged with Maritime Cooperative Services.[39] A strong regional structure had finally been achieved.

In addition to taking a little longer to achieve a strong regional positions, Maritimes Cooperative Services (its name changed to Coop Atlantic in 1978) also ultimately took a different perspective on service fee cooperatives. Cooperators in Atlantic Canada began to discuss the new consumer model in the 1960s, partly through the effective if distant missionary efforts of Ralph Staples and Rod Glen. Partly, the discussions developed because the wholesale, while making progress, was not moving ahead as rapidly as many wished. Partly, it was because the emphasis on continuous education, consumer control, local responsibility, and enlightened consumption resonated well with the movement's heritage in the region. Partly it was because the idea fitted well into the strong communal fabric of many communities in Atlantic Canada.

Nevertheless, there were intense debates over the viability of such an approach and then over practical issues as the idea gained support. A relatively widespread grassroots infatuation with the possibility forced the wholesale to develop a clear set of policies for the development of service fee stores; a skeptical, experienced group of managers insisted upon developing appropriate safeguards. The idea was tried, therefore, with some care and ultimately with some consistency and wholesale support. The result was that over twenty service fee cooperatives were in operation by 1980.

Nevertheless, even with this expansion, the movement in Atlantic Canada, like that in the West, was a long way from profoundly shaping consumption or from transforming the world. The overall trend was one of limiting horizons, not brave new worlds; it was, as in the West, becoming a matter of specializing in the markets large competitors left alone.

The blunting of grand objectives was also related to changes in the English-Canadian movement. Nationally, the consumer cooperative movement found itself increasingly isolated because of changes within the structure of the general Canadian cooperative movement, changes caused not so much by intent and animosity as by the gradual maturing of the other cooperative sectors. When the consumer movement had emerged it had done so largely within the shadow of the producer movement, even in Atlantic Canada. It had reached an understanding with farm organizations albeit not without some continuing tensions, most commonly over competition in the farm supply business. Consumer cooperatives, in turn, had been instrumental in the formation of many credit unions and in the development of the insurance and trust companies.

By the 1960s, though, many of the sister movements started in the 1930s, 1940s and 1950s had become powerful players in their own right within regional and national cooperative movements. Credit unions had grown with remarkable rapidity, insurance cooperatives had progressed, and the trust company had achieved some stability. Like the consumer cooperatives, these new organizations had developed their own space, created their own communications systems, and established their own democratic structures. Above all, they had fashioned their own managerial cultures appropriate to the kinds of business they undertook and in keeping with the industries within which they worked.

The result was a weakening of national cooperative consensus on purpose, priorities, and practice. Support for a common educational system dwindled; interest in common national activities varied in keeping with the urgency of issues around taxation and fees for the national organization. Much of the national vision that had moved the generation emanating from the Depression and the war dissipated amid local and provincial priorities and in the face of the inevitable challenges associated with developing the national financial system. In the process some of the natural enthusiasm also waned at the local level; human beings, particularly those who volunteer to build movements, respond to ideas as well as appeals for material advantage.

By 1980, therefore, the consumer cooperative movement was an established, even an old movement. Its history had been played out amid debates over how to relate to the spheres in which cooperatives functioned. It had wrestled with dilemmas offered by different perspectives on what were the appropriate roles for the movement. It had experienced fundamental change as institutions were shaped by different cultural paradigms. It had often experienced dramatic change and difficult debates as cooperative institutions went through different stages of development. The dynamics typical of cooperative enterprise help explain the successes of the English-Canadian consumer movement; they also help to explain its limitations and shortcomings.

Notes

1. "Some History of the Early Co-ops in Nova Scotia," *Canadian Co-operative Digest* (April 1960): 37-39.
2. See R. J MacSween, "Co-operation in Nova Scotia," (unpublished manuscript, Public Archives of Nova Scotia).
3. See G. S. Kealy and B. D. Palmer, *Dreaming of What Might Be* (Toronto, 1987), 365-69.

4. See Ian MacPherson, "The Search for the Commonwealth: The Co-operative Union of Canada, 1909-1939" (Ph.D. diss., University of Western Ontario, 1970), 276-345.

5. In this chapter, following normal Canadian practice, the word "Maritimes" refers to the provinces of New Brunswick, Nova Scotia, and Prince Edward Island; the words "Atlantic Canada" refers to these provinces plus Newfoundland and Labrador.

6. There was also a strong movement to organize the orchardists of the Annapolis Valley. While it achieved considerable success, it was focused largely upon matters of production and sale of apples and did not spark the development of consumer or other forms of cooperative endeavor.

7. There were some earlier local marketing cooperatives. See B. McCuthcheon, "The Birth of Agrarianism in the Prairie West," *Prairie Forum* (Nov. 1976), 79-94.

8. Brief, United Farmers of Canada (Saskatchewan Section) to the Royal Commission on Co-operatives, 1945, vol. V, 1587.

9. Keen drew his greatest inspiration from the writings of George Holyoake (his copies replete with considerable marginalia can be found in the library of the Canadian Cooperative Association) and from the works of Charles Gide and Beatrice Webb. For a brief autobiography, see George Keen, *The Birth of a Movement: Reminiscences of a Co-operator* (Montréal: undated, copy available in the CCA Library).

10. What Canadian cooperators—like those in other lands—considered the Rochdale rules varied significantly over time. Generally, the variations concerned the social goals of the original rules but political neutrality was also often at issue.

11. Alphonse Desjardins with the help of his wife, Dorimene, started the *caisses populaires* movement in 1900 in Lévis, Québec, across the St. Lawrence River from Québec City. In 1908 and 1909 he was instrumental in helping start the credit union movement in the United States.

12. M. H. Staples, *The Challenge of Agriculture: The Story of the UFO* (Toronto, 1921), 81-96.

13. There were earlier unsuccessful efforts by consumer societies to start wholesaling activities. See I. MacPherson, "The Search for the Commonwealth," 308-10.

14. For a more thorough treatment of the emergence of the wholesale and those that were developed in Manitoba and Alberta, see Brett Fairbairn, *Building a Dream: The Co-operative Retailing System in Western Canada, 1928-1988* (Saskatoon, 1989), 27-55. Much of the discussion of the western consumer movement is derived from this valuable study.

15. See Fairbairn, *Building a Dream*, 56-65.

16. Fairbairn, *Building a Dream*, 66. For a fuller description of the Refineries' background and early development see *ibid.*, 66-76.

17. For Fowler's description of the history of the refinery, see T. Phalen ed., *Co-operative Leadership: Harry L. Fowler* (Saskatoon, 1977), 95-108.

18. See A. V. Hill, *Tides of Change: A Story of the Fishermen's Co-operatives in British Columbia* (Vancouver, 1967), *passim*, for the history of the interrelationship between the fishing and consumer movement.

19. The Antigonish movement grew out of a program developed at St. Francis Xavier in the early years of this century aimed at helping people in fishing and agricultural communities improve their economic and social condition. From its beginnings in

eastern Nova Scotia it culminated in the formation of the Extension Department in 1928. Under the leadership of two priests, Moses Coady and Jimmy Tompkins, and a former educational leader, A. B. MacDonald, the Department involved a large number of women and men leaders in the organization of study clubs and co-operatives throughout the region. Its work, celebrated by the networks of the Christian churches and supported by several foundations, became known through much of North America and ultimately in many overseas development initiatives in the following five decades.

20. The historical analysis of the Antigonish movement is voluminous. A workman-like but useful description of it is Alexander Laidlaw, *Campus and Community, the Global Impact of the Antigonish Movement* (Montréal, 1961). A more recent study that focuses upon arguably the most dynamic of the movement's leaders is Jim Lotz, *Father Jimmy: The Life and Times of Jimmy Tompkins* (Wreck Cove, 1997).

21. Stefan Haley, *Tested by Fire: The Life and Work of W. H. McEwen* (Saskatoon, 1980), 153.

22. W. H. McEwen, *Faith, Hope and Co-operation: A Maritime Provinces Story* (Moncton, 1969), 52.

23. Ian MacPherson, *Each for All: A History of the Co-operative Movement in English Canada, 1900-1945* (Toronto, 1979), 169-70.

24. Haley, *Tested by Fire,* 173-77.

25. Ian MacPherson, "Better Tractors for Less Money: The Establishment of Canadian Co-operative Implements, Limited," *Manitoba History* (1987): 2-11, contains a description of the role of the consumer movement in the development of the farm machinery initiative.

26. See Fairbairn, *Building a Dream,* 130-32.

27. For a brief summary of the national efforts to create a national financial system for the cooperative movement, see Ian MacPherson, *The Story of Co-operative Insurance Services* (Regina, 1974), 1-49.

28. See Fairbairn, *Building a Dream,* 146-49 and Ian MacPherson, "An Act of Faith and Optimism: Creating a Co-operative College of Canada, 1951-1973," in M. R. Welton, ed., *Knowledge for the People: The Struggle for Adult Learning in English-Speaking Canada, 1828-1973* (Toronto, 1987), 178-93.

29. It may seem strange to those who knew him to include Harry Fowler in this list. He was not very good at managing everyday business activities and many of his roles were as an elected official (though he did serve as the manager of the refinery). He is best remembered as a visionary and an idealist. But, on the other hand, he was associated with virtually every major cooperative undertaking on the prairies and on a national level between 1934 and the late 1960s. If one thinks of cooperative entrepreneurship as being broader in its sources and leadership than entrepreneurship in capitalist firms, then he certainly belongs. He was one of the key individuals behind the creation of the modern cooperative movement in English Canada. See Terry Phalen, ed., *Co-operative Leadership* for a useful insight into Fowlers' activities and vision. Similarly, George Urwin was technically a director with the Saskatchewan wholesale but his influence was so pervasive and his involvement so deep that he really was a manager in all but name.

30. For an example of how "quiet," often informal government services could benefit the movement, see F. Waldo Walsh, *We Fought for the Little Man, My Sixty Years in Agriculture* (Moncton, 1978).

31. See Fairbairn, *Building a Dream*, 122-43 for a discussion of the rather difficult amalgamation process.

32. See S. Haley, *Tested by Fire*, 171-78 and 208-12.

33. By 1980, there were over 400 stores and more than 900,000 members in the western consumer cooperative movement united within the Federated system. The wholesale's total sales were $1,100,000,000 and that of local stores more than $1,900,000,000. See Appendices, Fairbairn, *Building a Dream*, 322-23.

34. See Fairbairn, *Building a Dream*, 171-205.

35. See I. MacPherson, *Building and Protecting the Co-operative Movement: A Brief History of the Co-operative Union of Canada, 1909-1984* (Ottawa, 1984), 158-93.

36. Fairbairn, *Building a Dream*, 242-44.

37. Interview with Rod Glen by Mariam Mctiernan, August 27, 1978. Archives, Credit Union Central of British Columbia.

38. The outstanding example of this trend in western Canada was the ill-fated effort in the 1970s to assist some small and troubled cooperatives by placing them under the central direction of a new regional cooperative, Westland Co-operatives. It failed because of some partly legitimate concerns about autonomy, an overly ambitious geographic "reach," inadequate consideration of how members might be involved, and a disputative rather than thoughtful discussion of the possibilities. See B. Fairbairn, *Building a Dream*, 225-28.

39. See S. Haley, *Tested by Fire*, 214-17 and 232-33.

Cooperative and Capitalist Commerce in Historical Perspective: A Selected Bibliography

1. Consumer Cooperation: Commerce and Culture

Adeyeye, Samuel. *The Co-operative Movement in Nigeria.* Gottingen, 1978.

Akira, Kurimoto. "The Cooperative Response to the Aging Society in Japan." *Review of International Cooperation* 90, no. 1 (1997): 18-24.

———. "Restructuring Consumer Coops and Coop Principles." *Review of International Cooperation* 86, no. 2 (1996): 6-74.

Ammirato, Piero. *La Lega: The Making of a Successful Cooperative Network.* Aldershot, 1996.

An Overview of the Swedish Cooperative Movement 1976 to 1984. Stockholm, 1986.

Aschoff, Gunther and Eckart Henningsen, *The German Cooperative System. Its History, Structure and Strength.* Frankfurt a.M., 1985.

Backstrom, Philip N. *Christian Socialism and Co-operation in Victorian England: Edward Vansittart Neale and the Co-operative Movement.* London, 1974.

Balawyder, Aloysius, ed. *Cooperative Movements in Eastern Europe.* Montclair, N.J., 1980.

Bernold, Monika. "Konsum, Politik und Geschlecht. Zur Feminisierung von Öffentlichkeit als Strategie und Paradoxon," in *Konsumgeschichte als Gesellschaftsgeschichte.* Edited by Helmut Kälble, Jürgen Kocka, and Hannes Siegrist. Frankfurt a.M., 1996.

Birchall, Johnston. *Co-op: The People's Business.* Manchester, 1994.

Blanc, Elsie Terry. *Cooperative Movement in Russia.* New York, 1924.

Bogardus, Emery S. *Dictionary of Cooperation.* New York and Chicago, 1948.

Bonner, Arnold. *British Co-operation.* Manchester, 1961.

Böök, Sven-Åke and Tore Johansson. *The Co-operative Movement in Sweden.* Stockholm, 1988.

Borgbjerg, F. J. *Kooperative Foretagender.* Copenhagen, 1909.

Brazda, Johann and Robert Schediwy. "Konsumgenossenschaften im Strukturwandel." *Wirtschaft und Gesellschaft. Wirtschaftspolitische Zeitschrift der Kammer für Arbeiter und Angetelle für Wien.* 1 (1989): 65.

Brazda, Johann and Robert Schediwy, eds. *Consumer Co-operatives in a Changing World.* Geneva, 1989.

Brewer, John and Roy Porter. *Consumption and the World of Goods*. London: 1993.

Brizon, P. and E. Poisson. *La Coopération*. Paris, 1913.

Cassau, Theodor. *The Consumers' Cooperative Movement in Germany*. New York, 1924.

———. *Die Konsumvereinsbewegung in Deutschland*. Munich, 1924.

Cassel, Gustav. *Grunddragen i penningväsendets utveckling*. Stockholm, 1931.

Chavez, MariaElena. "The Role of the ICA in the Advancement of Women in Cooperatives." *Review of International Cooperation* 89, no. 1 (1996): 42-51.

Christensen, Jens. *Rural Denmark 1750-1980*. Copenhagen, 1983.

Cole, G. D. H. *A Century of Co-operation*. Manchester, 1945.

Cowling, Ellis. *Co-operatives in America: Their Past, Present and Future*, 93. New York, 1943.

Cox, Craig. *Storefront Revolution: Food Coops and the Counterculture*. New Brunswick, 1994.

Davies, Margaret Llewelyn. *The Women's Co-operative Guild*. Kerksby Lonsdale, 1904.

DeBrouckère, Louis. *La Coopération, ses origines, sa nature, et ses grandes fonctions*. Brussels, 1927.

Dülfer, Eberhard, ed. *International Handbook of Cooperative Organizations*. Göttingen, 1994.

Ealter, Karl, ed. *Co-Operation and Charles Gide*. London, 1933.

Earle, John. *The Italian Cooperative Movement: A Portrait of the Lega Nazionale delle Cooperative e Mutue*. London, 1986.

Elldin, Harald. *Klipp och bakgrunder till kooperativt fostringsarbete under ett halvsekel*. Stockholm, 1950.

Ellmeier, Andreas. "Handel mit der Zunkunft. Zur Geschlechterpolitik der Konsumgenossenschaften," *L'Homme. Zeitschrift für feministische Geschichtswissenschaften* 6, no. 1 (1995): 62-77.

———. "Eva Singer-Meczes, Modellierung der sozialistischen Konsumentin. Konsumgenossenschaftliche, FrauenPolitik in den Zwanziger Jahren," *Zeitgeschichte* 11/12 (1989): 411, 424.

Faber, H. *Co-operation in Danish Agriculture*. London, 1931.

Fairbairn, Brett. *Building a Dream: The Co-operative Retailing System in Western Canada, 1928-1988*. Saskatoon, 1989.

———. *The Meaning of Rochdale: The Rochdale Pioneers and the Co-operative Principles*. Saskatoon, 1994.

Faust, Helmut. *Geschichte der Genossenschaftsbewegung: Ursprung und Aufbruch der Genossenschaftsbewegung in England, Frankreich und Deutschland sowie ihre weitere Entwicklung im deutschen Sprachraum*. 3rd ed. Frankfurt a.M., 1977.

Frank, Dana. *Purchasing Power: Consumer Organizing, Gender, and the Seattle Labor Movement, 1919-1929.* Cambridge, 1994.

Freundlich, Emmy. *Die Stellung der Frau in der Genossenschaftsbewegung.* Vienna, 1924.

Furlough, Ellen. *Consumer Cooperation in France: The Politics of Consumption, 1834-1930.* Ithaca, 1991.

Gaffin, Jean and David Thoms. *Caring and Sharing: The Centenary History of the Co-operative Women's Guild.* Manchester, 1983.

Gaumont, Jean. *Histoire générale de la coopération en France.* 2 vols. Paris, 1924.

———. *Les mouvements de la coopération ouvrière dans les banlieues parisiennes.* Paris, 1932.

Gide, Charles. *Fourier, précuseur de la coopération.* Paris, 1924.

Gjöres, Axel. *Svensk kooperation före ittiotalet.* Stockholm, 1919.

Gurney, Peter. *Co-operative culture and the politics of consumption in England, 1870-1930.* Manchester, 1996.

Haley, Stefan. *Tested by Fire: The life and Work of W.H. McEwen.* Saskatoon, 1980.

Hall, F. and W. P. Watkins, *Co-operation: A Survey of the History, Principles, and Organisation of the Co-operative Movement in Great Britain and Ireland.* Manchester, 19 .

Hamilton, G. K. *Om arbetsklassen och arbetare-föreningar.* Lund, 1865.

Harmaja, Laura. *Husmoderns ekonomiska gärning,* 1928, 3d. ed. Stockholm, 1937.

Harrison, J. F. C. *Robert Owen and the Owenites in Britain and America.* London, 1969.

Hasselman, Erwin. *Geschichte der Deutschen Konsumgenossenschaften.* Frankfurt, a.M., 1971.

———. *Consumers' Cooperation in Germany.* 3rd ed. Hamburg, 1961.

Hauch, Gabriella. "'Revolutionäre im Schlafrock' und Instrumente des Klasenkampfes'. Konsumgenossenschaften in der österreichischen Artbeiterbewegung vor 1914," *Arbeiterbewegung in Österreich und Ungarn bis 1914.* Ed. Wolfgang Maderthaner, Materialien zur Arbeiterbewegung 45.

Heckscher, Eli. *Tvångshushållning och "planhushållning."* Stockholm, 1934.

Hidekazu, Nomura, ed. *Seikyo: A Comprehensive Analysis of Consumer cooperatives in Japan.* Tokyo, 1993.

Hill, A. V. *Tides of Change: A Story of the Fishermen's Co-operatives in British Columbia.* Vancouver, 1967.

Holyoake, G. J. *The History of Co-operation.* vol. I, 1875. London, 1906.

———. *Self-Help by the People: History of Co-operation in Rochdale.* London, 1858.

International Cooperative Alliance. *Cooperation in the European Market Economies*. New York, 1967.

Isao, Takamura. *Principles of Cooperative Management*. Kobe, Japan, 1995.

Jackall, Robert and Henry M. Levin, eds. *Worker Cooperatives in America*. Berkeley, 1984.

Japanese Consumers' Cooperative Union. *Coop: Facts & Figures 1995*. Tokyo, 1996.

Jones, Anthony and William Moskoff. *Ko-ops: The Rebirth of Entrepreneurship in the Soviet Union*. Bloomington, 1991.

Jones, Ben. *Co-operative Production*. Oxford, 1894.

Kasmir, Sharryn. *The Myth of Mondragón: Cooperatives, Politics, and Working-Class Life in a Basque Town*. Albany, 1996.

Kautsky, Karl. *Consumvereine und Arbeiterbewegung*. Vienna, 1897.

Kayden, Eugene M. and Alexis N. Antsiferov. *The Cooperative Movement in Russia During the War*. New Haven, 1929.

Kinloch, J. and J. Butt. *History of the Scottish Co-operative Wholesale Society Limited*. Glasgow, 1981.

Klein, Fritz. *Selbsthilfe aus christlicher Verantwortung: Die Geschichte der christlichen. Konsumverein*. Recklinghausen, 1967.

Klinedinst, Mark and Sato Hitomi. "The Japanese Cooperative Sector." *Journal of Economic Issues* 38, no. 2, (1994): 511.

Knapp, Joseph G. *The Rise of American Cooperative Enterprise: 1620-1920*. U.S.A., 1969.

Kooperationens ställning inom svensk näringsliv. Stockholm, 1934.

Korp, Andreas. *Der Konsumverein Teesdorf. Ein Beitrag zur Frühgeschichte der österreichischen Genossenschaften*. Vienna, 1978.

———. *Stein auf Stein. 50 Jahre Großeinkaufsgesellschaft österreichischer Consumvereine 1905-1945*. Vienna, 1955.

Kress, Andrew J. *Introduction to the Cooperative Movement*. New York, 1941.

Lambert, Paul. *Studies in the Social Philosophy of Co-operation*. Manchester, 1963.

Lancaster, B. and P. Maguire, eds. *Towards the Co-operative Commonwealth*. Loughborough, 1996.

Lancaster, Bill. *Radicalism, Co-operation and Socialism: Leicester working-class politics, 1860-1906*. Leicester, 1987.

Larsen, A. D. "Arbejderkooperationens historie 1871-1923." *Arbejderhistorie*, 22 (1984): 25-29.

Leeman, F. W. *Co-operation in Nottingham. A History of 100 Years of Nottingham Co-operative Society Limited*. Nottingham, 1963.

Leikin, Steve. "The Practical Utopians: Cooperation and the American Labor Movement, 1860-1890." Ph.D. diss., University of California, Berkeley, 1992.

Ljungberg, C. E. *Om associationsväsendet i främmande länder med särskilt hänseende till de schultze-delitzschaska förskottsföreningarne.* Stockholm, 1865.

Lykke, Kaj. *Arbejderbevegelse og Arbejderkooperation i Danmark 1871-1898.* Copenhagen, 1974.

MacPherson, Ian. *Each for All: A History of the Co-operative Movement in English Canada, 1900-1945.* Toronto, 1979.

———. "An Act of Faith and Optimism: Creating a Co-operative College of Canada, 1951-1973." In *Knowledge for the People, 1828-1973*, M. R. Welton, ed. Toronto, 1987.

———. *The Story of Co-operative Insurance Services.* Regina, 1974.

———. *Building and Protecting the Co-operative Movement: A Brief History of the Co-operative Union of Canada, 1909-1984.* Ottawa, 1984.

Masayuki, Yamagishi, Lou Hammond Ketilson, Per-Olof Jonsson, Iain Macdonald, and Loris Ferini. "Joint Project on Participatory Democracy." *Review of International Cooperation* 88, no. 4 (1995): 27-43.

McEwen, W. H. *Faith, Hope and Co-operation: A Maritime Provinces Story.* Moncton, 1969.

Mehta, S. C. *Consumer Co-operation in India.* Delhi, 1964.

Myrdal, Gunnar and Alva Myrdal. *Kris i befolkningsfrågan.* Stockholm, 1935.

Myrdal, Gunnar. *Konjunktur och offentlig hushållning.* Stockholm, 1933.

North West Labour History 19 (1994/95). Special Issue on the history of consumer cooperation in England.

Ostergaard, G. N. and A. H. Halsey. *Power in Co-operatives: A Study of the Internal Politics of British Retail Societies.* Oxford, 1965.

Påhlman, Axel and Walter Sjin. *Arbetarföreningarna i Sverige 1850-1900.* Stockholm, 1944.

Parker, Florence E. "Consumers' Cooperation in the United States." In *The Annuals of the American Academy of Political and Social Science*, 98-99. May 1937.

Patera, Mario, ed. *Handbuch des österreichischen Genossenschaftswesens.* Vienna, 1986.

Pedersen, Clemens, ed. *The Danish Co-operative Movement.* Copenhagen, 1977.

Penin, Marc. *Charles Gide, 1847-1932. Lésprit critique.* Davis, 1998.

Pesthoff, Victor A. *Between Markets and Politics: Cooperatives in Sweden.* Boulder, 1991.

Phalen, T., ed. *Co-operative Leadership: Harry L. Fowler.* Saskatoon, 1977.

Poisson, Ernest. *The Co-operative Republic*, ix and 177. London, 1925.

Pollard, Sidney. "Nineteenth-century Co-operation: From Community Building to Shopkeeping." In *Essays in Labour History*, A. Briggs and J. Saville, eds. 1960.

————. "The Founding of the Co-operative Party." In *Essays in Labour History, 1886-1923*. Edited by Asa Briggs and John Saville. London, 1971.

Potter, Beatrice. *The Co-operative Movement in Great Britain*. London, 1891.

Prudhommeaux, Jean. *Coopération et pacification*. 71. Paris, 1904.

Purvis, M. "The Development of Co-operative Retailing in England and Wales, 1851-1901: A Geographical Study." *Journal of Historical Geography* 16 (1990): 314-31.

Ralph Nader Task Force on European Cooperatives. *Making Change? Learning From Europe's Consumer Cooperatives*. Washington, D.C., 1985.

Redfern, Percy. *The Story of the CWS*. Manchester, 1938.

Reid, Donald. *The Miners of Decazeville: A Genealogy of Deindustrialization*. Cambridge, 1985.

Richardson, William. *The CWS in War and Peace 1938-1976*. Manchester, 1977.

Rundbäck, Abraham. *Afhandling om konsumtionsföreningar*. Stockholm, 1869.

Rylander, Axel. *Konsumtionskredit: Nytt sekel - bättre varor*, Stockholm, 1900.

Sandgruber, Roman. *Die Anfänge der Konsumgesellschaft. Konsumgüterverbrauch, Lebensstandard und Alltagskultur in Österreich im 18. und 19. Jahrhundert*. Vienna, 1982.

Sato, Yoshiyuki. *Josei to Kyo-do- Kumiai no Shakai Gaku, The Sociology of Women and Cooperatives*. Tokyo.

Schildgen, Robert. *Toyohiko Kagawa: Apostle of Love and Social Justice*. Berkeley, 1988.

Schmidt, Franz. *Triumph einer Idee. 100 Jahre Konsumgenossenschaften*. Vienna, 1956.

Scott, Gillian. *Feminism and the Politics of Working Women: The Women's Co-operative Guild, 1880s to the Second World War*. London, 1998.

Seibert, Franz. *Die Konsumgenossenschaften in Österreich, Materialien zur Arbeiterbewegung* 11. Vienna, 1978.

Silber, Norman. *Test and Protect: The Influence of the Consumers' Union*. New York, 1983.

Singh, Mohinder. *Co-operatives in Asia*. New York, 1970.

Sjölin, Walter. *Svensk kooperation under 1800-talet*. Stockholm, 1960.

Sonnichsen, Albert. *Consumer's Cooperation*. New York, 1919.

Spann, Edward K. *Brotherly Tomorrows: Movements for a Cooperative Society in America, 1820-1920*. New York, 1989.

Taimni, K. K. *Consumers' Co-operatives in Third World Strategy for Development*, Poona, 1978.

Taylor, Barbara. *Eve and the New Jerusalem: Socialism and Feminism in the Nineteenth Century*. London, 1983.

Thomas, Henk and Chris Logan. *Mondragon: An Economic Analysis*. London, 1982.

Totomianz, T., ed. *Internationales Handwörterbuch des Genossenschaftswesens*. Berlin, 1928.

Vandervelde, Emile. *La coopération neutre et la coopération socialiste*. Paris, 1913.

Victor, Serwy. *Histoire du cooperation en Belgique*, 4 vols. Bruxelles, 1942-46.

Vukowitsch, Andreas. *100 Jahre Konsumgenossenschaften in Österreich*. Vienna, 1956.

———. *Geschichte des konsumgenossenschaftlichen Großeinkaufs in Osterreich*. Vienna, 1931.

———. *30 Jahre Zentralverband Österreischischer Konsumvereine*. Vienna, 1935.

Warbasse, James Peter. *Co-operative Democracy*. New York, 1923.

Warne, Colston E. *The Consumer Movement*. Edited by Richard Morse and Florence Snyder. Manhattan, Kansas, 1993.

Walton, John and Jenny Smith. "Property, Employment and the Co-operative Movement: The Social Structure of Co-operation in Sabden, 1923." *Transactions of the Historic Society of Lancashire and Cheshire* 134 (1985): 129-49.

Watkins, William. *The International Co-operative Alliance, 1895-1970*. London, 1970.

Webb, Cartherine. *The Woman with the Basket: the Story of the Women's Co-operative Guild*. Manchester, 1927.

Weuster, Arnulf. *Theorie der Konsumgenossenschaftsentwicklung: die deutschen Konsumgenossenschaften bis zum Ende der Weimarer Zeit*. Berlin, 1980.

Williams, C. Arthur. "Black Urban Consumer Cooperatives: Why They Fail." Ph.D. thesis, Rutgers University, 1977.

Woolf, Leonard S. *Socialism and Cooperation*. London, 1921.

Yeo, Stephen, ed. *New Views of Co-operation*. London, 1988.

2. Capitalist Commerce and Culture

Ambjörnsson, Ronny. *Den skötsamme arbetare*. Stockholm, 1988.

———. "The Conscientious Worker: Ideas and Ideals in a Swedish Working Class Culture." *History of European Ideas*. 1 (1989), 59-67.

Auslander, Leora. *Taste and Power: Furnishing Modern France*. Berkeley, 1996.

Benson, John. *The Rise of Consumer Society in Britain, 1880-1980.* NY, 1994.

Boddewyn, J. J. *Belgian Policy Toward Retailing since 1789.* East Lansing, 1978.

Brewer, John and Roy Porter, eds. *Consumption and the World of Goods.* London, 1993.

Campbell, Colin. *The Romantic Ethic and the Spirit of Modern Consumerism.* Oxford, 1987.

Cross, Gary. *Time and Money: The Making of Consumer Culture.* New York, 1993.

———. "Consumer History and Dilemmas of Working-Class History." *Labor History Review*, 62, no. 3 (1997), 261-74.

Douglas, Mary and Baron Isherwood. *The World of Goods: Towards an Anthropology of Consumption.* London, 1996.

Einhorn, Barbara and Eileen Yeo, eds. *Women and Market Societies: Crisis and Opportunity.* Aldershot, 1995.

Elias, Norbert. *Über den Prozess der Zivilisation: soziogenetische und psychologenetischeu Untersuchungen.* Basel, 1939.

Featherstone, Mike. *Consumer Culture and Postmodernism*, London, 1991.

Fine, Ben and Ellen Leopold. *The World of Consumption.* London, 1993.

Fontaine, Laurence. *History of Pedlars in Europe.* Durham, 1996.

Fox, Richard Wightman Fox and T. J. Jackson Lears, eds. *The Culture of Consumption.* New York, 1983.

Frow, John. *Time and Commodity Culture: Essays in Cultural Theory and Postmodernity.* Oxford, 1997.

Frykman, Jonas and Orvar Löfgren. *Culture-Builders: A Historical Anthropology of Middle-Class Life.* New Brunswick, 1987.

De Grazia, Victoria with Ellen Furlough. *The Sex of Things: Gender and Consumption in Historical Perspective.* Berkeley, 1996.

Habermas, Jurgen. *The Structural Transformation of the Public Sphere: An Inquiry into a Category of Bourgeois Society*, 1962; reprint Cambridge, Mass., 1991.

Hopkins, Eric. *Working-Class Self-Help in Nineteenth-Century England.* New York, 1995.

Howes, David, ed. *Cross Cultural Consumption: Global Markets, Local Realities.* London, 1996.

Kallen, Horace. *The Decline and Rise of the Consumer.* New York, 1936.

Kjergaard, Thorkild. "The Farmer Interpretation of Danish History." *Scandinavian Journal of History.* 10 (1985): 97-118.

Lancaster, Bill. *The Department Store: A Social History.* London, 1995.

Leach, William. *Land of Desire: Merchants, Power, and the Rise of a New American Culture.* NY, 1993.

Lears, T. J. Jackson. *Fables of Abundance: A Cultural History of Advertising in America*. NY, 1991.

Löfgren, Orvar. "Swedish Modern: Nationalizing Consumption and Aesthetics in the Welfare State." Rutgers Center for Historical Analysis, 1993.

Lury, Lury. *Consumer Culture*. New Brunswick, 1996.

Mackay, Hugh, ed. *Consumption and Everyday Life*. London, 1997.

McKendrick, Neil, John Brewer, and J. H. Plumb. *The Birth of a Consumer Society: The Commercialization of Eighteenth Century England*. Bloomington, 1982.

Miller, Daniel, ed. *Acknowledging Consumption: A Review of New Studies*. London, 1995.

Miller, Michael. *The Bon Marché: bourgeois Culture and the Department Store*. Princton.

Mort, Frank. *Cultures of Consumption: Masculinities and Social Space in Late Twentieth Century Britain*. London, 1996.

Moschis, George P. *Consumer Socialization: A Life-Cycle Perspective*. Lexington, Mass., 1987.

Ohlin, Bertil. *Den världsekonomiska depressionen*. Stockholm, 1931.

Richards, Thomas. *The Commodity Culture of Victorian England: Advertising and Spectacle, 1851-1914*. Stanford, 1990.

Shields, Rob. *Lifestyle Shopping: The Subject of Consumption*. London, 1992

Stearns, Peter N. "Stages of Consumerism: Recent Work on the Issues of Periodization," *Journal of Modern History* 69 (March 1997), 102-12.

Webb, Beatrice. *The Discovery of the Consumer*. New York, 1930.

Williams, Rosalind H. *Dream Worlds: Mass Consumtion in Late Nineteenth-Century France*. Berkeley, 1982.

Williamson, Judith. *Consuming Passsions: The Dynamics of Popular Culture*. London, 1986.

Index

About the Contributors

Peder Aléx is assistant professor at Umeå University, Sweden where he also received his Ph.D. His book, *The Rational Consumer: The Co-operative Union and Wholesale Society as a Public Educator*, was published in Swedish in 1994. His other publications include "Den rationella konsumenten" ("The Rational Consumer") in *Från hermetism till rationell distribution*, Idéhistoriska skrifter 14, Institutionen för idéhistoria, Umeå universitet (1993); "På jakt efter en rationell konsument" ("Searching for the Rational Consumer") in Aléx, ed., *Kooperation och välfärd, Kooperative årsbok 1995* (1994); and "Kivinnan med korgen—hemarbete och konsumentmakt" ("The Woman with the Basket: Domestic Work and Consumer Power") in Aléx, ed., *Världen och omvärlden, Kooperativ årsbok 1996* (1995).

Niels Finn Christiansen, M.A. in history, is senior lecturer at the University of Copenhagen, Center for the Study of Working Class Culture. He is the author of "Democracy and the Lower Middle Classes: Interwar Denmark," in Rudy Koshar, ed., *Splintered Classes: Politics and the Lower Middle Classes in Interwar Europe* (1990). Recent publications in Danish include a volume in a multi-volume "History of Denmark," covering the period 1900-1925, (1990); "Hartvig Frisch, a Political Biography" (1993); "The Spectre of Communism: The Left in Denmark 1848" (1998) (in Danish: *Kommunismens spøgelse—venstrefløjen i Danmark 1848*, which will be published in German as well).

Kathleen G. Donohue is assistant professor at the University of North Carolina at Charlotte. She received her doctoral degree at the University of Virginia. She is currently completing *Freedom From Want: the Idea of the Consumer and the Reconstruction of American Liberalism* for publication by Johns Hopkins University Press. Her article "What Gender Is the Consumer: The Role of Gender in Defining the Political" is scheduled to appear in the April 1999 issue of *The Journal of American Studies*.

Brett Fairbairn receieved a D.Phil. from Oxford University and is presently professor of history, University of Saskatchewan, Canada, where he teaches and does research and extension at the Centre for the Study of Co-operatives. He is author of *Democracy in the Undemocratic State: The German Reischstag Elections of 1898 and 1903* (1997); *Building a Dream: The Co-operative*

Retailing System in Western Canada, 1928-1988 (1989); and numerous papers and articles concerning cooperatives and social movements.

Ellen Furlough, who received her Ph.D. from Brown University, currently teaches European history at Kenyon College. Her publications include *Consumer Cooperation in France: The Politics of Consumption, 1830-1920* (1991) as well as articles and edited collections on aspects of consumer culture. Her current project analyzes twentieth-century French mass tourism and consumerism.

Ruth Grubel is professor at the School of Sociology at Kawansei Gakuin University in Nishinomiya, Japan. She has also taught at the University of Wisconsin-Whitewater and Hiroshima University, Japan. Her Ph.D. in political science is from the University of Nebraska-Lincoln. Local sources of foreign policy have been the primary focus of her research, and she has analyzed the international efforts of agricultural producers, U.S. state governments, and Japanese consumer cooperatives.

Peter Gurney was awarded a D.Phil. by the University of Sussex in 1989. He has published widely on the subject of consumer cooperation and working-class culture including *Co-operative culture and the politics of consumption in England, 1870-1930* (1996). He is presently a lecturer in history at the University of Huddersfield.

Gabriella Hauch is research sssociate at the Ludwig Boltzmann Institut fur Geschichte der Arbeiterbewegung at the Universitat Linz in Linz, Austria. She is the author of *Frau Biedermeier auf der Barrikaden: Frauenleben in der Weiner Revolution, 1848* (1990) and *Vom Frauenstandpunkt: Frauen in Parlament, 1919-1933* (1995) as well as the editor of two volumes of proceedings of the Internationale Tagung der Historiker der Arbeiterbewegung/International Conference of the Historians of the Labor Movement: *Arbeitsmigration und Arbeiterbewegung als historisches Problem/Stand der Forschung zu den Volksfrontregierungen in Spanien, Frankreich und Chile in den 30er Jahren* (1986) and *Geschlect, Klasse, Ethnizitat* (1993).

Steve Leikin received his Ph.D. in history from the University of California, Berkeley. He is currently a lecturer at Berkeley and at San Francisco State University. He was assistant editor of *The Salmon P. Chase Papers. Volume 1: Journals, 1829-1872* (1993) and of *The Salmon P. Chase Papers. Volume 2: Correspondence, 1823-1857* (1995). He is the author of "Biographical Sketch of Lawrence Dennis," *American National Biography* (forthcoming).

Ian MacPherson is professor of history and dean of humanities at the University of Victoria. The author of several books on the Canadian cooperative movement, including *Each for All: A History of the Co-operative Movement in English Canada, 1909-1945* (1979); *Building and Protecting the Co-operative Movement: A History of the Co-operative Union of Canada, 1909-1984* (1984); *Co-operation, Conflict and Consensus: B.C. Central and the Credit Union Movement to 1994* (1995); *Co-operative Principles for the 21st Century* (1995); and *Hands Around the Globe: The World Council of Credit Unions and the International Credit Union Movement to 1995* (1996). He has also been active as an elected official in numerous co-operative organization at the local, provincial, regional, national, and international levels. He chaired the process and wrote the documents by which the principles of the international cooperative movement were revised at the 1995 Congress of the International Co-operative Alliance.

Carl Strikwerda is professor of history and associate dean of the College of Liberal Arts and Sciences at the University of Kansas. He is the author of *A House Divided: Catholics, Socialists, and Flemish Nationalists in Nineteenth Century Belgium*, also published by Rowman and Littlefield; the coeditor with Camille Guerin-Gonzales of *The Politics of Immigrant Workers: Labor Activism and Migration in the World Economy Since 1830*; and author of "The Troubled Origins of European Economic Integration: International Iron and Steel and Labor Migration in the Era of World War I," *American Historical Review*, (1993).